Revolution, Democracy, Socialism

GET POLITICAL

www.plutobooks.com

Revolution, Democracy, Socialism
Selected Writings
V.I. Lenin
Edited by
Paul Le Blanc
9780745327600

Black Skin, White Masks
Frantz Fanon
Forewords by
Homi K.
Bhabha and
Ziauddin Sardar
9780745328485

Jewish History, Jewish Religion
The Weight of Three Thousand Years
Israel Shahak
Forewords by
Pappe / Mezvinsky/
Said / Vidal
9780745328409

The Communist Manifesto
Karl Marx and
Friedrich Engels
Introduction by
David Harvey
9780745328461

Theatre of the Oppressed
Augusto Boal
9780745328386

Catching History on the Wing
Race, Culture and Globalisation
A. Sivanandan
Foreword by
Colin Prescod
9780745328348

revolution democracy socialism

Selected Writings

V.I. LENIN

Edited and with an introduction by
Paul Le Blanc

PLUTO PRESS
www.plutobooks.com

First published 2008 by Pluto Press
345 Archway Road, London N6 5AA

www.plutobooks.com

British Library Cataloguing in Publication Data
A catalogue record for this book is available from the British Library

ISBN-13   978 0 7453 2761 7   Hardback
ISBN-13   978 0 7453 2760 0   Paperback

Library of Congress Cataloging in Publication Data applied for

10 9 8 7 6 5 4 3 2 1

Designed and produced for Pluto Press by
Chase Publishing Services Ltd, Sidmouth, EX10 9QG, England
Typeset by Stanford DTP Services, Northampton, England
Printed and bound by CPI Group (UK) Ltd, Croydon, CR0 4YY

CONTENTS

This volume is dedicated:

To the memory of my father Gaston (Gus) Le Blanc, a working-class organiser who first told me about Lenin,

To the memory of George Breitman, a revolutionary socialist scholar-activist who helped me tell others,

To the generations of fighters for a society of the free and equal, especially those who are young and those yet to come.

ACKNOWLEDGEMENTS

A number of friends and teachers and comrades, too numerous to mention, have contributed in innumerable ways to my ability and desire to help create this book.

Among those who offered direct encouragement and/or challenges and ideas are Anthony Arnove, Samantha (Sam) Ashman, Dennis Brutus, Sebastian Budgen, Nancy Ferrari, Geoffroy de Laforcade, Lars Lih, Michael Löwy, Michael Matambanadzo, Kevin Murphy, Immanuel Ness, August Nimtz, Bryan Palmer, Pierre Roussett, Helen Scott, George Shriver, and Michael Yates.

I am indebted to David Castle, Robert Webb, Alec Gregory and their colleagues at Pluto Press, and to Ray Addicott and Oliver Howard of Chase Publishing Services. Assistance of the staff of the Wright Library at La Roche College, and the intellectual engagement of many academic colleagues and students of that institution have helped sustain my efforts.

I have been especially inspired by activists with whom I have had the pleasure of working in Pittsburgh – particularly those who are members of the Anti-War Committee of the Thomas Merton Center, the International Socialist Organization, Solidarity, and the Workers International League.

I have been privileged, as well, to have been able to meet and draw strength from partisans of socialism while in Belgium, Brazil, Britain, Canada, China, France, India, Italy, the Netherlands, Nicaragua, and South Africa – and, along with those I know in the United States, they have brought to life for me, in their aspirations and struggles, much of the meaning of Lenin's own aspirations and struggles.

Part One:
Introductory Essay

1

TEN REASONS FOR NOT READING LENIN

Paul Le Blanc

> Lenin walks around the world,
> Black, brown and white receive him.
> Language is no barrier.
> The strangest tongues believe him.
> Langston Hughes[1]

This book draws together writings from someone generally acknowledged to have been one of the greatest revolutionary theorists and organisers in human history: Vladimir Ilyich Ulyanov, whose intimates knew him affectionately as 'Ilyich', but whom the world knew by his underground pseudonym – Lenin. He was the leader of the Bolshevik wing of the Russian socialist movement, and this wing later became the Russian Communist Party after coming to power in 1917 through a violent revolution (though less violent than the French Revolution or the American Civil War).

For millions he was seen as a liberator. Appropriated after his death by bureaucrats and functionaries in order to legitimate their tyranny in countries labelled 'Communist', he was at the same time denounced for being a wicked and cruel fanatic by defenders of power and privilege in capitalist countries – and with Communism's collapse at the close of the Cold War it is their powerful voices that achieved global domination. This book challenges that.

Lenin lived and died long ago, so one could ask why we should bother reading him in our very different world. This is indeed a good question. Here are ten good reasons for not reading Lenin:

1. The world is as it should be and all is going well.
2. Freedom, creative opportunities, and community exist for all.
3. Each person has a decisive say in the decisions affecting his or her life.
4. Oppression and exploitation do not exist.
5. The unequal structure of wealth and power in our society and in our world has nothing to do with the problems of humanity.
6. It is easy to figure out how to make the world a better place.
7. The history of struggles by workers and oppressed people is a waste of time.
8. The popular revolution of 1917 in Russia was a meaningless diversion.
9. It's good just to rely on what others say about someone as complex as Lenin.
10. Realities of the present and possibilities for the future have nothing to do with what happened in the past.

You may find the present volume helpful, however, if you reject these ten propositions. To reject the propositions does not mean that Lenin is right about everything, of course – but it does suggest that his ideas may have relevance for those developing an understanding of our history and our time.

The interpretation of 'Leninism' repeated over and over and over by liberals and conservatives goes like this: Lenin was the architect of a 'party of a new type' – the revolutionary vanguard party, led by Marxist intellectuals who were determined to use the working masses as a battering ram to take political power to bring about a total transformation of humanity – with predictably inhuman results.*

---

* According to liberal journalist David Remnick, Lenin held a 'view of man as modeling clay and sought to create a new model of human nature and behavior through social engineering of the most radical kind', and he goes on to quote conservative historian Richard Pipes that 'Bolshevism was the most audacious attempt in history to subject the entire life of a country to a master plan. It sought to sweep aside as useless rubbish the wisdom that mankind had accumulated over millennia.' David Remnick, 'Vladimir Ilyich Lenin', *Time/CBS News People of the Century: One Hundred Men and Women Who Shaped the Last One Hundred Years* (New York: Simon and Schuster, 1999), 51.

Indeed there are even Marxist-influenced democratic socialists who would argue that 'whoever wants to reach socialism by any other path than that of political democracy will inevitably arrive at conclusions that are absurd and reactionary both in the economic and political sense'. Are these the words of Keir Hardie or Rosa Luxemburg or Michael Harrington? No. Actually, these are the words of Lenin himself.[2]

There are other collections of Lenin's writings, but this one is organised for the purpose of highlighting the commitment to freedom and democracy that runs through his political thought from beginning to end. It also stresses his coherent analytical, strategic, and tactical orientation that retains some relevance for our own age of 'globalisation'. It is hoped that this volume can help scholars and students comprehend more clearly the early strength and success of Lenin's Bolsheviks. Both the grandeur and the tragedy of the Russian Revolution and the early years of Communism can thereby be thrown into bold relief – in contrast to the murderous dictatorship that later crystallised under the leadership of Joseph Stalin. This book may also be of use to those with an activist bent, especially those among the oppressed and exploited majorities of the Earth, who hope to pick up the banner of struggle for genuine democracy, global justice, and a society of the free and the equal.

In addition to providing an extensive but readable sampling of Lenin's major ideas *in his own words*, this book contains a succinct biography that connects these ideas to the historical realities from which they emerged. More, it examines some of the important criticisms levelled at Lenin by a variety of scholars and political opponents, among others. It offers a substantial interpretative essay exploring additional links of texts to historical contexts. And there is a bibliographical essay for those who want to get a sense of what other books they might consult for more information.

Lenin: A Succinct Biography

> The theory and practice of the vanguard party, of the one-party state, is not (repeat not) the central doctrine of Leninism. It is not the central doctrine, it is not even a special doctrine. It is not and it never was. ... Bolshevism, Leninism, did have central doctrines. One was theoretical, the inevitable collapse of capitalism into barbarism. Another was social, that on account of its place in society, its training and its numbers, only the working class could prevent the degradation and reconstruct society. Political action consisted in organizing a party to carry out these aims. These were the central principles of Bolshevism.
>
> C.L.R. James[3]

Vladimir Ilyich Ulyanov was born on 22 April 1870 (10 April, according to the Old Style calendar then used in Russia) in Simbursk (later renamed Ulyanovsk), a provincial town on the Volga River. He was the third of six children in what was at first a relatively happy family. His father, Ilya Nikolaevich Ulyanov, was a respected director of public schools. His mother, Maria Alexandrovna Blank, was the daughter of a physician and taught her children a love of reading and music. His father died in 1886, and in 1887 his beloved older brother, Alexander, was arrested and hanged for involvement in an unsuccessful plot by revolutionary university students to assassinate Tsar Alexander III.

At the end of 1887, Lenin himself was briefly arrested for involvement in a peaceful demonstration against the oppressive tsarist regime and for membership in a radical political group. A brilliant student, he had just entered the University of Kazan, but his involvement in protest activities resulted in his immediate expulsion and banishment to a small village near Kazan, where he lived under police surveillance. In 1888 he was permitted to return to Kazan, but he was denied entry to any university and therefore embarked on his own rigorous course of study. In 1891 he passed law examinations at the University of St Petersburg. Lenin worked as a lawyer for only a few months before becoming a full-time revolutionary.

The Making of a Revolutionary

At the time when Lenin became a revolutionary, impoverished peasants made up about 90 per cent of Russia's population. An expanding class of wage-workers and their families, created through the country's substantial industrial growth in the late nineteenth century, made up another 7 per cent. There was also a small 'middle-class' layer of professionals and well-to-do businessmen (the bourgeoisie), and at the very top a powerful landed aristocracy capped by an absolute monarchy. The country was characterised by a complete absence of democracy, limits on freedom of expression, the persecution of all religious minorities outside the official Russian Orthodox Church, severe limitations on the rights of women, and oppression of more than 100 national minorities that inhabited the Russian Empire – a notorious 'prison-house of nations'. Such conditions generated many revolutionary currents.

Lenin was deeply influenced by earlier nineteenth-century Russian revolutionaries, especially the writer Nikolai G. Chernyshevsky, as well as by the underground revolutionary populist movement known as the People's Will (Narodnaya Volya). This current was made up of idealistic activists who specialised in clandestine methods and sought to organise a peasant-based revolution and to establish a socialist society that would be based largely on the traditional commune, sometimes known as 'the mir', that had existed in peasant villages throughout Russia. Lenin drew upon this tradition, especially in his underground organisational concepts, but he was most profoundly attracted to the Western European working-class orientation developed by Karl Marx and Frederick Engels in such works as the *Communist Manifesto*, *Capital*, *Socialism: Utopian and Scientific*, etc. This orientation had been most forcefully injected into the Russian revolutionary movement by Georgi Plekhanov. Lenin became an influential voice among Russian Marxists, through his study *The Development of Capitalism in Russia* (1899) and many other works.

The Marxists argued that Russia was undergoing a capitalist transformation, that industrialisation was creating a factory-based proletariat, and that this working class would become the most effective force in the struggle to overthrow tsarism. Instead of engaging in terrorist activities (assassinations, etc.) against the tsar and his officials, as the People's Will had done, the Marxists argued that the working class should build trade unions to fight for better working conditions and living standards, should organise mass demonstrations to pressure for broader democratic and social reforms, and should organise their own political party to lead the struggle for a democratic revolution. Such a revolution would clear the way for the economic and political development of Russia (presumably through a capitalist economy and democratic republic). Then, when the working class became the majority, the process would culminate in a second revolution with a socialist character. The workers would take control of the economy and run it for the benefit of all. The Marxists believed that workers in other countries should and would be moving in a similar direction.

The Rise of Bolshevism

In 1898, the Marxists organised the Russian Social-Democratic Labour Party (RSDLP) to advance their orientation. Later, in 1901–02, the Populists organised the competing Socialist-Revolutionary (SR) Party. Both parties joined the international federation known as the Socialist (or Second) International. Lenin aimed many polemics against the SRs, but soon he also developed serious disagreements with others in the RSDLP. In the pages of the newspaper *Iskra* ('The Spark'), Lenin, Plekhanov, Julius Martov, and others criticised the so-called Economists, who urged that workers should concentrate only on economic issues at the workplace and that leadership of the democratic struggle should be left in the hands of pro-capitalist liberals. Lenin and the other '*Iskra*-ists' argued in favour of building a strong centralised party that would draw the various layers of the working class into a broad economic and political struggle to oppose all forms of oppression, overthrow tsarism, and advance the workers' interests.

Lenin popularised these ideas in *What Is To Be Done?*, published in 1902. The '*Iskra*-ists' won the day at the second congress of the RSDLP, held in Brussels and London in 1903. But before the congress was over they themselves had split into two organised factions – the Bolsheviks (from the Russian *bolshe*, meaning 'more', since they had gained a plurality of votes) and the Mensheviks (from the Russian word *menshe*, meaning 'less'). This split was analysed in Lenin's *One Step Forward, Two Steps Back* (1904). The Bolsheviks, led by Lenin, insisted on a more disciplined party than favoured by the Mensheviks, who became associated with Martov and Plekhanov. In addition, the Mensheviks favoured a coalition between workers and capitalists to overthrow tsarism, whereas Lenin (for example, in his 1905 polemic *Two Tactics of the Social Democracy in the Democratic Revolution*) insisted that a worker–peasant alliance, and the subsequent creation of a 'democratic dictatorship of the proletariat and the peasantry', would be necessary to achieve a genuinely democratic revolution in Russia.

In this period Lenin maintained a precarious existence in the revolutionary underground (where he married one of his closest comrades, Nadezhda Krupskaya, in 1898), in prison and Siberian exile, and in frugal circumstances as an exile outside Russia. He lived in Munich from 1900 to 1902, in London from 1902 to 1903, and in Geneva from 1903 to 1905. Lenin and Krupskaya played an essential role in co-ordinating the work of the underground Bolshevik organisation of the RSDLP, also facilitating the production and distribution of such revolutionary newspapers as *Vperyod* ('Forward') and *Proletary* ('The Proletarian').

From the 1905 Revolution to 1914

In 1905 a revolutionary upsurge sparked by a spontaneous uprising among the workers, after the tsar's troops fired on a peaceful demonstration in St Petersburg, and fuelled by hundreds of strikes and peasant insurgencies forced the tsarist regime to grant a number of important reforms, including greater political liberties and the creation of a weak parliamentary body called the Duma.

Although Lenin at first rejected participation in the Duma (he changed his position in 1906), he supported participation in the soviets (councils) of workers' deputies, spontaneously-formed democratic bodies arising in workplaces and workers' communities which had directed revolutionary activities. He also strongly favoured opening up the RSDLP, especially its Bolshevik wing, to a dramatic influx of radicalising workers. The political gap between Bolsheviks and Mensheviks narrowed, and the membership of the RSDLP soared. One left-wing Menshevik, Leon Trotsky, head of the St Petersburg soviet, even advanced (in articles written from 1904 through 1906) the idea of *permanent revolution* – that is, the concept that the democratic revolution would lead to workers taking political power with support from the peasants, initiating a transitional period to socialism, with the Russian revolution helping to generate workers' revolutions in more advanced industrial countries. While Lenin did not fully accept this notion at the time, it was later reflected in his perspectives for the 1917 revolution.

In late 1905 and throughout 1906, however, the forces of tsarist conservatism were able to stem the revolutionary tide and rescind many of the reforms granted earlier. Revolutionaries were once again forced underground or into exile, and many left-wing intellectuals became demoralised.

Differences between the Bolsheviks and the Mensheviks once again sharpened, yet Lenin also found himself in conflict with a group of Bolsheviks led by Alexander A. Bogdanov. These 'ultra-left' Bolsheviks denigrated trade union work and other reform activities (to which they counterposed 'armed struggle'), and also questioned the wisdom of the Bolsheviks running in elections and participating in the Duma. Lenin insisted that involvement in the Duma gave revolutionary socialists a powerful tool for legal agitation and education and that reform struggles enabled the working-class movement to grow in experience and political effectiveness. He wrote a philosophical work, *Materialism and*

Empirio-Criticism (1909), arguing against what he saw as serious philosophical revisions of Marxism being advanced by Bogdanov and others. At the same time, he was conducting a fierce struggle against the 'Liquidators', an influential current among the Mensheviks that wanted to replace all revolutionary underground organisational forms with strictly legal and reform-minded structures. Lenin was also sharply critical of 'conciliators', such as Trotsky and even some in the Bolsheviks' ranks, who attempted to maintain RSDLP unity. He had concluded that a cohesive and disciplined organisation, based on a revolutionary Marxist programme combining both legal and underground activity, could not be created by seeking compromises with socialists having a variety of orientations.

In 1912 Lenin and those who agreed with him definitively split with all other currents in the RSDLP and established their own distinct Bolshevik party. The new Bolshevik RSDLP published the newspaper *Pravda* ('Truth'). They had not only a coherent strategic orientation but, above all, a clear programme, highlighted by three demands: for an eight-hour work day, beneficial to the workers; for land reform, beneficial to the peasants; and for a democratic constituent assembly. These three demands were used to dramatise the need for a worker–peasant alliance in the democratic revolution. The Bolsheviks also had a serious and disciplined organisational structure that integrated legal reform efforts with revolutionary work. Between 1912 and 1914 Lenin's Bolsheviks outstripped all other currents in the Russian revolutionary movement, enjoying predominance among the organised workers.

Bolshevik successes coincided with a new wave of radicalisation among the dramatically growing Russian working class. Government violence against striking workers in the Lena gold fields in 1912, combined with population growth in the country's industrial centres marked by intensive exploitation of workers, generated considerable ferment and growing protests. By 1914 some observers concluded that Russia was on the verge of another revolutionary outbreak.

Imperialist World War

This militant upswing was checked, however, by the eruption of the First World War, which was used by the tsarist authorities to suppress all dissent. The socialist movement split into 'patriotic' and anti-war fragments, not only in Russia but in all countries involved in the conflict. In Russia only the more moderate 'patriotic' socialists were able to operate openly, thus managing to eclipse the now repressed Bolsheviks in the labour movement.

Lenin had moved to Krakow, in Austrian Poland, in 1912. After the outbreak of war in 1914 he was deported to Switzerland. Lenin, like many Marxists, had expected the outbreak of war. However, he was deeply shocked by the capitulation of the Second International's mass parties before the 'patriotic' demands of their respective ruling classes – in particular that of the German Social-Democratic Party (SPD), which he had previously considered the very model of an orthodox Marxist party in a more or less democratic parliamentary system. With the exception of Rosa Luxemburg, Karl Liebknecht and a few others, the bulk of the SPD leaders either endorsed German war aims or refrained from opposing the war effort. Lenin, along with Luxemburg and others on the revolutionary left, saw imperialism – the aggressive economic expansionism of the various 'great powers' – as the underlying cause of the ensuing slaughter. He was outraged that workers of the rival countries were being encouraged to kill each other in this conflict, and he never forgave Karl Kautsky, the German symbol of 'orthodox Marxism', for rationalising the betrayal of working-class internationalism.

In the period from 1914 to 1917 Lenin concentrated on efforts to build a revolutionary socialist opposition to the war. He joined with various anti-war socialist currents at the Zimmerwald and Kienthal conferences in criticising the failure of the Second International to remain true to its uncompromisingly anti-war statements, and he called for a new, revolutionary Third International. He also produced a study that explored the economic roots of the First World War, *Imperialism, the Highest Stage of Capitalism* (1916). In addition, he developed a critical analysis of nationalism, distinguishing between the nationalism of advanced and oppressive capitalist 'great powers' (which revolutionaries should not support) and the nationalism (which revolutionaries should support) of peoples oppressed and exploited by the 'great powers'. This view highlighted an orientation that was not common among previous Marxists – appreciating and supporting liberation struggles of oppressed 'non-white' peoples in Asia, Africa, and the Americas.

Lenin at this time also took issue with those non-Bolshevik revolutionaries, notably Luxemburg and Trotsky, whose policies were, in fact, closest to his own. Rejecting the emphasis of Luxemburg (in the 'Junius Pamphlet') and Trotsky (in *War and the International*) on calling for immediate peace and advocating a 'Socialist United States of Europe', he advanced the most intransigent possible slogan: 'Turn the Imperialist War into a Civil War'. Though only his closest associates, such as Gregory Zinoviev, accepted this slogan, it was very important to Lenin because it would make impossible any compromise with 'centrist' Social Democrats such as Kautsky and (in France) Jean Longuet, who by 1916 had retreated from their initial acceptance of the war yet were quite unwilling to make a clear break with the pro-war majorities of their parties. Only by splitting revolutionary socialists away from such compromisers would it be possible, he believed, to provide leadership to war-weary masses for a genuine socialist transformation.

Fall of Tsarism and Rise of 'Dual Power'

Within Russia, a growing disillusionment with the war generated a new upsurge of radicalism among the workers and peasants. A spontaneous uprising initiated by women workers on International Women's Day in Petrograd (as St Petersburg had been renamed in 1914) in March 1917 turned into a successful revolution when the Russian army – largely 'peasants in uniform' – joined with the insurgent workers and turned against the tsarist government. A situation of 'dual power' arose as the powers of the state were assumed by democratically elected councils (soviets) of workers' and soldiers' deputies and also by a pro-capitalist Provisional Government set up by politicians in the Duma. Many SRs and Mensheviks, and even some Bolsheviks, supported the Provisional Government. Lenin returned from exile in April 1917 to challenge this widespread orientation.

Immediately after the overthrow of the tsarist regime, Lenin had desperately sought to find ways to return to Russia. He was refused permission to travel by way of Great Britain and France, since the governments of those countries saw him as a threat to Russia's continued participation in the war. However, the German government – for similar reasons – allowed Lenin and all other Russian exiles to travel through Germany. Later, those hostile to Lenin were to use this (and also funds from Germany allegedly secured by the Bolsheviks) in order to slander him as a 'German agent'.

Upon his arrival in Petrograd, Lenin pointed out that the Provisional Government was unable to end Russian involvement in the war, could not guarantee that the workers in the cities would have enough to eat, and was unprepared to break up the nobility's large estates to give land to the peasants. Therefore, he argued, workers and revolutionaries should give no support to the Provisional Government. Instead they should demand 'all power to the soviets' and insist on 'peace, bread, and land'. The democratic revolution had to grow over into a working-class revolution supported by the peasantry. This development would stimulate the war-weary and radicalising workers of such countries as Germany, Austria-Hungary, and France to join their Russian comrades in socialist revolution.

These 'April Theses' shocked most of Russia's socialists, including many leading Bolsheviks, but quickly won over the rank-and-file of his party, as well as such former opponents as Trotsky. By July 1917 the Bolsheviks were in the lead of a militant mass demonstration against the Provisional Government, which was now headed by Alexander Kerensky, a moderate socialist. The demonstration erupted in violence, leading to repression by the Provisional Government. Many Bolsheviks (including the prestigious new recruit Trotsky) were arrested, and Lenin fled across the border to Finland. There he began writing his classic Marxist study *The State and Revolution*, which presented a libertarian and democratic vision of working-class revolution and the socialist future. Before he could complete this study, events had evolved to the point where Lenin found it possible to issue a practical appeal to the Bolshevik Central Committee for a revolutionary seizure of power.

Counter-revolutionary opponents played a key role in bringing about this turn in events. In September 1917 General Lavr Kornilov mounted a right-wing military coup designed to oust both the Provisional Government and the soviets. The Provisional Government freed all revolutionary militants from prison and gave them arms. Bolsheviks joined with Mensheviks, SRs, anarchists and others to defend the revolution. Kornilov was defeated, his troops melting away under the influence of revolutionary agitators.

Bolshevik Revolution and Russian Civil War

From hiding, Lenin urgently insisted to his comrades that the Bolsheviks launch an uprising to establish soviet power. Two of his own close followers, Gregory Zinoviev and Lev Kamenev, argued against so audacious a move, but they found themselves overwhelmed by revolutionary enthusiasm not only within the party but among growing sectors of the working class and peasantry. A split in the SRs resulted in a substantial left-wing faction that supported the Bolshevik demands. The soviets themselves – led once again, as in 1905, by Trotsky – now adopted the position of 'all power to the soviets' and organised a Military Revolutionary Committee under Trotsky's direction, which prepared an insurrection to overthrow the Provisional Government.

The stirring but relatively bloodless October Revolution in Russia, which was actually carried out on 7 November 1917 (according to the modern calendar), was seen as a beacon of hope by the discontented throughout the world. One of the central developments of the twentieth century, it led to the formation of the Union of Soviet Socialist Republics and to the rise of modern Communism.

Lenin was the leader of the first Soviet government, the Council of People's Commissars (*Soviet Narodnykh Komossarov*, or Sovnarkom), which consisted of a coalition of Bolsheviks (who soon renamed their organisation the Communist Party) and Left SRs. The new regime entered into peace negotiations with Germany to secure Russia's withdrawal from the First World War. The German government made harsh demands for territorial and financial concessions as a pre-condition for a peace settlement. Many revolutionaries, including the Left SRs and even a Left Communist faction in Lenin's own party, opposed the concessions and called for a revolutionary war against German imperialism.

Trotsky, who as leader of the Russian negotiating team at Brest-Litovsk had used the peace talks to expose German imperialist war aims and to appeal to the German masses 'over the heads' of their government, took an intermediary position, hoping that German military action against the infant Soviet republic would be blocked by mutinies and strikes by the German working class. Trotsky advocated refusal either to sign the Germans' Brest-Litovsk *diktat* or to resume the war with a virtually non-existent Russian army. This compromise position was initially adopted by the Soviet government, but the hoped-for mass strikes and mutinies failed to materialise, and, when the German military launched a devastating offensive, Trotsky withdrew his 'neither war nor peace' proposal and sided with Lenin.

Against angry opposition among many Bolsheviks and most Left SRs, Lenin insisted on Russia's need for peace and narrowly won acceptance of what were now even stiffer German demands, resulting in the Treaty of Brest-Litovsk (3 March 1918). The Left SRs withdrew from the government and assumed a stance of violent opposition. The Right SRs and even some Mensheviks were openly hostile as well. Pro-capitalist and pro-tsarist forces committed themselves to the overthrow of the new regime, as did a number of foreign governments, notably those of Great Britain, France, the United States, and Japan. At various times, in this period, foreign countries (including Britain, Czechoslovakia, Finland, France, Germany, Japan, Poland, Rumania, Serbia, Turkey, and the United States) intervened with military forces and aided counter-revolutionary Russian forces in an escalating, brutal civil war. Masses of workers and peasants joined the new Red Army to defend the gains of the revolution. Their efforts were hampered by economic collapse – hastened by premature nationalisations – and also by the inexperience and inevitable mistakes of the new government.

In 1918 some SRs carried out assassination attempts in which Lenin was badly wounded and other prominent Bolsheviks were killed. In response, a Red Terror of arrests and executions was launched against all perceived 'enemies of the revolution' by the Cheka (special security forces), set up on Lenin's initiative and directed by Felix Dzherzhinsky. Early in 1918 the Sovnarkom had dissolved what it felt to be an unrepresentative Constituent Assembly on the grounds that this institution had been superseded by a more thoroughgoing soviet democracy. By 1919, however, this democracy had largely evaporated. As a result of Communist repression of opposing left-wing parties and the relative disintegration of the working class as a political force (because the economy itself had largely disintegrated), the soviets became hollow shells that would rubber-stamp the decisions of the Sovnarkom and the Communist Party.

Brutal Communist policies were deepened in response to the murderous campaigns of anti-Communist counter-revolutionaries (known as 'the Whites' as opposed to the left-wing 'Reds'). Increasingly under the leadership of reactionary and pro-tsarist army officers, the Whites often combined anti-Communism with anti-democratic, anti-working class, anti-peasant, and anti-Semitic violence. Nonetheless, the Whites were given substantial material support from foreign governments hoping to put an end to what was a 'bad example' to their own working classes.

Lenin and the Russian Communists were convinced that the spread of socialist revolution to other countries was essential for the final victory of their own revolution. In 1919 they organised the first congress of the Communist International (the Third International), initiating the formation of Communist parties in countries throughout the world. Concerned that these new parties might fall prey to 'ultra-left' errors (such as attempting to seize power without majority working-class support or refusing to fight for 'mere' reforms), Lenin wrote *'Left-Wing' Communism, An Infantile Disorder* in 1920. At the second and third congresses of the Communist International he argued in favour of the 'united front' tactic, whereby Communists would join forces with more moderate Socialists to protect and advance workers' rights against capitalist and reactionary attacks. (This would also win support, among growing numbers of workers, for the Communists who would prove to be the most effective fighters for the workers' interests.) Lenin never gave up on the belief that the future of the new Soviet republic could be secured only through the spread of working-class revolution to other countries, but he never lived to see his hopes realised.

From 'War Communism' to New Economic Policy

During the Russian civil war, in Lenin's own opinion, he and his comrades had made terrible mistakes. In pushing back the foreign invaders, for example, the Red Army – with Lenin's support but over the objections of Red Army commander Trotsky – invaded Poland in hopes of generating a revolutionary uprising among the Polish workers and peasants. Instead, a fierce counter-attack drove the Russian forces from Polish soil.

Some of the greatest mistakes involved the implementation of what was called 'War Communism'. Sweeping nationalisations of industry formally placed the economy in the hands of the inexperienced state, and attempts at strict centralised planning introduced authoritarian and bureaucratic elements into the economy. Efforts were also made to pit 'poor peasants' against allegedly 'rich peasants' in order to establish state controls over agriculture. Such industrial and agricultural policies resulted in red tape, bottlenecks and shortages, and growing discontent among the workers and bitterness among the peasants.

Contrary to popular belief, these policies were hardly an attempted 'short-cut' to the ideal communist society of the future, which Marx had insisted could be achieved only after an extended period of high economic productivity, abundance, and genuinely democratic social control of the means of production. The policies of War Communism could reasonably be justified only as desperate emergency measures in the face of civil war and invasion. By 1921 the experience of War Communism had generated peasant revolts and an uprising of workers and sailors at the previously pro-Bolshevik Kronstadt naval base outside of Petrograd.

Lenin now led the way in adopting policies that had been urged by some Communists, including Trotsky. In 1921 the New Economic Policy (NEP) was established to allow small-scale capitalist production in the countryside and the reintroduction of market mechanisms into the economy as a whole. One Bolshevik theorist, Nikolai Bukharin, became closely identified in later years with the preservation of the NEP reforms. Such changes, together with the end of the civil war and foreign intervention, led to improvements in the economy and to the possibility of implementing important health, education, and social welfare policies beneficial to millions of people in the battered Soviet republic.

Yet at the same time, the Communist Party under Lenin also took measures to strengthen its monopoly of political power and even, as an emergency measure, to curtail democracy within the party itself, for the first time banning factions. In particular, a Workers Opposition headed by union leader Alexander Shlyapnikov and feminist intellectual Alexandra Kollontai – calling for greater working-class control over the state apparatus and economy – was prevented from expressing its views. These measures established precedents and the framework for the development of a permanently narrow and repressive dictatorship.

Lenin's Final Defeat and Legacy

Lenin grew increasingly alarmed that the Soviet republic was becoming 'bureaucratically degenerated', as he put it. Suffering from a stroke in May 1922, he recovered sufficiently in autumn to return to work, only to be felled by a second stroke in December. Throughout this period and into the early months of 1923 he focused attention on ways of overcoming the bureaucratic tyranny that was gripping the Communist Party and the Soviet government and of strengthening controls by workers and peasants over the state apparatus.

Lenin opposed the inclination of some party leaders to adopt repressive policies toward non-Russian nationalities. Chief among these particular leaders was Joseph Stalin, who became the party's general secretary in 1922. Also, while Lenin had seen the concept of *democratic centralism* as involving 'freedom of discussion, unity in action', Stalin and others who were now in charge of the party apparatus distorted the concept – so that a bureaucratic 'centralism' crowded out inner-party democracy – to inhibit questioning of and suppress opposition to their own policies.

Lenin sought an alliance with Trotsky to fight for his positions in the party, and he broke decisively with Stalin, whom he identified as being in the forefront of the trends he was opposing. In his last testament he urged that Stalin be removed from his positions of party leadership. But a third stroke in March 1923 completely incapacitated him. At his country home in the village of Gorki, outside Moscow, he suffered a last, fatal stroke on 21 January 1924. After an elaborate state funeral, Lenin's embalmed body was placed in a mausoleum in Moscow's Red Square.

He was mourned by millions in the Soviet Union and by Communists and other revolutionaries throughout the world, but much of Lenin's work was undone by (yet bombastically identified with) the later policies of the Stalin regime. Even in his lifetime, what he viewed as the 'dictatorship of the proletariat' – political rule by the working class – had, under difficult conditions, degenerated into a one-party dictatorship. But after his death it evolved into a ruthless bureaucratic tyranny which defended above all else the material and other privileges of the bureaucratic rulers.

Those who had been closest to Lenin found their authority eliminated by Stalin's political machine, and most of them were eventually killed in the purges during the 1930s, when many hundreds of thousands of real and imagined dissidents among the Communists and others were destroyed. Alternatives to this

Stalinist version of 'Leninism' were put forward, particularly by Trotsky and by Bukharin. But throughout the Communist International (dissolved by Stalin in 1943) and the world Communist movement, Stalin's orientation dominated. Even when Stalin was denounced in 1956 by later Communist leaders, the bureaucratic system and undemocratic methods with which he was associated remained in place.

With the collapse of the Soviet Union in 1991, questions arose about how much influence Lenin would continue to have as a symbol and as a theorist. Lenin concerned himself with many dimensions of political theory, but his distinctive contribution involved the conceptualisation and organisation of a party that proved capable of carrying out a socialist revolution in Russia in 1917. Even for many of his most severe critics, Lenin's political integrity and personal selflessness are beyond dispute, as is his place in history as one of the greatest revolutionary leaders of the twentieth century. What is hotly contested across the political spectrum, however, is his relevance for the future – which is, of course, related to how we are to interpret his life and thought and actions.

Lenin's Critics

[In the surrender of freedom to necessity, Marx] did what his teacher in revolution, Robespierre, had done before him and what his greatest disciple, Lenin, was to do after him in the most momentous revolution his teachings have yet inspired. It has become customary to view all these surrenders, and especially the last one through Lenin, as foregone conclusions, chiefly because we find it difficult to judge any of these men, and again most of all Lenin, in their own right, and not as mere forerunners. (It is perhaps noteworthy that Lenin, unlike Hitler and Stalin, has not yet found his definitive biographer, although he was not merely a 'better' but an incomparably simpler man; it may be because his role in twentieth-century history is so much more equivocal and difficult to understand.)

Hannah Arendt[4]

Among the revolutionaries of the twentieth century, according to the decidedly non-Leninist scholar Robert C. Tucker, Lenin was 'the most remarkable in many ways, and the most influential'.[5] Perhaps it is natural that he has consequently attracted innumerable battalions of critics, some incredibly ferocious. For those who wish to understand Lenin, it is necessary to make one's way through these battalions – and there is certainly much to learn by doing so.

There are many criticisms that can be made of Lenin. Yet the nature of the criticism is often difficult to separate from the political orientation of the critic. It will be impossible to offer a full survey, but four influential approaches can serve to illustrate the point:

- a conservative mode of criticism, rejecting the desirability of revolution in general and of the democratic and egalitarian ideals of socialism in particular, therefore condemning Lenin for his commitment to such things;
- a mode of criticism embracing the democratic and egalitarian ideals of socialism, but critical of Lenin's purported revolutionary utopianism that inadvertently brought about the opposite of these things;
- a mode of criticism giving lip-service to democratic ideals without a practical concern about their realisation, at the same time seeking to deny the existence of genuinely democratic qualities in Lenin – an orientation which was especially prevalent among scholars who had enlisted in the Cold War anti-Communist crusade of 1946–90;
- a mode of criticism associated with radical activists of the late twentieth and early twenty-first centuries, intensely engaged with practical concerns to advance toward a realisation of democratic and libertarian ideals, that sees Leninism as an obstacle to such realisation.

Conservative Critics

The conservative Stefan T. Possony, one of many biographers who disliked Lenin, described him this way:

Self-righteous, rude, demanding, ruthless, despotic, formalistic, bureaucratic, disciplined, cunning, intolerant, stubborn, one-sided, suspicious, distant, asocial, cold-blooded, ambitious, purposive, vindictive, spiteful, a grudgeholder, a coward who was able to face danger only when he deemed it unavoidable – Lenin was a complete law unto himself and he was entirely serene about it.

An even more famous conservative, Winston Churchill, while willing to acknowledge more attractive personal qualities in Lenin, explained in 1929:

> In the cutting off of the lives of men and women no Asiatic conqueror, not Tamerlane, not Genghis Khan, can match his fame …. Lenin was the Grand Repudiator. He repudiated everything. He repudiated God, King, Country, morals, treaties, debts, rents, interest, the laws and customs of centuries, all contracts written or implied, the whole structure – such as it is – of human society.

In the words of Possony, Lenin initiated 'the great world struggle between freedom and totalitarianism'. This is consistent with Churchill's 1919 judgement of Lenin and the Bolsheviks:

> Theirs is a war against civilized society which can never end. They seek as the first condition of their being the overthrow and destruction of all existing institutions and of every State and Government now standing in the world. They too aim at a worldwide and international league, but a league of the failures, the criminals, the unfit, the mutinous, the morbid, the deranged, and the distraught in every land; and between them and such order of civilization as we have been able to build up since the dawn of history there can, as Lenin rightly proclaims, be neither truce nor pact.[6]

It is important to note, however, that both Possony and Churchill – like many of their co-thinkers – are confident in the knowledge that some people, some classes, and some races are superior to others. They know, too, that revolutions designed to bring down those of superior intellectual and cultural qualities, in the name of utopian notions of equality and 'rule by the people', destroy the very fabric of civilisation, paving the way for chaos and tyranny. Obviously, from this standpoint, Lenin – committed to overturning the present social order to create a new and radically democratic society of the free and the equal – is a monster.[7]

Those of us who do not share the classical conservative assumptions may have grounds, therefore, to question this particular evaluation of Lenin. Certainly sharp critiques of the great revolutionary are not dependent on Churchill's reactionary eloquence or Possony's inclination toward character assassination. Indeed, those who actually knew him could not honestly agree with the personal denigrations of Lenin. According to so sharp a political opponent as the prominent Menshevik Raphael Abramovitch, who knew him personally and spent time visiting with him and his companion Nadezhda Krupskaya in their 1916 Swiss exile, 'it is difficult to conceive of a simpler, kinder and more unpretentious person than Lenin at home'. Another Menshevik leader, Julius Martov, concurred that there were not 'any signs of personal pride in Lenin's character', that he sought, 'when in the company of others, an opportunity to acquire knowledge rather than show off his own'.[8]

Interestingly, such comments were passed on in a largely forgotten early book by Isaac Don Levine, a Russian-born US journalist who became a well-known figure on the anti-Communist right. Uncompromisingly critical of Lenin, but permeated with a feel for the details of his life, Levine's 1924 portrait (undoubtedly a source for Churchill's 1929 remarks) transcends narrow political boundaries. Levine commented that the Communist leader 'derived genuine pleasure from associating with children and entertaining them', and that he had an 'effeminate weakness for cats, which he liked to cuddle and play with'. The knowledgeable journalist reported that other enthusiasms included bicycling, amateur photography, chess, skating, swimming, hunting – though Lenin was sometimes not inclined to actually shoot the animals he hunted ('well, he was so beautiful, you know', he said of a fox whose life he refused to take). According to the well-informed British agent Bruce Lockhart, he was 'the father of modern "hiking" … a passionate lover of outdoor life'. And, of course, Lenin embraced music

– contrary to the legend that he 'gave up Beethoven' in order to remain a 'hard' and unrelenting revolutionary. 'During his life in Switzerland Lenin immensely enjoyed the home concerts that the political emigrants improvised among themselves', Levine reported. 'When a player or singer was really gifted, Lenin would throw his head back on the sofa, lock his knees into his arms, and listen with an interest so absorbing that it seemed as if he were experiencing something very deep and mysterious.'[9]

There are other, more explicitly political qualities emphasised by the shrewd anti-Communist Levine – those of a personality 'concise in speech, energetic in action, and matter-of-fact', with an unshakeable faith in Marxism, although 'extraordinarily agile and pliant as to methods', with an 'erudition' that could be termed 'vast'. His 'capacity to back up his contentions [was] brilliant'. While he had an ability 'to readily acknowledge tactical mistakes and defeats', he was never willing to consider 'the possible invalidity of his great idea' (i.e., revolutionary Marxism). Levine concluded:

> The extraordinary phenomenon about Lenin is that he combined this unshakeable, almost fanatic, faith with a total absence of personal ambition, arrogance or pride. Unselfish and irreproachable in his character, of a retiring disposition, almost ascetic in his habits, extremely modest and gentle in his direct contact with people, although peremptory and derisive in his treatment of political enemies, Lenin could be daring and provocative in his policies ....[10]

Indeed, precisely such policies have been the focus of other critics.

Socialist Critics

In the 1962 account of old Menshevik Raphael Abramovitch, *The Soviet Revolution*, we find none of the character denigration of Lenin that seems so essential for such conservatives as Possony, but rather the charge that Lenin was insufficiently Marxist: 'Lenin had always combined an analytical Marxist outlook with a strong streak of romantic utopianism. After the February Revolution [which overthrew the monarchy in 1917] the utopianism became dominant.' For the Mensheviks, it had always been essential to see 'the bourgeois [i.e., capitalist] character of the coming Russian revolution and the historic necessity of political self-limitation of the Russian proletariat'.

Lenin's utopianism consisted of being perpetually inclined 'to make a bourgeois revolution without the bourgeoisie, against the bourgeoisie', and failing to realise that, in backward Russia, 'the numerically weak working-class, submerged as it was in the enormous mass of a hundred million peasants and the lower middle-class urban population, would, if it came to power, find itself completely incapable of assuming the burden of power within the framework of a bourgeois-democratic order emerging in the place of the autocracy'. Instead, by 1917 Lenin was foolishly leading a revolution of the workers, supported by the peasantry, to establish a radical democracy based on revolutionary councils (soviets), which would be a first step in the transition to socialism.

As things inevitably went wrong, Lenin's regime veered sharply away from its initial super-democracy. By the early 1920s, Julius Martov, the most prominent leader of the Mensheviks, offered the judgement that 'reality has shattered these illusions', that the utopian impatience of Lenin and the Bolsheviks had not brought the expected radical democracy but instead a chaos which caused the utopians to establish 'bureaucracy, police, a permanent army with commanding cadres that are independent of the soldiers, courts that are above control by the community, etc'.[11]

The Menshevik critique – that Lenin's rejection of their 'worker–capitalist alliance' notion led to disaster – is coherent, cogent, and seems to correspond to important aspects of Marxist theory and Russian reality. We have already seen, however, that it is hardly unanswerable. It was rejected by others aside from the Bolsheviks – by the substantial Left Socialist-Revolutionary Party, by most of the anarchists, and by some of the Mensheviks as well. It is worth giving attention to the testimony on this matter of two sometime-associates and sometime-critics of Lenin, Simon Liberman and Angelica Balabanoff.

Liberman was a Menshevik who (as with many revolutionaries) had come from a bourgeois background and so was in a position to monitor the actual views of the would-be capitalist partners in the proposed Menshevik worker–capitalist alliance. 'A majority of them were opposed to the tsarist regime, seeing in it as they did a feudalistic encumbrance', Liberman recalled. 'They felt that industrial capital was the lawful heir of this regime and should take over.' This was the good news – immediately overwhelmed by the bad:

> But it was the working class that represented the only real and fighting force of the revolution against tsarism and its feudalism. The industrialists were afraid of the workers and also of the peasants. They declared openly that they were ready and willing to make their peace with the tsarist regime in order to withstand the desires and demands of the working class and, in part, of the peasantry too.[12]

Angelica Balabanoff had been a highly respected figure in the Socialist International, a Russian revolutionary active in various European countries, who would work closely with Lenin upon returning to Russia after the overthrow of the tsar, only to break with him in the early 1920s as a frank critic. In her memoirs published in 1938, she explained:

> I had been trained, like most Marxists, to expect the social revolution to be inaugurated in one of the highly industrialized, vanguard countries, and at the same time Lenin's analysis of the Russian events seemed to me almost utopian. Later, after I had returned to Russia itself, I was to accept this analysis completely. I have never doubted since that if the revolutionaries – including many of the Mensheviks and Left Social Revolutionaries – had not convinced the peasants, workers, and soldiers of the need for a more far-reaching, Socialist revolution in Russia, Tsarism or some similar form of autocracy would have been restored.[13]

Of course, Liberman and Balabanoff themselves offered their own criticisms of Lenin's perspectives and policies (although with interesting and obvious respect for Lenin's goals and intellect and for positive qualities of his personality). Their criticisms focus on contributions they felt he made to the Soviet regime's authoritarian degeneration in the terrible civil war period. Regardless of what one makes of these various socialist critics of Lenin, there is a very practical-minded concern among them on how to advance the interests of the workers and the oppressed which flavours and informs their criticisms.

This is also very much the case with Lenin's greatest socialist critic, the brilliant revolutionary Marxist Rosa Luxemburg, especially in her insightful critique of 1918, 'The Russian Revolution' (which she wrote a few months before helping to found the German Communist Party, only to perish in the wake of an abortive effort to advance a workers' revolution in Germany). Commenting that 'only a party which knows how to lead, that is, to advance things, wins support in stormy times', she asserted that 'whatever a party could offer of courage, revolutionary far-sightedness and consistency in a historic hour, Lenin, Trotsky, and the other comrades have given in good measure'. But she reacted sharply to the authoritarian policies against opposition parties, insisting that 'freedom is always and exclusively for the one who thinks differently', and that 'only unobstructed, effervescing life … brings to light creative force' that 'corrects all mistaken attempts'. Emphasising the need of the labouring masses to exercise their control of society through 'general elections' with 'unrestricted freedom of press and assembly' and a 'free struggle of opinion', Luxemburg offered a dramatic elaboration:

> Socialist democracy is not something which begins only in the promised land after the foundations of socialist economy are created; it does not come as some sort of Christmas present for the worthy people who, in the interim, have loyally supported a handful of socialist dictators. Socialist democracy begins simultaneously with the beginnings of the destruction of class rule and the seizure of power by the socialist party.

It is the same thing as the dictatorship of the proletariat [i.e., political rule by the working class].

This is consistent not only with Marx but also the views expressed by Lenin himself not long before. Luxemburg did not blame the new Soviet regime for the collapse, under the impact of global isolation and foreign invasion, of the initially expansive soviet democracy. 'It would be demanding something superhuman from Lenin and his comrades if we should expect of them that under such circumstances they should conjure forth the finest democracy, the most exemplary dictatorship and a flourishing socialist economy', she wrote. Emergency measures sharply curtailing the norms of freedom and democracy were understandable and defensible. 'The danger begins only when they make a virtue of necessity and want to freeze into a complete theoretical system all the tactics forced upon them by these fatal circumstances, and want to recommend them to the international proletariat as a model of socialist tactics.' The growing inclination of Lenin, Trotsky and others to demonise dissent and dissenters, and to glorify the monopoly of power by the Russian Communist Party as 'the dictatorship of the proletariat', brought her sharp admonition: 'they render a poor service to international socialism for the sake of which they have fought and suffered; for they want to place in its storehouse as new discoveries all the distortions prescribed in Russia by necessity and compulsion'. Indeed, one could add that not only did this render poor service to international socialism, but (as more long-lived critics such as Balabanoff, Liberman, and others argued) it helped to establish a political culture in the beleaguered Soviet Republic that contributed to the crystallisation of what came to be known as Stalinism.[14]

Academic Critics

In contrast to Luxemburg and to the classical Menshevik critique (although certainly influenced by the Mensheviks' anti-Leninist offerings), there arose in the 1940s what seemed a deeper criticism of Lenin's orientation. It flourished through the 1950s and beyond

– down to the start of the twenty-first century. This new criticism was often consistent with liberal and even residual moderate-socialist sympathies, but was developed among scholars and ideologists who – unlike the early Mensheviks – were not inclined to build a socialist working-class movement, but instead were inclined to secure relatively comfortable intellectual niches in the US-led campaign of Cold War anti-Communism, as part of the global power struggle with the USSR. It has persisted among academics and intellectuals since the end of the Cold War who are not interested in revolutionary political activity – and this certainly has had an impact on the way many of them comprehend, explain, and garble Lenin's thought on 'the organisation question'.

What Lars Lih has recently dubbed 'the textbook interpretation' of Lenin has been based on a remarkably distorted reading of a specific passage in the 1902 pamphlet *What Is To Be Done?*, beginning with these words: 'We have said that there could not have been Social-Democratic consciousness among the workers. It would have to be brought to them from without.'[15] This is held up as the classic expression of what is said to be Lenin's shockingly arrogant and pernicious elitism. In a brilliant, massive, exhaustive study, *Lenin Rediscovered* (2006), Lih contextualises and explains the passage in question:

> Lenin is telling the story of how two great forces were moving toward each other in Russia during the 1890s. One force – the revolutionary intelligentsia inspired by Social Democracy – had been discussed in Chapter I of [*What Is To Be Done?*], so now, Lenin is going to tell us about the other force, that is, the great strike movement of the mid-1890s. He describes the strike movement, compliments the workers on their growing purposiveness, and asserts that the workers at this period were not yet convinced Social Democrats. The moral of the story is that the two forces needed each other and were moving towards each other with unstoppable force ...[16]

In the 'textbook interpretation' of anti-Communist scholars, however, a very different understanding is propagated. In a 1962 Cold War primer on *The Nature of Communism*, we find Robert

V. Daniels asserting that Lenin's pamphlet reflected 'a distinctly new conception of what the party ought to be and do'. Instead of a democratic mass workers' party of class struggle, Lenin's party 'was to be a tightly organised and disciplined body of "professional revolutionaries" dedicated to the promotion of a revolutionary mass movement'. Based on the premise that 'the masses, if left to themselves, would not become revolutionary', Leninism purportedly held that 'the working class movement would be made revolutionary only through the leadership of inspired intellectuals, guided by Marxism, who would impart to the workers the proper socialist mentality'. A.J. Polan summed it up even more succinctly in his 1984 text *Lenin and the End of Politics* when he claimed that Lenin's 1902 pamphlet 'argues the need for a revolutionary party to combat the consciousness of the people and supply them with scientific and revolutionary politics'.[17]

Adam Ulam, in his influential work *The Bolsheviks* (1965), has Lenin proclaiming: 'Socialist consciousness cannot exist among the workers.' This is used to buttress the notion that Lenin believed only revolutionary intellectuals such as himself were fit to lead ignorant workers (incapable of thinking socialist thoughts) in a socialist revolution … somehow. This incoherence is cleared away by Lih's explanatory restatement of Lenin's point: 'The Russian workers who carried out the heroic strikes of the mid-1890s did not yet have socialist awareness nor could we have expected them to.' This is an observation of what happened in the nineteenth century. Yet Ulam has Lenin making a sweeping generalisation about workers in general, an odd notion cropping up in the works of many others – for example, an earlier work by Alfred G. Meyer entitled *Leninism* (1956), telling us of Lenin's 'generally prevailing opinion was that the proletariat *was* not and *could* not be conscious', and James D. White more recently making the same point in *Lenin, The Practice and Theory of Revolution* (2001) – that in Lenin's view 'socialist consciousness *always* remained outside the working class because it could *never* see beyond its narrow material class interests'.[18]

This makes little sense. There is far too much material to the contrary in Lenin's writings and biography, and in the history of the Bolsheviks, to sustain such assertions. Logically it seems unlikely that Lenin would be devoting his writings and his life to fighting for socialism (rule by the people over the political and economic life of society) if he believed that the working-class majority is inherently incapable of being socialist. Nor can one explain how masses of thoughtful and capable workers would be drawn into the party of Lenin (as they were) if Lenin's ideas and organisation held them in such contempt. One cannot build a mass workers' party capable of making a revolution – which is what Lenin's Bolsheviks became – with the ideology attributed to him by the Cold War critics. Unlike the socialist critics, however, the academic critics are more concerned with attributing negative qualities to Lenin than with determining whether Lenin's perspectives do or do not make sense in the struggle for workers' liberation and the overcoming of an oppressive capitalist society. This obviously flavours their criticisms, and suggests the source of deficiencies in their analyses.

In the 1970s and 1980s, a far more serious set of studies emerged from a significant number of social historians who took the revolutionary workers' movement seriously, placed Lenin and his party in this context, and provided important insights – both positive and critical – into the meaning of 'Leninism'.[19]

With the collapse of the USSR in 1991, however, a powerful backlash was felt in the historiography of the Russian Revolution, not only revitalising old Cold War interpretations, but also injecting a pungent conservatism through such works as Richard Pipes's *The Russian Revolution* (1991), in which, as Peter Kenez observed, Lenin is 'the chief villain', portrayed – from youth to death – as 'an arrogant, anti-social, brutal creature'. Indeed, notes Kenez, 'the author's hatred of the revolutionaries is so great that he ceases to be a historian and becomes instead a prosecutor of revolutionaries'. His view of the majority of the people is in the classic conservative mould: 'irrational creatures driven by "anger, envy, resentments of every imaginable kind," that eventually blew off the "lid of awe and fear" that contained them', only to be manipulated by Lenin and other revolutionary intellectuals (in Ronald Suny's apt summary). Pipes offers an approach significantly to the right of most scholarship by Cold War and post-Cold War academics. But it is no more useful in helping us comprehend how one might change the world for the better, or in helping us understand how the Bolsheviks actually succeeded and failed in their own efforts to do so.[20]

Radical Activist Critics

There are a variety of criticisms offered by critics of Leninism who are radical activists of the late twentieth and early twenty-first centuries. Interestingly, many seem to involve a relatively uncritical acceptance of some or all of the other kinds of criticism we have touched on. All-too-often the criticisms seem to be superficial, ill-informed, and (as is the case with the academic critics and Cold War ideologists) not particularly coherent.

There are other intellectual streams that contemporary activists have drawn from, however, which are more coherent and penetrating, a prime example being that of anarchism. One of the most devastating eyewitness critiques of Lenin can be found in the eloquent memoir of Alexander Berkman, *The Bolshevik Myth* (1925), and one of the finest critical historians of the Russian Revolution is Paul Avrich, whose *The Russian Anarchists* and *Kronstadt 1921* (with a pro-anarchist orientation that advances rather than derailing serious scholarship) are essential reading. The most vibrant elements in these critiques, however, focus on the disasters of the civil war period and the authoritarian aftermath (which intersects with important criticisms of such socialist critics as Balabanoff and Liberman, and even pro-Bolshevik voices such as that of Victor Serge). While these critical targets are inseparable from the later history of Leninism, they are not part of its earlier history. It can even be argued that the criticisms of post-1917 problems are not necessarily inconsistent with the essentials of Lenin's thought that will be specified later in this introduction.[21]

Another challenge, to some extent overlapping with anarchist perspectives, questions more essential aspects of Lenin's orientation – (a) the Marxist view that the working class is a decisive force for advancing the revolutionary struggle, and (b) the notion that the workers (or any revolutionary force) should aim to take state power. Instead, principled activists should join with various oppressed populations to push back various aspects of capitalist 'globalisation' and to create a proliferation of 'free spaces', liberated zones, and oases of liberty and community, which will link with each other to create an increasingly better world. Whether this will prove a more effective and durable orientation than Lenin's, however, is by no means clear.[22]

A criticism targeting what appear to be other essential aspects of Lenin's thought has been expressed by some activists who were once part of one or another organisation identifying with the Leninist tradition. Among the most interesting of these is the critique articulated some years ago by socialist-feminist historian and activist Sheila Rowbotham, who raised a sharp question regarding the relationship between Leninist party and the broader social movements and non-party organisations in which its members function (trade unions, community organisations, women's liberation groups, anti-war coalitions, etc.). She wrote:

> The individual member will face a split loyalty between a commitment to an autonomous group and the [Leninist] organisation. The theory says the Party must be more important. The choice is either to get out of the organization (which seems from within to be leaving socialist politics itself), to ignore the center [i.e., the leadership of the Leninist organization] (in which case democratic centralism has proved unworkable), or to accept the line [of the Leninist organization even if you feel it would harm the autonomous group]. So however unsectarian this socialist may be, he or she has very stark choices and a political ideology which sanctions accepting party discipline more than helping to develop the self-activity of other people.

She adds: 'If you accept a high degree of centralization and define yourselves as [revolutionary] professionals concentrating above everything upon the central task of seizing power, you necessarily diminish the development of the self-activity and self-confidence of most of the people involved [in the broader autonomous group].'[23]

While there are certainly plenty of examples of members of one or another Leninist or would-be Leninist organisation functioning in a manipulative manner, to the detriment of a broader non-Leninist organisation, it is not the case that there is some 'iron law of Leninist manipulation'. In fact, there are also examples of the opposite type of behaviour – of open, honest, creative, principled Leninists helping to build trade unions, social movements, etc.

Testimony from US labour struggles of the 1930s provide counter-examples to what is suggested by Rowbotham. A veteran of the Women's Emergency Brigade, which emerged from the Great Flint Sit-Down Strike of 1937 and helped to build the United Auto Workers (UAW), commented some years later: 'I know that there was a Socialist Party and Communist Party helping to organize. Although I never belonged to a Party, I feel that had it not been for the education and the know-how that they gave us, we wouldn't have been able to do it.' A similar comment about the Trotskyist Dunne brothers, who helped organise a local of the Teamsters union, was made by Farrell Dobbs, who became one of the leaders of the 1934 Minneapolis General Strike: 'I was impressed with the way Grant and Miles had handled themselves during the strike. They appeared to know what had to be done and they had the guts to do it. ... I reasoned that if I joined a communist organization, I might be able to learn some of the things they knew.' The oldest of the three Dunne brothers on the scene – organiser and strike leader Vincent Raymond Dunne – matter-of-factly explained: 'Our policy was to organize and build strong unions, so workers could have something to say and assist in changing the present order into a socialist society.' As journalist and eyewitness Charles Rumford Walker commented, as many as 400 to 500 Minneapolis workers knew Ray Dunne personally as 'honest, intelligent, and selfless, and a damn good organizer for the truck drivers' union to have. They had always known him to be a Red; that was no news.' Such positive experience can be found in other contexts as well – which hardly eliminates the actuality of more problematical experiences.

The point is that such problems are not an automatic outcome of the Leninist organisational scheme.[24]

The Leninist Organisational Scheme and Democratic Centralism

We have already commented on the Cold War academics' special fixation on (and garbling of) Lenin's organisational perspectives. But their studies have so influenced the terms of the discussion among later critics on this important question that it may be fruitful to conclude the present section of our introduction with a further exploration (and clearing away) of their mystifications.

As Alfred G. Meyer explained in his influential 1956 study *Leninism*, although 'Lenin always carried the word "democracy" in his mouth, and was eager to show that he had not forsaken these democratic traditions', the fact was that 'all discussion was suspect to him, because it was a waste of time and because it might threaten the unity of the party in action'. Robert V. Daniels concurred in *The Nature of Communism* (1962) that Lenin's preference was for 'the revolutionary party as a disciplined, conspiratorial elite', despite his desire to appear democratic. 'The formula Lenin found for the resolution of the problem has become famous', according to Meyer. 'It is the principle of "democratic centralism"', which projected 'the party as a genuinely collectivist organization, freely, consciously, and joyfully submitting to the leadership imposed upon it by senior members.' Daniels concurred: 'Lenin would not be constrained by democratic scruples; "democratic centralism," implicitly far more centralism than democratic, was his formula for combining the ideal and the practical.'[25]

This interpretation has continued to reverberate into the twenty-first century in accounts provided by capable and respected scholars in works produced for college and university courses (and which naturally influence student activists as well). 'Lenin's professional revolutionaries were to be organized in a conspiratorial, centralized, and hierarchical network', according to Michael Kort's *The Soviet Colossus* (2006), and 'the party was to tell the working class what to do, and the party's central committee was to govern the party', with this leading body functioning according to '"democratic centralism," a term he first used in 1905', but which 'turned out to be far more centralist than democratic'. In *Socialism in Russia* (2002), John Gooding writes that 'because the workers were not capable of being an effective revolutionary force', Lenin argued for a revolutionary party that 'had to be small, disciplined, conspiratorial and hierarchical: an elite of professional and utterly dedicated Marxist revolutionaries' – in short 'a dominant party leading a passive working class'. As David Marples puts it in *Lenin's Revolution* (2000), 'what was required was a system of "democratic centralism," whereby the main decisions would be taken by a small party of committed and experienced revolutionaries working through a party central committee', with 'the rule of a minority party over the workers that would ultimately result in a dictatorship'.[26]

This is a myth. Lenin's conceptions were not what these scholars say they are.

In defence of the academics (and especially those writing during the Cold War), the most influential example of 'Leninism' of the time was that of the world Communist movement, led by the Communist Party of the Soviet Union, with an ideology that had been grotesquely transformed during the predominance of Joseph Stalin and his co-thinkers from the late 1920s through the early 1950s. According to Stalin, Lenin's approach to organisation specified:

(a) that the Party is a higher form of the class organization of the proletariat as compared with the other forms of proletarian organization (labor unions, cooperative societies, state organizations) and, moreover, its function was to generalize and direct the work of these organizations; (b) that the dictatorship of the proletariat may be realized only through the party as its directing force; (c) that the dictatorship of the proletariat may be complete only if it is led by a single party, the Communist Party; and (d) that without iron discipline in the Party, the tasks of the dictatorship of the proletariat to crush the exploiters and to transform class society into socialist society cannot be fulfilled.[27]

The place of 'democratic centralism' within the Stalinist scheme of things involved the membership 'democratically' passing on ideas and information to the central leadership and then 'democratically' discussing how to carry out the leadership's decisions. This comes through in comments by one of Stalin's spokesmen, V.G. Sorin, in the early 1930s. 'The Party is governed by leaders', he explained. 'If the party is the vanguard of the working class then the leaders are the advanced post of this vanguard.' Sorin emphasised that

> the special feature of the Communist Party is its strictest discipline, i.e., the unconditional and exact observance by all members of the party of all directives coming from their Party organizations. Discipline, firm and unrelenting, is necessary not only during the period of underground work and struggle against tsarism, not only during civil war, but even during peaceful times.

Sorin concluded: 'The stricter the discipline, the stronger the party, the more dangerous is it to the capitalists.'[28]

This is the opposite of the original meaning of the term, which was *not* an invention of Lenin's 'vanguardist' Bolsheviks within the Russian Social-Democratic Labour Party (RSDLP). Actually, the term *democratic centralism* was introduced into the Russian socialist movement in the revolutionary year 1905 by Lenin's factional adversaries, the Mensheviks, as the RSDLP was acquiring a mass base in the Russian working class, and the Mensheviks and Bolsheviks were moving closer together.

A Menshevik resolution asserted that 'the RSDLP must be organized according to the principle of democratic centralism', that 'actions affecting the organization as a whole ... must be decided upon by all the members of the organization', and that 'decisions of lower-level organizations [such a party branch] are not to be implemented if they contradict the decisions of higher organizations [such as a national convention or party congress]'. A Bolshevik resolution almost a month later, 'recognizing as indisputable the principle of democratic centralism', called for 'the broad implementation of the elective principle', adding that 'while granting elected centers full powers in matters of ideological and practical leadership, they are at the same time subject to recall, their actions are given broad publicity, and they are to be strictly accountable [to the membership] for these activities'.[29]

Lenin summarised it as 'freedom of discussion, unity of action'. In Lenin's opinion, the revolutionary party 'must be united, but in these united organizations there must be wide and free discussion of party questions, free comradely criticism and assessment of events in Party life'. This would include, he stressed in 1906, 'guarantees for the rights of all minorities and for all loyal opposition, ... recognizing that all party functionaries must be elected, accountable to the Party and subject to recall'. He explained that 'the principle of democratic centralism and autonomy for local Party organizations implies universal and full *freedom to criticize* so long as this does not disturb the unity of a definite *action*', although there was an expectation that a significant degree of loyalty to the party, its programme, and its organisational statutes would provide the framework of (and constraints for) such local autonomy and freedom to criticise.[30]

Lenin's organisational perspectives for a revolutionary working-class party (discussed at length and with extensive documentation in *Lenin and the Revolutionary Party*) could be summarised in the following eight points:

1. The workers' party must, first of all, be based on a revolutionary Marxist programme and must exist to apply that programme to reality in a way that will advance the struggle for socialism.

2. The members of that party must be activists who agree with the basic programme, who are collectively developing and implementing the programme, and who collectively control the organisation as a whole.

3. To the extent that it is possible (given tsarist repression, for example), the party should function openly and democratically, with the elective principle operating from top to bottom.

4. The highest decision-making body of the party is the *party congress* or convention, made up of delegates democratically elected by each local party unit. The congress should meet at least every two years and should be preceded by a full discussion (in written discussion bulletins and in special meetings) throughout the party on all questions that party members deem important.

5. Between congresses, a *central committee* – elected by and answerable to the congress – should ensure the cohesion and co-ordinate the work of the party on the basis of the party programme and the decisions of the congress. It may set up subordinate, interim bodies (such as a political committee and organisation bureau) to help oversee the weekly and even daily functioning of the organisation. These leadership bodies have the responsibility to keep all local units and the membership informed of all party experiences, activities, and decisions; members and local units also have the responsibility to keep the leadership informed of their experiences and activities.

6. It is assumed that within the general framework of the revolutionary programme there will be shades of difference on various theoretical, programmatic, tactical and practical questions. These should be openly discussed and debated, particularly before party congresses. Depending on time, place and circumstance, such differences can be aired publicly. All members should be encouraged to participate in this discussion process and should have an opportunity to make their views known to the party as a whole. Groupings will sometimes form around one or another viewpoint or even around a full-fledged platform that certain members believe the party should adopt. This provides a basis for ongoing political clarity and programmatic development that are essential to the party's health and growth.

7. All questions should be decided on the basis of democratic vote (majority rule), after which the minority is expected to function loyally in the party, and particularly to avoid undermining the specific actions decided on. The organisation

as a whole learns through the success, partial success, or failure of policies that are adopted and tested in practice.

8. Local units of the party must operate within the framework of the party programme and of the decisions of the party as a whole, but within that framework they must operate under the autonomous and democratic control of the local membership.

Taken together, these points indicate the way that a revolutionary vanguard organisation would function according to the principle of democratic centralism as elaborated by Lenin. It also describes, more or less, the way the Bolsheviks functioned until the early 1920s.[31]

It remains for us to trace the contexts in which the actual Leninist orientation triumphed and in which it was defeated and distorted, and also to ponder ways in which it may be relevant so many decades later.

His Time and Ours

> Read Lenin again (be careful).
> C. Wright Mills[32]

Lenin has been described as 'the architect of twentieth-century totalitarianism' and 'the author of mass terror and even the first concentration camps ever built on the European continent', who 'created a model not merely for his successor, Stalin, but for Mao, for Hitler, for Pol Pot'.[33] This is a powerful indictment that should be confronted before we decide whether we want to spend much of our time with the writings of this man.

In fact, there is ample non-Leninist testimony available to demonstrate the falseness of this indictment. As two of Lenin's political opponents, David Dallin and Boris Nicolaevsky, pointed out in their 1947 classic *Forced Labor in Soviet Russia*, 'the Communist party came to power as the great heir to an age-old revolutionary movement in which lofty ideals and humanitarian goals were the inspiring stimuli to self-sacrifice and devotion to the political cause'. In *The Origins of Totalitarianism* Hannah Arendt observed 'that Lenin suffered his greatest defeat' when, in the horrific civil war period following the 1917 revolution, the vitality of the democratic councils (soviets) of working people – which he had projected as central to the new revolutionary regime – was destroyed, with the supreme power passing into the hands of the party bureaucracy.[34]

On the matter of Lenin founding the first concentration camps, Arendt has demonstrated that it was instead the impeccably anti-Bolshevik European imperialists – engaged in an extensive 'civilising' mission to pump wealth out of colonies in Africa and Asia – who, long before 1917, had first created concentration camps in defence of their empires among mostly non-white peoples: 'These camps corresponded in many respects to the concentration camps at the beginning of totalitarian rule; they were used for "suspects" whose offenses could not be proved and who could not be sentenced by ordinary process of law.' Drawing on a rich array of sources, including Rosa Luxemburg's *The Accumulation of Capital* (as Arendt notes, a work of 'brilliant insight'), Arendt demonstrates what many Cold War anti-Communists refused to acknowledge: that the imperialism of the advanced capitalist powers has been responsible for much of the authoritarianism and inhumanity associated with the twentieth-century 'totalitarianism'. More recent studies have amply documented the continuing brutality of more modern, non-colonial variants of imperialism down to the present day. Lenin was one of the sharpest analysts and opponents of imperialism in its various forms, highlighting the importance of, and lending support to, national liberation struggles against imperialist domination around the world.[35]

Similarly, Dallin and Nicolaevsky have demonstrated that in Russia it is hardly the case that Lenin invented systematic state-sponsored forced labour camps. These had been established and maintained, years before Lenin was born, by the tsarist monarchy of which he was a mortal enemy. Nor is it the case that things got qualitatively worse under Lenin. Dallin and Nicolaevsky note that while 30,000 was the maximum number of camp inmates on the eve of the First World War, the number had shot up to 50,000 by

1917 – *before* the Revolution. Under Lenin's regime the camps continued to exist. One can certainly raise critical points about this, but there was not the massive expansion that some have alleged. As late as 1928, according to Robert Conquest's *The Great Terror*, the number of people in the camps was 30,000.[36]

Lenin can be associated with what came to be known as 'the Red Terror' of the civil war period (1918–21), involving policies which a number of revolutionaries sympathetic with Lenin's goals have sharply challenged. But the fact remains that 'Lenin's Terror was the product of the years of war and violence, of the collapse of society and administration, of the desperate acts of rulers precariously riding the flood, and fighting for control and survival', as anti-Communist scholar Robert Conquest points out. 'Stalin, on the contrary, attained complete control at a time when general conditions were calm. ... It was in cold blood, quite deliberately and unprovokedly, that Stalin started a new cycle of suffering.' It was Stalin's vicious 'revolution from above' in the early 1930s – the forced collectivisation of land and rapid industrialisation – that sent the population of the gulag, according to Conquest, up to 600,000 by 1930 and into the millions in following years. While new evidence has meant that Conquest's figure of 7 million has to be revised downward to something more like 1 to 2 million, the overall pattern he traced is generally accepted by serious scholars of various persuasions. As Conquest and many others have documented, the camps of the 1930s became far more brutal and lethal than had been the case in the 1920s and before 1917.[37]

Stalin and Stalinists have sought to associate Lenin and Leninism with this murderous regime, and anti-Communists down to the present day have happily followed suit. The reality was emphasised eloquently at the time of this 'revolution from above', however, by one of the last significant oppositionists, Mikhail N. Riutin, a veteran Bolshevik and one-time follower of Nikolai Bukharin. Riutin observed that 'the main cohort of Lenin's comrades has been removed from the leading positions, and some of them are in prisons and exile; others have capitulated, still others, demoralized and humiliated, carry on a miserable existence, and finally, some, those who have degenerated completely, have turned into loyal servants of the dictator'. In his view, 'the most evil enemy of the party and the proletarian dictatorship, the most evil counter-revolutionary and provocateur could not have carried out the work of destroying the party and socialist construction better than Stalin has done'. And it is certainly the case that methods of Stalinism created a so-called 'socialism' that was hated by millions and incapable of enduring.[38]

Contrary to what Lenin's modern-day detractors insist, we have to push past this grotesque and murderous bureaucratic tyranny, with its anti-Leninist 'Leninism', in order to find who Lenin actually was and what he actually thought. And in doing that, we will discover ideas far more durable, far more useful for our own time, than the sterile caricatures attributed to him.

Lenin and Marxism

It has often been asserted that Lenin – far from adhering to the ideas of Karl Marx – believed 'that the scientific doctrine of Marxism must be supplemented by a revolutionary faith and that the Social Democratic Party [which he sought to transform] must also become like a military order', as Adam Ulam has put it in his influential account *The Bolsheviks*. We are told that because of this Lenin sought 'to infuse Marxists with ... revolutionary fire and conspiratorial discipline', and that 'most of Lenin's colleagues began to sense that there was something new in his Marxism' as early as 1902.[39]

Far more accurate, however, are those scholars who insist, with Neil Harding in his sharply critical study *Leninism*, that 'the lineage of Leninism lies firmly within the Russian and European Marxist traditions, and that Leninism, as a distinctive ideology, did not exist until 1914'. Harding adds that 'the passion and commitment of Leninism ... derived from its insistence that, in all essentials, Marx was right'. This is a point worth giving attention to if we truly wish to understand the actualities of Lenin's thought. This means that it makes sense, first of all, to review essential aspects of Karl Marx's own perspectives that can be found at the core of Lenin's outlook.[40]

Marx had taught that revolutionary change is possible and necessary. The nature of capitalism itself makes this so. The advance of technology and productivity – thanks to the dynamics of capitalist development – has drawn the different regions of our planet together and created a sufficient degree of social wealth, or economic surplus, to make possible a decent, creative, free existence and meaningful self-development for each and every person. Yet the dynamics of capitalist development, related to the *accumulation process* (i.e., the need for capitalists to make more and more profits), are so destructive of human freedom and dignity that it is necessary to move to a different form of economic life. What's more, the natural trend of capitalist development has been creating a working-class majority in more and more sectors of the world, and the nature of the working class makes a socialist future both possible and necessary: *possible* because a majority class, essential to the functioning of capitalism, has the potential power to lay hold of the technology and resources of the economy to bring about a socialist future; *necessary* because the economic democracy of socialism is required to ensure the dignity, the freedom, and the survival of the working-class majority and humanity in general.

According to Marx, it will be possible to win a working-class majority to this perspective if revolutionaries develop a clear understanding of the capitalist reality that is creating the possibility and necessity for socialism, and help others – especially among the growing working class – to understand that reality. An essential part of this process of creating a socialist majority among the working class would involve helping to organise the workers themselves around serious struggles to improve the condition of the working class (a better economic situation, an expansion of democratic rights, etc.). Not only will this result in life-giving improvements for the workers, but it will also give them a sense of their power and their ability to bring about change, and their organisational and class-struggle experience will enable them to struggle more effectively in the future.

In order to advance its interests, the working class must organise itself not only as an economic movement but also as a political movement, and it must be politically independent from the capitalists and other upper-class elements organised in various liberal, conservative, and hybrid political parties. The workers must utilise their trade unions, reform organisations, and political party to struggle for political power. When they are able to win political power (which will have to be organised in more radically democratic structures than those developed by the capitalist politicians), this will constitute a working-class revolution, and they should use this revolutionary power to begin the transition from a capitalist to a socialist economy. In this entire process, the workers must ally themselves with all labouring people (especially farmers, peasants, etc.), and with all of the oppressed, whose liberation must be part of the working-class political programme.

Because capitalism is a global system, the struggle of the working class for a better life and for socialism must be global, and the development of socialism can only be accomplished on a global scale. The global and exploitative expansiveness inherent in capitalism is laid out clearly in the *Communist Manifesto*. Workers of all countries will have to unite in a multi-faceted international movement to bring a better future into being.

Marx approached the organisation question with a high degree of seriousness. According to the *Communist Manifesto*, Communists are the most advanced and resolute section of the working-class movement, seeking to push forward all the others – because they are the most theoretically clear element within the working class, with a definite understanding of 'the line of march, the conditions, and the ultimate general results of the proletarian movement'. There is a need for democratic, cohesive, effective organisations of working-class activists to play this role. There are radical insights and militant upsurges that naturally and spontaneously animate the working class in its struggles – but much serious work needs to be done to help draw together and deepen such insights into consistent class consciousness, and to sustain and broaden such upsurges into consistent class struggle that can lead to socialism.[41]

Lenin's Triumph

Lenin did more than most other twentieth-century Marxists to articulate a powerful orientation among those adhering to classical Marxism. He is important for serious-minded socialists because of what Georg Lukács stressed as the core of his thought – a deep belief in 'the actuality of revolution'. In contrast to so many would-be socialists, he does not see the capitalist status quo as the solid and unshakeable ground of our being. Rather, his starting point is the opposite – that the continuing development of capitalism creates the basis for working-class revolution. This means not that revolution is about to erupt at every given moment, but that every person and every issue can and must be seen in relationship to the fundamental practical problem of advancing the struggle for revolution. What this means, for a Marxist like Lenin, is utilising his revolutionary Marxism, as Lukács put it, 'to establish firm guide-lines for all questions on the daily agenda, whether they were political or economic, involved theory or tactics, agitation or organization'.[42]

Until the explosion of the First World War, as leader of the Bolshevik wing of the Russian Social-Democratic Labour Party (RSDLP), Lenin was also inclined to follow the 'orthodox Marxist' notion that a working-class socialist revolution would not be possible in backward, overwhelmingly agrarian Russia, a predominantly peasant land languishing under the yoke and lash of the autocratic monarchy of the Tsars and the landed aristocracy. At the time of the 1905 uprising in Russia, he was in accord with the Menshevik faction of the RSDLP (and in disagreement with the revolutionary maverick Leon Trotsky) in arguing that 'under the present social and economic order this democratic revolution in Russia will not weaken but strengthen the domination of the bourgeoisie', and 'will, for the first time, make it possible for the bourgeoisie to rule as a class'. This would establish the basis for the sort of capitalist development and industrial modernisation that Marx and Engels had described in the *Communist Manifesto*. At the same time, Lenin and others in the RSDLP insisted that 'the democratic revolution ... clears the ground for a new class struggle', and that for the working class 'the struggle for political liberty and a democratic republic in a bourgeois society is only one of the necessary stages in the struggle for the social revolution which will overthrow the bourgeois system'.[43]

A central difference distinguishing Lenin's Bolsheviks from many Mensheviks in 1905 (and even more afterward) was the fact that he did not seek a worker–capitalist alliance as a means for overthrowing tsarism. The exploiters of the working class could not be counted on to help advance the interests of the workers, he insisted. The bourgeois liberals could be counted on only to make what Lenin called 'a wretched deal' with the forces of monarchy and reaction (as they had done, for example, amid Europe's revolutionary upsurges of 1848). Instead, he advocated a worker–peasant alliance. As he put it: 'Only the proletariat can be a consistent fighter for democracy. It can become a victorious fighter for democracy only if the peasant masses join its struggle.'[44] This revolutionary alliance, Lenin argued, should result in a revolutionary worker–peasant regime (what he called 'the revolutionary-democratic dictatorship of the proletariat and the peasantry'), that would carry through the most consistent demolition of the old tsarist order. Then matters could be turned over to a bourgeois republic based on an industrialising capitalist economy that would – in turn – allow for the growth of a working-class majority that could push for greater and greater democracy, with struggles that would ultimately culminate in a socialist order based on industrial abundance.

With the imperialist slaughter of the First World War, the so-called 'orthodox' Social-Democratic Party of Germany – whose norms Lenin believed he was adapting to Russian conditions – capitulated to the war effort, along with most of the other parties of the Socialist International, or Second International, with which socialist parties around the world were affiliated. This war-time betrayal caused Lenin to re-evaluate and revise his own Marxism. It is in this period that he engaged more seriously, in his 'Philosophical Notebooks', with the dialectical thought of Hegel. It has been argued that this decisively contributed to his analysis of imperialism, to his sharpened perspectives on the complex dynamics of nationalism (and on the right of oppressed nations to self-determination), and to his deepened perspectives on the questions of the state and revolution.[45] And he dramatically deepened his commitment to revolutionary democracy and to its unbreakable link with the class struggle and with the struggle for socialism. In a manner reminiscent of Leon Trotsky's 1906 formulations of the theory of permanent revolution, Lenin articulated an approach of integrating reform struggles with revolutionary strategy and, combined with this, a conceptualisation of democratic struggles flowing into socialist revolution. He also saw the horrific slaughter and carnage of the First World War as generating a powerful reaction among masses of people world-wide against the leaders and the system that had led them into this calamity – which would now create a context in which revolutionary upsurges could be expected in a number of countries.[46]

In some ways this prediction proved more accurate than even Lenin anticipated. February/March 1917, before the war's end, saw the overthrow of the tsar by a mass uprising of workers joined by soldiers and sailors, setting the stage for a confused dance of two newly-formed power centres – a network of democratic councils (soviets) established by the workers and their allies, and a Provisional Government composed of pro-capitalist politicians joined by moderate socialist allies.

In this context, Lenin composed his unfinished theoretical symphony, *The State and Revolution*. This work constitutes – first of all – a brilliant contribution to Marxist scholarship, but building on the excavation of the actual views of Marx and Engels, Lenin projects a vision of a workers' state in which government is directly and genuinely a manifestation of 'rule by the people' – a modern Marxist version of Athenian democracy.[47] This is in harmony with his incredible, radically democratic public writings and polemics of 1917.

Lenin and his comrades relentlessly advanced the demand of 'all power to the soviets', leading to a second revolution of October/ November to turn the slogan into reality. This soviet seizure of power was, in fact, made up of multi-faceted insurgencies, pushed forward by not only the Bolsheviks but also Left Socialist-Revolutionaries, anarchists, and even some Mensheviks, as well as revolutionary independents, among the workers and their allies in the military (many of whom were 'peasants in uniform', as Trotsky noted). The uprisings in the cities and towns were buttressed by ferment in the peasant villages and supplemented by the radicalism of oppressed nationalities throughout the Russian Empire.[48] After the Provisional Government's overthrow, Lenin appealed to the labouring masses throughout Russia:

> Comrades, workers, soldiers, peasants – all toilers! Take immediately all local power into your hands .... Little by little, with the consent of the majority of peasants, we shall march firmly and unhesitatingly toward the victory of Socialism, which will fortify the advance-guards of the working class of the most civilised countries, and give to the peoples an enduring peace, and free them from every slavery and every exploitation.[49]

In contrast to the fiction that the Bolsheviks were intent upon establishing a new tyranny, the new regime was radically democratic. Menshevik Simon Liberman later recounted that the Soviet government 'began by abrogating the death penalty at the front (behind the lines it had been abolished de facto even before the November revolution). Opposition newspapers of sundry political hues continued to be published, criticizing Lenin's government, day in and day out. The opposition parties existed and functioned pretty much as before.' In the near future, we will see, things would dramatically shift – but Liberman observed that 'when, two months after the November revolution, the Cheka or Soviet secret police office ... was first established, it was empowered to investigate, but not to punish, political crimes'.[50] Of course, within several months the escalation of events would dramatically broaden what the Cheka considered a 'political crime', and it would do far more than 'investigating'.

It was by no means clear that the new revolutionary regime that Lenin was leading would be able to survive. And there were terrible mistakes being made by the Bolshevik-led regime every day. 'Of course, we make mistakes. There cannot be a revolution without errors', Lenin commented to Liberman. 'But we are learning from our errors and are glad when we can correct them. ... Our government may not last long, but these decrees will be part of history. Future revolutionaries will learn from them ....' Making reference to the short-lived Paris Commune, fruit of a workers' uprising in 1871, he added: 'We ourselves keep the decrees of the Paris Commune before our eyes as a model.'[51]

A key to the revolution's survival and success, Lenin and his comrades were convinced, would be the spread of revolution throughout Europe and beyond. Some have dismissed this as an utterly unrealistic expectation. It is worth recalling, however, the recollections of the US Communist-turned-conservative, Bertram D. Wolfe, who – even as an aging anti-Communist – could not dispel a sense of excitement from his memories of 1919:

The opportunities for American radicalism of all varieties seemed immense in that year of interregnum between all-out war and what was supposed to be all-out peace. Millions of soldiers were being demobilized and hundreds of thousands of those who had risked their lives at the front were finding that there were no jobs waiting for them at home. Europe was in turmoil: crowns were tumbling and ancient empires falling; there were revolutions, still not defined in their nature, in Russia, Germany, Austria-Hungary, then a Communist revolution in Hungary itself and another in Bavaria; soldiers were carrying their arms from the front and imposing their will insofar as they knew what they willed. A strike wave unprecedented in our history swept through America: the Seattle General Strike grew out of a protest at the closing down of the shipyards; the Lawrence Textile Strike; the national coal strike; and, wonder of wonders, the Boston police strike; the great steel strike involving 350,000; the battles of the workers in many industries to keep wages abreast of the high cost of living, and of the employers to end the wartime gains of the labor movement

[and] to establish or restore the [non-union] open shop. Not until the Great Depression [of the 1930s] would the labor movement again show so much militancy.[52]

It was to help channel such energy into successful revolutions that Lenin and his co-thinkers in 1919 established the Communist International (or Third International) to organise and support revolutionary parties in all countries. But the results were not consistent with Lenin's hopes. Although the dozens of newly formed Communist parties would attract millions of workers, peasants, and others to struggle under the banner of the hammer and sickle, in some cases writing heroic pages in the histories of more than one country, the upsurges in other lands did not bring to the side of revolutionary Russia the expected new partners in socialist progress. The industrial capitalist nations – Germany most of all – were shaken by revolutionary tremors but remained capitalist.[53]

Just as no other durable revolutions were achieved in Lenin's lifetime, so would the radically democratic soviet state prove unable to endure for more than several months.

Lenin's Tragedy

Of course, the disastrous conditions already facing the new Soviet republic, and the horrific intensification of difficulties guaranteed by powerful internal and external enemies, ensured the destruction of any necessary pre-conditions for a democratic order. 'The faith which Lenin had placed in the Soviets was rendered altogether illusory by the circumstances of revolution and civil war', Ralph Miliband has noted, adding: 'Whether they could have fulfilled even some of his expectations had circumstances been more favorable is an open question.'[54]

In an important comparative study of violence and terror in the French and Russian revolutions entitled *The Furies*, Arno Mayer outlines the dialectic of revolution and counter-revolution. Unlike many who simply condemn the murderous violence of Lenin and the Bolsheviks, Mayer sees the no less murderous violence of the powerful anti-Bolsheviks as an essential element in the equation. He comments that Bolsheviks 'were unprepared for the enormity of the crisis', and also were 'caught unawares by its Furies, which they were not alone to quicken'. At the same time, he reflects: 'It may well be that by virtue of its eventual costs and cruelties, this resolve to fight a civil war became the original sin or primal curse of Bolshevik governance during the birth throes of the Russian Revolution.'[55]

The wonderful quality of Lenin's Marxism especially in 1915– 17 was the unity of revolutionary strategy and revolutionary goal – each permeated by a vibrant, uncompromising working-class militancy, insurgent spirit, and radical democracy. This is worthy of the great symphonies of narrative and analysis that the finest representatives of the revolutionary Marxist tradition have produced. This was Lenin's triumph, culminating in the Bolshevik Revolution.

Lenin's tragedy is that this broke down in practice in 1918 – not simply because of the debilitating and murderous violence, but because the simple solution of 'workers' democracy' became problematical when the abstract visions were brought down to the level of concrete realities. In the midst of the chaotic realities of 1918 and after, workers' committees and councils in the factories and neighbourhoods did not have enough information and knowledge, nor enough skill, practical experience, and resources to make and carry out decisions for the purpose of running a national economy, developing adequate social services throughout the country, formulating a coherent foreign policy, or even running a factory. This was especially so in the context of the overwhelming destructiveness of the First World War, the various and unrelenting foreign military interventions against the revolution, the economic blockade, and the horrors of civil war.

At least 1 million people died in the combat and violence of the Russian civil war, and several million more died from disease, hunger, and cold – largely the result of massive aid that Britain, France, and the United States gave to the counter-revolutionary armies of Admiral Kolchak and General Denikin, and also the economic embargo imposed by the world's capitalist powers.

Winston Churchill, who, as British Minister of War, played a central role in helping to co-ordinate the Allied intervention against the Bolsheviks, while lamenting (several years later) over the failure to overturn the revolutionary regime, argued that his efforts were not in vain. 'The Bolsheviks were absorbed during the whole of 1919 in the conflicts with Kolchak and Denikin. Their energy was turned upon the internal struggle', he noted, adding: 'A breathing space of inestimable importance was afforded to the whole line of newly liberated countries which stood upon the western borders of Russia.' He emphasised: 'By the end of 1920 the "Sanitary Cordon" which protected Europe from the Bolshevik infection was formed by living national organisms vigorous in themselves, hostile to the disease and immune through experience against its ravages.'[56]

What Churchill neglects to say is that the 'vigorous' anti-Communist regimes he so admired (and which his government helped to put in place) were, in fact, violent right-wing dictatorships which (like the counter-revolutionary armies in Russia) had few qualms about massive human rights violations, the repression of workers' organisations, and a sometimes systematic and murderous anti-Semitism. While Churchill frowned on the anti-Semitic policies, his happy acceptance of all the rest should not be surprising from someone who admiringly contrasted 'the far-seeing realism of Mussolini' and his fascist dictatorship in Italy to the 'sub-human doctrine and superhuman tyranny' of Communism.[57]

In the face of counter-revolutionary intervention and onslaught and economic collapse, the Bolsheviks (who renamed their organisation the Russian Communist Party) established a one-party dictatorship. The rights of speech, press, assembly and association – providing the possibility of spreading confusion, or of putting forward super-revolutionary but unworkable alternatives, or of fomenting counter-revolution – were suppressed. This meant the suppression of Mensheviks, anarchists, Left Socialist-Revolutionaries, Right Socialist-Revolutionaries, liberals, priests, and others. Only the dictatorship of the Communist Party could be tolerated.

There was a cumulative momentum from early 1918 onward leading to this identification of 'dictatorship of the proletariat' (working-class rule) with Communist political monopoly, but the logic of this development was codified most clearly in Lenin's remarks of 1921 on 'The Tax in Kind', which notes, first of all, that 'with enormous difficulty, and in the course of desperate struggles, the Bolsheviks have trained a proletarian vanguard that is capable of governing; they have created and successfully defended the dictatorship of the proletariat'. Then he indicates the existence of three elements on the political scene – 'the steeled and tempered vanguard of the only revolutionary class [i.e., the working-class Communists]; the vacillating petty-bourgeois element [i.e., left-wing opponents of the Bolsheviks among the workers, peasants, and intellectuals – Mensheviks, Socialist-Revolutionaries, and anarchists]; and the Milyukovs, the capitalists and landowners, lying in wait abroad and supported by the world bourgeoisie'. Lenin sees the 'vacillating petty-bourgeois element' as incapable of providing a coherent and practical alternative to either the dictatorship of the bourgeoisie or the dictatorship of the proletariat. Regardless of their intentions, Bolshevism's left-wing critics and opponents were spreading confusion and disunity that threatened to undermine the struggle to maintain working-class rule. 'Ruin, want and the hard conditions of life give rise to vacillation: one day for the bourgeoisie, the next for the proletariat. Only the steeled proletarian vanguard is capable of withstanding and overcoming this vacillation.'[58]

This reflected a powerful element of truth in the situation – but it also stood as a defence of brutal policies fraught with terrible contradictions, abuses, and crimes. A one-time ally of the Bolsheviks, the heroic Left Socialist-Revolutionary leader Maria Spiridonova, wrote an open letter from a Bolshevik prison giving some sense of this moral disaster. 'Your party had great tasks and began them finely', she recalled. 'The October Revolution, in which we marched side by side, was bound to conquer, because its foundations and watchwords were rooted in historical reality and were solidly supported by all the working masses.' But by November 1918 this had all changed:

In the name of the proletariat you have wiped out all the moral achievements of our Revolution. Things that cry aloud to Heaven have been done by the provincial Chekas, by the All-Russian Cheka. A blood-thirsty mockery of the souls and bodies of men, torture and treachery, and then – murder, murder without end, done without inquiry, on denunciation only, without waiting for any proof of guilt.[59]

This was acknowledged even by partisans of the Bolshevik cause, even as they defended the Bolsheviks. As eyewitness journalist from the United States, Albert Rhys Williams, wrote in his 1921 classic *Through the Russian Revolution*:

'Repressions, tyranny, violence', cry the enemies. 'They have abolished free speech, free press, free assembly. They have imposed drastic military conscription and compulsory labor. They have been incompetent in government, inefficient in industry. They have subordinated the Soviets to the Communist Party. They have lowered their Communist ideals, changed and shifted their program and compromised with the capitalists'.

Some of these charges are exaggerated. Many can be explained. But they cannot all be explained away. Friends of the Soviet grieve over them. Their enemies have summoned the world to shudder and protest against them. ...

While abroad hatred against the Bolsheviks as the new 'enemies of civilization' mounted from day to day, these selfsame Bolsheviks were straining to rescue civilization in Russia from total collapse.[60]

Yet a key problem, identified by Bolshevik partisans even closer to the realities, was the growth of a bureaucracy that absorbed Bolsheviks, now calling themselves Communists, into itself while moving in a direction inconsistent with the goals for which the Revolution was made. 'The economic power in the hands of the proletarian state of Russia is quite adequate to ensure the transition to communism', Lenin commented in 1922, but he added that

what is lacking is culture among the stratum of the Communists who perform administrative functions. If we take Moscow with its

4,700 Communists in responsible positions, and if we take that huge bureaucratic machine, that gigantic heap, we must ask: who is directing whom? I doubt very much whether it can truthfully be said that the Communists are directing that heap. To tell the truth, they are not directing, they are being directed.[61]

Victor Serge later recalled:

'Totalitarianism' did not yet exist as a word; as an actuality it began to press hard on us, even without our being aware of it. What with the political monopoly, the Cheka [secret police], and the Red Army, all that now existed of the 'Commune-State' of our dreams was a theoretical myth. The war, the internal measures against counter-revolution, and the famine (which had created a bureaucratic rationing-apparatus) had killed off Soviet democracy. How could it revive and when? When the Party lived in the certain knowledge that the slightest relaxation of its authority could give the day to reaction.[62]

The last few years of Lenin's life involved much that seems to have swept him far from the political trajectory that he followed from the 1890s through 1917. Yet he never repudiated the revolutionary-democratic orientation that had guided him. Despite contradictions (introduced by the contradictory reality), he remained true to the goal of a socialism rooted in political freedom. This was the basis for his belated efforts to challenge and eliminate the influence of Stalin – although this brutalised and pathological individual was hardly the root of the problem. Lenin also sought to bring more workers and peasants into the government, especially as watchdogs over the functioning of the state, although ultimately this seems to have done little more than add another layer to the growing bureaucracy. The dilemma of a regime founded in the spirit of socialist democracy yet evolving as a bureaucratic dictatorship, as Lenin himself recognised, could only be resolved by the spread of revolution bringing more advanced industrial countries into the socialist orbit, creating a material basis for the economic and cultural development of a socialist society.

As other socialist revolutions were blocked, however, the growing contradictions overwhelmed revolutionary Russia. Some have insisted that the only positive solution would have been provided by the opening of significantly more democratic political space. Instead, the contradictions were to be resolved by new layers in the state and party (as well as corrupted elements of the older layers), identifying with Stalin's leadership, who were increasingly prepared to dispense with political freedom as a core value (while also dispensing with comrades and others not inclined to do so). At the same time, this rising bureaucratic layer continued to utilise a degraded variant of Marxism, and from 1924 onward they made full use of the symbol of the now-dead Lenin to justify the new order that they were building. Such an order both extended and fatally undermined aspects of the 1917 triumph, and ultimately proved not to be durable. Moshe Lewin has commented that 'the year 1924 [marks] the end of "Bolshevism"', adding:

> For a few more years one group of old Bolsheviks after another was to engage in rearguard actions in an attempt to rectify the course of events in one fashion or another. But their political tradition and organization, rooted in the history of Russian and European Social-Democracy, were rapidly swept aside by the mass of new members and new organizational structures which pressed that formation into an entirely different mold. The process of the party's conversion into an apparatus – careers, discipline, ranks, abolition of all political rights – was an absolute scandal for the oppositions of 1924–28. But their old party was dead. People should not be misled by old names and ideologies: in a fluid political context, names last longer than substances.[63]

One can raise questions about how inevitable the triumph of Stalinist dictatorship was in 1924. The perceptive political philosopher Hannah Arendt commented in her classic *The Origins of Totalitarianism* that

> there is no doubt that Lenin suffered his greatest defeat when, at the outbreak of the civil war, the supreme power that he originally

planned to concentrate in the Soviets definitely passed into the hands of the party bureaucracy; but even this development, tragic as it was for the course of the revolution, would not necessarily have led to totalitarianism.

Surveying various countervailing tendencies in the early 1920s, she concludes:

> At the moment of Lenin's death [in 1924] the roads were still open. The formation of workers, peasants, and [in the wake of the New Economic Policy] middle classes need not necessarily have led to the class struggle which had been characteristic of European capitalism. Agriculture could still be developed on a collective, cooperative, or private basis, and the national economy was still free to follow a socialist, state-capitalist, or free-enterprise pattern. None of these alternatives would have automatically destroyed the new structure of the country.[64]

These are matters which serious historians are still sorting through, with much divergent interpretation on the table and much work remaining to be done. What this volume seeks to present is a survey of Lenin's political thought which gives a sense of its varied strands, and which is true to the profoundly democratic thrust of his theory and practice, so terribly battered by horrific complexities in the final years of his life.

Essentials of Lenin's Thought

Whether one ends up embracing or rejecting Lenin's overall orientation, the point that sociologist C. Wright Mills once made about Marx is also true of Lenin: 'To study his work today and then come back to our own concerns is to increase our chances of confronting them with useful ideas and solutions.'[65]

As we can see from some of his earliest writings, Lenin's starting-point is a belief in the *necessary interconnection* of socialist theory and practice with the working class and labour movement. The working class cannot adequately defend its actual interests and overcome its oppression, in his view, without embracing the goal of socialism – an economic system in which the economy is socially owned and democratically controlled in order to meet the needs of all people. Inseparable from this is a basic understanding of *the working class as it is*, which involves a grasp of the diversity and unevenness of working-class experience and consciousness.

This calls for the development of a practical revolutionary approach seeking to connect, in serious ways, with the various sectors and layers of the working class. It involves the understanding that different approaches and goals are required to reach and engage one or another worker, or group or sector or layer of workers. This means thoughtfully utilising various forms of educational and agitational literature, and developing different kinds of speeches and discussions, in order to connect the varieties of working-class experience, and, most important, to help initiate or support various kinds of practical struggles. The more 'advanced' or vanguard layers of the working class must be rallied not to narrow and limited goals (in the spirit of 'Economism' and 'pure and simple trade unionism'), but to an expansive sense of solidarity and common cause which has the potential for drawing the class as a whole into the struggle for its collective interests. This fundamental orientation is the basis for most of what Lenin has to say in this volume. It is the basis of other key perspectives that one can find in these writings:

- an understanding of the necessity of working-class political independence in political and social struggles, and the need for its supremacy (or hegemony) if such struggles are to triumph;
- an understanding of the necessity for socialist and working-class support for struggles of all who suffer oppression;
- a coherent conception of organisation that is practical, democratic, and revolutionary;
- the development of the united front tactic, in which diverse political forces can work together for common goals, without revolutionary organisations undermining their ability to pose effective revolutionary perspectives to the capitalist status quo;

- an intellectual and practical seriousness (and lack of dogmatism or sectarianism) in utilising Marxist theory;
- an approach of integrating reform struggles with revolutionary strategy;
- a remarkable understanding of the manner in which democratic struggles flow into socialist revolution;
- a commitment to a worker–peasant alliance;
- a profound analysis of imperialism and nationalism;
- a vibrantly revolutionary internationalist approach.

Generations of revolutionary activists have found much of value in these ideas, and this in regions throughout the world. Coming out of such a quintessentially American radical formation as the Industrial Workers of the World (IWW), James P. Cannon later recalled the powerful impact of 'the ideas of the Russian Bolsheviks' among US left-wing activists in the wake of the First World War and the 1917 Revolution: 'The power the Russians exerted in that early time was ideological, not administrative. They changed and reshaped the thinking of the young American communists by explanation, not by command; and the effect was clarifying and enlightening, and altogether beneficent for the American movement.' IWW leader 'Big Bill' Haywood commented in an interview with Max Eastman that the Leninist party was consistent with key insights of American radicalism: 'You remember I used to say that all we needed was fifty thousand real IWW's, and then about a million members to back them up? Well, isn't that a similar idea? At least I always realized that the essential thing was to have an organization of *those who know*.'[66]

There have been, since the Russian Revolution of 1917, innumerable efforts – inspired by Lenin's ideas and example – to create such revolutionary organisations of 'those who know'. Some of these efforts have contributed to the writing of inspiring pages in the history of the labour movements and working-class struggles of various countries, although many have also been undermined and fatally compromised by the later impact of Stalinism in the world Communist movement.

The fact is, however, that even anti-Stalinist variants of would-be Leninist organisations (often amounting to what Tariq Ali once called 'toy Bolshevik parties') have all-too-often shown themselves to be quite different from, and inferior to, the revolutionary-democratic Bolsheviks of 1917. This brings us to some concluding comments regarding the use and misuse of Lenin's ideas.

Be Careful

In his 1960 'Letter to the New Left', left-wing academic C. Wright Mills – down-to-earth and honest – advised: 'Read Lenin again (be careful).'[67] This can be interpreted in various ways, but one aspect of being careful involves getting clear on the profound difference between 'the Leninism of Lenin' and the immediate possibilities that we face in a context that is, in some ways, qualitatively different from his. To transpose the texts that come from Lenin and his time into our very different reality can lead to serious political confusion.

Lenin's Bolsheviks came into being within a very specific context. They were part of a broad global working-class formation, part of a developing labour movement, and part of an evolving labour-radical subculture. To try to duplicate some variant of the Leninist party today, outside of such a context, will create something that cannot function as the Bolsheviks functioned in early Russia, nor can it function in the way the early Communists functioned in the 1920s or in the 1930s. In the 1950s, after decades of attempting to apply Lenin's ideas to US realities, James P. Cannon commented:

> The conscious socialists should act as a 'leaven' in the instinctive and spontaneous movement of the working class. ... The leaven can help the dough to rise and eventually become a loaf of bread, but it can never be a loaf of bread itself. ... Every tendency, direct or indirect, of a small revolutionary party to construct a world of its own, outside and apart from the real movement of the workers in the class struggle, is sectarian.[68]

This dovetails with ideas put forward by Lenin himself, in the excerpt from 'Left-Wing' Communism, An Infantile Disorder, contained in this volume. The experience of many activists influenced by Lenin from the 1950s down to the present (2008) demonstrates that efforts to create Leninist parties all-too-often degenerate into the construction of sects, with well-meaning activists penned up in a world of their own, separate and apart from the working class.

A layer of the working class that is permeated by a sub-culture that helps to nourish a certain level of class consciousness must exist if something like 'the Leninism of Lenin' is to come into being. A genuinely revolutionary vanguard organisation cannot exist abstracted from such a reality. Only through the development of that broad vanguard layer and subculture could the context be recreated that will allow for the development of an effective revolutionary vanguard party – a twenty-first-century variant of what the Bolshevik party was, but also reflecting some of the difficult lessons of the post-1917 period.[69]

Related to this is the perspective recently advanced by Sheila Cohen, with experience in both British and US labour activism, a perspective that

> starts with the continuing, unassailable reality of the working-class struggle, in all sections and under all circumstances. Rather than turning aside from that reality and its uncomfortable implications, those [revolutionaries] who seek a lasting resurgence within the [labor] movement are urged to start with the concrete conditions workers face, the organization and resistance they build in response to those conditions, and the direct democracy and class struggle politics contained within these structures, these 'ramparts,' of rank-and-file resistance. In advocating a mutually reinforcing unity to replace the 'unbridgeable gulf' between radical intellectuals and workplace activists, this argument centers on the crucial need to build a class-conscious leadership *within* the working class – ready, perhaps, for the next upsurge. Possibly, in these circumstances, workers will be better equipped to take the independent, united action needed to get their power back.[70]

Similar views are expressed by a working-class South African 'township' activist who has been on the cutting edge of the global justice movement that has challenged the imperialist thrust of modern-day 'globalisation', Trevor Ngwane. 'Some in the anti-globalization movement say that the working-class is finished, that the social movements or even "civil society" itself are now the leading force for change', he has observed. 'But if we're honest, some of these social movements consist of nothing more than an office and a big grant from somewhere or other. They can call a workshop, pay people to attend, give them a nice meal and then write up a good report. They build nothing on the ground.' He finds the abstraction of 'civil society' even more problematical, 'expanding to the business sector and to NGOs [non-governmental organisations dealing with social issues] tendering for contracts for private government services'.[71]

Ngwane embraces aspects of the global justice movement (such as the World Social Forum) that involve dialogue, information-sharing, and co-ordinated efforts between activists like himself of various countries – but he stresses that 'the working class … remains a key component of any alternative left strategy'. A majority of workers are not in trade unions, and problems faced by workers extend well beyond the workplace. This requires seeing the class struggle as something larger than union struggles. He adds that 'the high level of unemployment is a real problem here. It does make workers more cautious. We need to organize both the employed and the unemployed, to overcome capital's divide-and-conquer tactics.' As a township activist, he emphasises, 'in the end we had to get down to the most basic questions: what are the problems facing people on the ground that unite us most? In Soweto, it's electricity. In another area, it is water. We've learned that you have to actually organize – to talk to people, door to door; to connect with the masses.' For Ngwane, however, this is necessarily linked with 'the issue of political power', and ultimately 'targeting state power'. He concludes his discussion of local grassroots organising with the comment that 'you have to build with a vision. From Day One we argued that electricity cuts are the result of privatization. Privatization …

reflects the demands of global capital. ... We cannot finally win this immediate struggle unless we win that greater one.' He then comes back to the essential point: 'But still, connecting with what touches people on a daily basis, in a direct fashion, is the way to move history forward.'[72]

The points that Ngwane and Cohen make are consistent with the points made by Lenin's companion Nadezhda Krupskaya many years before, when she described how some of his comrades asserted that revolutionary struggle precluded the struggle for 'mere reforms'. Such a view, she insisted, was 'fallacious', because 'it would mean giving up all practical work, standing aside from the masses instead of organizing them on real-life issues'. Referring to the actual history of the Bolsheviks, she insisted on the very same connections we find in the comments of Cohen and Ngwane: 'Prior to the Revolution of 1905 the Bolsheviks showed themselves capable of making good use of every legal possibility, of forging ahead and rallying the masses behind them under the most adverse conditions. Step by step, beginning with the campaign for tea service and ventilation, they had led the masses up to the national armed insurrection.' The interplay of the practical and the principled, of the real struggles of the workers and oppressed with the revolutionary goal are here at the heart of Bolshevism: 'The ability to adjust oneself to the most adverse conditions and at the same time to stand out and maintain one's high-principled positions – such were the traditions of Leninism.'[73]

An accurate understanding of 'the Leninism of Lenin' – for scholars studying the history of Russia and its 1917 revolution, no less than for activists who wish to change the world in the twenty-first century – requires an understanding of these dynamics. Scholars can certainly not hope to comprehend the history of the twentieth century without understanding the actual meaning of what one of that century's greatest revolutionaries thought and did. The hope for the future may lie with those who are able to utilise the positive (and negative) lessons from the Leninist experience in the struggles of the twenty-first century.

Further Reading

A delightful, and actually rather good, 'comic book' introduction to Lenin can be found in Richard Appignanesi and Oscar Zarate, *Introducing Lenin and the Russian Revolution* (London: Icon Books, 1997). Also useful for 'beginners' may be an article I wrote, for *Encarta On-Line Encyclopedia* on 'The Russian Revolutions of 1917'. More critical is S.A. Smith's *The Russian Revolution, A Very Short Introduction* (Oxford: Oxford University Press, 2002). A rich source of primary and secondary materials for students is provided in Ronald G. Suny and Arthur Adams (eds), *The Russian Revolution and Bolshevik Victory* (Lexington, MA: D.C. Heath and Co., 1990).

A key assumption of the present volume is that the actual ideas and activities of Lenin continue to be important for an understanding of 'what happened in history', and also that they continue to be relevant for our own time. This notion is supported by such new scholarship as Lars T. Lih, *Lenin Rediscovered: 'What Is to Be Done?' in Context* (Leiden, Netherlands: Brill, 2006), which is a truly marvellous work of historical excavation, and the challenging essays in Sebastian Budgen, Stathis Kouvelakis, and Slavoj Žižek (eds), *Lenin Reloaded: Toward a Politics of Truth* (Durham, NC: Duke University Press, 2007). Unlike the works cited in the preceding paragraph, neither is for beginners, but each is well worth the attention of serious scholars.

In some ways more accessible may be three related books of mine, designed for scholars and activists alike: *Lenin and the Revolutionary Party* (Atlantic Highlands, NJ: Humanities Press, 1993; reprinted by Humanity Books), which examines the development of Lenin's organisational perspectives in relation to his political analysis and strategic thought, and within the context of the revolutionary workers' movement of Russia; *From Marx to Gramsci, A Reader in Revolutionary Marxist Politics* (Amherst, NY: Humanity Books, 1996), which places Lenin in relationship with other representatives of revolutionary Marxism – Marx and Engels, Luxemburg, Trotsky, and Gramsci; and *Marx, Lenin, and the Revolutionary Experience: Studies of Communism and*

Radicalism in the Age of Globalization (New York: Routledge, 2006), which explores the relationship of Leninism to Stalinism, and also considers the relevance of Lenin to realities of the twenty-first century.

Lenin's Life and Ideas

As of 2008, the best single life of Lenin in English is by a thoughtful professional biographer (neither Marxist nor anti-Marxist) striving for a balanced account – Ronald W. Clark, *Lenin: A Biography* (New York: Harper and Row, 1988). Also worthwhile is Lars T. Lih, *Lenin* (London: Reaktion, forthcoming). Three other volumes, read in succession, constitute a fairly reliable political biography: Leon Trotsky, *The Young Lenin* (Garden City, NY: Doubleday, 1972), N.K. Krupskaya, *Reminiscences of Lenin* (New York: International Publishers, 1970), and Moshe Lewin, *Lenin's Last Struggle* (New York: Vintage Books, 1970).

Other major biographies range from the deification presented in P.N. Pospelov et al., *Lenin, A Biography* (Moscow: Progress Publishers, 1965) to the Cold War hatchet-jobs of Stefan Possony's *Lenin: The Compulsive Revolutionary* (Chicago: Henry Regnery Co., 1964) and Robert Payne's *The Life and Death of Lenin* (New York: Simon and Schuster, 1964). Better than this, but disappointing each in their own way, are Louis Fischer's *The Life of Lenin* (New York: Harper and Row, 1965), which is far from thorough and deals mostly with his later years, and Robert Service's *Lenin, A Biography* (Cambridge, MA: Harvard University Press, 2000), which claims a balance that it doesn't achieve, and as scholarship seems quite inferior to his earlier three-volume critical study *Lenin: A Political Life*, 3 vols (Bloomington: Indiana University Press, 1985–95). An older, not always reliable work by a Menshevik opponent (and who therefore had the virtue of writing about something of which he knew, despite having an axe to grind) is David Shub's *Lenin, A Biography* (Harmondsworth, UK: Penguin, 1966) – superior to other Cold War products but now rather dated. Less 'dated' in some ways is the product of an 'official' academician, Dmitri Volkogonov, who, as a member of the Communist Party of the Soviet Union, routinely lauded Lenin but – with the collapse of Communism, employed by the anti-Communist regime of Boris Yeltsin – produced the hostile *Lenin: Life and Legacy* (New York: HarperCollins, 1994).

In a different category, and still quite valuable, are: Tony Cliff, *Lenin*, 3 vols (London: Bookmarks, 1986); Neil Harding, *Lenin's Political Thought*, 2 vols (New York: St Martin's Press, 1975, 1981); Marcel Liebman, *Leninism Under Lenin* (London: Merlin Press, 1980); and Ernst Fischer and Franz Marek, *The Essential Lenin* (New York: Seabury Press, 1972). A fine, richly informative essay is Ernest Mandel, 'The Leninist Theory of Organization', in his collection *Revolutionary Marxism and Social Reality: Selected Essays*, edited by Steve Bloom (Atlantic Highlands, NJ: Humanities Press, 1994).

Far more negative surveys of Lenin's thought can be found in: Alfred G. Meyer's Cold War classic *Leninism* (New York: Frederick A. Praeger, 1962), presenting Lenin as an elitist and totalitarian; Neil Harding's disillusioned dismissal, *Leninism* (Durham, NC: Duke University Press, 1996); and James D. White's *Lenin: The Practice and Theory of Revolution* (New York: Palgrave Macmillan, 2001), which seems to recycle Meyer's interpretation.

Overview of Lenin's Historical Context

The immediate contexts in which Lenin's ideas had impact (and were then badly distorted) are the subject of a number of valuable works. Quite excellent is Ronald G. Suny's textbook account, *The Soviet Experiment: Russia, the Soviet Union, and the Successor States* (New York: Oxford University Press, 1998). Crucial are interpretations by Moshe Lewin – *The Making of the Soviet System: Essays on the Interwar History of Russia* (New York: Pantheon Books, 1985), *Russia, USSR, Russia: The Drive and Drift of a Superstate* (New York: The New Press, 1995), and *The Soviet Century* (London: Verso, 2005). An older but still quite valuable work is E.H. Carr's *The Bolshevik Revolution*, 3 vols (Harmondsworth, UK: Penguin, 1966) and *The Interregnum* (Harmondsworth, UK: Penguin, 1969). Also rather good is the trilogy, popularly written by a capable historian, W. Bruce Lincoln: *In War's Dark Shadow: The Russians Before the Great War* (New York: Simon and Schuster, 1983), *Passage Through Armageddon: The Russians in War and Revolution 1914–1918* (New York: Simon and Schuster, 1986), and *Red Victory: A History of the Russian Civil War* (New York: Simon and Schuster, 1989).

Workers' Party and Workers' Revolution

The fact that Lenin was part of the workers' movement, that the Bolshevik party was primarily a workers' party, and that the Bolshevik revolution was a workers' revolution has often been obscured. It comes through in such memoirs as: Cecilia Bobrovskaya, *Twenty Years in Underground Russia* (Chicago: Proletarian Publishers, 1976); Semen Kanatchikov, *A Radical Worker in Tsarist Russia* (Stanford, CA: Stanford University Press, 1986); O. Piatnitsky, *Memoirs of a Bolshevik* (New York: International Publishers, 1931); F.F. Raskolnikov, *Kronstadt and Petrograd in 1917* (London: New Park, 1985); Alexander Shlyapnikov, *On the Eve of 1917* (London: Allison and Busby, 1982). Gregory Zinoviev's brief *History of the Bolshevik Party from the Beginnings to February 1917, A Popular Outline* (London: New Park, 1973) contains additional information on this (and much else).

The working-class dimension also comes through in Mark D. Steinberg (ed.) *Voices of Revolution, 1917* (New Haven, CT: Yale University Press, 2001), as well as with an invaluable body of social history that includes: Victoria E. Bonnell, *Roots of Rebellion: Workers' Politics and Organizations in St Petersburg and Moscow, 1900–1914* (Berkeley: University of California Press, 1983); Ralph Carter Elwood, *Russian Social Democracy in the Underground* (Assen, Netherlands: Van Gorcum and Co., 1974); Leopold H. Haimson, 'The Problem of Social Stability in Urban Russia, 1905–1917', 2 parts, *Slavic Review*, vol. 23, no. 4 (December 1964), and vol. 24, no. 1 (March 1965); Tsuyoshi Hasegawa, *The February Revolution: Petrograd 1917* (Seattle: University of Washington Press, 1981); Rose Glickman, *Russian*

Factory Women: Workplace and Society, 1880–1914 (Berkeley: University of California Press, 1984); Diane Koenker, *Moscow Workers and the 1917 Revolution* (Princeton, NJ: Princeton University Press, 1981); David Mandel, *The Petrograd Workers and the Fall of the Old Regime* (New York: St Martin's Press, 1984), and *The Petrograd Workers and the Soviet Seizure of Power* (New York: St Martin's Press, 1984); S.A. Smith, *Red Petrograd: Revolution in the Factories, 1917–1918* (Cambridge: Cambridge University Press, 1985); Reginald E. Zelnick (ed.), *Workers and Intelligentsia in Late Imperial Russia: Realities, Representations, Reflections* (Berkeley: International and Area Studies, University of California at Berkeley, 1999).

On the 1905 'dress rehearsal' for the Russian Revolution, valuable sources include Leon Trotsky, *1905* (New York: Vintage Books, 1971), Solomon Schwarz, *The Russian Revolution of 1905: The Workers' Movement and the Formation of Bolshevism and Menshevism* (Chicago: Chicago University Press, 1967), Laura Engelstein, *Moscow, 1905: Working-Class Organization and Political Conflict* (Stanford, CA: Stanford University Press, 1982), and Abraham Ascher, *The Revolution of 1905*, 2 vols (Stanford, CA: Stanford University Press, 1988).

A primary focus for anyone interested in Lenin, obviously, will be on the Russian Revolution of 1917. An outstanding eyewitness account by a sympathetic journalist from the United States can be found in John Reed, *Ten Days That Shook the World* (New York: Boni and Liveright, 1919). Other classic accounts can be found in Victor Serge, *The Year One of the Russian Revolution* (Chicago: Holt, Rinehart and Winston, 1972), and Leon Trotsky, *The History of the Russian Revolution*, Three Volumes in One (New York: Simon and Schuster, 1936). Consistent with these accounts is the two-volume work by yet another US journalist, William H. Chamberlin, *The Russian Revolution, 1917–1921*, 2 vols (New York: Grosset and Dunlap, 1965), which also covers the brutalising civil war (1918–21). Two more recent works of scholarship – Alexander Rabinowitch, *The Bolsheviks Come to Power: The Revolution of 1917 in Petrograd* (New York: W.W. Norton, 1976) and Rex A. Wade, *The Russian Revolution,*

1917 (Cambridge: Cambridge University Press, 2000) – richly corroborate the other accounts mentioned here, as do materials cited in the previous paragraphs of this section.

After the Revolution

A sharp and well-argued critique of Lenin's post-1917 policies is advanced in Samuel Farber, *Before Stalinism: The Rise and Fall of Soviet Democracy* (London: Verso, 1990), while a capable defence of Lenin's policies is mounted by John Rees (in debate with Samuel Farber and Robert Service) in the slim but lively and well-documented *In Defence of October: A Debate on the Russian Revolution* (London: Bookmarks, 1997). These matters are taken up by other works cited in previous paragraphs, and also – from 'participant-observers' maintaining a critical-minded 'Bolshevik-Leninist' standpoint – in Victor Serge, *Russia Twenty Years After* (Atlantic Highlands, NJ: Humanities Press, 1996) and Leon Trotsky, *The Revolution Betrayed* (New York: Doubleday Doran, 1937). Also worth consulting is Arno J. Mayer's massive and very fine book, providing a useful comparative perspective, *The Furies: Violence and Terror in the French and Russian Revolutions* (Princeton, NJ: Princeton University Press, 2000).

The three works just mentioned consider the rise of what has been called 'Stalinism', which is dealt with quite well in a number of important studies. Indispensable are Robert C. Tucker's *Stalin as Revolutionary: 1879–1929* (New York: W.W. Norton, 1974) and *Stalin in Power: The Revolution From Above, 1928–1941* (New York: W.W. Norton, 1992). Another key source is Roy Medvedev's *Let History Judge: The Origins and Consequences of Stalinism* (New York: Columbia University Press, 1989). Also see Sheila Fitzpatrick, *Everyday Stalinism: Ordinary Life in Extraordinary Times, Soviet Russia in the 1930s* (New York: Oxford University Press, 2000), and Lewis Siegelbaum and Andrei Sokolov, *Stalinism as a Way of Life, A Narrative in Documents* (New Haven, CT: Yale University Press, 2000). More general surveys of Soviet history by Ronald Suny and Moshe Lewin, cited earlier, help to round out the story.

Lenin's Writings

There are presently four one-volume selections of Lenin's writings easily available in English. *Essential Works of Lenin*, edited by Henry M. Christman (Dover, 1987) is an inexpensive compilation consisting of excerpts from *The Development of Capitalism in Russia*, and three works in their entirety – *What Is To Be Done?*, *Imperialism,The Highest Stage of Capitalism*, and *The State and Revolution*. More comprehensive is *The Lenin Anthology*, edited by Robert C. Tucker (New York: W.W. Norton, 1975), which includes an extensive and fairly representative selection, including more or less complete versions of *The State and Revolution* and *'Left-Wing' Communism, An Infantile Disorder*. The most limited, if creative, collection is *Revolution at the Gates: Selected Writings of Lenin from 1917*, edited by Slavoj Žižek (London: Verso, 2002) – half the volume consisting of some of Lenin's most dynamic short pieces within a nine-month time span, the other half consisting of Žižek's radically edgy 'Afterword', packed with modern/post-modern cultural analogies and analysis. Last, and least, is *The Unknown Lenin: From the Secret Archive*, edited by Richard Pipes (New Haven, CT: Yale University Press, 1996), a conservative assault that has been lambasted by knowledgeable scholars as a single-minded, sloppy, stilted effort to 'expose' Lenin as simply a fanatical and murderous totalitarian. A scholarly and devastating critique of what Pipes has done can be found in Lars T. Lih, 'Review of Richard Pipes, *The Unknown Lenin* and *V.I. Lenin: Neizvestnye dokumenty, 1891–1922*', *Canadian-American Slavic Studies*, vol. 35, nos 2–3, 2001, 301–6.

Most of Lenin's writings in English can be found in the *Collected Works*, 45 volumes (Moscow: Progress Publishers, 1960–70). Quite handy are his *Selected Works*, 3 vols (New York: International Publishers, 1967), containing most of his major works and much else; unfortunately, at present this edition is out of print.

Notes to Part One

1. Langston Hughes, 'Lenin', in Gregory Zlobin et al. (eds), *Lenin in Profile, World Writers and Artists on Lenin* (Moscow: Progress Publishers, 1975), 265.

2. V.I. Lenin, 'Two Tactics of Social-Democracy in the Democratic Revolution', *Collected Works*, Vol. 9 (Moscow: Progress Publishers, 1962), 29.

3. C.L.R. James, 'Lenin and the Vanguard Party', in Anna Grimshaw (ed.), *The C.L.R. James Reader* (Oxford: Blackwell, 1992), 327–8. This section is based on material prepared by the author for *Colliers Encyclopedia* (1995) and *International Encyclopedia of Revolution and Protest*, ed. by Immanuel Ness et al. (Oxford: Blackwell, 2009, forthcoming).

4. Hannah Arendt, *On Revolution* (London: Penguin Books, 1990), 65.

5. Robert C. Tucker, 'Lenin and Revolution', in Robert C. Tucker (ed.), *The Lenin Anthology* (New York: W.W. Norton, 1975), xxv.

6. Stefan T. Possony, *Lenin: The Compulsive Revolutionary* (Chicago: Henry Regnery Co., 1964), vii, 392; Winston S. Churchill, *The Aftermath: The World Crisis 1918–1928* (New York: Charles Scribner's Sons, 1929), 64–6; Martin Gilbert, *Winston S. Churchill, Volume IV: 1916–1922, The Striken World* (Boston: Houghton Mifflin, Co., 1975), 903.

7. A classic articulation of the conservative outlook can be found in Russell Kirk, *The Conservative Mind: From Burke to Eliot* (Chicago: Henry Regnery Co., 1960). Possony's elitism and racism are spelled out 'scientifically' in Nathaniel Weyl and Stefan Possony, *The Geography of Intellect* (Chicago: Henry Regnery Co., 1963), 144, 147, 266, 267, 268, 271, 288, 289. On Churchill's, see the ample quotations and documentation in Clive Ponting, *Churchill* (London: Sinclair-Stevenson, 1994).

8. Both quoted in Isaac Don Levine, *The Man Lenin* (New York: Thomas Seltzer, 1924), 13, 36.

9. Ibid., 157, 160, 176. For more extensive examination of the anti-music legend, see Paul Le Blanc, *Marx, Lenin, and the Revolutionary Experience: Studies of Communism and Radicalism in the Age of Globalization* (New York: Routledge, 2006), 83–5.

10. Levine, *The Man Lenin*, 179, 192, 193. Levine's conservative trajectory (inspired by disillusioned libertarianism rather than traditionalist elitism) is indicated in Richard Gid Powers, *Not Without Honor: The History of American Anticommunism* (New York: Free Press, 1996), 99, 149, 229, 230.

11. Raphael Abramovitch, *The Soviet Revolution* (New York: International Universities Press, 1962), 210, 214, 216; Julius Martov, 'Dictatorship of the Minority', in Irving Howe (ed.), *Essential Works of Socialism* (New York: Bantam Books, 1971), 261, 262. A 1903–21 survey of the Mensheviks, with snippets from their writings, is provided in Abraham Ascher (ed.), *The Mensheviks in the Russian Revolution* (Ithaca, NY: Cornell University Press, 1976). Also see Ziva Galili's excellent *The Menshevik Leaders in the Russian Revolution: Social Realities and Political Strategies* (Princeton, NJ: Princeton University Press, 1989). An indispensable intellectual history of post-1917

Menshevism can be found in André Liebich, *From the Other Shore: Russian Social Democracy After 1921* (Cambridge, MA: Harvard University Press, 1998).

12. Simon Liberman, *Building Lenin's Russia* (Chicago: University of Chicago Press, 1945), 55–6.

13. Angelica Balabanoff, *My Life as a Rebel* (Bloomington: Indiana University Press, 1973), 144.

14. Rosa Luxemburg, 'The Russian Revolution', in Mary-Alice Waters (ed.), *Rosa Luxemburg Speaks* (New York: Pathfinder Press, 1970), 374–5, 389–90, 391, 393–5. In their valuable anthology, *The Rosa Luxemburg Reader* (New York: Monthly Review Press, 2005), editors Peter Hudis and Kevin Anderson follow anti-Communist Bertram D. Wolfe in suggesting a strong connection between Luxemburg's pre-First World War criticisms of Lenin (when she participated in factional disputes within the Russian socialist movement) and her later critique. Wolfe's key points can be found on pages 11–16 and 22 of his 'Introduction' to Rosa Luxemburg, *The Russian Revolution and Leninism or Marxism?* (Ann Arbor, MI: University of Michigan Press, 1961). This interpretation seems to me not to be warranted by the facts – see my essay 'Luxemburg and Lenin on Organization', in Paul Le Blanc (ed.), *Rosa Luxemburg, Reflections and Writings* (Amherst, NY: Humanity Books, 1999).

15. Lars T. Lih, *Lenin Rediscovered: 'What Is To Be Done?' in Context* (Leiden, Netherlands: Brill, 2006), 375.

16. Ibid., 645.

17. Robert V. Daniels, *The Nature of Communism* (New York: Vintage Books, 1962), 19–20; A.J. Polan, *Lenin and the End of Politics* (London: Metheun, 1984), 9.

18. Adam B. Ulam, *The Bolsheviks* (New York: Macmillan Co., 1965), 179; Alfred G. Meyer, *Leninism* (New York: Frederick A. Praeger, 1962), 29; James D. White, *Lenin, The Practice and Theory of Revolution* (Basingstoke: Palgrave Macmillan, 2001), 60, emphases added; Lih, *Lenin Rediscovered*, 647–8.

19. The classic survey remains Ronald G. Suny, 'Toward a Social History of the October Revolution', *American Historical Review*, vol. 99, no. 1, February 1983. Samples can be found in Daniel H. Kaiser (ed.), *The Workers' Revolution in Russia, 1917: The View From Below* (Cambridge: Cambridge University Press, 1987).

20. Richard Pipes, *The Russian Revolution* (New York: Alfred A. Knopf, 1990), 26; Peter Kenez, 'The Prosecution of Soviet History: A Critique of Richard Pipes', *'The Russian Revolution'*, *The Russian Review*, vol. 50, no. 3, July 1991, 346, 348; Ronald Grigor Suny, 'Revision and Retreat in the Historiography of 1917: Social History and Its Critics', *The Russian Review*, vol. 53, no. 2, April 1994, 171.

21. Alexander Berkman, *The Bolshevik Myth, Diary 1920–1922* (New York: Boni and Liveright, 1925); Paul Avrich, *The Russian Anarchists* (New York: W.W. Norton, 1978); Paul Avrich, *Kronstadt 1921* (New York: W.W. Norton, 1974). Limitations of anarchism are suggested in Le Blanc, *Marx, Lenin and the Revolutionary Experience*, 199–219.

22. Important works mapping out perspectives going in this direction include: Ernesto Laclau and Chantal Mouffe, *Hegemony and Socialist Strategy: Towards a Radical Democratic Politics*, 2nd edn (London: Verso, 2001); John Holloway, *Change the World Without Taking Power*, 2nd edn (London: Pluto Press, 2005); Michael Hardt and Antonio Negri, *Empire* (Cambridge, MA: Harvard University Press, 2001).

23. This passage is drawn from Paul Le Blanc, *Lenin and the Revolutionary Party* (Amherst, NY: Humanity Books, 1993), 353–4; Rowbotham's comments are in the essay 'The Women's Movement and Organizing for Socialism', in Sheila Rowbotham, *Dreams and Dilemmas, Collected Writings* (London: Virago, 1983), 316–38.

24. The quote from the Women's Emergency Brigade veteran can be found in the documentary film produced by Lorraine Gray and Lyn Goldfarb, *With Babies and Banners: Story of the Women's Emergency Brigade* (The Women's Labor History Film Project/ New Day Films, 1978), which can be supplemented with Sol Dollinger and Genora Johnson Dollinger, *Not Automatic: Women and the Left in the Forging of the Auto Workers' Union* (New York: Monthly Review Press, 2000); Farrell Dobbs, *Teamster Rebellion* (New York: Monad/ Pathfinder, 1972), 24–5; V.R. Dunne and Walker are quoted in Paul Le Blanc, *A Short History of the U.S. Working Class: From Colonial Times to the Twenty-First Century* (Amherst, NY: Humanity Books, 1999), 85. Also see Paul Le Blanc, 'Revolutionary Vanguards in the United States During the 1930s', in John Hinshaw and Paul Le Blanc (eds), *U.S. Labor in the Twentieth Century: Studies in Working-Class Struggle and Insurgency* (Amherst, NY: Humanity Books, 2000); Alan Wald, 'African Americans, Culture, and Communism: National Liberation and Socialism', in Paul Le Blanc (ed.), *Black Liberation and the American Dream: The Struggle for Racial and Economic Justice* (Amherst, NY: Humanity Books, 2003); Fred Halstead, *Out Now: A Participant's Account of the American Movement Against the Vietnam War* (New York: Monad/Pathfinder Press, 1978).

25. Meyer, *Leninism*, 92–3, 96; Daniels, *The Nature of Communism*, 88.

26. Michael Kort, *The Soviet Colossus, History and Aftermath*, 6th edn (Armonk, NY: M.E. Sharpe, 2006), 64, 65, 66; John Gooding, *Socialism in Russia: Lenin and his Legacy, 1890–1991* (New York: Palgrave Macmillan, 2002), 37; David R. Marples, *Lenin's Revolution: Russia, 1917–1921* (Harlow, UK: Longman, 2000), 9.

27. Joseph Stalin, 'Interview With the First American Labor Delegation in Russia', in *What is Leninism?* (New York: International Publishers, 1926), 46.

28. Quoted in Le Blanc, *Lenin and the Revolutionary Party*, 5; see V. Sorin, 'Lenin's Teachings About the Party', *The Party Organizer*, May, June and July 1931.

29. Quoted in Le Blanc, *Lenin and the Revolutionary Party*, 128–9.

30. Lenin, 'Report on the Unity Congress of the RSDLP', and 'Freedom to Criticize and Unity of Action', *Collected Works*, Vol. 10 (Moscow: Progress Publishers, 1962), 380, 442–3; Lenin, 'Social Democrats and the Duma Elections', *Collected Works*, Vol. 11 (Moscow: Progress Publishers, 1962), 434.

31. Le Blanc, *Lenin and the Revolutionary Party*, 127–41. For substantial discussions of these issues, also see 'Vanguard Parties' and 'The Leninist

Theory of Organization' in Ernest Mandel, *Revolutionary Marxism and Social Reality in the 20th Century, Collected Essays*, ed. by Steve Bloom (Atlantic Highlands, NJ: Humanities Press, 1994).

32. C. Wright Mills, 'The New Left', in *Power, Politics and People: Collected Essays*, ed. by Irving L. Horowitz (New York: Ballantine Books, 1963), 259. Portions of this section draw from Le Blanc, *Marx, Lenin, and the Revolutionary Experience*.

33. David Remnick, 'Vladimir Ilyich Lenin', *Time/CBS News People of the Century: One Hundred Men and Women Who Shaped the Last One Hundred Years* (New York: Simon and Schuster, 1999), 50.

34. David Dallin and Boris Nicolaevsky, *Forced Labor in Soviet Russia* (New Haven, CT: Yale University Press, 1947), 154; Hannah Arendt, *The Origins of Totalitarianism* (New York: Meridian Books, 1958), 318.

35. Arendt, *Origins of Totalitarianism*, 440, 148, 123–302; Rosa Luxemburg, *The Accumulation of Capital* (London: Routledge, Kegan and Paul, 1953). Applying Lenin's somewhat similar but somewhat different analysis to more recent realities are Harry Magdoff, *Imperialism: From the Colonial Age to the Present* (New York: Monthly Review Press, 1978), John Rees *Imperialism and Resistance* (London: Routledge, 2006), and John Bellamy Foster, *Naked Imperialism: The U.S. Pursuit of Global Dominance* (New York: Monthly Review Press, 2006). Key portions of Lenin's *Imperialism, The Highest Stage of Capitalism* and related material on national liberation are available in this anthology.

36. Dallin and Nicolaevsky, *Forced Labor in Soviet Russia*, 191; Robert Conquest, *The Great Terror: A Reassessment* (Oxford: Oxford University Press, 1990), 311.

37. Conquest, *The Great Terror*, 251. On new research and revised figures, and related matters, regarding the camps under Stalin, see Moshe Lewin, *Russia, USSR, Russia: The Drive and Drift of a Superstate* (New York: The New Press, 1995), and Oleg V. Khlevniuk, *The History of the Gulag: From Collectivization to the Great Terror* (New Haven, CT: Yale University Press, 2004).

38. Vladimir Brovkin, *Russia After Lenin: Politics, Culture, and Society 1921–1929* (London: Routledge, 1998), 209; Robert W. Thurston, *Life and Terror in Stalin's Russia* (New Haven, CT: Yale University Press, 1996), 13. For excerpts of the Riutin Platform, 'Stalin and the Crisis of the Proletarian Dictatorship', see J. Arch Getty and Oleg V. Naumov, *The Road to Terror: Stalin and the Self-Destruction of the Bolsheviks, 1932–1939* (New Haven, CT: Yale University Press, 1999), 54–8.

39. Ulam, *The Bolsheviks*, 177, 181. Perhaps to shield Marxism and socialism from the powerful post-Communist impulse to say 'goodbye to Lenin', it has become increasingly fashionable, since 1991, among many Marx scholars to insist on the divide between Marx and Lenin, a position often associated previously with what has been called 'Western Marxism' – although this would have been rejected by two of its 'foundational' figures, Georg Lukács and Antonio Gramsci.

40. Neil Harding, *Leninism* (Durham, NC: Duke University Press, 1996), 17–18, 272. The view that Lenin's perspectives are in harmony with those of Marx,

and the perception of Lenin as a radically democratic thinker, have received increasing support from recent research of such scholars as Sebastien Budgen, Alex Callinicos, Stathis Kovelakis, Paul Le Blanc, Lars T. Lih, Kevin Murphy, August M. Nimtz, Jr., Bryan Palmer, John Rees, Slavoj Žižek, and others. The position is also presented in such older works as: David Riazanov, *Karl Marx and Friedrich Engels* (New York: Monthly Review Press, 1974); Sidney Hook, *Towards the Understanding of Karl Marx, A Revolutionary Interpretation* (New York: John Day Co., 1933); Leo Huberman, *Man's Worldly Goods* (New York: Monthly Review Press, 1963); Edmund Wilson, *To the Finland Station* (New York: Farrar, Straus and Giroux, 1972); Christopher Hill, *Lenin and the Russian Revolution* (New York: Viking/Penguin, 1978); Ernst Fischer and Franz Marek, *The Essential Lenin* (New York: Seabury Press, 1972); E.H. Carr, *The Russian Revolution, From Lenin to Stalin* (New York: The Free Press, 1979); and Ernest Mandel, *The Place of Marxism in History* (Atlantic Highlands, NJ: Humanities Press, 1994).

41. The foregoing summary is largely drawn from Michael D. Yates, 'Interview with Paul Le Blanc', *MRzine*, 28 August 2006 (http://mrzine.monthlyreview. org/yates.280806.html). Useful works on this outlook include: Ernst Fischer and Franz Marek, *How to Read Karl Marx* (New York: Monthly Review Press, 1996); Hal Draper, *Karl Marx's Theory of Revolution*, 6 vols (New York: Monthly Review Press, 1977–); August M. Nimitz, Jr., *Marx and Engels: Their Contribution to the Democratic Breakthrough* (Albany: State University of New York, 2000); and Paul Le Blanc, *From Marx to Gramsci, A Reader in Revolutionary Marxist Politics* (Amherst, NY: Humanity Books 1996).

42. Georg Lukács, *Lenin: A Study on the Unity of His Thought* (Cambridge, MA: MIT Press, 1971), 9–13.

43. Lenin, quoted in Le Blanc, *Lenin and the Revolutionary Party*, 103–4.

44. Ibid., 104.

45. See Michael Löwy, 'From the Great Logic of Hegel to the Finland Station in Petrograd', *Critique*, no. 6, Spring 1976, reprinted in Michael Löwy, *On Changing the World: Essays in Political Philosophy, From Karl Marx to Walter Benjamin* (Atlantic Highlands, NJ: Humanities Press, 1992); Kevin Anderson, *Lenin, Hegel, and Western Marxism, A Critical Study* (Urbana: University of Illinois Press, 1995); and John Rees, *The Algebra of Revolution: The Dialectic and the Classical Marxist Tradition* (London: Routledge, 1998), 170–1, 184–92. In *Reminiscences of Lenin* (New York: International Publishers, 1970), 328–30, his lifelong companion Nadezhda Krupskaya, recounts how this was a decisive period in the development of his thought.

46. See Le Blanc, *From Marx to Gramsci*, for exploration of Lenin's political common ground and interrelationship with Marx and Engels, Luxemburg, Trotsky, and Gramsci. Recent, scholarly, and insightful explorations of Trotsky's perspectives, including some discussion of Lenin, can be found in Bill Dunn and Hugo Radice (eds), *100 Years of Permanent Revolution, Results and Prospects* (London: Pluto Press, 2006).

47. For discussion of Lenin's work, see Ralph Miliband, 'Lenin's *The State and Revolution*', in *Class Power and State Power, Political Essays* (London: Verso, 1983), 154–66. On the Marxist idealisation of Athenian democracy, see

Richard N. Hunt, *The Political Ideas of Marx and Engels*, vol. I (Pittsburgh: University of Pittsburgh Press, 1974), 82–4, and vol. II (Pittsburgh: University of Pittsburgh Press, 1984), 253–6, and also C.L.R. James, *Any Cook Can Govern* (Detroit: Bewick, 1988).

48. See, for example: John Reed, *Ten Days that Shook the World* (New York: International Publishers, 1926); Leon Trotsky, *History of the Russian Revolution*, Three Volumes in One (New York: Simon and Schuster, 1936); Alexander Rabinowitch, *The Bolsheviks Come to Power: The Revolution of 1917 in Petrograd* (New York: W.W. Norton, 1976). An excellent survey of the scene, drawing together much recent scholarship, can be found in Rex A. Wade, *The Russian Revolution 1917* (Cambridge: Cambridge University Press, 2000). My own summation of events can be found in 'The Russian Revolutions of 1917', in *The Encarta On-Line Encyclopedia*.

49. Quoted in Reed, *Ten Days that Shook the World*, 363–4.

50. Liberman, *Building Lenin's Russia*, 4–5.

51. Ibid., 7–8.

52. Bertram D. Wolfe, *A Life in Two Centuries: An Autobiography* (New York: Stein and Day, 1981), 228–9. A decisive element in the expectation of the revolution's international expansion was Germany. The expectation was based on actual possibilities – which are documented in Pierre Broué, *The German Revolution 1917–1923* (Leiden/Boston: Brill, 2005), as are the reasons why the possibilities were not realised, thereby paving the way for Hitler's rise to power.

53. For sketches of these realities, see Alfred Rosmer, *Moscow Under Lenin* (New York: Monthly Review Press, 1972) and Helmut Gruber, *International Communism in the Era of Lenin, A Documentary History* (Greenwich, CT: Fawcett, 1967). For more elaborate detail and incredibly rich accumulations of information, see the unfinished multi-volume project under the editorship of John Riddell and others – *Lenin's Struggle for a Revolutionary International, Documents: 1907–1916, The Preparatory Years* (New York: Monad Press, 1984); *German Revolution and the Debate on Soviet Power: Documents, 1918–1919: Preparing the Founding Congress* (New York: Monad Press, 1986); *Founding the Communist International: Proceedings and Documents of the First Congress, March 1919* (New York: Monad Press, 1988); *Workers of the World and Oppressed Peoples Unite: Proceedings and Documents of the Second Congress of the Communist International, 1920*, 2 vols (New York: Monad Press, 1991); and Leon Trotsky, *First Five Years of the Communist International*, 2 vols (New York: Pathfinder Press, 1997).

54. Ralph Miliband, *Marxism and Politics* (Oxford: Oxford University Press, 1977), 141.

55. Arno J. Mayer, *The Furies: Violence and Terror in the French and Russian Revolutions* (Princeton, NJ: Princeton University Press, 2000), 230.

56. Ronald G. Suny, *The Soviet Experiment: Russia, the USSR, and the Successor States* (New York: Oxford University Press, 1998), 56–95; Churchill, *The Aftermath*, 288.

57. Arno J. Mayer, *Why Did the Heavens Not Darken? The 'Final Solution' in History* (New York: Pantheon Books, 1988), 64–89; Churchill, *The Aftermath*, 487.

58. V.I. Lenin, 'The Tax in Kind', *Collected Works*, Vol. 32 (Moscow: Progress Publishers, 1965), 360, 361. Pavel Milyukov was a pro-capitalist leader of the liberal Constitutional Democrats (Kadets), a former leader of the Provisional Government, and from exile a partisan of civil war to overthrow soviet rule.

59. Isaac Steinberg, *Spiridonova, Revolutionary Terrorist* (Freeport, NY: Books for Libraries Press, 1971), 235–6. For detailed documentation, see George Leggett, *The Cheka: Lenin's Political Police* (Oxford: Clarendon Press, 1981). From a critical Bolshevik standpoint, see Victor Serge, *Memoirs of a Revolutionary* (London: Writers and Readers, 1984) and his splendid novel *Conquered City* (London: Writers and Readers, 1978). Also see the devastating accounts written by a veteran of the Red Cavalry, Isaac Babel, in *Collected Stories* (New York: Meridian Press, 1971).

60. Albert Rhys Williams, *Through the Russian Revolution* (New York: Monthly Review Press, 1967), 276–7, 278.

61. V.I. Lenin, 'Political Report of the Central Committee of the R.C.P. (B.) March 27 [1922]', *Collected Works*, Vol. 33 (Moscow: Progress Publishers, 1965), 288.

62. Serge, *Memoirs of a Revolutionary*, 132–3. For a useful, critical overview, see S.A. Smith, *The Russian Revolution, A Very Short Introduction* (Oxford: Oxford University Press, 2002). A path-breaking work that emphasises the qualitative difference between the 1917 'revolution from below' and the later Stalinist 'revolution from above' is Kevin Murphy's *Revolution and Counterrevolution: Class Struggle in a Moscow Metal Factory* (New York: Berghahn Books, 2005).

63. Moshe Lewin, *The Soviet Century* (London: Verso, 2005), 308. Prominent among Leninists criticising Lenin for tightening the dictatorship rather than opening up democratic space in 1921 was Ernest Mandel – for example, in his 'Introduction' to my book *Lenin and the Revolutionary Party*, xxiv–xxxii.

64. Arendt, *The Origins of Totalitarianism*, 318–19. Arendt's views find support in a recent study by the thoroughly anti-Leninist scholar Vladimir Brovkin, *Russia After Lenin*, 222, and in the valuable scholarship gathered in the following volumes: Diane P. Koenker, William G. Rosenberg, and Ronald Grigor Suny (eds), *Party, State, and Society in the Russian Civil War: Explorations in Social History* (Bloomington: Indiana University Press, 1989); Sheila Fitzpatrick, Alexander Rabinowitch, and Richard Stites (eds), *Russia in the Era of NEP: Explorations in Soviet Society* (Bloomington: Indiana University Press, 1991); R.W. Davies (ed.), *From Tsarism to the New Economic Policy* (Ithaca, NY: Cornell University Press, 1991).

65. C. Wright Mills, *The Marxists* (New York: Dell Publishing Co., 1961), 35.

66. James P. Cannon, *The First Ten Years of American Communism* (New York: Lyle Stuart, 1962), 304, 317–18. An outstanding work of recent scholarship on this reality can be found in Bryan Palmer's invaluable *James P. Cannon and the Origins of the American Revolutionary Left* (Urbana: University of Illinois Press, 2007).

67. Mills, *Power, Politics and People: Collected Essays*, 259.

68. James P. Cannon, 'Engels and Lenin on the Party' [Letter to V.R. Dunne, 14 January 1955], *Bulletin in Defense of Marxism*, no. 19, June 1985, 29–30.

69. This and the preceding three paragraphs draw from Le Blanc, *Marx, Lenin, and the Revolutionary Experience*, 150–1, and Le Blanc, *Lenin and the Revolutionary Party*, 344, 348–9.
70. Sheila Cohen, *Ramparts of Resistance: Why Workers Lost Their Power and How to Get It Back* (London: Pluto Press, 2006), 221.
71. Trevor Ngwane, 'Sparks in the Township', in Tom Mertes (ed.), *A Movement of Movements: Is Another World Really Possible?* (London: Verso, 2004), 132–3.
72. Ibid., 133, 134. On the World Social Forum, see the volume containing Ngwane's comments, plus José Corrêa Leite, *The World Social Forum: Strategies of Resistance* (Chicago: Haymarket Books, 2005).
73. Krupskaya, *Reminiscences of Lenin*, 167.

Part Two:
Lenin's Selected Writings, 1895–1923

The first edition of Lenin's *Collected Works* was begun in the early 1920s under the editorship of Lev Kamenev, a seasoned Bolshevik who had worked with Lenin for many years. '"The way to make a proletarian revolution is not told in any book", Vladimir Ilyich was fond of saying', wrote Kamenev, in his own way pushing against the Lenin cult that was already engulfing the Soviet Union, a development that would have sickened and horrified his old comrade. 'The teaching of Lenin was created in the course of the struggle', he commented, and 'every attempt … to create any kind of a "Handbook" of Leninism, a collection of formulae applicable to all questions at any time – will certainly fail. Nothing would be more foreign to Lenin in his work than any tendency to catechism.'[1]

Early in 1923, another of Lenin's comrades, Karl Radek, recalled that, after the 1917 revolution, 'when Vladimir Ilyich once observed me glancing through a collection of his articles in the year 1903, which had just been published, a sly smile crossed his face, and he remarked with a laugh: "It is very interesting to read what stupid fellows we were!"' This dovetails with Kamenev's comment that each of Lenin's writings 'is permeated through and through with the anxieties and lessons of a particular historical situation … written under great pressure and … concerned with a given situation'. Interactions with accumulating experience and knowledge, interactions with comrades and opponents, interactions of theory and practice caused Lenin's perspectives to evolve up to the end of his life. Kamenev wrote: 'We can only approach the real science of Lenin through a consideration of his complete works in the light of contemporary events.'[2]

The selections offered here are by no means meant to stand in for Lenin's 'complete works' – it will be well worth one's time to read the complete versions of materials excerpted in this volume, and to examine texts that are not represented here at all. At the same time, these selections do give a sense of essential strands of Lenin's thought, and in particular the continuity of his contributions as a revolutionary-democratic theorist. Still, it is important to keep in mind Kamenev's stricture that we consider Lenin's works 'in the light of contemporary events'. There is, however, an ambiguity in Kamenev's comment. Does he mean relating Lenin's works to events contemporary to Lenin or to ourselves? Perhaps the most fruitful answer would be – both. This would compel us to consider differences and similarities between Lenin's situation and our own.[3]

The readings that follow are drawn from the English edition of Lenin's *Collected Works*, 45 volumes (Moscow: Progress Publishers, 1960–70). Lars T. Lih, who has produced an important new translation of Lenin's *What Is To Be Done?*, has suggested modest alterations in the Moscow translation, and these have been incorporated into this volume's excerpts from that work.

Notes

1. L.B. Kamenev, 'The Literary Legacy of Ilyitch', *Communist International*, no. 1 in 1924, 68. This can be found, along with an extensive collection of writings by Lenin and other Marxists, on the invaluable Marxists Internet Archive, www.marxists.org.
2. Karl Radek, 'On Lenin', *International Socialist Review*, vol. 34, no. 10, November 1973, 29; Kamenev, 'The Literary Legacy of Ilyitch', 69.
3. These comments are drawn from Paul Le Blanc, *Lenin and the Revolutionary Party* (Amherst, NY: Humanity Books, 1993), 64, 344–5.

2
MARXIST PROGRAMME AND REVOLUTIONARY ORGANISATION

In 1895, a 25-year-old revolutionary Marxist, V.I. Ulyanov, travelled to Switzerland to make contact with the small but influential Emancipation of Labour Group headed by the prestigious 'father of Russian Marxism' George Plekhanov, travelling then to establish contacts with the socialist movement in France, Austria, and Germany. He then returned to Russia to help organise and lead a cluster of socialist and working-class activists in the clandestine St Petersburg Union of Struggle for the Emancipation of the Working Class. Within several months he was arrested, but while in jail he composed the 'Draft and Explanation of a Programme for the Social-Democratic Party', sketching a classical Marxist conception of the political programme that should guide the workers' movement. This programme is presented here in full, with an excerpt from the 'explanation' elaborating on the nature of 'working-class consciousness'.

Sentenced to Siberian exile in 1897, Ulyanov began working on a major study, *The Development of Capitalism in Russia*, published in 1899 under the name Vladimir Ilyin. The excerpts presented here shed light on how the capitalist mode of production was becoming increasingly dominant in Russia's economy, even within the cracks and crevices of the 'pre-capitalist' rural economy. In contrast to the *Narodniks* (populist intellectuals), Ulyanov saw this as a progressive advance over the static, patriarchal way of life characterising the traditional Russian peasantry. He saw his analyses as validating the classical Marxist focus on the working class as a revolutionary force, and – especially with his expansive conceptions of the 'rural proletariat' and the plight of the 'middle peasantry' – also suggesting possibilities of a worker–peasant alliance.

At the close of the nineteenth century, there arose in the world socialist movement an increasingly influential trend to revise the theoretical and political orientation mapped out by Karl Marx and Frederick Engels. Spearheaded by Eduard Bernstein in the German Social-Democratic Party, it asserted that the class struggle between workers and capitalists would neither have to intensify nor culminate in a socialist revolution. Instead, an accumulation of reforms could gradually eliminate the negative features of capitalism.

Ulyanov followed the world's most prominent Marxists, particularly Karl Kautsky in Germany and George Plekhanov in Russia, in defending the revolutionary Marxist orientation. He took special aim at elements in and around his own organisation, the newly formed Russian Social-Democratic Labour Party (RSDLP), who urged a limitation of workers to focusing on trade union activities and economic reform struggles – an orientation which came to be called 'Economism'. The last three items in this chapter, all published in 1899, are polemics against this trend. 'Our Programme' and 'Our Immediate Task' are presented in their entirety. In *A Retrograde Trend in Russian Social Democracy*, we find an insistence on the need to 'Fuse Socialism with the Workers' Movement', the title we have given to the excerpt presented here.

1895–96: Draft and Explanation of a Programme for the Social-Democratic Party*

Draft Programme

A.

1. Big factories are developing in Russia with ever-growing rapidity, ruining the small handicraftsmen and peasants, turning them into propertyless workers and driving ever-increasing numbers of the people to the cities, factory and industrial villages and townlets.

2. This growth of capitalism signifies an enormous growth of wealth and luxury among a handful of factory owners, merchants and landowners, and a still more rapid growth of the poverty and oppression of the workers. The improvements in production and the machinery introduced in the big factories, while facilitating a rise in the productivity of social labour, serve to strengthen the power of the capitalists over the workers, to increase unemployment and with it to accentuate the defenceless position of the workers.

3. But while carrying the oppression of labour by capital to the highest pitch, the big factories are creating a special class of workers which is enabled to wage a struggle against capital, because their very conditions of life are destroying all their ties with their own petty production, and, by uniting the workers through their common labour and transferring them from factory to factory, are welding masses of working folk together. The workers are beginning a struggle against the capitalists, and an intense urge for unity is appearing among them. Out of the isolated revolts of the workers is growing the struggle of the Russian working class.

4. This struggle of the working class against the capitalist class is a struggle against all classes who live by the labour of others, and against all exploitation. It can only end in the passage of political power into the hands of the working class, the transfer

---

* *Collected Works*, Vol. 2: 95–112–117.

of all the land, instruments, factories, machines, and mines to the whole of society for the organisation of socialist production, under which all that is produced by the workers and all improvements in production must benefit the working people themselves.

5. The movement of the Russian working class is, according to its character and aims, part of the international (Social-Democratic) movement of the working class of all countries.

6. The main obstacle in the struggle of the Russian working class for its emancipation is the absolutely autocratic government and its irresponsible officials. Basing itself on the privileges of the landowners and capitalists and on subservience to their interests, it denies the lower classes any rights whatever and thus fetters the workers' movement and retards the development of the entire people. That is why the struggle of the Russian working class for its emancipation necessarily gives rise to the struggle against the absolute power of the autocratic government.

B.

1. The Russian Social-Democratic Party declares that its aim is to assist this struggle of the Russian working class by developing the class-consciousness of the workers, by promoting their organisation, and by indicating the aims and objects of the struggle.

2. The struggle of the Russian working class for its emancipation is a political struggle, and its first aim is to achieve political liberty.

3. That is why the Russian Social-Democratic Party will, without separating itself from the working-class movement, support every social movement against the absolute power of the autocratic government, against the class of privileged landed nobility and against all the vestiges of serfdom and the social-estate system which hinder free competition.

4. On the other hand, the Russian Social-Democratic workers' party will wage war against all endeavours to patronise the labouring

classes with the guardianship of the absolute government and its officials, all endeavours to retard the development of capitalism, and consequently the development of the working class.

5. The emancipation of the workers must be the act of the working class itself.

6. What the Russian people need is not the help of the absolute government and its officials, but emancipation from oppression by it.

C.

Making these views its starting-point, the Russian Social-Democratic Party demands first and foremost:

1. The convening of a Zemsky Sobor made up of representatives of all citizens so as to draw up a constitution.

2. Universal and direct suffrage for all citizens of Russia who have reached 21 years of age, irrespective of religion or nationality.

3. Freedom of assembly and organisation, and the right to strike.

4. Freedom of the press.

5. Abolition of social estates, and complete equality of all citizens before the law.

6. Freedom of religion and equality of all nationalities. Transfer of the registration of births, marriages and deaths to independent civic officials, independent, that is, of the police.

7. Every citizen to have the right to prosecute any official, without having to complain to the latter's superiors.

8. Abolition of passports, full freedom of movement and residence.

9. Freedom of trades and occupations and abolition of guilds.

D.

For the workers, the Russian Social-Democratic Party demands:

1. Establishment of industrial courts in all industries, with elected judges from the capitalists and workers, in equal numbers.

2. Legislative limitation of the working day to 8 hours.

3. Legislative prohibition of night work and shifts. Prohibition of work by children under 15 years of age.

4. Legislative enactment of national holidays.

5. Application of factory laws and factory inspection to all industries throughout Russia, and to government factories, and also to handicraftsmen who work at home.

6. The Factory Inspectorate must be independent and not be under the Ministry of Finance. Members of industrial courts must enjoy equal rights with the Factory Inspectorate in ensuring the observance of factory laws.

7. Absolute prohibition everywhere of the truck system.

8. Supervision, by workers' elected representatives, of the proper fixing of rates, the rejection of goods, the expenditure of accumulated fines and the factory-owned workers' quarters.
   A law that all deductions from workers' wages, whatever the reason for their imposition (fines, rejects, etc.), shall not exceed the sum of 10 kopeks per ruble all told.

9. A law making the employers responsible for injuries to workers, the employer being required to prove that the worker is to blame.

10. A law making the employers responsible for maintaining schools and providing medical aid to the workers.

E.

For the peasants, the Russian Social-Democratic Party demands:

1. Abolition of land redemption payments and compensation to the peasants for redemption payments made. Return to the peasants of excess payments made to the Treasury.

2. Return to the peasants of their lands cut off in 1861.

3. Complete equality of taxation of the peasants' and landlords' lands.

4. Abolition of collective responsibility and of all laws that prevent the peasants from doing as they will with their lands.

Explanation of the Programme

... **B. 1.** This is the most important, the paramount, point of the programme, because it indicates what should constitute the activity of the Party in defending the interests of the working class, the activity of all class-conscious workers. It indicates how the striving for socialism, the striving for the abolition of the age-old exploitation of man by man, should be linked up with the popular movement engendered by the living conditions created by the large-scale factories.

The Party's activity must consist in promoting the workers' class struggle. The Party's task is not to concoct some fashionable means of helping the workers, but to join up with the workers' movement, to bring light into it, to assist the workers in the struggle they themselves have already begun to wage. The Party's task is to uphold the interests of the workers and to represent those of the entire working-class movement. Now, what must this assistance to the workers in their struggle consist of?

The programme says that this assistance must consist, firstly, in developing the workers' class-consciousness. We have already spoken of how the workers' struggle against the employers becomes the class struggle of the proletariat against the bourgeoisie.

What is meant by workers' class-consciousness follows from what we have said on the subject. The workers' class-consciousness means the workers' understanding that the only way to improve their conditions and to achieve their emancipation is to conduct a struggle against the capitalist and factory-owner class created by the big factories. Further, the workers' class-consciousness means their understanding that the interests of all the workers of any particular country are identical, that they all constitute one class, separate from all the other classes in society. Finally, the class-consciousness of the workers means the workers' understanding that to achieve their aims they have to work to influence affairs of state, just as the landlords and the capitalists did, and are continuing to do now.

By what means do the workers reach an understanding of all this? They do so by constantly gaining experience from the very struggle that they begin to wage against the employers and that increasingly develops, becomes sharper, and involves larger numbers of workers as big factories grow. There was a time when the workers' enmity against capital only found expression, in a hazy sense of hatred of their exploiters, in a hazy consciousness of their oppression and enslavement, and in the desire *to wreak vengeance* on the capitalists. The struggle at that time found expression in isolated revolts of the workers, who wrecked buildings, smashed machines, attacked members of the factory management, etc. That was the *first*, the initial, form of the working-class movement, and it was a necessary one, because hatred of the capitalist has always and everywhere been the first impulse towards arousing in the workers the desire to defend themselves. The Russian working-class movement has, however, already outgrown this original form. Instead of having a hazy hatred of the capitalist, the workers have already begun to understand the antagonism between the interests of the working class and of the capitalist class. Instead of having a confused sense of oppression, they have begun to distinguish *the ways and means* by which capital oppresses them, and are revolting against various forms of oppression, placing limits to capitalist oppression, and protecting themselves against the capitalist's greed. Instead of wreaking vengeance on the capitalists they are now turning to the fight for concessions, they are beginning to face the capitalist class with one demand after another, and are demanding improved working conditions, increased wages and shorter working hours.

Every strike concentrates all the attention and all the efforts of the workers on some particular aspect of the conditions under which the working class lives. Every strike gives rise to discussions about these conditions, helps the workers to appraise them, to understand what capitalist oppression consists in in the particular case, and what means can be employed to combat this oppression. Every strike enriches the experience of the entire working class. If the strike is successful it shows them what a strong force working-class unity is, and impels others to make use of their comrades' success. If it is not successful, it gives rise to discussions about the causes of the failure and to the search for better methods of struggle. This transition of the workers to the steadfast struggle for their vital needs, the fight for concessions, for improved living conditions, wages and working hours, now begun all over Russia, means that the Russian workers are making tremendous progress, and that is why the attention of the Social-Democratic Party and all class-conscious workers should be concentrated mainly on this struggle, on its promotion. Assistance to the workers should consist in showing them those most vital needs for the satisfaction of which they should fight, should consist in analysing the factors particularly responsible for worsening the conditions of different categories of workers, in explaining factory laws and regulations the violation of which (added to the deceptive tricks of the capitalists) so often subject the workers to double robbery. Assistance should consist in giving more precise and definite expression to the workers' demands, and in making them public, in choosing the best time for resistance, in choosing the method of struggle, in discussing the position and the strength of the two opposing sides, in discussing whether a still better choice can be made of the method of fighting (a method, perhaps, like addressing a letter to the factory owner, or approaching the inspector, or the doctor, according to circumstances, where direct strike action is not advisable, etc.).

We have said that the Russian workers' transition to such struggle is indicative of the tremendous progress they have made. This struggle places (leads) the working-class movement on to the high road, and is the certain guarantee of its further success. The mass of working folk learn from this struggle, firstly, how to recognise and to examine one by one the methods of capitalist exploitation, to compare them with the law, with their living conditions, and with the interests of the capitalist class. By examining the different forms and cases of exploitation, the workers learn to understand the significance and the essence of exploitation as a whole, learn to understand the social system based on the exploitation of labour by capital. Secondly, in the process of this struggle the workers test their strength, learn to organise, learn to understand the need for and the significance of organisation. The extension of this struggle and the increasing frequency of clashes inevitably lead to a further extension of the struggle, to the development of a sense of unity, a sense of solidarity – at first among the workers of a particular locality, and then among the workers of the entire country, among the entire working class. Thirdly, this struggle develops the workers' political consciousness. The living condition of the mass of working folk places them in such a position that they do not (cannot) possess either the leisure or the opportunity to ponder over problems of state. On the other hand, the workers' struggle against the factory owners for their daily needs automatically and inevitably spurs the workers on to think of state, political questions, questions of how the Russian state is governed, how laws and regulations are issued, and whose interests they serve. Each clash in the factory necessarily brings the workers into conflict with the laws and representatives of state authority. In this connection the workers hear 'political speeches' for the first time. At first, from, say, the factory inspectors, who explain to them that the trick employed by the factory owner to defraud them is based on the exact meaning of the regulations, which have been endorsed by the appropriate authority and give the employer a free hand to defraud the workers, or that the factory owner's oppressive measures are quite lawful, since he is merely availing himself of his rights, giving effect to such and such a law, that has been endorsed by the state authority that sees to its implementation. The political explanations of Messrs the Inspectors are occasionally supplemented by the still more beneficial 'political explanations' of the minister, who reminds the workers of the feelings of 'Christian love' that they owe to the factory owners for their making millions out of the workers' labour. Later, these explanations of the representatives of the state authority, and the workers' direct acquaintance with the facts showing for whose benefit this authority operates, are still further supplemented by leaflets or other explanations given by socialists, so that the workers get their political education in full from such a strike. They learn to understand not only the specific interests of the working class, but also the specific place occupied by the working class in the state. And so the *assistance* which the Social-Democratic Party can render to the class struggle of the workers should be: to develop the workers' class-consciousness by assisting them in the fight for their most vital needs.

The second type of *assistance* should consist, as the programme states, in promoting the organisation of the workers. The struggle we have just described necessarily requires that the workers be organised. Organisation becomes necessary for strikes, to ensure that they are conducted with great success, for collections in support of strikers, for setting up workers' mutual benefit societies, and for propaganda among the workers, the distribution among them of leaflets, announcements, manifestoes, etc. Organisation is still more necessary to enable the workers to defend themselves against persecution by the police and the gendarmerie, to conceal from them all the workers' contacts and associations and to arrange the delivery of books, pamphlets, newspapers, etc. To assist in all this – such is the Party's second task.

The third consists in indicating the real aims of the struggle, i.e., in explaining to the workers what the exploitation of labour by capital consists in, what it is based on, how the private ownership of the land and the instruments of labour leads to the poverty of the working masses, compels them to sell their labour to the capitalists and to yield up gratis the entire surplus produced by the worker's labour over and above his keep, in explaining, furthermore, how this exploitation inevitably leads to the class struggle between the workers and the capitalists, what the conditions of this struggle and its ultimate aims are – in a word, in explaining what is briefly stated in the programme.

1897–99: The Development of Capitalism in Russia[*]

Chapter II, Part XIII. Conclusions from Chapter II ('The Differentiation of the Peasantry')

Let us sum up the main points that follow from the data examined above:

1. The social-economic situation in which the contemporary Russian peasantry find themselves is that of commodity economy. Even in the central agricultural belt (which is most backward in this respect as compared with the south-eastern border regions or the industrial gubernias), the peasant is completely subordinated to the market, on which he is dependent as regards both his personal consumption and his farming, not to mention the payment of taxes.

2. The system of social-economic relations existing among the peasantry (agricultural and village-community) shows us the presence of all those contradictions which are inherent in every commodity, economy and every order of capitalism: competition, the struggle for economic independence, the grabbing of land (purchasable and rentable), the concentration of production in the hands of a minority, the forcing of the majority into the ranks of the proletariat, their exploitation by a minority through the medium of merchant's capital and the hiring of farm labourers. There is not a single economic phenomenon among the peasantry that does not bear this contradictory form, one specifically peculiar to the capitalist system, i.e., that does not express a struggle and antagonism of interests, that does not imply advantage for some and disadvantage for others. It is the case with the renting of land, the purchase of land and with 'industries' in their diametrically opposite types; it is also the case with the technical progress of farming.

We attach cardinal importance to this conclusion, not only as regards capitalism in Russia, but also as regards the significance

[*] *Collected Works*, Vol. 3: Ch. II, 172–3, 177–8, 181; Ch. V, 381–3; Ch. VII, 541–51; Ch. VIII, 596–600.

of the Narodnik doctrine in general. It is these contradictions that show us clearly and irrefutably that the system of economic relations in the 'community' village does not at all constitute a special economic form ('people's production', etc.), but is an ordinary petty-bourgeois one. Despite the theories that have prevailed here during the past half-century, the Russian community peasantry are not antagonists of capitalism, but, on the contrary, are its deepest and most durable foundation. The deepest – because it is here, remote from all 'artificial' influences, and in spite of the institutions which restrict the development of capitalism, that we see the constant formation of the elements of capitalism within the 'community' itself. The most durable – because agriculture in general, and the peasantry in particular, are weighed down most heavily by the traditions of the distant past, the traditions of patriarchal life, as a consequence of which the transformative effects of capitalism (the development of the productive forces, the changing of all social relations, etc.) manifest themselves here most slowly and gradually.

3. The sum-total of all the economic contradictions among the peasantry, constitutes what we call the differentiation of the peasantry. The peasants themselves very aptly and strikingly characterise this process with the term 'depeasantising'. This process signifies the utter dissolution of the old, patriarchal peasantry and the creation of *new types* of rural inhabitants. ...

4. The differentiation of the peasantry, which develops the latter's extreme groups at the expense of the middle 'peasantry', creates two new types of rural inhabitants. The feature common to both types is the commodity, money character of their economy. The first new type is the rural bourgeoisie or the well-to-do peasantry. These include the independent farmers who carry on commercial agriculture in all its varied forms (the principal ones of which we shall describe in Chapter IV), then come the owners of commercial and industrial establishments, the proprietors of commercial enterprises, etc. The combining of commercial agriculture with commercial and industrial enterprises is the type of 'combination of agriculture with industries' that is specifically peculiar to *this*

peasantry. From among these well-to-do peasants a class of capitalist farmers is created, since the renting of land for the sale of grain plays (in the agricultural belt) an enormous part in their farms, often a more important part than the allotment. The size of the farm, in the majority of cases, requires a labour force larger than that available in the family, for which reason the formation of a body of farm labourers, and still more of day labourers, is a necessary condition for the existence of the well-to-do peasantry.[1] The spare cash obtained by these peasants in the shape of net income is either directed towards commercial operations and usury, which are so excessively developed in our rural districts, or, under favourable conditions, is invested in the purchase of land, farm improvements, etc. In a word, these are small agrarians. Numerically, the peasant bourgeoisie constitute a small minority of the peasantry, probably not more than one-fifth of the total number of households (which is approximately three-tenths of the population), although, of course, the proportion fluctuates considerably according to district. But as to their weight in the sum-total of peasant farming, in the total quantity of means of production belonging to the peasantry, in the total amount of produce raised by the peasantry, the peasant bourgeoisie are undoubtedly predominant. They are the masters of the contemporary countryside.

5. The other new type is the rural proletariat, the class of *allotment-holding wage-workers*. This covers the poor peasants, including those that are completely landless; but the most typical representative of the Russian rural proletariat is the allotment-holding farm labourer, day labourer, unskilled labourer, building worker or other allotment-holding worker. Insignificant farming on a patch of land, with the farm in a state of utter ruin (particularly evidenced by the leasing out of land), inability to exist without the sale of labour-power (= 'industries' of the indigent peasants), an

1. Let us note that the employment of wage-labour is not an essential feature of the concept 'petty bourgeoisie'. This concept covers all independent production for the market, where the social system of economy contains the contradictions described by us above, particularly where the mass of producers are transformed into wage-workers.

extremely low standard of living (probably lower even than that of the worker without an allotment) – such are the distinguishing features of this type. One must assign not less than half the total peasant households (which is approximately four-tenths of the population) to membership of the rural proletariat, i.e., all the horseless and a large part of the one-horse peasants (this, of course, is only a wholesale, approximate calculation, one subject to more or less considerable modifications in the different areas, according to local conditions). ...

6. The intermediary link between these post-Reform types of 'peasantry' is the *middle peasantry*. It is distinguished by the *least* development of commodity production. The independent agricultural labour of this category of peasant covers his maintenance in perhaps only the best years and under particularly favourable conditions, and that is why his position is an extremely precarious one. In the majority of cases the middle peasant cannot make ends meet without resorting to loans, to be repaid by labour-service, etc., without seeking 'subsidiary' employment on the side, which also consists partly in the sale of labour-power, etc. Every crop failure flings masses of the middle peasants into the ranks of the proletariat. In its social relations this group fluctuates between the top group, towards which it gravitates but which only a small minority of lucky ones succeed in entering, and the bottom group, into which it is pushed by the whole course of social evolution. We have seen that the peasant bourgeoisie *oust* not only the bottom group, but also the middle group, of the peasantry. Thus a process specifically characteristic of capitalist economy takes place, the middle members are swept away and the extremes are reinforced – the process of 'depeasantising'.

7. *The differentiation of the peasantry creates a home market for capitalism*. In the bottom group, this formation of a market takes place on account of articles of consumption (the market of personal consumption). The rural proletarian, by comparison with the middle peasantry, *consumes less*, and, moreover, consumes food of worse quality (potatoes instead of bread, etc.), *but buys more*. The formation and development of a peasant bourgeoisie

creates a market in twofold fashion: firstly and mainly on account of means of production (the market of productive, consumption), since the well-to-do peasant strives to convert into capital those means of production which he 'gathers' from both landlords 'in straitened circumstances' and peasants in the grip of ruin. Secondly, a market is also created here on account of personal consumption, due to the expansion of the requirements of the more affluent peasants. ...

Chapter V, Part IX. Some Remarks on the Pre-Capitalist Economy of Our Countryside

The essence of the problem of the 'destiny of capitalism in Russia' is often presented as though the prime importance attaches to the question: *how fast?* (i.e. how fast is capitalism developing?). Actually, however, far greater importance attaches to the question: *how exactly?* and to the question: *where from?* (i.e., what was the nature of the pre-capitalist economic system in Russia?). The principal errors of Narodnik economics are the false replies given to precisely these two questions, i.e., in a wrong presentation of exactly how capitalism is developing in Russia, in a false idealisation of the pre-capitalist order. In Chapter II (and partly in III) and in the present one we have examined the most primitive stages of capitalism in small-scale agriculture and in the small peasant industries; in doing so we could not avoid many references to the features of the pre-capitalist order. If we now try to summarise these features we shall arrive at the conclusion that the pre-capitalist countryside constituted (from the economic point of view) *a network of small local markets which linked up tiny groups of small producers, severed from each other by their separate farms, by the innumerable medieval barriers between them, and by the remnants of medieval dependence.*

As to the scattered nature of the small producers, it stands out in boldest relief in their differentiation both in agriculture and in industry, which we established above. But their fragmentation is far from being confined to this. Although united by the village community into tiny administrative, fiscal and land-holding associations, the peasants are split up by a mass of diverse divisions into grades, into categories according to size of allotment, amount of payments, etc. Let us take, for example, the Zemstvo statistical returns for Saratov Gubernia; there the peasants are divided into the following grades: gift-land, owner, full owner and state peasants, state peasants with community holdings, state peasants with quarter holdings, state peasants that formerly belonged to landlords, appanage, state-land tenant, and landless peasants, owners who were formerly landlords' peasants, peasants whose farmsteads have been redeemed, owners who are former appanage peasants, colonist freeholder, settler, gift-land peasants who formerly belonged to landlords, owners who were former state peasants, manumitted, those who did not pay quitrent, free tiller, temporarily bound, former factory-bound, etc.; further, there are registered peasants, migrant, etc. All these grades differ in the history of their agrarian relations, in size of allotments, amount of payments, etc., etc. And within the grade there are innumerable differences of a similar kind: sometimes even the peasants of one and the same village are divided into two quite distinct categories: 'Mr X's former peasants' and 'Mrs Y's former peasants'. All this diversity was natural and necessary in the Middle Ages, in the remote past; at the present time however, the preservation of the social-estate exclusiveness of the peasant communities is a crying anachronism and greatly worsens the conditions of the toiling masses, while at the same time not in the least safeguarding them against the burdens of the new, capitalist era. The Narodniks usually shut their eyes to this fragmentation, and when the Marxists express the view that the splitting up of the peasantry is progressive, the Narodniks confine themselves to hackneyed outcries against 'supporters of land dispossession', thereby covering up the utter fallacy of their views about the pre-capitalist countryside. One has only to picture to oneself the amazing fragmentation of the small producers, an inevitable consequence of patriarchal agriculture, to become convinced of this progressiveness of capitalism, which is shattering to the very foundations the ancient forms of economy and life, with their age-old immobility and routine, destroying the settled life of the peasants who vegetated behind their medieval partitions, and creating new social classes striving of necessity towards contact, unification, and active participation in the whole of the economic (and not only economic) life of the country, and of the whole world.

If we take the peasants who are handicraftsmen or small industrialists we shall find the same thing. Their interests do not transcend the bounds of the small area of surrounding villages. Owing to the insignificant area covered by the local market they do not come into contact with the industrialists of other districts; they are in mortal terror of 'competition', which ruthlessly destroys the patriarchal paradise of the small handicraftsmen and industrialists, who live lives of stagnant routine undisturbed by anybody or anything. With respect to these small industrialists, competition and capitalism perform a useful historical function by dragging them out of their backwoods and confronting them with all the issues that already face the more developed strata of the population.

A necessary attribute of the small local markets is, apart from primitive forms of artisan production, primitive forms of merchant's and usury capital. The more remote a village is, the further away it is from the influence of the new capitalist order, from railways, big factories and large-scale capitalist agriculture, the greater the monopoly of the local merchants and usurers, the more they subjugate the surrounding peasantry, and the cruder the forms of this subjugation. The number of these small leeches is enormous (when compared with the meagre produce of the peasants), and there is a rich variety of local names to designate them. ... The predominance of natural economy, which accounts for the scarcity and dearness of money in the countryside, results in the assumption of an importance by all these 'kulaks' out of all proportion to the size of their capital. The dependence of the peasants on the money owners inevitably acquires the form of bondage. Just as one cannot conceive of developed capitalism without large-scale merchant's capital in the form of commodities or money so the pre-capitalist village is inconceivable without small traders and buyers-up, who are the 'masters' of the small local markets. Capitalism draws these markets together, combines them into a big national market, and then into a world market, destroys the primitive forms of bondage and personal dependence, develops in depth and in breadth the contradictions which in a rudimentary form are also to be observed among the community peasantry – and thus paves the way for their resolution. ...

Chapter VII, Part XII. Three Stages in the Development of Capitalism in Russian Industry

Let us now sum up the main conclusions to be drawn from the data on the development of capitalism in our industry.[2]

There are three main stages in this development: small commodity-production (small, mainly peasant industries); capitalist manufacture; and the factory (large-scale machine industry). The facts utterly refute the view widespread here in Russia that 'factory' and 'handicraft' industry are isolated from each other. On the contrary, such a division is purely artificial. The connection and continuity between the forms of industry mentioned is of the most direct and intimate kind. The facts quite clearly show that the main trend of small commodity-production is towards the development of capitalism, in particular, towards the rise of manufacture; and manufacture is growing with enormous rapidity before our very eyes into large-scale machine industry. Perhaps one of the most striking manifestations of the intimate and direct connection between the consecutive forms of industry is the fact that many of the big and even the biggest factory owners were at one time the smallest of small industrialists and passed through all the stages from 'popular production' to 'capitalism'. Savva Morozov was a peasant serf (he purchased his freedom in 1820), a cowherd, a carter, a worker weaver, a handicraft weaver who used to journey to Moscow on foot in order to sell his goods to buyers-up; then he became the owner of a small establishment, a work-distributing office, a factory. When he died in 1862, he and his numerous sons owned two large factories. In 1890, the four

---

2. Confining ourselves, as stated in the preface, to the post-Reform period, we leave aside the forms of industry that were based on the labour of the serf population.

factories belonging to his descendants employed 39,000 workers, producing goods to the value of 35 million rubles. In the silk industry of Vladimir Gubernia, a number of big factory owners were formerly worker weavers or 'handicraft' weavers. The biggest factory owners in Ivanovo-Voznesensk (the Kuvayevs, Fokins, Zubkovs, Kokushkins, Bobrovs and many others) were formerly handicraftsmen. The brocade factories in Moscow Gubernia all grew out of handicraft workrooms. The factory owner Zavyalov, of Pavlovo district, still had in 1864 'a vivid recollection of the time when he was a plain employee of craftsman Khabarov'. Factory owner Varypayev used to be a small handicrafts-man. Kondratov was a handicraftsman who used to walk to Pavlovo carrying his wares in a bag. Millowner Asmolov used to be a pedlars' horse-driver; then a small trader, then proprietor of a small tobacco workshop, and finally owner of a factory with a turnover of many millions. And so on and so forth. It would be interesting to see how, in these and similar cases, the Narodnik economists would determine where 'artificial' capitalism begins and 'people's' industry ends.

The three main forms of industry enumerated above differ first of all in their systems of technique. Small commodity-production is characterised by its totally primitive, hand technique that remained unchanged almost from time immemorial. The small producer in industry remains a peasant who follows tradition in his methods of processing raw material. Manufacture introduces division of labour, which effects a substantial change in technique and transforms the peasant into a factory-hand, a 'labourer performing one detailed operation'. But production by hand remains, and, on its basis, progress in methods of production is inevitably very slow. Division of labour springs up spontaneously and is passed on by tradition just as peasant labour is. Large-scale machine industry alone introduces a radical change, throws manual skill overboard, transforms production on new, rational principles, and systematically applies science to production. So long as capitalism in Russia did not organise large-scale machine industry, and in those industries in which it has not done so yet, we see almost complete stagnation in technique, we see the employment of the same hand-loom and the same watermill or windmill that were used in production centuries ago. On the other hand, in industries subordinated to the factory we observe a complete technical revolution and extremely rapid progress in the methods of machine production.

We see that the different stages of the development of capitalism are connected with different systems of technique. Small commodity-production and manufacture are characterised by the prevalence of small establishments, from among which only a few large ones emerge. Large-scale machine industry completely eliminates the small establishments. Capitalist relationships arise in the small industries too (in the form of workshops employing wage-workers and of merchant's capital), but these are still poorly developed and are not crystallised in sharp oppositions between the groups participating in production. Neither big capital nor extensive proletarian strata as yet exist.

In manufacture we see the rise of both. The gulf between the one who owns the means of production and the one who works now becomes very wide. 'Wealthy' industrial settlements spring up, the bulk of whose inhabitants are poor working people. A small number of merchants, who do an enormous business buying raw materials and selling finished goods, and a mass of detail workers living from hand to mouth – such is the general picture of manufacture. But the multitude of small establishments, the retention of the tie with the land, the adherence to tradition in production and in the whole manner of living – all this creates a mass of intermediary elements between the extremes of manufacture and retards the development of these extremes. In large-scale machine industry all these retarding factors disappear; the acuteness of social contradictions reaches the highest point. All the dark sides of capitalism become concentrated, as it were: the machine, as we know, gives a tremendous impulse to the greatest possible prolongation of the working day; women and children are drawn into industry; a reserve army of unemployed is formed (and must be formed by virtue of the conditions of factory production), etc. However, the socialisation of labour effected on a vast scale by the factory, and the transformation of the sentiments and conceptions of the people it employs (in particular, the destruction of patriarchal and petty-bourgeois traditions) cause a reaction: large-scale machine industry, unlike the preceding stages, imperatively calls for the planned regulation of production and public control over it (a manifestation of the latter tendency, is factory legislation).

The very character of the development of production changes at the various stages of capitalism. In the small industries this development follows in the wake of the development of peasant economy; the market is extremely narrow, the distance between the producer and the consumer is short, and the insignificant scale of production easily adapts itself to the slightly fluctuating local demand. That is why industry at this stage is characterised by the greatest stability, but this stability is tantamount to stagnation in technique and the preservation of patriarchal social relationships tangled up with all sorts of survivals of medieval traditions. The manufactories work for a big market – sometimes for the whole country – and, accordingly, production acquires the instability characteristic of capitalism, an instability which attains the greatest intensity under factory production. Large-scale machine industry can only develop in spurts, in alternating periods of prosperity and of crisis. The ruin of small producers is tremendously accelerated by this spasmodic growth of the factory; the workers are drawn into the factory in masses during a boom period, and are then thrown out. The formation of a vast reserve army of unemployed, ready to undertake any kind of work, becomes a condition for the existence and development of large-scale machine industry. In Chapter II we showed from which strata of the peasantry this army is recruited, and in subsequent chapters we indicated the main types of occupations for which capital keeps these reserves ready. The 'instability' of large-scale machine industry has always evoked, and continues to evoke, reactionary complaints from individuals who continue to look at things through the eyes of the small producer and who forget that it is this 'instability' alone that replaced the former stagnation by the rapid transformation of methods of production and of all social relationships.

One of the manifestations of this transformation is the separation of industry from agriculture, the liberation of social relations in industry from the traditions of the feudal and patriarchal system that weigh down on agriculture. In small commodity-production the industrialist has not yet emerged at all from his peasant shell; in the majority of cases he remains a farmer, and this connection between small industry and small agriculture is so profound that we observe the interesting law of the parallel differentiation of the small producers in industry and in agriculture. The formation of a petty bourgeoisie and of wage-workers proceeds simultaneously in both spheres of the national economy, thereby preparing the way, at both poles of differentiation, for the industrialist to break with agriculture. Under manufacture this break is already very considerable. A whole number of industrial centres arise that do not engage in agriculture. The chief representative of industry is no longer the peasant, but the merchant and the manufactory owner on the one hand, and the 'artisan' on the other. Industry and the relatively developed commercial intercourse with the rest of the world raise the standard of living and the culture of the population; the peasant is now regarded with disdain by the manufactory workman. Large-scale machine industry completes this transformation, separates industry from agriculture once and for all, and, as we have seen, creates a special class of the population totally alien to the old peasantry and differing from the latter in its manner of living, its family relationships and its higher standard of requirements, both material and spiritual. In the small industries and in manufacture we always find survivals of patriarchal relations and of diverse forms of personal dependence, which, in the general conditions of capitalist economy, exceedingly worsen the condition of the working people, and degrade and corrupt them. Large-scale machine industry, which concentrates masses of workers who often come from various parts of the country, absolutely refuses to tolerate survivals of patriarchalism and personal dependence, and is marked by a truly 'contemptuous attitude to the past'. It is this break with obsolete tradition that is one of the substantial conditions which have created the possibility and evoked the necessity of regulating production

and of public control over it. In particular, speaking of the transformation brought about by the factory in the conditions of life
of the population, it must be stated that the drawing of women
and juveniles into production is, at bottom, progressive. It is
indisputable that the capitalist factory places these categories of
the working population in particularly hard conditions, and that
for them it is particularly necessary to regulate and shorten the
working day, to guarantee hygienic conditions of labour, etc.; but
endeavours completely to ban the work of women and juveniles in
industry, or to maintain the patriarchal manner of life that ruled
out such work, would be reactionary and utopian. By destroying
the patriarchal isolation of these categories of the population
who formerly never emerged from the narrow circle of domestic,
family relationships, by drawing them into direct participation in
social production, large-scale machine industry stimulates their
development and increases their independence, in other words,
creates conditions of life that are incomparably superior to the
patriarchal immobility of pre-capitalist relations.[3]

3. 'The poor woman-weaver follows her father and husband to the factory and works
alongside of them and independently of them. She is as much a breadwinner as
the man is.' 'In the factory ... the woman is quite an independent producer, apart
from her husband.' Literacy spreads among the women factory workers with
remarkable rapidity. (*Industries of Vladimir Gubernia*, III, 113, 118, 112 and
elsewhere.) Mr Kharizomenov is perfectly right in drawing the following conclusion:
industry destroys 'the economic dependence of the woman on the family ... and
on the husband. ... At the factory, the woman is the equal of the man; this is the
equality of the proletarian. ... The capitalisation of industry is an important factor
in woman's struggle for her independence in the family.' 'Industry creates a new
position for the woman in which she is completely independent of her family and
husband.' (*Yuridichesky Vestnik*, 1883, No. 12, pp. 582, 596.) In the *Statistical
Returns for Moscow Gubernia* (Vol. VII, Pt. II, Moscow, 1882, pp. 152, 138–139),
the investigators compare the position of women engaged in making stockings by
hand and by machine. The daily earnings of hand workers are about 8 kopeks, and of
machine workers, 14 to 30 kopeks. The working woman's conditions under machine
production are described as follows; '... Before us is a free young woman, hampered
by no obstacles, emancipated from the family and from all that constitutes the peasant
woman's conditions of life, a young woman who at any moment may leave one place
for another, one employer for another, and may at any moment find herself without
a job ... without a crust of bread. ... Under hand production, the knitter's earnings
are very meagre, insufficient to cover the cost of her food, earnings only acceptable
if she, as a member of an allotment-holding and farming family, enjoys in part the
product of that land; under machine production the working woman, in addition
to food and tea, gets earnings which enable ... her to live away from the family and
to do without the family's income from the land. ... Moreover, the woman worker's
earnings in machine industry, under present conditions, are more secure.'

The settled character of the population is typical of the first two stages of industrial development. The small industrialist, remaining a peasant, is bound to his village by his farm. The artisan under manufacture is usually tied to the small, isolated industrial area which is created by manufacture. In the very system of industry at the first and second stages of its development there is nothing to disturb this settled and isolated condition of the producer. Intercourse between the various industrial areas is rare. The transfer of industry to other areas is due only to the migration of individual small producers, who establish new small industries in the outlying parts of the country. Large-scale machine industry, on the other hand, necessarily creates mobility of the population; commercial intercourse between the various districts grows enormously; railways facilitate travel. The demand for labour increases on the whole – rising in periods of boom and falling in periods of crisis, so that it becomes a necessity for workers to go from one factory to another, from one part of the country to another. Large-scale machine industry creates a number of new industrial centres, which grow up with unprecedented rapidity, sometimes in unpopulated places, a thing that would be impossible without the mass migration of workers. Further on we shall speak of the dimensions and the significance of the so-called outside non-agricultural industries. At the moment we shall limit ourselves to a brief presentation of Zemstvo sanitation statistics for Moscow Gubernia. An inquiry among 103,175 factory workers showed that 53,238, or 51.6 per cent of the total, were born in the uyezd in which they worked. Hence, nearly half the workers had migrated from one uyezd to another. The number of workers who were born in Moscow Gubernia was 66,038, or 64 per cent. More than a third of the workers came from other gubernias (chiefly from gubernias of the central industrial zone adjacent to Moscow Gubernia). A comparison of the different uyezds shows the most highly industrialised ones to be marked by the lowest percentage of locally-born workers. For example, in the poorly industrialised Mozhaisk and Volokolamsk uyezds from 92 to 93 per cent of the factory workers are natives of the uyezd where they work. In the very highly industrialised Moscow,

Kolomna and Bogorodsk uyezds the percentage of locally-born workers drops to 24 per cent, 40 per cent, and 50 per cent. From this the investigators draw the conclusion that 'the considerable development of factory production in an uyezd encourages the influx of outside elements'. These facts show also (let us add) that the movement of industrial workers bears the same features that we observed in the movement of agricultural workers. That is to say, industrial workers, too, migrate not only from localities where there is a surplus of labour, but also from those where there is a shortage. For example, the Bronnitsi Uyezd attracts 1,125 workers from other uyezds of Moscow Gubernia and from other gubernias, while at the same time providing 1,246 workers for the more highly industrialised Moscow and Bogorodsk uyezds. Hence, workers leave not only because they do not find 'local occupations at hand', but also because they make for the places where conditions are better. Elementary as this fact is, it is worth while giving the Narodnik economists a further reminder of it, for they idealise local occupations and condemn migration to industrial districts, ignoring the progressive significance of the mobility of the population created by capitalism.

The above-described characteristic features which distinguish large-scale machine industry from the preceding forms of industry may be summed up in the words – socialisation of labour. Indeed, production for an enormous national and international market, development of close commercial ties with various parts of the country and with different countries for the purchase of raw and auxiliary materials, enormous technical progress, concentration of production and of the population in colossal enterprises, demolition of the worn-out traditions of patriarchal life, creation of mobility of the population, and improvement of the worker's standard of requirements and his development – all these are elements of the capitalist process which is increasingly socialising production in the country, and with it those who participate in production.

On the problem of the relation of large-scale, machine industry in Russia to the home market for capitalism, the data given above lead to the following conclusion. The rapid development of factory industry in Russia is creating an enormous and ever-growing market for means of production (building/materials, fuel, metals, etc.) and is increasing with particular rapidity the part of the population engaged in making articles of productive and not personal consumption. But the market for articles of personal consumption is also growing rapidly, owing to the growth of large-scale machine industry, which is diverting an increasingly large part of the population from agriculture into commercial and industrial occupations. As for the home market for factory-made products, the process of the formation of that market was examined in detail in the early chapters of this book. ...

Chapter VIII, Part VI. The 'Mission' of Capitalism

We still have, in conclusion, to sum up on the question which in literature has come to be known as that of the 'mission' of capitalism, i.e., of its historical role in the economic development of Russia. Recognition of the progressiveness of this role is quite compatible (as we have tried to show in detail at every stage in our exposition of the facts) with the full recognition of the negative and dark sides of capitalism, with the full recognition of the profound and all-round social contradictions which are inevitably inherent in capitalism, and which reveal the historically transient character of this economic regime. It is the Narodniks – who exert every effort to show that an admission of the historically progressive nature of capitalism means an apology for capitalism – who are at fault in underrating (and sometimes in even ignoring) the most profound contradictions of Russian capitalism, by glossing over the differentiation of the peasantry, the capitalist character of the evolution of our agriculture, and the rise of a class of rural and industrial allotment-holding wage-labourers, by glossing over the complete predominance of the lowest and worst forms of capitalism in the celebrated 'handicraft' industries.

The progressive historical role of capitalism may be summed up in two brief propositions: increase in the productive forces of social labour, and the socialisation of that labour. But both these facts manifest themselves in extremely diverse processes in different branches of the national economy.

The development of the productive forces of social labour is to be observed in full relief only in the epoch of large-scale machine industry. Until that highest stage of capitalism was reached, there still remained hand production and primitive technique, which developed quite spontaneously and exceedingly slowly. The post-Reform epoch differs radically in this respect from previous epochs in Russian history. The Russia of the wooden plough and the flail, of the water-mill and the hand-loom, began rapidly to be transformed into the Russia of the iron plough and the threshing machine, of the steam-mill and the power-loom. An equally thorough transformation of technique is seen in every branch of the national economy where capitalist production predominates. This process of transformation must, by the very nature of capitalism, take place in the midst of much that is uneven and disproportionate: periods of prosperity alternate with periods of crisis, the development of one industry leads to the decline of another, there is progress in one aspect of agriculture in one area and in another aspect in another area, the growth of trade and industry outstrips the growth of agriculture, etc. A large number of errors made by Narodnik writers spring from their efforts to prove that this disproportionate, spasmodic, feverish development is not development.

Another feature of the development by capitalism of the social productive forces is that the growth of the means of production (productive consumption) outstrips by far the growth of personal consumption: we have indicated on more than one occasion how this is manifested in agriculture and in industry. This feature springs from the general laws of the realisation of the product in capitalist society, and fully conforms to the antagonistic nature of this society.

The socialisation of labour by capitalism is manifested in the following processes. Firstly, the very growth of commodity-production destroys the scattered condition of small economic units that is characteristic of natural economy and draws together the small local markets into an enormous national (and then world) market. Production for oneself is transformed into production for the whole of society; and the greater the development of capitalism, the stronger becomes the contradiction between this collective character of production and the individual character of appropriation. Secondly, capitalism replaces the former scattered production by an unprecedented concentration both in agriculture and in industry. That is the most striking and outstanding, but not the only, manifestation of the feature of capitalism under review. Thirdly, capitalism eliminates the forms of personal dependence that constituted an inalienable component of preceding systems of economy. In Russia, the progressive character of capitalism in this respect is particularly marked, since the personal dependence of the producer existed in our country (and partly continues to exist to this day), not only in agriculture, but in manufacturing industry ('factories' employing serf labour), in the mining and metallurgical industries, in the fishing industry, etc. Compared with the labour of the dependent or bonded peasant, the labour of the hired worker is progressive in all branches of the national economy. Fourthly, capitalism necessarily creates mobility of the population, something not required by previous systems of social economy and impossible under them on anything like a large scale. Fifthly, capitalism constantly reduces the proportion of the population engaged in agriculture (where the most backward forms of social and economic relationships always prevail), and increases the number of large industrial centres. Sixthly, capitalist society increases the population's need for association, for organisation, and lends these organisations a character distinct from those of former times. While breaking down the narrow, local, social-estate associations of medieval society and creating fierce competition, capitalism at the same time splits the whole of society into large groups of persons occupying different positions in production, and gives a tremendous impetus to organisation within each such group. Seventhly, all the above-mentioned changes effected in the old economic system by capitalism inevitably lead also to a change in the mentality of the population. The spasmodic character of economic development, the rapid transformation of the methods of production and the enormous concentration of production, the disappearance of all forms of personal dependence and patri-archalism in relationships, the mobility of the population, the influence of the big industrial centres, etc. – all this cannot but lead to a profound change in the very character of the producers, and we have had occasion to note the corresponding observations of Russian investigators.

Turning now to Narodnik economics, with whose representatives we have constantly had to polemise, we may sum up the causes of our differences with them as follows. First, we cannot but regard as absolutely wrong the Narodniks' very conception of the process of capitalist development in Russia, and their notion of the system of economic relationships that preceded capitalism in Russia; and what is particularly important, from our point of view, is their ignoring of the capitalist contradictions in the structure of peasant economy (both agricultural and industrial). Furthermore, whether the development of capitalism in Russia is slow or rapid, depends entirely on what we compare this development with. If we compare the pre-capitalist epoch in Russia with the capitalist (and that is the comparison which is needed for arriving at a correct solution of the problem), the development of social economy under capitalism must be considered as extremely rapid. If, however, we compare the present rapidity of development with that which could be achieved with the general level of technique and culture as it is today, the present rate of development of capitalism in Russia really must be considered as slow. And it cannot but be slow, for in no single capitalist country has there been such an abundant survival of ancient institutions that are incompatible with capitalism, retard its development and immeasurably worsen the condition of the producers who 'suffer not only from the development of capitalist production but also from the incompleteness of that development'. Finally, perhaps the profoundest cause of disagreement with the Narodniks is the difference in our fundamental views on social and economic processes. When studying the latter, the Narodnik usually draws conclusions that point to some moral; he does not set out to present the sum total of social and economic relationships as the result of the mutual relations between these groups, which have different interests and different historical roles. ... If the writer of these lines has succeeded in providing some material for clarifying these problems, he may regard his labours as not having been fruitless.

1899: Our Programme[*]

International Social-Democracy is at present in a state of ideological wavering. Hitherto the doctrines of Marx and Engels were considered to be the firm foundation of revolutionary theory, but voices are now being raised everywhere to proclaim these doctrines inadequate and obsolete. Whoever declares himself to be a Social-Democrat and intends to publish a Social-Democratic organ must define precisely his attitude to a question that is preoccupying the attention of the German Social-Democrats and not of them alone.

We take our stand entirely on the Marxist theoretical position: Marxism was the first to transform socialism from a Utopia into a science, to lay a firm foundation for this science, and to indicate the path that must be followed in further developing and elaborating it in all its parts. It disclosed the nature of modern capitalist economy by explaining how the hire of the labourer, the purchase of labour-power, conceals the enslavement of millions of propertyless people by a handful of capitalists, the owners of the land, factories, mines, and so forth. It showed that all modern capitalist development displays the tendency of large-scale production to eliminate petty production and creates conditions that make a socialist system of society possible and necessary. It taught us how to discern, beneath the pall of rooted customs, political intrigues, abstruse laws, and intricate doctrines – the *class struggle*, the struggle between the propertied classes in all their variety and the propertyless mass, the *proletariat*, which is at the head of all the propertyless. It made clear the real task of a revolutionary socialist party: not to draw up plans for refashioning society, not to preach to the capitalists and their hangers-on about improving the lot of the workers, not to hatch conspiracies, *but to organise the class struggle of the proletariat*

---

[*]   *Collected Works*, Vol. 4: 210–14.

and to lead this struggle, the ultimate aim of which is the conquest of political power by the proletariat and the organisation of a socialist society.

And we now ask: Has anything new been introduced into this theory by its loud-voiced 'renovators' who are raising so much noise in our day and have grouped themselves around the German socialist Bernstein? *Absolutely nothing.* Not by a single step have they advanced the science which Marx and Engels enjoined us to develop; they have not taught the proletariat any new methods of struggle; they have only retreated, borrowing fragments of backward theories and preaching to the proletariat, not the theory of struggle, but the theory of concession – concession to the most vicious enemies of the proletariat, the governments and bourgeois parties who never tire of seeking new means of baiting the socialists. Plekhanov, one of the founders and leaders of Russian Social-Democracy, was entirely right in ruthlessly criticising Bernstein's latest 'critique'; the views of Bernstein have now been rejected by the representatives of the German workers as well (at the Hanover Congress).

We anticipate a flood of accusations for these words; the shouts will rise that we want to convert the socialist party into an order of 'true believers' that persecutes 'heretics' for deviations from 'dogma', for every independent opinion, and so forth. We know about all these fashionable and trenchant phrases. Only there is not a grain of truth or sense in them. There can be no strong socialist party without a revolutionary theory which unites all socialists, from which they draw all their convictions, and which they apply in their methods of struggle and means of action. To defend such a theory, which to the best of your knowledge you consider to be true, against unfounded attacks and attempts to corrupt it is not to imply that you are an enemy of *all* criticism. We do not regard Marx's theory as something completed and inviolable; on the contrary, we are convinced that it has only laid the foundation stone of the science which socialists *must* develop in all directions if they wish to keep pace with life. We think that an *independent* elaboration of Marx's theory is especially essential for Russian socialists; for this theory provides only general *guiding* principles, which, *in particular*, are applied in England differently than in France, in France differently than in Germany, and in Germany differently than in Russia. We shall therefore gladly afford space in our paper for articles on theoretical questions and we invite all comrades openly to discuss controversial points.

What are the main questions that arise in the application to Russia of the programme common to all Social-Democrats? We have stated that the essence of this programme is to organise the class struggle of the proletariat and to lead this struggle, the ultimate aim of which is the conquest of political power by the proletariat and the establishment of a socialist society. The class struggle of the proletariat comprises the economic struggle (struggle against individual capitalists or against individual groups of capitalists for the improvement of the workers' condition) and the political struggle (struggle against the government for the broadening of the people's rights, i.e., for democracy, and for the broadening of the political power of the proletariat). Some Russian Social-Democrats (among them apparently those who direct *Rabochaya Mysl*) regard the economic struggle as incomparably the more important and almost go so far as to relegate the political struggle to the more or less distant future. This standpoint is utterly false. All Social-Democrats are agreed that it is necessary to organise the economic struggle of the working class, that it is necessary to carry on agitation among the workers on this basis, i.e., to help the workers in their day-to-day struggle against the employers, to draw their attention to every form and every case of oppression and in this way to make clear to them the necessity for combination. But to forget the political struggle for the economic would mean to depart from the basic principle of international Social-Democracy, it would mean to forget what the entire history of the labour movement teaches us. The confirmed adherents of the bourgeoisie and of the government which serves it have even made repeated attempts to organise purely economic unions of workers and to divert them in this way from 'politics', from socialism. It is quite possible that the Russian Government, too, may undertake something of the kind, as it has always endeavoured to throw some paltry sops or, rather, sham sops, to the people, only to turn their thoughts away from the fact that they are oppressed and without rights. No economic struggle can bring the workers any lasting improvement, or can even be conducted on a large scale, unless the workers have the right freely to organise meetings and unions, to have their own newspapers, and to send their representatives to the national assemblies, as do the workers in Germany and all other European countries (with the exception of Turkey and Russia). But in order to win these rights it is necessary to wage a *political struggle*. In Russia, not only the workers, but all citizens are deprived of political rights. Russia is an absolute and unlimited monarchy. The tsar alone promulgates laws, appoints officials and controls them. For this reason, *it seems* as though in Russia the tsar and the tsarist government are independent of all classes and accord equal treatment to all. But *in reality* all officials are chosen exclusively from the propertied class and all are subject to the influence of the big capitalists, who make the ministers dance to their tune and who achieve whatever they want. The Russian working class is burdened by a double yoke; it is robbed and plundered by the capitalists and the landlords, and to prevent it from fighting them, the police bind it hand and foot, gag it, and every attempt to defend the rights of the people is persecuted. Every strike against a capitalist results in the military and police being let loose on the workers. Every economic struggle necessarily becomes a political struggle, and Social-Democracy must indissolubly combine the one with the other into a *single class struggle of the proletariat*. The first and chief aim of such a struggle must be the conquest of political rights, *the conquest of political liberty*. If the workers of St Petersburg alone, with a little help from the socialists, have rapidly succeeded in wringing a concession from the government – the adoption of the law on the reduction of the working day – then the Russian working class as a whole, led by a single Russian Social-Democratic Labour Party, will be able, in persistent struggle, to win incomparably more important concessions.

The Russian working class is able to wage its economic and political struggle alone, even if no other class comes to its aid. But in the political struggle the workers do not stand alone. The people's complete lack of rights and the savage lawlessness of the bashi-bazouk officials rouse the indignation of all honest educated people who cannot reconcile themselves to the persecution of free thought and free speech; they rouse the indignation of the persecuted Poles, Finns, Jews, and Russian religious sects; they rouse the indignation of the small merchants, manufacturers, and peasants, who can nowhere find protection from the persecution of officials and police. All these groups of the population are incapable, separately, of carrying on a persistent political struggle. But when the working class raises the banner of this struggle, it will receive support from all sides. Russian Social-Democracy will place itself at the head of all fighters for the rights of the people, of all fighters for democracy, and it will prove invincible!

These are our fundamental views, and we shall develop them systematically and from every aspect in our paper. We are convinced that in this way we shall tread the path which has been indicated by the Russian Social-Democratic Labour Party in its published *Manifesto*.

1899: Our Immediate Task[*]

The Russian-working-class movement is today going through a period of transition. The splendid beginning achieved by the Social-Democratic workers' organisations in the Western area, St Petersburg, Moscow, Kiev, and other cities was consummated by the formation of the Russian Social-Democratic Labour Party (spring 1898). Russian Social-Democracy seems to have exhausted, for the time being, all its strength in making this tremendous step forward and has gone back to the former isolated functioning of separate local organisations. The Party has not ceased to exist, it has only withdrawn into itself in order to gather strength and put the unification of all Russian Social-Democrats on a sound footing. To effect this unification, to evolve a suitable form for it and to get rid completely of narrow local isolation – such is the immediate and most urgent task of the Russian Social-Democrats.

[*]   *Collected Works*, Vol. 4: 215–20.

We are all agreed that our task is that of the organisation of the proletarian class struggle. But what is this class struggle? When the workers of a single factory or of a single branch of industry engage in struggle against their employer or employers, is this class struggle? No, this is only a weak embryo of it. The struggle of the workers becomes a class struggle only when all the foremost representatives of the entire working class of the whole country are conscious of themselves as a single working class and launch a struggle that is directed, not against individual employers, but against the *entire class* of capitalists and against the government that supports that class. Only when the individual worker realises that he is a member of the entire working class, only when he recognises the fact that his petty day-to-day struggle against individual employers and individual government officials is a struggle against the entire bourgeoisie and the entire government, does his struggle become a class struggle. 'Every class struggle is a political struggle' – these famous words of Marx are not to be understood to mean that any struggle of workers against employers must *always be* a political struggle. They must be understood to mean that the struggle of the workers against the capitalists inevitably *becomes* a political struggle *insofar as* it becomes a *class* struggle. It is the task of the Social-Democrats, by organising the workers, by conducting propaganda and agitation among them, to *turn* their spontaneous struggle against their oppressors into the struggle of the whole class, into the struggle of a definite political *party* for definite political and socialist ideals. This is something that cannot be achieved by local activity alone.

Local Social-Democratic activity has attained a fairly high level in our country. The seeds of Social-Democratic ideas have been broadcast throughout Russia; workers' leaflets – the earliest form of Social-Democratic literature – are known to all Russian workers from St Petersburg to Krasnoyarsk, from the Caucasus to the Urals. All that is now lacking is the unification of all this local work into the work of a single *party*. Our chief drawback, to the overcoming of which we must devote all our energy, is the narrow 'amateurish' character of local work. Because of this amateurish character many manifestations of the working-class movement in Russia remain purely local events and lose a great deal of their significance as examples for the whole of Russian Social-Democracy, as a stage of the whole Russian working-class movement. Because of this amateurishness the consciousness of their community of interests throughout Russia is insufficiently inculcated in the workers, they do not link up their struggle sufficiently with the idea of Russian socialism and Russian democracy. Because of this amateurishness the comrades' varying views on theoretical and practical problems are not openly discussed in a central newspaper, they do not serve the purpose of elaborating a common programme and devising common tactics for the Party, they are lost in narrow study-circle life or they lead to the inordinate exaggeration of local and chance peculiarities. Enough of our amateurishness! We have attained sufficient maturity to go over to *common action*, to the elaboration of a common Party programme, to the joint discussion of our Party tactics and organisation.

Russian Social-Democracy has done a great deal in criticising old revolutionary and socialist theories; it has not limited itself to criticism and theorising alone; it has shown that its programme is not hanging in the air but is meeting the extensive spontaneous movement among the people, that is, among the factory proletariat. It has now to make the following, very difficult, but very important, step – to elaborate an organisation of the movement adapted to our conditions. Social-Democracy is not confined to simple service to the working-class movement: it represents '*the combination of socialism and the working-class movement*' (to use Karl Kautsky's definition which repeats the basic ideas of the *Communist Manifesto*); the task of Social-Democracy is to bring definite socialist ideals to the spontaneous working-class movement, to connect this movement with socialist convictions that should attain the level of contemporary science, to connect it with the regular political struggle for democracy as a means of achieving socialism – in a word, to fuse this spontaneous movement into one indestructible whole with the activity of the *revolutionary party*. The history of socialism and democracy in Western Europe, the history of the Russian revolutionary movement, the experience of our working-class movement – such is the *material* we must master to elaborate a purposeful organisation and purposeful tactics for our Party. 'The analysis' of this material must, however, be done independently, since there are no ready-made models to be found anywhere. On the one hand, the Russian working-class movement exists under conditions that are quite different from those of Western Europe. It would be most dangerous to have any illusions on this score. On the other hand, Russian Social-Democracy differs very substantially from former revolutionary parties in Russia, so that the necessity of learning revolutionary technique and secret organisation from the old Russian masters (we do not in the least hesitate to admit this necessity) does not in any way relieve us of the duty of assessing them critically and elaborating our own organisation independently.

In the presentation of such a task there are two main questions that come to the fore with particular insistence: (1) How is the need for the complete liberty of local Social-Democratic activity to be combined with the need for establishing a single – and, consequently, a centralist – party? Social-Democracy draws its strength from the spontaneous working-class movement that manifests itself differently and at different times in the various industrial centres, the activity of the local Social-Democratic organisations is the *basis* of all Party activity. If, however, this is to be the activity of isolated 'amateurs', then it cannot, strictly speaking, be called Social-Democratic, since it will not be the organisation and leadership of the *class* struggle of the proletariat. (2) How can we combine the striving of Social-Democracy to become a revolutionary party that makes the struggle for political liberty its chief purpose with the determined refusal of Social-Democracy to organise political conspiracies, its emphatic refusal to 'call the workers to the barricades' (as correctly noted by P.B. Axelrod), or, in general, to impose on the workers this or that 'plan' for an attack on the government, which has been thought up by a company of revolutionaries?

Russian Social-Democracy has every right to believe that it has provided the *theoretical* solution to these questions; to dwell on this would mean to repeat what has been said in the article, 'Our Programme'. It is now a matter of the *practical* solution to these questions. This is not a solution that can be made by a single person or a single group; it can be provided only by the organised activity of Social-Democracy as a whole. We believe that the most urgent task of the moment consists in undertaking the solution of these questions, for which purpose we must have as our immediate aim *the founding of a Party organ that will appear regularly and be closely connected with all the local groups*. We believe that *all* the activity of the Social-Democrats should be directed to this end throughout the whole of the forthcoming period. Without such an organ, local work will remain narrowly 'amateurish'. The formation of the Party – if the correct representation of that Party in a certain newspaper is not organised – will to a considerable extent remain bare words. An economic struggle that is not united by a central organ cannot become the *class* struggle of the entire Russian proletariat. It is impossible to conduct a political struggle if the Party as a whole fails to make statements on all questions of policy and to give direction to the various manifestations of the struggle. The organisation and disciplining of the revolutionary forces and the development of revolutionary technique are impossible without the discussion of all these questions in a central organ, without the collective elaboration of certain *forms and rules for the conduct of affairs*, without the establishment – through the central organ – of every Party member's *responsibility* to the entire Party.

In speaking of the necessity to concentrate *all* Party forces – all literary forces, all organisational abilities, all material resources, etc. – on the foundation and correct conduct of the organ of the whole Party, we do not for a moment think of pushing other forms of activity into the background – e.g., local agitation, demonstrations, boycott, the persecution of spies, the bitter campaigns against individual representatives of the bourgeoisie and the government, protest strikes, etc., etc. On the contrary, we are convinced that all these forms of activity constitute the *basis* of the Party's activity, but, *without* their unification through an organ of the whole Party, these forms of revolutionary struggle *lose nine-tenths of their significance*; they do not lead to the creation of common Party experience, to the creation of Party traditions and continuity. The Party organ, far from competing with such activity, will exercise tremendous influence on its extension, consolidation, and systematisation.

The necessity to concentrate *all* forces on establishing a regularly appearing and regularly delivered organ arises out of the peculiar situation of Russian Social-Democracy as compared with that of Social-Democracy in other European countries and with that of the old Russian revolutionary parties. Apart from newspapers, the workers of Germany, France, etc., have numerous other means for the public manifestation of their activity, for organising the movement – parliamentary activity, election agitation, public meetings, participation in local public bodies (rural and urban), the open conduct of trade unions (professional, guild), etc., etc. *In place of all of that*, yes, *all* of that, we must be served – until we have won political liberty – by a revolutionary newspaper, without which *no* broad organisation of the entire working-class movement is possible. We do not believe in conspiracies, we renounce individual revolutionary ventures to destroy the government; the words of Liebknecht, veteran of German Social-Democracy, serve as the watchword of our activities: '*Studieren, propagandieren, organisieren*' – Learn, propagandise, organise – and the pivot of this activity can and must be only the *organ of the Party*.

But is the regular and more or less stable establishment of such an organ possible, and under what circumstances is it possible? We shall deal with this matter next time.

1899: Fuse Socialism With the Workers' Movement[*]

At first socialism and the working-class movement existed separately in all the European countries. The workers struggled against the capitalists, they organised strikes and unions, while the socialists stood aside from the working-class movement, formulated doctrines criticising the contemporary capitalist, bourgeois system of society and demanding its replacement by

[*]   *Collected Works*, Vol. 4: 257–9, 280–3.

another system, the higher, socialist system. The separation of the working-class movement and socialism gave rise to weakness and underdevelopment in each: the theories of the socialists, unfused with the workers' struggle, remained nothing more than utopias, good wishes that had no effect on real life; the working-class movement remained petty, fragmented, and did not acquire political significance, was not enlightened by the advanced science of its time. For this reason we see in all European countries a constantly growing urge to *fuse* socialism with the working-class movement in a single *Social-Democratic* movement. When this fusion takes place the class struggle of the workers becomes *the conscious struggle of the proletariat* to emancipate itself from exploitation by the propertied classes, it is evolved into a higher form of the socialist workers' movement – *the independent working-class Social-Democratic party*. By directing socialism towards a fusion with the working-class movement, Karl Marx and Frederick Engels did their greatest service: they created a revolutionary theory that explained the necessity for this fusion and gave socialists the task of organising the class struggle of the proletariat.

Precisely this is what happened in Russia. In Russia, too, socialism has been in existence for a long time, for many decades, *standing aside* from the struggle of the workers against the *capitalists*, aside from the workers' strikes etc. On the one hand, the socialists did not understand Marx's theory, they thought it inapplicable to Russia; on the other, the Russian working-class movement remained in a purely embryonic form. When the South-Russian Workers' Union was founded in 1875 and the North-Russian Workers' Union in 1878, those workers' organisations did not take the road chosen by the Russian socialists; they demanded political rights for the people, they wanted to wage a struggle for those rights, but at that time the Russian socialists mistakenly considered the political struggle a deviation from socialism. However, the Russian socialists did not hold to their undeveloped, fallacious theory. They went forward, accepted Marx's teaching, and evolved a theory of workers' socialism applicable to Russia – the theory of the Russian Social-Democrats. The foundation of

Russian Social-Democracy was the great service rendered by the Emancipation of Labour group, Plekhanov, Axelrod, and their friends.[4] Since the foundation of Russian Social-Democracy (1883) the Russian working-class movement – in each of its broader manifestations – has been drawing closer to the Russian Social-Democrats in an effort to merge with them. The founding of the Russian Social-Democratic Labour Party (in the spring of 1898) marked the biggest step forward towards this fusion. At the present time the *principal task* for all Russian socialists and all class-conscious Russian workers is to strengthen this fusion, consolidate and organise the Social-Democratic Labour Party. He who does not wish to recognise this fusion, he who tries to draw some sort of artificial line of demarcation between the working-class movement and Social-Democracy in Russia renders no service but does *harm* to workers' socialism and the working-class movement in Russia. …

The history of the working-class movement in all countries shows that the better-situated strata of the working class respond to the ideas of socialism more rapidly and more easily. From among these come, in the main, the advanced workers that every working-class movement brings to the fore, those who can win the confidence of the labouring masses, who devote themselves entirely to the education and organisation of the proletariat, who accept socialism consciously, and who even elaborate independent socialist theories. Every viable working-class movement has brought to the fore such working-class leaders, its own Proudhons, Vaillants, Weitlings, and Bebels. And our Russian working-class movement promises not to lag behind the European movement in this respect. At a time when educated society is losing interest in honest, illegal literature, an impassioned desire for knowledge and for socialism is growing among the workers, real heroes are coming to the fore from amongst the workers, who, despite their wretched living conditions, despite the stultifying penal

---

4. The fusion of Russian socialism with the Russian working-class movement has been analysed historically in a pamphlet by one of our comrades, *The Red Flag in Russia. A Brief History of the Russian Working-Class Movement*. The pamphlet will shortly be off the press.

servitude of factory labour, possess so much character and will-power that they study, study, study, and turn themselves into conscious Social-Democrats – 'the working-class intelligentsia'. This 'working-class intelligentsia' already exists in Russia, and we must make every effort to ensure that its ranks are regularly reinforced, that its lofty mental requirements are met and that leaders of the Russian Social-Democratic Labour Party come from its ranks. The newspaper that wants to become the organ of all Russian Social-Democrats must, therefore, be at the level of the advanced workers; not only must it not lower its level artificially, but, on the contrary, it must raise it constantly, it must follow up all the tactical, political, and theoretical problems of world Social-Democracy. Only then will the demands of the working-class intelligentsia be met, and it itself will take the cause of the Russian workers and, *consequently*, the cause of the Russian revolution, into its own hands.

After the numerically small stratum of advanced workers comes the broad stratum of average workers. These workers, too, strive ardently for socialism, participate in workers' study circles, read socialist newspapers and books, participate in agitation, and differ from the preceding stratum only in that they cannot become fully independent leaders of the Social-Democratic working-class movement. The average worker will not understand some of the articles in a newspaper that aims to be the organ of the Party, he will not be able to get a full grasp of an intricate theoretical or practical problem. This does not at all mean that the newspaper must lower itself to the level of the mass of its readers. The newspaper, on the contrary, must raise their level and help promote advanced workers from the middle stratum of workers. Such workers, absorbed by *local* practical work and interested mainly in the events of the working-class movement and the immediate problems of agitation, should connect their every act with thoughts of the entire Russian working-class movement, its historical task, and the ultimate goal of socialism, so that the newspaper, the mass of whose readers are average workers, must connect socialism and the political struggle with every local and narrow question.

Lastly, behind the stratum of average workers comes the mass that constitutes the lower strata of the proletariat. It is quite possible that a socialist newspaper will be completely or well-nigh incomprehensible to them (even in Western Europe the number of Social-Democratic voters is much larger than the number of readers of Social-Democratic newspapers), but it would be absurd to conclude from this that the newspaper of the Social-Democrats should adapt itself to the lowest possible level of the workers. The only thing that follows from this is that different forms of agitation and propaganda must be brought to bear on these strata – pamphlets written in more popular language, oral agitation, and chiefly – leaflets on local events. The Social-Democrats should not confine themselves even to this; it is quite possible that the first steps towards arousing the consciousness of the lower strata of the workers will have to take the form of legal educational activities. It is very important for the *Party* to make use of this activity, guide it in the direction in which it is most needed, send out legal workers to plough up virgin fields that can later be planted by Social-Democratic agitators. Agitation among the lower strata of the workers should, of course, provide the widest field for the personal qualities of the agitator and the peculiarities of the locality, the trade concerned, etc. 'Tactics and agitation must not be confused', says Kautsky in his book against Bernstein. 'Agitational methods must be adapted to individual and local conditions. Every agitator must be allowed to select those methods of agitation that he has at his disposal. One agitator may create the greatest impression by his enthusiasm, another by his biting sarcasm, a third by his ability to adduce a large number of instances, etc. While being adapted to the agitator, agitation must also be adapted to the public. The agitator must speak so that he will be understood; he must take as a starting-point something well known to his listeners. All this is self-evident and is not merely applicable to agitation conducted among the peasantry. One has to talk to cabmen differently than to sailors, and to sailors differently than to printers. *Agitation* must be *individualised* but our *tactics*, our political *activity* must be *uniform*.' These words from a leading representative of Social-Democratic theory contain a superb assessment of agitation as part of the general activity of the party. These words show how unfounded are the fears of those who think that the formation of a revolutionary party conducting a political struggle will interfere with agitation, will push it into the background and curtail the freedom of the agitators. On the contrary, only an organised party can carry out widespread agitation, provide the necessary guidance (and material) for agitators on all economic and political questions, make use of every local agitational success for the instruction of all Russian workers, and send agitators to those places and into that *milieu* where they can work with the greatest success. It is only in an organised party that people possessing the capacities for work as agitators will be able to dedicate themselves wholly to this task – to the advantage both of agitation and of the other aspects of Social-Democratic work. From this it can be seen that whoever forgets political agitation and propaganda on account of the economic struggle, whoever forgets the necessity of organising the working-class movement into the struggle of a political party, will, aside from everything else, deprive himself of even an opportunity of successfully and steadily attracting the lower strata of the proletariat to the working-class cause.

3
BIRTH OF BOLSHEVISM

At the beginning of 1900, Ulyanov's term of Siberian internal exile ended, and he soon chose to live in voluntary external exile in order to more freely carry out revolutionary work. He was soon to be joined by his close comrade and companion, Nadezhda Krupskaya – the two had married in 1898, while both were in Siberia. In 1901 he chose the pseudonym by which he would be known to the world – Lenin.

The crystallisation of the political current that Lenin would lead within the Russian Social-Democratic Labour Party (RSDLP) took place within this period extending from the dawn of the twentieth century to the revolutionary upsurge of 1905. We can see that Lenin's writings of these years are fully consistent with the classical Marxism advanced in his earlier writings – but there is also a growing emphasis on certain distinctive themes that would be essential to 'Leninism'. Initially, however, he was – with George Plekhanov, Julius Martov, and others – simply one of the most forceful and articulate leaders of a revolutionary Marxist current in the RSDLP.

'The Urgent Tasks of Our Movement' (1900) was a major article in the first issue of this current's newspaper, *Iskra* (Spark), focusing on: the need for a more highly organised and centralised party of revolutionaries who will 'devote the whole of their lives, not only their spare evenings', to the struggle; the need to combine political and economic demands; and the need to reject reformism and instead to interweave reform struggles into an uncompromising working-class revolutionary strategy. The excerpts here from his famous pamphlet *What Is To Be Done? Burning Questions of Our Movement*, are a fierce polemic against what he perceived as a de-centralising and reformist 'Economist' trend in the RSDLP (particularly the rival newspaper *Rabocheye Dyelo* [Workers' Cause] and one of its spokesmen, Alexander S. Martynov). But the pamphlet also surveys recent experiences of the revolutionary and workers' struggles, elaborating on the qualities that he and others in the *Iskra* trend believed must characterise the revolutionary workers' party that the RSDLP should become. The beginning of 1903 saw the publication of another important work, *To the*

Rural Poor, excerpted here, which shows Lenin taking the lead in analysing and reaching out to Russia's vast peasantry as a key ally of the working class in the struggle against tsarist tyranny.

The further consolidation of the RSDLP became increasingly important in the face of very different revolutionary organisations that were also taking shape in this period. There was the Socialist-Revolutionary Party (SRs), blending elements of Marxism with the peasant orientation of the Narodniks plus a penchant for individual terrorism that was alien to the Marxist RSDLP. Breaking off from the rightward end of the RSDLP were elements that moved to form the liberal Constitutional Democrats (KDs, or Kadets), which sought to replace tsarism with a democratic republic based on a modernising capitalism. In July and August 1903, an extended Second Congress of the RSDLP was held in Brussels and London, through which the *Iskra*-ites intended to make the RSDLP into a powerful Marxist force.

While those around *Iskra* did indeed dominate the proceedings of the RSDLP Second Congress, a totally unexpected but incredibly bitter split took place in their ranks during the last phase of the Congress. A minority (Menshevik) faction led by Martov and a majority (Bolshevik) faction led by Lenin seemed locked in irreconcilable conflict, with the prestigious Plekhanov aligned initially with the Bolsheviks, but after the Congress switching to the Mensheviks, which then placed *Iskra* under their control. The myth is that the split revolved around Martov's desire for a broad definition of party membership and Lenin's desire for a narrower definition (Lenin lost this vote). But the explosion was actually ignited around Lenin's winning proposal to reduce the *Iskra* editorial board from six to three (Plekhanov, Lenin, Martov), which would have removed two venerable older comrades, Pavel Axelrod and Vera Zasulich, from the board. Stunned by this split, but convinced of the correctness of his positions, Lenin explained his side of the story at length in *One Step Forward, Two Steps Back*, which is also the title of a shorter piece reprinted here responding to Rosa Luxemburg's pro-Menshevik critique of his longer pamphlet. (This great Marxist's sympathies for the Mensheviks would quickly and dramatically erode, but the article she wrote, 'Organisational Questions of Russian Social Democracy', has been recycled often, including under a title – 'Leninism or Marxism?' – fashioned long after her death.)

Although at first believing that no principled differences divided the Bolshevik and Menshevik factions of the RSDLP, Lenin dramatically changed his mind when the Menshevik *Iskra* proposed a campaign to focus on encouraging pro-capitalist liberals to push for democratic reforms through the Zemstvos (local government bodies). In the sharply worded 1904 polemic

'The Zemstvo Campaign and Iskra's Plan', Lenin argued – in the words of the title created for the excerpt offered here – 'Against Subordination to Liberalism'. A principled difference had now opened up between Mensheviks and Bolsheviks, the former favouring a worker–capitalist alliance, the latter counterposing to this a worker–peasant alliance.

1900: The Urgent Tasks of Our Movement[*]

Russian Social-Democracy has repeatedly declared the immediate political task of a Russian working-class party to be the overthrow of the autocracy, the achievement of political liberty. This was enunciated over 15 years ago by the representatives of Russian Social-Democracy – the members of the Emancipation of Labour group. It was affirmed two and a half years ago by the representatives of the Russian Social-Democratic organisations that, in the spring of 1898, founded the Russian Social-Democratic Labour Party. Despite these repeated declarations, however, the question of the political tasks of Social-Democracy in Russia is prominent again today. Many representatives of our movement express doubt as to the correctness of the above-mentioned solution of the question. It is claimed that the economic struggle is of predominant importance; the political tasks of the proletariat are pushed into the background, narrowed down, and restricted, and it is even said that to speak of forming an independent working-class party in Russia is merely to repeat somebody else's words, that the workers should carry on only the economic struggle and leave politics to the intelligentsia in alliance with the liberals. The latest profession of the new faith (the notorious *Credo*) amounts to a declaration that the Russian proletariat has not yet come of age and to a complete rejection of the Social-Democratic programme. *Rabochaya Mysl* (particularly in its *Separate Supplement*) takes practically the same attitude. Russian Social-Democracy is passing through a period of vacillation and doubt bordering on self-negation. On the one hand, the working-class movement is being sundered from socialism, the workers are being helped to carry on the economic struggle, but nothing, or next to nothing, is done to explain to them the socialist aims and the political tasks of the movement as a whole. On the other hand, socialism is being sundered from the labour movement; Russian socialists are again beginning to talk more and more about the struggle against the government having to be carried on entirely by the intelligentsia because the workers confine themselves to the economic struggle.

[*] *Collected Works*, Vol. 4: 366–71.

In our opinion the ground has been prepared for this sad state of affairs by three circumstances. First, in their early activity, Russian Social-Democrats restricted themselves merely to work in propaganda circles. When we took up agitation among the masses we were not always able to restrain ourselves from going to the other extreme. Secondly, in our early activity we often had to struggle for our right to existence against the Narodnaya Volya adherents, who understood by 'politics' an activity isolated from the working-class movement and who reduced politics purely to conspiratorial struggle. In rejecting this sort of politics, the Social-Democrats went to the extreme of pushing politics entirely into the background. Thirdly, working in the isolation of small local workers' circles, the Social-Democrats did not devote sufficient attention to the necessity of organising a revolutionary party which would combine all the activities of the local groups and make it possible to organise the revolutionary work on correct lines. The predominance of isolated work is naturally connected with the predominance of the economic struggle.

These circumstances resulted in concentration on one side of the movement only. The 'economist' trend (that is, if we can speak of it as a 'trend') has attempted to elevate this narrowness to the rank of a special theory and has tried to utilise for this purpose the fashionable Bernsteinism and the fashionable 'criticism of Marxism', which peddles old bourgeois ideas under a new label. These attempts alone have given rise to the danger of a weakening of connection between the Russian working-class movement and Russian Social-Democracy, the vanguard in the struggle for political liberty. The most urgent task of our movement is to strengthen this connection.

Social-Democracy is the combination of the working-class movement and socialism. Its task is not to serve the working-class movement passively at each of its separate stages, but to represent the interests of the movement as a whole, to point out to this movement its ultimate aim and its political tasks, and to safeguard its political and ideological independence. Isolated from Social-Democracy, the working-class movement becomes petty and inevitably becomes bourgeois. In waging only the economic struggle, the working class loses its political independence; it becomes the tail of other parties and betrays the great principle. 'The emancipation of the working classes must be conquered by the working classes themselves.' In every country there has been a period in which the working-class movement existed apart from socialism, each going its own way; and in every country this isolation has weakened both socialism and the working-class movement. Only the fusion of socialism with the working-class movement has in all countries created a durable basis for both. But in every country this combination of socialism and the working-class movement was evolved historically, in unique ways, in accordance with the prevailing conditions of time and place. In Russia, the necessity for combining socialism and the working-class movement was in theory long ago proclaimed, but it is only now being carried into practice. It is a very difficult process and there is, therefore, nothing surprising in the fact that it is accompanied by vacillations and doubts.

What lesson can be learned from the past?

The entire history of Russian socialism has led to the condition in which the most urgent task is the struggle against the autocratic government and the achievement of political liberty. Our socialist movement concentrated itself, so to speak, upon the struggle against the autocracy. On the other hand, history has shown that the isolation of socialist thought from the vanguard of the working classes is greater in Russia than in other countries, and that if this state of affairs continues, the revolutionary movement in Russia is doomed to impotence. From this condition emerges the task which the Russian Social-Democracy is called upon to fulfil – to imbue the masses of the proletariat with the ideas of socialism and political consciousness, and to organise a revolutionary party inseparably connected with the spontaneous working-class movement. Russian Social-Democracy has done much in this direction, but much more still remains to be done. With the growth of the movement, the field of activity for Social-Democrats becomes wider; the work becomes more varied, and an increasing number of activists in the movement will concentrate their efforts upon the fulfilment of various special tasks which the daily needs of propaganda and agitation bring to the fore. This phenomenon is quite natural and is inevitable, but it causes us to be particularly concerned with preventing these special activities and methods of struggle from becoming ends in themselves and with preventing preparatory work from being regarded as the main and sole activity.

Our principal and fundamental task is to facilitate the political development and the political organisation of the working class. Those who push this task into the background, who refuse to subordinate to it all the special tasks and particular methods of struggle, are following a false path and causing serious harm to the movement. And it is being pushed into the background, firstly, by those who call upon revolutionaries to employ only the forces of isolated conspiratorial circles cut off from the working-class movement in the struggle against the government. It is being pushed into the background, secondly, by those who restrict the content and scope of political propaganda, agitation, and organisation; who think it fit and proper to treat the workers to 'politics' only at exceptional moments in their lives, only on festive occasions; who too solicitously substitute demands for partial concessions from the autocracy for the political struggle against the autocracy; and who do not go to sufficient lengths to ensure that these demands for partial concessions are raised to the status of a systematic, implacable struggle of a revolutionary, working-class party against the autocracy.

'Organise!' *Rabochaya Mysl* keeps repeating to the workers in all keys, and all the adherents of the 'economist' trend echo the cry. We, of course, wholly endorse this appeal, but we will not fail to add: organise, but not only in mutual benefit societies, strike funds, and workers' circles; organise also in a political party; organise for the determined struggle against the autocratic government and against the whole of capitalist society. Without such organisation the proletariat will never rise to the class-conscious struggle; without such organisation the working-class movement is doomed to impotency. With the aid of nothing but funds and study circles and mutual benefit societies the working class will never be able to fulfil its great historical mission – to emancipate itself and the whole of the Russian people from political and economic slavery. Not a single class in history has achieved power without producing its political leaders, its prominent representatives able to organise a movement and lead it. And the Russian working class has already shown that it can produce such men and women. The struggle which has developed so widely during the past five or six years has revealed the great potential revolutionary power of the working class; it has shown that the most ruthless government persecution does not diminish, but, on the contrary, increases the number of workers who strive towards socialism, towards political consciousness, and towards the political struggle. The congress which our comrades held in 1898 correctly defined our tasks and did not merely repeat other people's words, did not merely express the enthusiasm of 'intellectuals'. ... We must set to work resolutely to fulfil these tasks, placing the question of the Party's programme, organisation, and tactics on the order of the day. We have already set forth our views on the fundamental postulates of our programme, and, of course, this is not the place to develop them in detail. We propose to devote a series of articles in forthcoming issues to questions of organisation, which are among the most burning problems confronting us. In this respect we lag considerably behind the old workers in the Russian revolutionary movement. We must frankly admit this defect and exert all our efforts to devise methods of greater secrecy in our work, to propagate systematically the proper methods of work, the proper methods of deluding the gendarmes and of evading the snares of the police. We must train people who will devote the whole of their lives, not only their spare evenings, to the revolution; we must build up an organisation large enough to permit the introduction of a strict division of labour in the various forms of our work. Finally, with regard to questions of tactics, we shall confine ourselves to the following: Social-Democracy does not tie its hands, it does not restrict its activities to some one preconceived plan or method of political struggle; it recognises all methods of struggle, provided they correspond to the forces at the disposal of the Party and facilitate the achievement of the best results possible under the given conditions. If we have a strongly organised party, a single strike may turn into a political demonstration, into a political victory over the government. If we have a strongly organised party, a revolt in a single locality may grow into a victorious revolution. We must bear in mind that the struggles with the government for partial demands and the gain of certain concessions are merely light skirmishes with the enemy, encounters between outposts, whereas the decisive battle is still to come. Before us, in all its strength, towers the enemy fortress which is raining shot and shell upon us, mowing down our best fighters. We must capture this fortress, and we will capture it, if we unite all the forces of the awakening proletariat with all the forces of the Russian revolutionaries into one party which will attract all that is vital and honest in Russia. Only then will the great prophecy of the Russian worker-revolutionary, Pyotr Alexeyev, be fulfilled: 'The muscular arm of the working millions will be lifted, and the yoke of despotism, guarded by the soldiers' bayonets, will be smashed to atoms!'

1902: What Is To Be Done?*

In the previous chapter we pointed out how *universally* absorbed the educated youth of Russia was in the theories of Marxism in the middle of the nineties. In the same period the strikes that followed the famous St Petersburg industrial war of 1896 assumed a similar general character. Their spread over the whole of Russia clearly showed the depth of the newly awakening popular movement, and if we are to speak of the 'spontaneous element' then, of course, it is this strike movement which, first and foremost, must be regarded as spontaneous. But there is spontaneity and spontaneity. Strikes occurred in Russia in the seventies and sixties (and even in the first half of the nineteenth century), and they were accompanied by the 'spontaneous' [or elemental] destruction of machinery, etc. Compared with these 'revolts', the strikes of the nineties might even be described as 'conscious', to such an extent do they mark the progress which the working-class movement made in that period. This shows that the 'spontaneous element', in essence, represents

* *Collected Works*, Vol. 5: 374–6, 396–7, 405–6, 409–10, 412–13, 422–3, 426–9.

nothing more nor less than consciousness in an *embryonic form*. Even the primitive revolts expressed the awakening of consciousness to a certain extent. The workers were losing their age-long faith in the permanence of the system which oppressed them and began ... I shall not say to understand, but to sense the necessity for collective resistance, definitely abandoning their slavish submission to the authorities. But this was, nevertheless, more in the nature of outbursts of desperation and vengeance than of *struggle*. The strikes of the nineties revealed far greater flashes of consciousness; definite demands were advanced, the strike was carefully timed, known cases and instances in other places were discussed, etc. The revolts were simply the resistance of the oppressed, whereas the systematic strikes represented the class struggle in embryo, but only in embryo. Taken by themselves, these strikes were simply trade union struggles, not yet Social-Democratic struggles. They marked the awakening antagonisms between workers and employers; but the workers were not, and could not be, conscious of the irreconcilable antagonism of their interests to the whole of the modern political and social system, i.e., theirs was not yet Social-Democratic consciousness. In this sense, the strikes of the nineties, despite the enormous progress they represented as compared with the 'revolts', remained a purely elemental movement.

We have said that *there could not have been* Social-Democratic consciousness among the workers. It would have to be brought to them from without. The history of all countries shows that the working class, exclusively by its own effort, is able to develop only trade-union consciousness, i.e., the conviction that it is necessary to combine in unions, fight the employers, and strive to compel the government to pass necessary labour legislation, etc. The theory of socialism, however, grew out of the philosophic, historical, and economic theories elaborated by educated representatives of the propertied classes, by intellectuals. By their social status, the founders of modern scientific socialism, Marx and Engels, themselves belonged to the bourgeois intelligentsia. In the very same way, in Russia, the theoretical doctrine of Social-Democracy arose altogether independently of the spontaneous growth of the working-class movement; it arose as a natural and inevitable outcome of the development of thought among the revolutionary socialist intelligentsia. In the period under discussion, the middle nineties, this doctrine not only represented the completely formulated programme of the Emancipation of Labour group, but had already won over to its side the majority of the revolutionary youth in Russia.

Hence, we had both the elemental awakening of the working masses, their awakening to conscious life and conscious struggle, and a revolutionary youth, armed with Social-Democratic theory and straining towards the workers. In this connection it is particularly important to state the oft-forgotten (and comparatively little-known) fact that, although the *early* Social-Democrats of that period *zealously carried on economic agitation* (being guided in this activity by the truly useful indications contained in the pamphlet *On Agitation*, then still in manuscript), they did not regard this as their sole task. On the contrary, *from the very beginning* they set for Russian Social-Democracy the most far-reaching historical tasks, in general, and the task of overthrowing the autocracy, in particular. ...

And so, we have become convinced that the fundamental error committed by the 'new trend' in Russian Social-Democracy is its bowing to spontaneity and its failure to understand that the spontaneity of the masses demands a high degree of consciousness from us Social-Democrats. The greater the spontaneous upsurge of the masses and the more widespread the movement, the more rapid, incomparably so, the demand for greater consciousness in the theoretical, political, and organisational work of Social-Democracy.

The elemental upsurge of the masses in Russia proceeded (and continues) with such rapidity that the young Social-Democrats proved unprepared to meet these gigantic tasks. This unpreparedness is our common misfortune, the misfortune of *all* Russian Social-Democrats. The upsurge of the masses proceeded and spread with uninterrupted continuity; it not only continued in the places where it began, but spread to new localities and to new strata of the population (under the influence of the working-class movement, there was a renewed ferment among the student youth, among the intellectuals generally, and even among the peasantry). ...

Revolutionary Social-Democracy has always included the struggle for reforms as part of its activities. But it utilises 'economic' agitation for the purpose of presenting to the government, not only demands for all sorts of measures, but also (and primarily) the demand that it cease to be an autocratic government. Moreover, it considers it its duty to present this demand to the government on the basis, not of the economic struggle *alone*, but of all manifestations in general of public and political life. In a word, it subordinates the struggle for reforms, as the part to the whole, to the revolutionary struggle for freedom and for socialism. ...

The propagandist, dealing with, say, the question of unemployment, must explain the capitalistic nature of crises, the cause of their inevitability in modern society, the necessity for the transformation of this society into a socialist society, etc. In a word, he must present 'many ideas', so many, indeed, that they will be understood as an integral whole only by a (comparatively) few persons. The agitator, however, speaking on the same subject, will take as an illustration a fact that is most glaring and most widely known to his audience, say, the death of an unemployed worker's family from starvation, the growing impoverishment, etc., and, utilising this fact, known to all, will direct his efforts to presenting *a single idea* to the 'masses', e.g., the senselessness of the contradiction between the increase of wealth and the increase of poverty; he will strive to *rouse* discontent and indignation among the masses against this crying injustice, leaving a more complete explanation of this contradiction to the propagandist. Consequently, the propagandist operates chiefly by means of the *printed* word; the agitator by means of the *spoken* word. The propagandist requires qualities different from those of the agitator. Kautsky and Lafargue, for example, we term propagandists; Bebel and Guesde we term agitators. ...

In reality, it is possible to 'raise the activity of the working masses' *only* when this activity is *not restricted* to 'political agitation on an economic basis'. A basic condition for the necessary expansion of political agitation is the organisation of *comprehensive* political exposure. *In no way* except by means of such exposures *can* the masses be trained in political consciousness and revolutionary activity. Hence, activity of this kind is one of the most important functions of international Social-Democracy as a whole, for even political freedom does not in any way eliminate exposures; it merely shifts somewhat their sphere of direction. Thus, the German party is especially strengthening its positions and spreading its influence, thanks particularly to the untiring energy with which it is conducting its campaign of political exposure. Working-class consciousness cannot be genuine political consciousness unless the workers are trained to respond to *all cases* of tyranny, oppression, violence, and abuse, no matter *what class* is affected – unless they are trained, moreover, to respond from a Social-Democratic point of view and no other. The consciousness of the working masses cannot be genuine class-consciousness, unless the workers learn, from concrete, and above all from topical, political facts and events to observe *every* other social class in *all* the manifestations of its intellectual, ethical, and political life; unless they learn to apply in practice the materialist analysis and the materialist estimate of *all* aspects of the life and activity of *all* classes, strata, and groups of the population. Those who concentrate the attention, observation, and consciousness of the working class exclusively, or even mainly, upon itself alone are not Social-Democrats; for the self-knowledge of the working class is indissolubly bound up, not solely with a fully clear theoretical understanding – or rather not so much with the theoretical, as with the practical, understanding – of the relationships between *all* the various classes of modern society, acquired through the experience of political life. For this reason the conception of the economic struggle as the most widely applicable means of drawing the masses into the political movement, which our Economists preach, is so extremely harmful and reactionary in its practical significance. In order to become a Social-Democrat, the worker must have a clear picture in his mind of the economic nature and the social and political features of the landlord and the priest, the high state official and the peasant, the student and the vagabond; he must know their strong and weak points, he must grasp the meaning of all the catchwords and sophisms by which each class and each stratum *camouflages* its selfish strivings and its real 'inner workings'; he must understand what interests are reflected by certain institutions and certain laws and how they are reflected. But this 'clear picture' cannot be obtained from any book. It can be obtained only from living examples and from exposures that follow close upon what is going on about us at a given moment; upon what is being discussed, in whispers perhaps, by each one in his own way; upon what finds expression in such and such events, in such and such statistics, in such and such court sentences, etc., etc. These comprehensive political exposures are an essential and *fundamental* condition for training the masses in revolutionary activity.

Why do the Russian workers still manifest little revolutionary activity in response to the brutal treatment of the people by the police, the persecution of religious sects, the flogging of peasants, the outrageous censorship, the torture of soldiers, the persecution of the most innocent cultural undertakings, etc.? Is it because the 'economic struggle' does not 'stimulate' them to this, because such activity does not 'promise palpable results', because it produces little that is 'positive'? To adopt such an opinion, we repeat, is merely to direct the charge where it does not belong, to blame the working masses for one's own philistinism (or Bernsteinism). We must blame ourselves, our lagging behind the mass movement, for still being unable to organise sufficiently wide, striking, and rapid exposures of all the shameful outrages. When we do that (and we must and can do it), the most backward worker will understand, *or will feel*, that the students and religious sects, the peasants and the authors are being abused and outraged by those same dark forces that are oppressing and crushing him at every step of his life. Feeling that, he himself will be filled with an irresistible desire to react, and he will know how to hoot the censors one day, on another day to demonstrate outside the house of a governor who has brutally suppressed a peasant uprising, on still another day to teach a lesson to the gendarmes in surplices who are doing the work of the Holy Inquisition, etc. As yet we have done very little, almost nothing, *to bring* before the working masses prompt exposures on all possible issues. Many of us as yet do not recognise this as our *bounden duty* but trail spontaneously in the wake of the 'drab everyday struggle', in the narrow confines of factory life. ...

Class political consciousness can be brought to the workers *only from without*, that is, only from outside the economic struggle, from outside the sphere of relations between workers and employers. The sphere from which alone it is possible to obtain this knowledge is the sphere of relationships of *all* classes and strata to the state and the government, the sphere of the interrelations between *all* classes. For that reason, the reply to the question as to what must be done to bring political knowledge to the workers cannot be merely the answer with which, in the majority of cases, the practical workers, especially those inclined towards Economism, mostly content themselves, namely: 'To go among the workers.' To bring political knowledge to the *workers* the Social-Democrats must go *among all classes of the population*; they must dispatch units of their army *in all directions*. ...

Let us take the type of Social-Democratic study circle that has become most widespread in the past few years and examine its work. It has 'contacts with the workers' and rests content with this, issuing leaflets in which abuses in the factories, the government's partiality towards the capitalists, and the tyranny of the police are strongly condemned. At workers' meetings the discussions never, or rarely ever, go beyond the limits of these subjects. Extremely rare are the lectures and discussions held on the history of the revolutionary movement, on questions of the government's home and foreign policy, on questions of the economic evolution of Russia and of Europe, on the position of the various classes in modern society, etc. As to systematically acquiring and extending contact with other classes of society, no one even dreams of that. In fact, the ideal leader, as the majority of the members of such circles picture him, is something far more in the nature of a trade-union secretary than a socialist political leader. For the secretary of any, say English, trade union always helps the workers to carry on the economic struggle, he helps them to expose factory abuses, explains the injustice of the laws and of measures that hamper the freedom to strike and to picket (i.e., to warn all and sundry that a strike is proceeding at a certain factory), explains the partiality of arbitration court judges who belong to the bourgeois classes, etc., etc. In a word, every trade-union secretary conducts and helps to conduct 'the economic struggle against the employers and the government'. It cannot be too strongly maintained that *this is still* not Social-Democracy, that the Social-Democrat's ideal should not be the trade-union secretary, but *the tribune of the people*, who is able to react to every manifestation of tyranny and oppression, no matter where it appears, no matter what stratum or class of the people it affects; who is able to generalise all these manifestations and produce a single picture of police violence and capitalist exploitation; who is able to take advantage of every event, however small, in order to set forth *before all* his socialist convictions and his democratic demands, in order to clarify for *all* and everyone the world-historic significance of the struggle for the emancipation of the proletariat. ...

For it is not enough to call ourselves the 'vanguard', the advanced contingent; we must act in such a way that *all* the other contingents recognise and are obliged to admit that we are marching in the vanguard. And we ask the reader: Are the representatives of the other 'contingents' such fools as to take our word for it when we say that we are the 'vanguard'? Just picture to yourselves the following: a Social-Democrat comes to the 'contingent' of Russian educated radicals, or liberal constitutionalists, and says, We are the vanguard; 'the task confronting us now is, as far as possible, to lend the economic struggle itself a political character'. The radical, or constitutionalist, if he is at all intelligent (and there are many intelligent men among Russian radicals and constitutionalists), would only smile at such a speech and would say (to himself, of course, for in the majority of cases he is an experienced diplomat): 'Your "vanguard" must be made up of simpletons. They do not even understand that it is our task, the task of the progressive representatives of bourgeois democracy to lend the workers' economic struggle *itself* a political character. Why, we too, like the West-European bourgeois, want to draw the workers into politics, *but only into trade-unionist, not into*

Social-Democratic politics. Trade-unionist politics of the working class is precisely *bourgeois politics* of the working class, and this "vanguard's" formulation of its task is the formulation of trade-unionist politics! Let them call themselves Social-Democrats to their heart's content, I am not a child to get excited over a label. But they must not fall under the influence of those pernicious orthodox doctrinaires, let them allow "freedom of criticism" to those who unconsciously are driving Social-Democracy into trade-unionist channels.' ...

But if we desire to be front-rank democrats, we must make it our concern *to direct* the thoughts of those who are dissatisfied only with conditions at the university, or in the Zemstvo etc., to the idea that the entire political system is worthless. We must take upon ourselves the task of organising an all-round political struggle under the leadership of *our* Party in such a manner as to make it possible for all oppositional strata, to render their fullest support to the struggle and to our Party. We must train our Social-Democratic practical workers to become political leaders, able to guide all the manifestations of this all-round struggle, able at the right time to 'dictate a positive programme of action' for the aroused students, the discontented Zemstvo people, the incensed religious sects, the offended elementary school-teachers, etc., etc. ...

Iskra desires to *elevate* the trade-unionist politics of the working class (to which through misconception, through lack of training, or through conviction, our practical workers frequently confine themselves) to the level of Social-Democratic politics. *Rabocheye Dyelo*, however, desires *to degrade* Social-Democratic politics to trade-unionist politics. Moreover, it assures the world that the two positions are 'entirely compatible within the common cause'. *O, sancta simplicitas!*

1903: To the Rural Poor*

7. The Class Struggle in the Countryside

What is the *class struggle*? It is a struggle of one part of the people against the other; a struggle waged by the masses of those who have

---

*   *Collected Works*, Vol. 6: 421–8.

no rights, are oppressed and engage in toil, against the privileged, the oppressors and drones; a struggle of the wage-labourers, or proletarians, against the property-owners, or bourgeoisie. This great struggle has always gone on and is now going on in the Russian countryside too, although not everyone sees it, and although not everyone understands its significance. In the period of serfdom the entire mass of the peasants fought against their oppressors, the landlord class, which was protected, defended, and supported by the tsarist government. The peasants were then unable to unite and were utterly crushed by ignorance; they had no helpers and brothers among the urban workers; nevertheless they fought as best they could. They were not deterred by the brutal persecution of the government, were not daunted by punitive measures and bullets, and did not believe the priests, who tried with all their might to prove that serfdom was approved by Holy Scripture and sanctioned by God (that is what Metropolitan Philaret actually said!); the peasants rose in rebellion, now in one place and now in another, and at last the government yielded, fearing a general uprising of all the peasants.

Serfdom was abolished, but not altogether. The peasants remained without rights, remained an inferior, tax-paying, 'black' social-estate, remained in the clutches of serf bondage. Unrest among the peasants continues; they continue to seek complete, real freedom. Meanwhile, after the abolition of serfdom, a new class struggle arose, the *struggle of the proletariat against the bourgeoisie*. Wealth increased, railways and big factories were built, the towns grew still more populous and more luxurious, but all this wealth was appropriated by a very few, while the people became poorer all the time, became ruined, starved, and had to leave their homes to go and hire themselves out for wages. The urban workers started a great, new struggle of all the poor against all the rich. The urban workers have united in the *Social-Democratic Party* and are waging their struggle stubbornly, staunchly, and solidly, advancing step by step preparing for the great final struggle, and demanding political liberty for all the people.

At last the peasants, too, lost patience. In the spring of last year, 1902, the peasants of Poltava, Kharkov, and other gubernias rose against the landlords, broke open their barns, shared the contents among themselves, distributed among the starving the grain that had been sown and reaped by the peasants but appropriated by the landlords, and demanded a new division of the land. The peasants could no longer bear the endless oppression, and began to seek a better lot. The peasants decided – and quite rightly so – that it was better to die fighting the oppressors than to die of starvation without a struggle. But they did not win a better lot for themselves. The tsarist government proclaimed them common rioters and robbers (for having taken from the robber landlords grain which the peasants themselves had sown and reaped!); the tsarist government sent troops against them as against an enemy, and the peasants were defeated; peasants were shot down, many were killed; peasants were brutally flogged, many were flogged to death; they were tortured worse than the Turks torture their enemies, the Christians. The tsar's envoys, the governors, were the worst torturers, real executioners. The soldiers raped the wives and daughters of the peasants. And after all this, the peasants were tried by a court of officials, were compelled to pay the landlords 800,000 rubles, and at the trials, those infamous secret trials, trials in a torture chamber, counsels for the defence were not even allowed to tell how the peasants had been ill-treated and tortured by the tsar's envoys, Governor Obolensky, and the other servants of the tsar.

The peasants fought in a just cause. The Russian working class will always honour the memory of the martyrs who were shot down and flogged to death by the tsar's servants. Those martyrs fought for the freedom and happiness of the working people. The peasants were defeated, but they will rise again and again, and will not lose heart because of this first defeat. The class-conscious workers will do all in their power to inform the largest possible number of working people in town and country about the peasants' struggle and to help them prepare for another and more successful struggle. The class-conscious workers will do all in their power to help the peasants *clearly to understand why the first peasant uprising* (1902) *was crushed and what must be done in order to secure victory for the peasants and workers and not for the tsar's servants.*

The peasant uprising was crushed because it was an uprising of an ignorant and politically unconscious mass, an uprising without clear and definite *political* demands, i.e., without the demand for a change in the political order. The peasant uprising was crushed because *no preparations had been made for it*. The peasant uprising was crushed because the rural proletarians had not yet allied themselves with the urban proletarians. Such were the three causes of the peasants' first failure. To be successful an insurrection must have a conscious political aim; preparations must be made for it in advance; it must spread throughout the whole of Russia and be in alliance with the urban workers. And every step in the struggle of the urban workers, every Social-Democratic pamphlet or newspaper, every speech made by a class-conscious worker to the rural proletarians will bring nearer the time when the insurrection will be repeated and end in victory.

The peasants rose without a conscious political aim, simply because they could not bear their sufferings any longer, because they did not want to die like dumb brutes, without resistance. The peasants had suffered so much from every manner of robbery, oppression, and torment that they could not but believe, if only for a moment, the vague rumours about the tsar's mercy; they could not but believe that every sensible man would regard it as just that grain should be distributed among starving people, among those who had worked all their lives for others, had sown and reaped, and were now dying of starvation, while the 'gentry's' barns were full to bursting. The peasants seemed to have forgotten that the best land and all the factories had been seized by the rich, by the landlords and the bourgeoisie, precisely for the purpose of compelling the starving people to work for them. The peasants forgot that not only do the priests preach sermons in defence of the rich class, but the entire tsarist government, with its host of bureaucrats and soldiers, rises in its defence. The tsarist government reminded the peasants of that. With brutal cruelty, the tsarist government showed the peasants what state power is, whose servant and whose protector it is. We need only remind the peasants of this lesson more often, and they will easily understand why it is necessary to *change the political order*, and why we need *political liberty*. Peasant uprisings will have a conscious political aim when that is understood by larger and larger numbers of people, when every peasant who can read and write and who thinks for himself becomes familiar with the *three principal demands* which must be fought for first of all. The first demand – the convocation of *a national assembly of deputies for the purpose of establishing popular elective government in Russia in place of the autocratic government*. The second demand – *freedom for all to publish all kinds of books and newspapers*. The third demand – *recognition by law of the peasants' complete equality of rights with the other social-estates, and the institution of elected peasant committees with the primary object of abolishing all forms of serf bondage*. Such are the chief and fundamental demands of the Social-Democrats, and it will now be very easy for the peasants to understand them, to understand *what to begin with* in the struggle for the people's freedom. When the peasants understand these demands, they will also understand that long, persistent and persevering *preparations* must be made in advance for the struggle, not in isolation, but together with the workers in the towns – the Social-Democrats.

Let every class-conscious worker and peasant rally around himself the most intelligent, reliable, and fearless comrades. Let him strive to explain to them what the Social-Democrats want, so that every one of them may understand the struggle that must be waged and the demands that must be advanced. Let the class-conscious Social-Democrats begin gradually, cautiously, but unswervingly, to teach the peasants the doctrine of Social-Democracy, give them Social-Democratic pamphlets to read and explain those pamphlets at small gatherings of trustworthy people.

But the doctrine of Social-Democracy must not be taught from books alone; every instance, every case of oppression and injustice we see around us must be used for this purpose. The Social-Democratic doctrine is one of struggle against all oppression, all robbery, all injustice. Only he who knows the causes of oppression and who *all his life fights every case of oppression* is a real Social-Democrat. How can this be done? When they gather in their town or village, class-conscious Social-Democrats must themselves decide how it must be done to the best advantage of the entire working class. To show how it must be done I shall cite one or two examples. Let us suppose that a Social-Democratic worker has come on a visit to his village, or that some urban Social-Democratic worker has come to any village. The entire village is in the clutches of the neighbouring landlord, like a fly in a spider's web; it has always been in this state of bondage and cannot escape from it. The worker must at once pick out the most sensible, intelligent, and trustworthy peasants, those who are seeking justice and will not be frightened by the first police agent who comes along, and explain to them the causes of this hopeless bondage, tell them how the landlords cheated the peasants and robbed them with the aid of the committees of nobles, tell them how strong the rich are and how they are supported by the tsarist government, and also tell them about the demands of the Social-Democratic workers. When the peasants understand all these simple things they must all put their heads together and discuss whether it is possible to put up united resistance to the landlord, whether it is possible to put forward the first and principal demands (in the same way as the urban workers present their demands to the factory owners). If the landlord holds one big village, or several villages, in bondage, the best thing would be to obtain through trustworthy people, a *leaflet* from the nearest Social-Democratic committee. In the leaflet the Social-Democratic committee will correctly describe, from the very beginning, the bondage the peasants suffer from and formulate their most immediate demands (reduction of rent paid for land, proper rates, and not half-rates, of pay for winter hire, or less persecution for damage done by straying cattle or various other demands). From such a leaflet all peasants who can read and write will get to know very well what the issue is, and those who cannot read will have it explained to them. The peasants will then clearly see that the Social-Democrats support them, that the Social-Democrats condemn all robbery. The peasants will then begin to understand what relief, if only slight, but relief for all that, can be obtained now, at once, if all stand together, and what big improvements for the whole country they must seek to obtain by a great struggle in conjunction with the Social-Democratic workers in the towns. The peasants will then prepare more and more for that great struggle; they will learn how to find trustworthy people and how to stand unitedly for their demands. Perhaps they may sometimes succeed in organising a strike, as the urban workers do. True, this is more difficult in the countryside than in the towns, but it is sometimes possible for all that; in other countries there have been successful strikes, for instance, in the busy seasons, when the landlords and rich farmers are badly in need of hands. If the rural poor are prepared to strike, if an agreement has long been reached about the general demands, if those demands have been explained in leaflets, or properly explained at meetings, all will stand together, and the landlord will have to yield, or at least put some curb on his greed. If the strike is unanimous and is called during the busy season, the landlord, and even the authorities with their troops, will find it hard to do anything – time will be lost, the landlord will be threatened with ruin, and he will soon become more tractable. Of course, strikes are a new thing, and new things do not come off well at first. The urban workers, too, did not know how to fight unitedly at first; they did not know what demands to put forward in common; they simply went out to smash machinery and wreck a factory. But now the workers have learned to conduct a united struggle. Every new job must first be learned. The workers now understand that immediate relief can be obtained only if they stand together; meanwhile, the people are getting used to offering united resistance and are preparing more and more for the great and decisive struggle. Similarly, the peasants will learn to stand up to the worst robbers, to be united in their demands for some measure of relief and to prepare gradually, persistently, and everywhere for the great battle for freedom. The number of class-conscious workers and peasants will constantly grow, and the unions of rural Social-Democrats will become stronger and stronger; every case of bondage to the landlord, of extortion by the priest, of police brutality and bureaucratic oppression, will increasingly serve to open the eyes of the people, accustom them to putting up united resistance and to the idea that it is necessary to change the political order by force.

At the very beginning of this pamphlet we said that at the present time the urban workers come out into the streets and squares and publicly demand *freedom*, that they inscribe on their banners and cry out: 'Down with the autocracy!' The day will soon come when the urban workers will rise not merely to march shouting through the streets, but for the great and final struggle; when the workers will declare as one man: 'We shall win freedom, or die in the fight!'; when the places of the hundreds who have been killed, fallen in the fight, will be taken by thousands of fresh and still more resolute fighters. And the peasants, too, will then rise all over Russia and go to the aid of the urban workers, will fight to the end for the freedom of the workers and peasants. The tsar's hordes will be unable to withstand that onslaught. Victory will go to the working people, and the working class will march along the wide, spacious road to the liberation of all working people from any kind of oppression. The working class will use its freedom to fight for socialism!

1904: One Step Forward, Two Steps Back – Reply to Rosa Luxemburg*

Comrade Rosa Luxemburg's article in Nos. 42 and 43 of the *Neue Zeit* is a criticism of my Russian book on the crisis in our Party.[1] I cannot but thank our German comrades for their attention to our Party literature and their attempts to acquaint German Social-Democrats with it, but I must point out that Rosa Luxemburg's *Neue Zeit* article does not acquaint the reader with my book, but with something else. This may be seen from the following instances. Comrade Luxemburg says, for example, that my book is a clear and detailed expression of the point of view of 'intransigent centralism'. Comrade Luxemburg thus supposes that I defend one system of organisation against another. But actually that is not so.

---

* *Collected Works*, Vol. 7: 472–83.
1. *One Step Forward, Two Steps Back*.

From the first to the last page of my book, I defend the elementary principles of any conceivable system of party organisation. My book is not concerned with the difference between one system of organisation and another, but with how any system is to be maintained, criticised, and rectified in a manner consistent with the party idea. Rosa Luxemburg further says that 'according to his [Lenin's] conception, the Central Committee has the right to organise all the local Party committees'. Actually that is not so. What my views on this subject are can be documentarily proved by the draft Rules of Party Organisation which I proposed. In that draft there is nothing about any right to organise the local committees. That right was introduced into the Party Rules by the commission elected by the Party Congress to frame them, and the Congress adopted the commission's text. But besides myself and one other majority adherent, the commission included three members of the Congress minority, so that in this commission which gave the Central Committee the right to organise the local committees, it was my opponents that had the upper hand. Comrade Luxemburg has confused two different things. In the first place, she has confused my organisational draft with the modified draft of the commission and with the Rules of Organisation as actually adopted by the Congress; secondly, she has confused the defence of a specific point relating to a specific clause of the Rules (in that defence I was by no means intransigent, for I did not object at the plenary session to the amendment made by the commission) with the defence of the thesis (truly 'ultra-centralist', is it not?) that Rules adopted by a Party congress must be adhered to until amended by a subsequent congress. This thesis (a 'purely Blanquist' one, as the reader may readily observe) I did indeed defend in my book quite 'intransigently'. Comrade Luxemburg says that in my view 'the Central Committee is the only active nucleus of the Party'. Actually that is not so. I have never advocated any such view. On the contrary, my opponents (the Second Party Congress minority) charged in their writings that I did not sufficiently uphold the independence of the Central Committee, that I made it too subordinate to the editorial board of the Central Organ and the Party Council, bodies located abroad. To these charges I replied in my book that when the Party majority had the upper hand in the Party Council, the latter never made any attempt to interfere with the Central Committee's independence, but that when the Party council became a weapon of the minority, this did immediately happen. Comrade Rosa Luxemburg says that there are no two opinions among the Russian Social-Democrats as to the need for a united party, and that the whole controversy is over the degree of centralisation. Actually that is not so. If Comrade Luxemburg had taken the trouble to acquaint herself with the resolutions of the many local Party committees that constitute the majority, she would readily have seen (which incidentally is also clear from my book) that our controversy has principally been over whether the Central Committee and Central Organ should represent the trend of the majority of the Party Congress, or whether they should not. About this 'ultra-centralist' and 'purely Blanquist' demand the worthy comrade says not a word, she prefers to declaim against mechanical subordination of the part to the whole, against slavish submission, blind obedience, and other such bogeys. I am very grateful to Comrade Luxemburg for explaining the profound idea that slavish submission is very harmful to the Party, but I should like to know: does the comrade consider it normal for supposed party central institutions to be dominated by the minority of the Party Congress? – can she imagine such a thing? – has she ever seen it in any party? Comrade Luxemburg fathers on me the idea that all the conditions already exist in Russia for forming a large and extremely centralised workers' party. Again an error of fact. Nowhere in my book did I voice such an idea, let alone advocate it. The thesis I advanced expressed and expresses something else: I insisted, namely, that all the conditions already existed for expecting Party Congress decisions to be observed, and that the time was past when a Party institution could be supplanted by a private circle. I brought proof that certain academics in our Party had shown themselves inconsistent and unstable, and that they had no right to lay the blame for their own lack of discipline upon the Russian proletarians. The Russian workers have already pronounced repeatedly, on various occasions, for observance of the Party Congress decisions. It is nothing short of laughable when Comrade Luxemburg proclaims such a view 'optimistic' (should it not rather be considered 'pessimistic'?) without uttering a single word about the factual basis of my thesis. Comrade Luxemburg declares that I glorify the educational influence of the factory. That is not so. It was my opponent, not I, who said that I pictured the Party as a factory. I properly ridiculed him and proved with his own words that he confused two different aspects of factory discipline, which, unfortunately, is the case with Comrade Luxemburg too.

Comrade Luxemburg says that I characterised my standpoint more acutely, perhaps, than any of my opponents could have done when I defined a revolutionary Social-Democrat as a Jacobin who has identified himself with the organisation of the class-conscious workers. Yet another error of fact. It was P. Axelrod, not I, who first started talking about Jacobinism. He was the first to liken our Party trends to those of the days of the great French Revolution. I merely observed that the parallel could only be allowed in the sense that the division of present-day Social-Democracy into a revolutionary and an opportunist wing corresponded to some extent to the division into Montagnards and Girondists. The old *Iskra*, which the Party Congress endorsed, often drew such a parallel. Just because it recognised this division, the old *Iskra* fought against the opportunist wing in our Party, against the *Rabocheye Dyelo* trend. Rosa Luxemburg here confuses *comparison* of the two revolutionary trends of the eighteenth and the twentieth century with identification of those trends. If I say, for example, that the Jungfrau stands in the same relation to the Little Scheidegg as a house of four storeys to one of two, that does not mean I identify a four-storey house with the Jungfrau. Comrade Luxemburg leaves completely out of sight the factual analysis of the different trends in our Party. Yet the greater half of my book is devoted precisely to this analysis, based on the minutes of our Party Congress, and in the preface I call special attention to the fact. Rosa Luxemburg sets out to talk about the present position in our Party while totally ignoring our Congress, which was what really laid our Party's foundation. A rash enterprise, it has to be said! Particularly since I point out a hundred times in my book that my opponents ignore our Party Congress and by so doing leave all their assertions devoid of all foundation of fact.

Comrade Luxemburg commits exactly the same basic error. She repeats naked words without troubling to grasp their concrete meaning. She raises bogeys without informing herself of the actual issue in the controversy. She puts in my mouth commonplaces, general principles and conceptions, absolute truths, and tries to pass over the relative truths, pertaining to perfectly definite facts, with which alone I operate. And then she rails against set formulas and invokes the dialectics of Marx! It is the worthy comrade's own article that consists of nothing but manufactured formulas and runs counter to the ABC of dialectics. This ABC tells us that there is no such thing as abstract truth, truth is always concrete. Comrade Rosa Luxemburg loftily ignores the concrete facts of our Party struggle and engages in grandiloquent declamation about matters which it is impossible to discuss seriously. Let me cite one last example from Comrade Luxemburg's second article. She quotes my remark that the way the Rules of Organisation are formulated can make them a more or a less trenchant weapon against opportunism. Just what formulations I talked about in my book and all of us talked about at the Congress, of that she does not say a word. What the controversy at the Party Congress was, and against whom I advanced my theses, she does not touch on in the slightest. Instead, she favours me with a whole lecture on opportunism … in the parliamentary countries! But about the peculiar, specific varieties of opportunism in Russia, the shades which it has taken on there and with which my book is concerned, we find not a word in her article. The upshot of all these very brilliant arguments is 'Party Rules are not meant in themselves [?? understand this who can!] to be a weapon of resistance to opportunism, but only an outward instrument for exerting the dominant influence of the actually existing revolutionary-proletarian majority of the Party.' Quite so. But how this actually existing majority of our Party was formed Rosa Luxemburg does not say, yet that is exactly what I talk about in my book. Nor does she say what influence it was that Plekhanov and I defended with the help of this outward instrument. I can only add that never and nowhere have I talked such nonsense as that the Party Rules are a weapon 'in themselves'.

The best way to answer this kind of presentation of my views will be to set forth the concrete facts of our Party struggle. Anyone will then be able to see how ill Comrade Luxemburg's abstract commonplaces and formulas sort with the concrete facts.

Our Party was founded in Russia in the spring of 1898 at a congress of representatives of several Russian organisations. It was named the Russian Social-Democratic Labour Party, *Rabochaya Gazeta* was made the Central Organ, and the Union of Russian Social-Democrats Abroad became the Party's foreign representative. Very soon after the congress, the Central Committee of the Party was arrested. *Rabochaya Gazeta* had to cease publication after its second issue. The whole Party became a shapeless conglomeration of local Party organisations (known as committees). The only bond between these local committees was an ideological, purely spiritual one. A period of disunity, vacillation, and splits was bound to set in again. The intellectuals, who in our Party made up a much larger percentage than in the West-European parties, had taken up Marxism as a new vogue. This vogue very soon gave place to slavish acceptance of the bourgeois criticism of Marx, on the one hand, and an infatuation for a purely trade-unionist labour movement (strikeism – Economism), on the other. The divergence between the intellectual-opportunist and proletarian-revolutionary trends led to a split in the Union Abroad. The newspaper *Rabochaya Mysl*, and the *Rabocheye Dyelo* magazine published abroad, expressed (the latter in somewhat lesser degree) the standpoint of Economism, they belittled the importance of political struggle and denied the existence of a bourgeois-democratic element in Russia. The 'legal' critics of Marx – Messrs. Struve, Tugan-Baranovsky, Bulgakov, Berdyaev; and the rest – swung all the way to the Right. Nowhere in Europe do we find Bernsteinism arriving so speedily at its logical consummation – the formation of a liberal group – as was the case in Russia. There, Mr Struve began with 'criticism' in the name of Bernsteinism and ended by setting up the liberal magazine *Osvobozhdeniye*, liberal in the European sense of the term. Plekhanov and his friends, who broke away from the Union Abroad, met with support from the founders of *Iskra* and *Zarya*. These two publications waged (even Comrade Luxemburg has heard something about that) a 'brilliant three-year campaign' against the opportunist wing of the Party, a campaign of the Social-Democratic 'Mountain' against the Social-Democratic 'Gironde' (the expression belongs to the old *Iskra*), a campaign against *Rabocheye Dyelo* (Comrades Krichevsky, Akimov, Martynov, and others), against the Jewish Bund, against the organisations in Russia that eagerly espoused this trend (notably the St Petersburg so-called Workers' Organisation and the Voronezh Committee).

It became more and more obvious that the purely ideological bond between the committees was not enough. The need to create a really united party, that is, to effect what was only foreshadowed in 1898, asserted itself more and more insistently. Finally, at the end of 1902 an Organising Committee was formed to convene the Second Party Congress. This Organising Committee, which was largely set up by the *Iskra* organisation in Russia, also included a representative of the Jewish Bund. In the autumn of 1903 the Second Congress was at last held; it ended, on the one hand, in the Party's formal unification, and on the other, in a split into 'majority' and 'minority'. That division did not exist before the Congress. Only a detailed analysis of the struggle at the Congress can explain this division. Unfortunately, the supporters of the minority (including Comrade Luxemburg) shy away fearfully from any such analysis.

In my book, presented to the German reader by Comrade Luxemburg in such a singular manner, I devote over a hundred pages to a close study of the Congress minutes (which make up a volume of some 400 pages). This analysis caused me to divide the delegates, or rather votes (we had delegates with one vote and with two), into four main groups: (1) majority *Iskra*-ists (adherents of the trend of the old *Iskra*) – 24 votes; (2) minority *Iskra*-ists – nine votes; (3) 'Centre' (also referred to ironically as the 'Marsh') – ten votes; and, lastly, (4) anti-*Iskra*-ists – eight votes, making 51 votes in all. I analyse the part played by these groups in *all* the voting at the Congress, and prove that on all issues (of programme, of tactics, and of organisation) the Congress was an arena of struggle between the *Iskra*-ists, and the anti-*Iskra*-ists, with the 'Marsh' making various zigzags. Anyone even slightly familiar with our Party's history is bound to see that it could not have been otherwise. But all supporters of the minority (including Rosa Luxemburg) modestly close their eyes to this struggle. Why? Because this struggle makes manifest the utter falsity of the minority's present political position. Throughout the struggle at the Party Congress, on dozens of questions, in dozens of votes, the *Iskra*-ists fought the anti-*Iskra*-ists and the 'Marsh', which sided the more definitely with the anti-*Iskra*-ists, the more concrete the matter at issue, the more positively it affected the fundamentals of Social-Democratic activity, the more tangibly it involved putting into practice the old *Iskra*'s long-standing plans. The anti-*Iskra*-ists (particularly Comrade Akimov and the St Petersburg Workers' Organisation delegate, Comrade Brouckère, who always agreed with him, and nearly always Comrade Martynov and the five delegates of the Jewish Bund) were against recognising the trend of the old *Iskra*. They defended the old separate organisations and voted against their subordination to the Party, their fusion into the Party (the Organising Committee incident, the dissolution of the *Yuzhny Rabochy* group – the leading group of the 'Marsh', and so on). They fought against centralistic Rules of Organisation (14th sitting of the Congress) and accused *all* the *Iskra*-ists at that time of wanting to introduce 'organised distrust', 'emergency laws', and other such horrors. *All* the *Iskra*-ists, without exception, laughed at it then; it is remarkable that Comrade Rosa Luxemburg should now take these bogeys seriously. On the great majority of questions the *Iskra*-ists carried the day; they predominated at the Congress, as is clear from the figures given above. But during the second half of the Congress, when less fundamental issues were being decided, the anti-*Iskra*-ists had the better of it – some of the *Iskra*-ists voted with them. That was the case, for example, with regard to proclaiming equality of all languages in our programme; on this point the anti-*Iskra*-ists nearly succeeded in defeating the Programme Committee and getting their formulation carried. It was also the case over Paragraph 1 of the Rules, when the anti-

Iskra-ists and the 'Marsh' put through Martov's formulation. According to this formulation, Party members are not only those who belong to Party organisations (the formulation defended by Plekhanov and myself), but also all persons working under the control of Party organisations.

The same thing happened in the elections to the Central Committee and the editorial board of the Central Organ. The compact majority consisted of 24 *Iskra*-ists, and they put through the long since planned reconstitution of the editorial board; of the six former editors, three were elected. The minority consisted of nine *Iskra*-ists, ten members of the 'Centre', and one anti-*Iskra*-ist (the other seven anti-*Iskra*-ists, representing the Jewish Bund and *Rabocheye Dyelo*, had withdrawn from the Congress by then). This minority was so displeased with the elections that it decided to take no part in the rest of the elections. Comrade Kautsky was quite right when he said that the reconstitution of the editorial board was the main cause of the struggle that followed. But his view that I (*sic*!) 'expelled' three comrades from the editorial board can only be attributed to his being totally uninformed about our Congress. In the first place, non-election is far from the same thing as expulsion, and I certainly had no power at the Congress to expel anyone; and secondly, Comrade Kautsky seems to have no inkling that the fact of a coalition between the anti-*Iskra*-ists, the 'Centre', and a small section of the *Iskra* adherents had political implications too and could not fail to influence the outcome of the elections. Anyone who does not wilfully close his eyes to what happened at our Congress is bound to see that our new division into minority and majority is only a variant of the old division into a proletarian-revolutionary and an intellectual-opportunist wing of our Party. That is a fact, and there is no explaining or laughing it away.

Unfortunately, after the Congress the principles involved in this division were obscured by squabbling over co-optation: the minority would not work under the control of the central institutions unless the three ex-editors were again co-opted. This fight went on for two months. The weapons used were boycott and disruption of the Party. Twelve committees (out of the 14 that spoke out on the subject) severely condemned these methods of struggle. The minority would not even accept the proposal, made by Plekhanov and myself, that they should set forth their point of view in *Iskra*. At the Congress of the League Abroad the thing was carried to the length of showering the members of the central bodies with personal insults and abuse (autocrats, bureaucrats, gendarmes, liars, etc., etc.). They were accused of suppressing individual initiative and wanting to introduce slavish submission, blind obedience, and so on. Plekhanov's attempts to characterise these minority methods of struggle as anarchistic did not avail. After this Congress Plekhanov came out with his epoch-making article against me, 'What Should Not Be Done' (in No. 52 of *Iskra*). In this article he said that fighting revisionism did not necessarily mean fighting the revisionists; and it was clear to all that he was referring to our minority. He further said that one should not always fight the anarchistic individualism so deeply ingrained in the Russian revolutionary, that at times some concessions were a better way to subdue it and avoid a split. I resigned from the editorial board as I could not share this view, and the minority editors were co-opted. Then followed a fight for co-optation to the Central Committee. My offer to conclude peace on the basis of the minority keeping the Central Organ and the majority the Central Committee was rejected. The fight went on, they were fighting 'on principle' against bureaucracy, ultra-centralism, formalism, Jacobinism, Schweitzerism (I was dubbed a Russian Schweitzer), and other such bogeys. I ridiculed all these accusations in my book and pointed out that they were either just a matter of squabbling about co-optation, or (if they were to be recognised, conditionally, as involving 'principles') nothing but opportunist, Girondist phrases. The present minority are only repeating what Comrade Akimov and other acknowledged opportunists said at our Congress against the centralism of all the adherents of the old *Iskra*.

The committees in Russia were outraged at the conversion of the Central Organ into the organ of a private circle, an organ of co-optation squabbling and Party scandal. A number of resolutions expressing the severest censure were passed. Only the so-called

St Petersburg Workers' Organisation already mentioned and the Voronezh Committee (both of them supporters of Comrade Akimov's trend) pronounced their satisfaction *in principle* at the trend of the new *Iskra*. Demands to have the Third Party Congress summoned became ever more numerous.

The reader who takes the trouble to make a first-hand study of the struggle in our Party will readily see that, concretely and practically, Comrade Rosa Luxemburg's talk about 'ultra-centralism', about the need for centralisation to be gradual, and the like, is a mockery of our Congress, while abstractly and theoretically (if one can speak here of theory at all) it is nothing but a vulgarisation of Marxism, a perversion of true Marxian dialectics, etc.

The latest phase in our Party struggle is marked by the fact that the majority members have in part been ousted from the Central Committee, in part rendered useless, reduced to nonentities. (This happened owing to changes in the Central Committee's composition, etc.) The Party Council (which after the co-optation of the old editors likewise fell into the minority's hands) and the present Central Committee have condemned all agitation for summoning the Third Congress and are taking the path of personal deals and negotiations with some members of the minority. Organisations which dared to commit such a crime as to agitate for a congress – as for instance a certain agent body of the Central Committee – have been dissolved. A campaign against the summoning of the Third Congress has been proclaimed by the Party Council and the new Central Committee all along the line. The majority have replied with the slogan 'Down with Bonapartism!' (that is the title of a pamphlet by Comrade Galyorka, who speaks for the majority). More and more resolutions are being passed declaring that Party institutions which fight against a congress are anti-Party and Bonapartist. How hypocritical was all the minority's talk against ultra-centralism and in favour of autonomy is obvious from the fact that a new majority publishing house started by myself and another comrade (which issued the above-named pamphlet by Comrade Galyorka and some others) has been declared outside the Party. This new publishing house affords the majority their only opportunity of propagating their views, for the columns of *Iskra* are as good as closed to them. Yet – or rather just because of it – the Party Council has made the above ruling, on the purely formal grounds that our publishing house has not been authorised by any Party organisation.

It need hardly be said how greatly positive work has been neglected, how greatly the prestige of Social-Democracy has suffered, how greatly the whole Party is demoralised by this nullification of all the decisions, all the elections made by the Second Congress, and this fight which Party institutions accountable to the Party are waging against the convening of the Third Congress.

1904: Against Subordination to Liberals[*]

Now let us examine the new *Iskra*'s plan. The editors acknowledge that we must make full use of all material showing the irresolution and half-heartedness of the liberal democrats and the antagonism of interests between the liberal bourgeoisie and the proletariat, must do so 'in accordance with the fundamental demands of our programme'. 'But,' the editors continue, '*but* within the framework of the struggle with absolutism, notably in its present phase, our attitude towards the liberal bourgeoisie is *determined by the task* of spurring it to greater boldness and inducing it to join in the demands which the proletariat, led by the Social-Democrats, *will put forward* [? has put forward?].' We have italicised the particularly strange words in this strange tirade. For what is it if not strange to contrast criticism of half-heartedness and analysis of antagonistic interests, on the one hand, and the task of spurring these people to greater boldness and inducing them to join, on the other? How can we spur the liberal democrats to greater boldness except by relentless analysis and devastating criticism of the half-heartedness of their democracy? Insofar as the bourgeois (liberal) democrats intend to act as democrats, and are forced to act as democrats, they necessarily seek the support of the widest possible sections of the people. This inevitably

[*] *Collected Works*, Vol. 7: 499–500, 501, 503, 514–15.

produces the following contradiction. The wider these sections of the people, the more representatives are there among them of the proletarian and semi-proletarian strata, who demand the complete democratisation of the political and social system – such complete democratisation as would threaten to undermine very important pillars of all bourgeois rule (the monarchy, the standing army, the bureaucracy). Bourgeois democrats are by their very nature incapable of satisfying these demands, and are therefore, by their very nature, doomed to irresolution and half-heartedness. By criticising this half-heartedness, the Social-Democrats keep prodding the liberals on and winning more and more proletarians and semi-proletarians, and partly petty bourgeois too, from liberal democracy to working-class democracy. How then is it possible to say: we must criticise the half-heartedness of the liberal bourgeoisie, *but* (but!) our attitude towards it is determined by the task of spurring it to greater boldness? Why, that is plain muddle-headedness, which shows that its authors are either marching backward, reverting to the days when the liberals did not come forward openly at all, when they had still to be roused, stirred, induced to open their mouths – or else are slipping into the idea that one can 'spur' the liberals to greater boldness by subtracting from the boldness of the proletarians. ...

[The liberals] are afraid of the revolutionary socialist aims of the 'extreme' parties, they are afraid of leaflets, those first harbingers of independent revolutionary action by the proletariat, which will not stop, will not lay down its arms until it has overthrown the rule of the bourgeoisie. This fear is not inspired by ludicrous bogeys, but by the actual nature of the working-class movement; and it is a fear ineradicable from the hearts of the bourgeoisie (not counting a few individuals and groups, of course). And that is why the new *Iskra*'s talk about the discrediting tactics of intimidating the Zemstvo-ists and representatives of the bourgeois opposition rings so false. Afraid of leaflets, afraid of anything that goes beyond a qualified-franchise constitution, the liberal gentry will always stand in fear of the slogan 'a democratic republic' and of the call for an armed uprising of the people. But the class-conscious proletariat will indignantly reject the very idea that we could renounce this slogan and this call, or could in general be guided in our activity by the panic and fears of the bourgeoisie. ...

The [*Iskra*] editors denounce the discrediting tactics of seeking to extort from the Zemstvo-ists 'a formal promise to present our demands to the government'. Over and above the absurdities already noted, the very idea that 'our' demands, the demands of working-class democrats, should be presented to the government by liberal democrats is a peculiar one. On the one hand, the liberal democrats, being bourgeois democrats, can never identify themselves with 'our' demands, can never uphold them sincerely, consistently, and resolutely. Even if the liberals gave, and gave 'voluntarily', a formal promise to present our demands, it is a foregone conclusion that they would fail to keep that promise, would betray the proletariat. On the other hand, if we should be strong enough to exert serious influence on the bourgeois democrats generally and the Zemstvo gentlemen in particular, we should be quite strong enough to present our demands to the government ourselves. ...

We, the party of the proletariat, should, of course, 'go to all classes of the population', openly and vigorously championing our programme and our immediate demands before the people at large; we should seek to present these demands to the Zemstvo gentlemen too; but our focal point and guiding thread must be pressure on the government, not on the Zemstvo-ists. ...

What the working class must do is to broaden and strengthen its organisation and redouble its agitation among the masses, making the most of every vacillation of the government, propagating the idea of an uprising, demonstrating the necessity for it from the example of all those half-hearted and foredoomed 'steps' about which so much fuss is now being made. It need hardly be said that the workers' response to the Zemstvo petitions must be to call meetings, scatter leaflets, and – where there are forces enough – organise demonstrations to present all the Social-Democratic demands, regardless of the 'panic' of Mr Trubetskoy and his like or of the philistines' cries about levers for reaction. And if one is really to risk talking in advance, and from abroad at that, about a possible and (desirable higher type of *mass* demonstration (because demonstrations not of a mass nature are altogether without significance); if one is really to discuss before what particular premises the demonstrators' forces should be concentrated – we would point to the premises where the business of police persecution of the working-class movement is carried on, to the police, gendarmerie, censorship headquarters, to the places where political 'offenders' are confined. The way for the workers to give serious support to the Zemstvo petitions is not by concluding agreements about the conditions on which the Zemstvo-ists would have a right to speak in the name of the people, but by striking a blow at the people's enemies. And there need be little doubt that the idea of such a demonstration will meet with the sympathy of the proletariat. The workers nowadays hear magniloquent phrases and lofty promises on every hand, they see a real – infinitesimal but nonetheless real – extension of freedom for 'society' (a slackening of the curb on the Zemstvos, the return of banished Zemstvo-ists, an abatement of the ferocity against the liberal press); but they see nothing whatever that gives *their* political struggle more freedom. Under pressure of the revolutionary onslaught of the *proletariat* the government has allowed the *liberals* to talk a little about freedom! The condition of the slaves of capital, downtrodden and deprived of rights, now comes home to the proletarians more clearly than ever. The workers do not have any regular widespread organisations for the relatively free (by Russian standards) discussion of political matters; nor halls to hold meetings in; nor newspapers of their own; and their exiled and imprisoned comrades are not coming back. The workers see now that the liberal bourgeois gentry are setting about dividing the bearskin, the skin of the bear which the workers have not yet killed, but which they, and they alone, have seriously wounded. They see that, at the very start of dividing the skin in anticipation, these liberal bourgeois gentry already snap and snarl at the 'extreme parties', at the 'enemies at home' – the relentless enemies of bourgeois rule and bourgeois law and order. And the workers will rise still more fearlessly, in still greater numbers, to finish off the bear, to win by force *for themselves* what is promised as charity to the liberal bourgeois gentry – freedom of assembly, freedom of the workers' press, full political freedom for a broad and open struggle for the complete victory of socialism.

4

1905: CHALLENGES OF THE REVOLUTIONARY UPSURGE

Russia's revolutionary upsurge of 1905 was sparked by working-class protests influenced by Father Georgi Gapon, a Russian Orthodox priest who organised tea rooms and social activities in St Petersburg's working-class neighbourhoods. Although financed and supported by the tsarist regime, Gapon was drawn into a sincere concern for the workers' plight and was increasingly influenced by working-class activists animated by notions of trade unionism, democracy, and socialism. Gapon helped them draw up a petition appealing to Tsar Nicholas II to help the workers overcome their oppression and exploitation. In January tens of thousands of men, women and children – carrying religious icons and portraits of the tsar, singing hymns and the anthem 'God Save the Tsar' – brought the petition to the Winter Palace. They were met by troops who fired upon them, resulting in hundreds of casualties. This generated not only shock but popular rage and insurgencies throughout the country which shook the tsarist empire. In the face of incredible radicalisation and militant actions by the workers, the tsar felt compelled to offer economic and political concessions.

Writing in the Bolshevik faction's newspaper *Vperyod* (Forward), Lenin gave an account and evaluation of this situation in the article 'The Beginning of the Revolution in Russia'. The new situation swelled the memberships of the various revolutionary organisations – both the Bolshevik and Menshevik wings of the RSDLP, the Socialist-Revolutionary Party, and others – and the RSDLP now enjoyed the mass working-class base it had sought since its founding seven years before. In February a radicalised Father Gapon issued an appeal for a unified revolutionary uprising, to which Lenin responded positively in another *Vperyod* article, 'A Militant Agreement for the Uprising'. Here he articulated essential principles which would become associated with the key conception of the *united front*.

In April the RSDLP held its Third Congress in London, where tactical and strategic perspectives were sharply debated between the Bolshevik and

Menshevik factions. In the wake of this, Lenin wrote *Two Tactics of Social Democracy in the Democratic Revolution*, excerpts of which are reproduced here. (Lenin's use of the word 'tactics' here corresponds to what would later commonly be called *strategy* – which could be defined as an overall plan of action which can be advanced by discrete tactical methods.) The most fundamental difference in strategic orientation dividing Bolsheviks from Mensheviks – a worker–peasant alliance instead of a worker–capitalist alliance – was the focal-point of Lenin's polemic. Both factions believed that Russia required a *bourgeois-democratic revolution* (replacing tsarism with political democracy and an unfettered capitalist economy), which they believed would prepare the way for working-class growth and industrial development, providing the material basis for the socialist revolution of the future. But while the Mensheviks saw the revolution culminating in a liberal democratic government dominated by capitalist elements, Lenin argued for a strongly radical regime of workers and peasants – what he called a 'democratic dictatorship of the proletariat and the peasantry' – that would uncompromisingly sweep aside all vestiges of the old tsarist order. As one rank-and-file Bolshevik of the time later reminisced:

It would be a dictatorship of the proletariat and the peasantry which would continue until the convening of a Constituent Assembly, and after that precisely because of this dictatorship of the proletariat and the peasantry and the opportunities for influence it provided, a true democratic republic would be set up: capitalism would be maintained but with very strong footholds for socialism within the framework of a democratized capitalistic Russia.[1]

In the course of the revolutionary upsurge, democratic councils of workers – soviets – formed and played a profoundly important part in the struggles of 1905. Open to members of all parties, the soviets helped to co-ordinate working-class action and also played a governing role in the working-class districts. Some members of the Bolshevik faction were suspicious of these new entities and were inclined to reject the soviets in favour of urging workers simply to join and follow the RSDLP (and especially the Bolshevik faction). This is in stark contrast to the very positive Bolshevik attitude toward the soviets in 1917. In 'Our Tasks and the Soviet of Workers' Deputies', written in Stockholm as Lenin was making his way back to Russia from exile, and excerpted here, he comes out in favour of involvement in the soviets, which are seen as a revolutionary-democratic expression of the Russian working class. It was written for the new legal Bolshevik newspaper, *Novoya Zhizn*

(New Life), but a number of leading Bolsheviks did not agree with it, so it was not published.

A significant feature of the revolutionary upsurge was the importance of religious beliefs for many of the insurgents. In 'Socialism and Religion' (published in *Novoya Zhizn*) Lenin bluntly restates a common Marxist rejection of religion as inconsistent with science and the intellectual achievements of the Enlightenment, and also reiterates the revolutionary-democratic demand for separation of church and state, especially important in the face of the close and official link between the tsarist regime and the Russian Orthodox Church. At the same time, he emphasises the importance of defending religious freedom (especially from state persecution), stressing the need to work with and assist religious revolutionary activists, and positively noting the acceptance of religious activists into the ranks of the RSDLP.

There were many currents and counter-currents during the revolutionary year of 1905. The tsarist regime wavered between unleashing savage repression and mobilising extreme reactionary sentiments in the population through an organisation known as the Black Hundreds (which glorified the desire 'to kill revolutionists and Jews'[2]), and on the other hand – in the face of the rising revolutionary wave of workers, peasants, and other social sectors – finally issued the 'October Manifesto' which seemed to promise a democratic constitution, going so far as to establish (with many limitations, to be sure) a representative assembly, the Duma. At the same time, Tsar Nicholas and those around him had no intention of actually making a transition away from monarchist autocracy, and were obviously prepared to assert their authority, violently and murderously – which they did in the bloody suppression of the uprising of the Moscow soviet in December, and in the quelling of various peasant disturbances.

Notes

1. Interview with George Denike (who later became a Menshevik) in Leopold H. Haimson (ed.), *The Making of Three Russian Revolutionaries, Voices from the Menshevik Past* (Cambridge: Cambridge University Press, 1987), 338.
2. Interview with Boris I. Nicolaevsky, in ibid., 276.

1905: The Beginning of the Revolution in Russia*

Geneva, Wednesday, 25 (12) January

Events of the greatest historical importance are developing in Russia. The proletariat has risen against tsarism. The proletariat was driven to revolt by the government. There can hardly be any doubt now that the government deliberately allowed the strike movement to develop and a wide demonstration to be started more or less without hindrance in order to bring matters to a point where military force could be used. Its manoeuvre was successful. Thousands of killed and wounded – such is the toll of Bloody Sunday, 9 January, in St Petersburg. The army defeated unarmed workers, women, and children. The army vanquished the enemy by shooting prostrate workers. 'We have taught them a good lesson!' the tsar's henchmen and their European flunkeys from among the conservative bourgeoisie say with consummate cynicism.

Yes, it was a great lesson, one which the Russian proletariat will not forget. The most uneducated, backward sections of the working class, who naively trusted the tsar and sincerely wished to put peacefully before 'the tsar himself' the petition of a tormented people, were all taught a lesson by the troops led by the tsar or his uncle, the Grand Duke Vladimir.

The working class has received a momentous lesson in civil war; the revolutionary education of the proletariat made more progress in one day than it could have made in months and years of drab, humdrum, wretched existence. The slogan of the heroic St Petersburg proletariat, 'Death or freedom!' is reverberating throughout Russia. Events are developing with astonishing rapidity. The general strike in St Petersburg is spreading. All industrial, public, and political activities are paralysed. On Monday, 10 January, still more violent clashes occurred between the workers and the military. Contrary to the mendacious government reports, blood is flowing in many parts of the capital. The workers of Kolpino are rising. The proletariat is arming itself and the people. The workers are said to have seized the Sestroretsk Arsenal. They

* *Collected Works*, Vol. 8: 97–100.

are providing themselves with revolvers, forging their tools into weapons, and procuring bombs for a desperate bid for freedom. The general strike is spreading to the provinces. Ten thousand have already ceased work in Moscow, and a general strike has been called there for tomorrow (Thursday, 13 January). An uprising has broken out in Riga. The workers are demonstrating in Lodz, an uprising is being prepared in Warsaw, proletarian demonstrations are taking place in Helsingfors. Unrest is growing among the workers and the strike is spreading in Baku, Odessa, Kiev, Kharkov, Kovno, and Vilna. In Sevastopol, the naval stores and arsenals are ablaze, and the troops refuse to shoot at the mutineers. Strikes in Revel and in Saratov. Workers and reservists clash with the troops in Radom.

The revolution is spreading. The government is beginning to lose its head. From the policy of bloody repression it is attempting to change over to economic concessions and to save itself by throwing a sop to the workers or promising the nine-hour day. But the lesson of Bloody Sunday cannot be forgotten. The demand of the insurgent St Petersburg workers – the immediate convocation of a Constituent Assembly on the basis of universal, direct, and equal suffrage by secret ballot – must become the demand of all the striking workers. Immediate overthrow of the government – this was the slogan with which even the St Petersburg workers who had believed in the tsar answered the massacre of 9 January; they answered through their leader, the priest Georgi Gapon, who declared after that bloody day: 'We no longer have a tsar. A river of blood divides the tsar from the people. Long live the fight for freedom!'

Long live the revolutionary proletariat! say we. The general strike is rousing and rallying increasing masses of the working class and the urban poor. The arming of the people is becoming an immediate task of the revolutionary moment.

Only an armed people can be the real bulwark of popular liberty. The sooner the proletariat succeeds in arming, and the longer it holds its fighting positions as striker and revolutionary, the sooner will the army begin to waver; more and more soldiers will at last begin to realise what they are doing and they will join sides with the people against the fiends, against the tyrant, against the murderers of defenceless workers and of their wives and children. No matter what the outcome of the present uprising in St Petersburg may be, it will, in any case, be the first step to a wider, more conscious, better organised uprising. The government may possibly succeed in putting off the day of reckoning, but the postponement will only make the next step of the revolutionary onset more stupendous. This will only mean that the Social-Democrats will take advantage of this postponement to rally the organised fighters and spread the news about the start made by the St Petersburg workers. The proletariat will join in the struggle, it will quit mill and factory and will prepare arms for itself. The slogans of the struggle for freedom will be carried more and more widely into the midst of the urban poor and of the millions of peasants. Revolutionary committees will be set up at every factory, in every city district, in every large village. The people in revolt will overthrow all the government institutions of the tsarist autocracy and proclaim the immediate convocation of a Constituent Assembly.

The immediate arming of the workers and of all citizens in general, the preparation and organisation of the revolutionary forces for overthrowing the government authorities and institutions – this is the practical basis on which revolutionaries of every variety can and must unite to strike the common blow. The proletariat must always pursue its own independent path, never weakening its connection with the Social-Democratic Party, always bearing in mind its great, ultimate objective, which is to rid mankind of all exploitation. But this independence of the Social-Democratic proletarian party will never cause us to forget the importance of a common revolutionary onset at the moment of actual revolution. We Social-Democrats can and must act independently of the bourgeois-democratic revolutionaries and guard the class independence of the proletariat. But we must go hand in hand with them during the uprising, when direct blows are being struck at tsarism, when resistance is offered the troops, when the bastilles of the accursed enemy of the entire Russian people are stormed.

The proletariat of the whole world is now looking eagerly towards the proletariat of Russia. The overthrow of tsarism in Russia, so valiantly begun by our working class, will be the turning-point in the history of all countries, it will facilitate the task of the workers of all nations, in all states, in all parts of the globe. Let, therefore, every Social-Democrat, every class-conscious worker bear in mind the immense tasks of the broad popular struggle that now rest upon his shoulders. Let him not forget that he represents also the needs and interests of the whole peasantry, of all who toil, of all who are exploited, of the whole people against their enemy. The proletarian heroes of St Petersburg now stand as an example to all.

Long live the revolution!

Long live the insurgent proletariat!

1905: A Militant Agreement for the Uprising[*]

Revolutsionnaya Rossiya, No. 58, says: 'May the spirit of fighting unity now at long last pervade the ranks of the revolutionary socialist groups, which are torn by fratricidal animosity, and may it revive the consciousness of socialist solidarity which has been so criminally sapped. ... Let us spare the revolutionary forces as much as we can and increase their effectiveness by means of a concerted attack!'

We have often had occasion to protest against the tyranny of the phrase among the Socialists-Revolutionaries and we must do so again. Why these frightful words, gentlemen, about 'fratricidal animosity' and so forth? Are they worthy of a revolutionary? Now of all times, when the real fight is on, when blood is flowing – the blood of which *Revolutsionnaya Rossiya* speaks in such flamboyant terms, these grotesque exaggerations about 'fratricidal animosity' ring false than ever. Spare the forces, say you? But surely this is done by a united, welded organisation which is at one on questions of principle, and not by lumping together heterogeneous elements. Strength is not spared but wasted by

*   *Collected Works*, Vol. 8: 156–66.

such barren attempts at lumping. To achieve a 'fighting unity' in deed and not merely in word, we must know clearly, definitely, and *from experience* exactly wherein and to what extent we *can* be united. *Without* this, all talk of fighting unity will be mere words, words, words; *this* knowledge, incidentally, comes from the very controversy, struggle, and animosity of which you speak in such 'frightful' terms. Would it really be better if we hushed up the differences that divide vast sections of Russian public opinion and Russian socialist thought? Was it only the 'cult of discord' that provoked the bitter struggle between Narodism, that nebulous ideology of the democratic bourgeoisie woven of socialistic dreams, and Marxism, the ideology of the proletariat? Nonsense, gentlemen; you only make yourselves ridiculous by saying such things, by continuing to regard as an 'insult' the Marxist view that Narodism and your 'social-revolutionism' are essentially bourgeois-democratic. We shall inevitably argue, differ, and quarrel also in the future revolutionary committees in Russia, but surely we must learn from history. We must not have unexpected, unintelligible, and muddled disputes at a time when action is called for; we must be prepared to argue on fundamental issues, to know the points of departure of each trend, to anticipate possible unity or possible antagonism. The history of revolutionary epochs provides many, all too many, instances of tremendous harm caused by hasty and half-baked experiments in 'fighting unity' that sought to lump together the most heterogeneous elements in the committees of the revolutionary people, but managed thereby to achieve *mutual friction* and *bitter disappointment.*

We want to profit by this lesson of history. Marxism, which to you seems a narrow dogma, is to us the quintessence of this historical lesson and guidance. We see in the *independent*, uncompromisingly Marxist party of the revolutionary proletariat the sole pledge of socialism's victory and the road to victory that is most free from vacillations. We shall never, therefore, not even at the most revolutionary moments, forgo the complete independence of the Social-Democratic Party or the complete intransigence of our ideology.

You believe this *rules out* fighting unity? You are mistaken. You can see from the resolution of our Second Congress that we do not renounce agreements for the struggle and in the struggle. In *Vperyod*, No. 4, we stressed the fact that the beginning of the revolution in Russia undoubtedly brings closer the moment when such agreements can be practically implemented. A joint struggle of the revolutionary Social-Democrats and the revolutionary elements of the democratic movement is inevitable and indispensable in the era of the fall of the autocracy. We think that we should serve the cause of future militant agreements better if, instead of indulging in bitter recriminations, we sanely and coolly weighed the conditions under which they would become possible and the likely limits of their 'jurisdiction', if one may use the term. We began this work in *Vperyod*, No. 3, in which we undertook a study of the progress of the Socialist-Revolutionary Party from Narodism to Marxism.

'The masses took to arms themselves', *Revolutsionnaya Rossiya* wrote in connection with the Ninth of January. 'Sooner or later, without doubt, the question of arming the masses will be decided.' 'That is when the fusion between terrorism and the mass movement, to which we are striving by word and deed in accordance with the entire spirit of our Party tactics, will be manifested and realised in the most striking manner.' (We would remark parenthetically that we would gladly put a question mark after the word 'deed'; but let us proceed with the quotation.) 'Not so long ago, before our own eyes, these two factors of the movement were separate, and this separateness deprived them of their full force.'

What is true is true! Exactly! Intelligentsia terrorism and the mass movement of the working class *were separate, and this separateness deprived them of their full force*. That is precisely what the revolutionary Social-Democrats have been saying all along. For this very reason they have always been opposed to terrorism and to all the vacillations towards terrorism which members of the intellectualist wing of our Party have often displayed. For this reason precisely the old *Iskra* took a position against terrorism when it wrote in issue No. 48: 'The terrorist struggle of the *old type* was the riskiest form of revolutionary struggle, and those who engaged in it had the reputation of being resolute, self-sacrificing people. ... Now, however, when demonstrations develop into acts of open resistance to the government, ... the old terrorism ceases to be an exceptionally daring method of struggle. ... Heroism has now come out into the open; the true heroes of our time are now the revolutionaries who lead the popular masses, which are rising against their oppressors. ... The terrorism of the great French Revolution ... began on July 14, 1789, with the storming of the Bastille. Its strength was the strength of the revolutionary movement of the people. ... *That* terrorism was due, not to disappointment in the strength of the mass movement, but, on the contrary, to unshakable faith in its strength. ... The history of *that* terrorism is exceedingly instructive for the Russian revolutionary.'

Yes, a thousand times yes! The history of *that* terrorism is instructive in the extreme. Instructive, too, are the quoted passages from *Iskra*, which refer to an epoch of 18 months ago. These quotations show us, in their full stature, the ideas which even the Socialists-Revolutionaries, under the influence of the revolutionary lessons, would like to arrive at. They remind us of the importance of *faith* in the mass movement; they remind us of revolutionary tenacity, which comes only from high principles and which alone can safeguard us against the 'disappointments' induced by a prolonged *apparent* standstill of the movement. Now, after the Ninth of January, there can be no question, on the face of it, of any 'disappointments' in the mass movement. But only on the face of it. We should distinguish between the momentary 'attraction' evoked by a striking display of mass heroism and the steadfast, reasoned convictions that link inseparably the entire activity of the Party with the movement of the masses, owing to the paramount importance which is attached to the principle of the class struggle. We should bear in mind that the revolutionary movement, however high its level since the Ninth of January, still has many stages to pass through before our socialist and democratic parties will be reconstructed on a new basis in a free Russia. And through all these stages, through all the vicissitudes of the struggle, we must maintain the ties between Social-Democracy and the class struggle of the proletariat unbroken, and we must see to it that they are continuously strengthened and made more secure.

It seems to us, therefore, a gross exaggeration for *Revolutsionnaya Rossiya* to assert that 'the pioneers of the armed struggle were swallowed up in the ranks of the roused masses …'. This is the desirable future rather than the reality of the moment. The assassination of Sergei in Moscow on 17 (4) February, which has been reported by telegraph this very day, is obviously an act of terrorism of the old type. The pioneers of the armed struggle have *not yet* been swallowed up in the ranks of the roused masses. Pioneers with bombs evidently lay in wait for Sergei in Moscow while, the masses (in St Petersburg), without pioneers, without arms, without revolutionary officers, and without a revolutionary staff 'flung themselves in implacable fury upon bristling bayonets', as this same *Revolutsionnaya Rossiya* expresses it. The separateness of which we spoke above *still exists*, and the individual intellectualist terror shows all the more strikingly its inadequacy in face of the growing realisation that 'the masses have risen to the stature of individual heroes, that mass heroism has been awakened in them' (*Revolutsionnaya Rossiya*, No. 58). The pioneers should submerge among the masses *in actual fact*, that is, exert their selfless energies in real inseparable connection with the insurgent masses, and proceed with them in the literal, not figurative, symbolical, sense of the word. That this is essential can hardly be open to doubt now. That it is possible has been proved by the Ninth of January and by the deep unrest which is still smouldering among the working-class masses. The fact that this is a new, higher, and more difficult task in comparison with the preceding ones cannot and should not stop us from meeting it at once in a practical way.

Fighting unity between the Social-Democratic Party and the revolutionary-democratic party – the Socialist-Revolutionary Party, might be one way of facilitating the solution of this problem. Such unity will be all the more practicable, the sooner the pioneers of the armed struggle are 'swallowed up' in the ranks of the insurgent masses, the more firmly the Socialists-Revolutionaries follow the path which they themselves have charted in the words, 'May these beginnings of fusion between revolutionary terrorism and the mass movement grow and strengthen, may the masses act as quickly as possible, armed cap-à-pie with terrorist methods of struggle!' With a view to bringing about speedily such a fighting unity, we take pleasure in publishing the following letter which we have received from Georgi Gapon:

An Open Letter to the Socialist Parties of Russia

The bloody January days in St Petersburg and the rest of Russia have brought the oppressed working class face to face with the autocratic regime, headed by the blood-thirsty tsar. The great Russian revolution has begun. All to whom the people's freedom is really dear must either win or die. Realising the importance of the present historic moment, considering the present state of affairs, and being above all a revolutionary and a man of action, I call upon all the socialist parties of Russia to enter immediately into an agreement among themselves and to proceed to the armed uprising against tsarism. All the forces of every party should be mobilised. All should have a single technical plan of action. Bombs and dynamite, individual and mass terror – every thing that can help the popular uprising. The immediate aim is the over throw of the autocracy, a provisional revolutionary government which will at once amnesty all fighters for political and religious liberties, at once arm the people, and at once convoke a Constituent Assembly on the basis of universal, equal, and direct suffrage by secret ballot. To the task, comrades! Onward to the fight! Let us repeat the slogan of the St Petersburg workers on the Ninth of January – Freedom or Death! Delay and disorder now are a crime against the people, whose interests you are defending. Having given all of myself to the service of the people, from whom I myself am sprung (the son of a peasant), and having thrown in my lot irrevocably with the struggle against the oppressors and exploiters of the working class, I shall naturally be heart and soul with those who will undertake the real business of actually liberating the proletariat and all the toiling masses from the capitalist yoke and political slavery.

Georgi Gapon

On our part, we consider it necessary to state our view of this letter as clearly and as definitely as possible. We consider that the 'agreement' it proposes is possible, useful, and essential. We welcome the fact that Gapon speaks explicitly of an 'agreement', since only through the preservation of complete independence by each separate party on points of principle and organisation can the efforts at a fighting unity of these parties rest on hope. We must be very careful, in making these endeavours, not to spoil things by vainly trying to lump together heterogeneous elements. We shall inevitably have to *getrennt marschieren* (march separately), but we can *vereint schlagen* (strike together) more than once and particularly now. It would be desirable, from our point of view, to have this agreement embrace the *revolutionary* as well as the socialist parties, for there is nothing socialistic in the immediate aim of the struggle, and we must not confound or allow anyone ever to confound the immediate democratic aims with our ultimate aims of socialist revolution. It would be desirable, and from our point of view *essential*, for the agreement that, instead of a general call for '*individual* and mass terror', it should be stated openly and definitely that this joint action pursues the aim of a direct and actual *fusion* between terrorism and the uprising of the masses. True, by adding the words 'everything that can help the popular uprising', Gapon clearly indicates his desire to make even individual terror subservient to this aim; but this desire, which suggests the idea that we noted in *Revolut-sionnaya Rossiya*, No. 58, should be expressed more definitely and embodied in absolutely unequivocal practical decisions. We should like, finally, to point out, regardless of the readability of the proposed agreement, that Gapon's extra-party stand seems to us to be another negative factor. Obviously, with so rapid a conversion from faith in the tsar and petitioning of the tsar to revolutionary aims, Gapon was not able to evolve for himself immediately a clear revolutionary outlook. This is inevitable, and the faster and broader the revolution develops, the more often will this kind of thing occur. Nevertheless, complete clarity and definiteness in the relations between parties, trends, and shades are absolutely necessary if a temporary agreement among them is to be in any way successful. Clarity and definiteness will be needed at every practical step; they will be the pre-condition for definiteness and the absence of vacillation in the real, *practical* work. The beginning of the revolution in Russia will probably lead to the emergence upon the political arena of many people and perhaps trends representing the view that the slogan 'revolution' is, for 'men of action', a quite adequate definition of their aims and their methods of operation. Nothing could be more fallacious than this opinion. The extra-party position, which seems higher, or more convenient, or more 'diplomatic', is in actual fact *more vague*, more obscure, and inevitably fraught with inconsistencies and vacillations in practical activity. In the interests of the revolution our ideal should by no means be that all parties, all trends and shades of opinion fuse in a revolutionary chaos. On the contrary, the growth and spread of the revolutionary movement, its constantly deeper penetration among the various classes and strata of the people, will inevitably give rise (all to the good) to constantly newer trends and shades. Only full clarity and definiteness in their mutual relations and in their attitude towards the position of the revolutionary proletariat can guarantee maximum success for the revolutionary movement. Only full clarity in mutual relations can guarantee the success of an agreement to achieve a common immediate aim.

This immediate aim is *outlined* quite correctly, in our opinion, in Gapon's letter, namely: (1) the overthrow of the autocracy; (2) a provisional revolutionary government; (3) the immediate amnesty to all fighters for political and religious liberties, including, of course, the right to strike, etc.; (4) the immediate arming of the people; and (5) the immediate convocation of an All-Russian Constituent Assembly on the basis of universal, equal, and direct suffrage by secret ballot. The immediate translation into life by the revolutionary government of complete equality for all citizens and complete political freedom during elections is, of course, taken for granted by Gapon; but this might have been stated explicitly. It would be advisable also to include in the general policy of the provisional government the establishment everywhere of revolutionary peasant committees for the purpose of supporting the democratic revolution and putting into effect its various measures. The success of the revolution depends largely on the revolutionary activity of the peasantry itself, and the various socialist and revolutionary-democratic parties would probably agree on a slogan such as we have suggested.

It is to be hoped that Gapon, whose evolution from views shared by a politically unconscious people to revolutionary views proceeds from such profound personal experiences, will achieve the clear revolutionary outlook that is essential for a man of politics. It is to be hoped that his appeal for a militant agreement for the uprising will meet with success, and that the revolutionary proletariat, side by side with the revolutionary democrats, will strike at the autocracy and overthrow it all the more quickly and surely, and with the least sacrifices.

1905: Two Tactics of Social Democracy in the Democratic Revolution[*]

The degree of Russia's economic development (an objective condition), and the degree of class-consciousness and organisation of the broad masses of the proletariat (a subjective condition inseparably bound up with the objective condition) make the immediate and complete emancipation of the working class impossible. Only the most ignorant people can close their eyes to the bourgeois nature of the democratic revolution which is now taking place; only the most naive optimists can forget how little as yet the masses of the workers are informed about the aims of socialism and the methods of achieving it. We are all convinced that the emancipation of the working classes must be won by the working classes themselves; a socialist revolution is out of the question unless the masses become class-conscious and organised, trained, and educated in an open class struggle against the entire bourgeoisie. Replying to the anarchists' objections that we are putting off the socialist revolution, we say: we are not putting it off, but are taking the first step towards it in the only possible way, along the only correct path, namely, the path of a democratic republic. Whoever wants to reach socialism by any other path than that of political democracy, will inevitably arrive at conclusions that are absurd and reactionary both in the economic and the political sense. If any workers ask us at the appropriate moment why we should not go ahead and carry out our maximum programme we shall answer by pointing out how far from socialism the masses of the democratically-minded people still are, how undeveloped class antagonisms still are, and how unorganised the proletarians still are. Organise hundreds of thousands of workers all over Russia; get the millions to sympathise with our programme! Try to do this without confining yourselves to high-sounding but hollow anarchist phrases – and you will see at once that achievement of this organisation and the spread of this socialist enlightenment depend on the fullest possible achievement of democratic transformations. ...

Let us return to the resolution on a provisional government. We have shown that new-*Iskra*-ist tactics does not push the revolution forward – the possibility of which they would like to ensure by their resolution – but pull it back. We have shown that it is precisely this tactics that *ties the hands* of Social-Democracy in the struggle against the inconsistent bourgeoisie and does not prevent its being dissolved in bourgeois democracy. The false premises of the resolution naturally lead to the following false conclusion: 'Therefore, Social-Democracy must not set itself the aim of seizing or sharing power in the provisional government, but must remain the party of extreme revolutionary opposition.' Consider the first half of this conclusion, which contains a statement of aims. Do the new-*Iskra*-ist declare that the revolution's decisive victory over tsarism is the aim of Social-Democratic activity? They do. They are unable correctly to formulate the conditions of a decisive victory, and lapse into the [liberal] *Osvobozhdeniye* formulation, but they do set themselves this aim. Further, do they associate a provisional government with insurrection? Yes, they do so directly by stating that a provisional government 'will emerge from a victorious popular insurrection'. Finally, do they set themselves the aim of guiding the insurrection? Yes, they do. Like Mr Struve they evade the admission that an insurrection is an urgent necessity, but at the same time, unlike Mr Struve, they say that 'Social-Democracy strives to *subordinate* it (the insurrection) to its influence and *leadership* and to use it in the interests of the working class'.

How nicely this hangs together, does it not? We set ourselves the *aim* of subordinating the insurrection of both the proletarian and *non-proletarian* masses to our influence and our leadership, and of using it in our interests. Hence, we set ourselves the aim of loading, in the insurrection, both the proletariat, and the revolutionary bourgeoisie and petty bourgeoisie ('the non-proletarian groups'), i.e., of '*sharing*' the leadership of the insurrection between the Social-Democracy and the revolutionary bourgeoisie. We set ourselves the aim of securing *victory* for the insurrection, which is to lead to the establishment of a provisional government ('which will emerge from a victorious popular insurrection'). *Therefore ...* therefore we must not set ourselves the aim of seizing power or of sharing it in a provisional revolutionary government!! ...

The basic idea here is the one repeatedly formulated by *Vperyod*, which has stated that we must not be afraid (as Martynov is) of Social-Democracy's complete victory in a democratic revolution, i.e., of a revolutionary-democratic dictatorship of the proletariat and the peasantry, for such a victory will enable us to rouse Europe; after throwing off the yoke of the bourgeoisie, the socialist proletariat of Europe will in its turn help us to accomplish the socialist revolution. But see how the new-*Iskra* rendering impairs this idea. We shall not dwell on details; on the absurd assumption that power could 'fall' into the hands of a class-conscious party which considers seizure of power harmful tactics; on the fact that in Europe the conditions for socialism have reached not a certain degree of maturity, but maturity in general; on the fact that our Party programme knows no socialist reforms, but only the socialist revolution. Let us take the principal and basic difference between *Vperyod*'s idea and the one presented in the resolution. *Vperyod* set the revolutionary proletariat of Russia an active task: winning the battle for democracy and using this victory to bring the revolution into Europe. The resolution fails to grasp this link between our 'decisive victory' (not in the new-*Iskra* sense) and the revolution in Europe, and, therefore, it does not speak of the tasks of the proletariat or the prospects of the *latter*'s victory, but of one of the possibilities in general: 'in the event of the revolution spreading ...'. *Vperyod* pointedly and definitely indicated – and this was incorporated in the resolution of the Third Congress of the Russian Social-Democratic Labour Party – how 'governmental power' can and must 'be utilised' in the interests of the proletariat, bearing in mind what can be achieved immediately, at a given stage of social development, and what must first be achieved as a democratic prerequisite of the struggle for socialism. Here, too, the resolution lags hopelessly behind when it states: 'will be able to prepare itself to utilise', but fails to say *how* it will be able, *how* it will prepare itself, and to utilise *for what purpose*. We have no doubt, for instance, that the new-*Iskra*-ist may be 'able to prepare themselves to utilise' their leading position in the Party, but the point is that so far their experience of that utilisation, their preparation, does not hold out much hope of possibility becoming reality. ...

Vperyod stated quite definitely wherein lies the real 'possibility of retaining power' – namely, in the revolutionary-democratic dictatorship of the proletariat and the peasantry; in their joint mass strength, which is capable of outweighing all the forces of counter-revolution; in the inevitable concurrence of their interests in *democratic* reforms. Here, too, the resolution of the Conference gives us nothing positive; it merely evades the issue. Surely, the possibility of retaining power in Russia must be determined by the composition of the social forces in Russia herself, by the circumstances of the democratic revolution now taking place in our country. A victory of the proletariat in Europe (it is still quite a far cry from bringing the revolution into Europe to the victory of the proletariat) will give rise to a desperate counter-revolutionary struggle on the part of the Russian bourgeoisie – yet the resolution of the new-*Iskra*-ists does not say a word about this counter-revolutionary force whose significance was appraised in the resolution of the RSDLP's Third Congress. If, in our fight for a republic and democracy, we could not rely upon the peasantry as well as upon the proletariat, the prospect of our 'retaining power' would be hopeless. But if it is not hopeless, if the 'revolution's decisive victory over tsarism' opens up such a possibility, then we must indicate it, call actively for its transformation into reality, and issue practical slogans not only *for the contingency* of the revolution being brought into Europe, but also *for the purpose* of taking it there. The reference made by tail-ist Social-Democrats to the 'limited historical scope of the Russian revolution' merely serves to cover up their limited understanding of the aims of this democratic revolution, and of the proletariat's leading role in it! ...

The proletariat must carry the democratic revolution to completion, allying to itself the mass of the peasantry in order to crush the autocracy's resistance by force and paralyse the bourgeoisie's instability. The proletariat must accomplish the socialist revolution, allying to itself the mass of the semi-proletarian elements of the population, so as to crush the bourgeoisie's resistance by force and paralyse the instability of the peasantry and the petty bourgeoisie. ...

The depth of the rift among present-day Social-Democrats on the question of the path to be chosen can at once be seen by comparing the Caucasian resolution of the new-*Iskra* supporters with the resolution of the Third Congress of the Russian Social-Democratic Labour Party. The Congress resolution says: the bourgeoisie is inconsistent and will without fail try to deprive us of the gains of the revolution. Therefore, make more energetic preparations for the fight, comrades and workers! Arm yourselves, win the peasantry over to your side! We shall not, without a struggle, surrender our revolutionary gains to the self-seeking bourgeoisie. The resolution of the Caucasian new-*Iskra* supporters says: the bourgeoisie is inconsistent and may recoil from the revolution. Therefore, comrades and workers, please do not think of joining a provisional government, for, if you do, the bourgeoisie will certainly recoil, and the sweep of the revolution will thereby be diminished!

One side says: advance the revolution to its consummation despite resistance or passivity on the part of the inconsistent bourgeoisie.

The other side says: do not think of independently advancing the revolution to completion, for if you do, the inconsistent bourgeoisie will recoil from it.

Are these not two diametrically opposite paths? ...

In its social and economic essence, the democratic revolution in Russia is a bourgeois revolution. It is, however, not enough merely to repeat this correct Marxist proposition. It has to be properly understood and properly applied to political slogans. In general, all political liberty founded on present-day, i.e., capitalist, relations of production is bourgeois liberty. The demand for liberty expresses primarily the interests of the bourgeoisie. Its representatives were the first to raise this demand. Its supporters have everywhere used like masters the liberty they acquired, reducing it to moderate and meticulous bourgeois doses, combining it with the most subtle suppression of the revolutionary proletariat in peaceful times, and with savage suppression in times of storm.

But only rebel Narodniks, anarchists, and Economists could conclude therefrom that the struggle for liberty should be negated or disparaged. These intellectualist-philistine doctrines could be foisted on the proletariat only for a time and against its will. The proletariat has always realised instinctively that it needs political liberty, needs it more than anyone else, although the immediate effect of that liberty will be to strengthen and organise the bourgeoisie. It is not by evading the class struggle that the proletariat expects to find its salvation, but by developing it, by extending its scope, its consciousness, organisation, and resoluteness. Whoever disparages the tasks of the political struggle transforms the Social-Democrat from a tribune of the people into a trade union secretary. Whoever disparages the proletarian tasks in a democratic bourgeois revolution transforms the Social-Democrat from a leader of the people's revolution into a leader of a free labour union.

Yes, the *people's* revolution. Social-Democracy has fought, and is quite rightly fighting, against the bourgeois-democratic abuse of the word 'people'. It demands that this word shall not be used to cover up failure, to understand class antagonisms within the people. It insists categorically on the need for complete class independence for the party of the proletariat. However, it does not divide the 'people' into 'classes' so that the advanced class will become locked up within itself, will confine itself within narrow limits and emasculate its activity for fear that the economic rulers of the world will recoil; it does that so that the advanced class, which does not suffer from the half-heartedness, vacillation, and indecision of the intermediate classes, should fight with all the greater energy and enthusiasm for the cause of the whole people, at the head of the whole people. ...

Revolutions are the locomotive of history, said Marx. Revolutions are festivals of the oppressed and the exploited. At no time are the mass of the people in a position to come forward so actively as creators of a new social order, as at a time of revolution. At such times the people are capable of performing miracles, if judged by the limited, philistine yardstick of gradualist progress. But it is essential that leaders of the revolutionary parties, too, should advance their aims more comprehensively and boldly at such a time, so that their slogans shall always be in advance of the revolutionary initiative of the masses, serve as a beacon, reveal to them our democratic and socialist ideal in all its magnitude and splendour, and show them the shortest and most direct route to complete, absolute, and decisive victory.

1905: Our Tasks and the Soviet of Workers' Deputies[*]

It seems to me that Comrade Radin is wrong in raising the question, in No. 5 of *Novaya Zhizn* (I have seen only five issues of the virtual Central Organ of our RSDLP): the Soviet of Workers' Deputies or the Party? I think that it is wrong to put the question in this way and that the decision must *certainly* be *both* the Soviet of Workers' Deputies *and* the Party. The only question – and a highly important one – is how to divide, and how to combine, the tasks of the Soviet and those of the Russian Social-Democratic Labour Party.

I think it would be inadvisable for the Soviet to adhere wholly to any one party. As this opinion will probably surprise the reader,

[*]   *Collected Works*, Vol. 10: 19–24.

I shall proceed straightway to explain my views (stating again and most emphatically that it is the opinion of an onlooker).

The Soviet of Workers' Deputies came into being through the general strike, in connection with the strike, and for its aims. Who led the strike and brought it to a victorious close? The *whole* proletariat, which includes non-Social-Democrats – fortunately a minority. What were the aims of the strike? They were both economic and political. The economic aims concerned the *whole* proletariat, all workers, and partly even all working people, not the wage-workers alone. The political aims concerned all the people, or rather all the peoples, of Russia. These aims were to free all the peoples of Russia from the yoke of the autocracy, survivals of serfdom, a rightless status, and police tyranny.

Let us go further. Should the proletariat continue its economic struggle? By all means; there is no disagreement over this point among Social-Democrats, nor could there be any. Should this struggle be conducted only by the Social-Democrats or only under the Social-Democratic banner? I do not think so; I still hold the view I have expressed (in entirely different, now outdated conditions, it is true) in *What Is To Be Done?*, namely, that it is inadvisable to limit the composition of the trade unions, and hence of those taking part in the trade union, economic struggle, to members of the Social-Democratic Party. It seems to me that the Soviet of Workers' Deputies, as an organisation representing all occupations, should *strive* to include deputies from *all* industrial, professional and office workers, domestic servants, farm labourers, etc., from *all* who want and are able to fight in common for a better life for the whole working people, from all who have at least an elementary degree of political honesty, from all but the Black Hundreds. As for us Social-Democrats, we shall do our best, first, to have all our Party organisations represented on all trade unions as fully as possible and, secondly, to use the struggle we are waging jointly with our fellow-proletarians, irrespective of their views, for the tireless, steadfast advocacy of the *only* consistent, the only truly proletarian world outlook, *Marxism*. To propagate it, to carry on this propaganda and agitation work, we shall by all means preserve, strengthen and expand our completely independent, consistently principled class party of the class-conscious proletariat, i.e., the Russian Social-Democratic Labour Party. Every step in the proletarian struggle, if inseparably linked with our Social-Democratic, methodical and organised, activities, will bring the *masses* of the working class in Russia and the Social-Democrats ever closer together.

This aspect of the problem, concerning the economic struggle, is comparatively simple and hardly gives rise to any particular disagreement. But the other aspect, concerning political leadership and the political struggle, is a different matter. And yet, at the risk of surprising the reader still more, I must say here and now that in this respect, too, I think it inadvisable to demand that the Soviet of Workers' Deputies should accept the Social-Democratic programme and join the Russian Social-Democratic Labour Party. It seems to me that to lead the political struggle, *both* the Soviet (*reorganised* in a sense to be discussed forthwith) *and* the Party are, to an equal degree, absolutely necessary.

I may be wrong, but I believe (on the strength of the incomplete and only 'paper' information at my disposal) that politically the Soviet of Workers' Deputies should be regarded as the embryo of a *provisional revolutionary government*. I think the Soviet should proclaim itself the provisional revolutionary government of the whole of Russia as early as possible, or should *set up* a provisional revolutionary government (which would amount to the same thing, only in another form).

The political struggle has just reached a stage of development where the forces of revolution and counter-revolution are roughly equal and where the tsar's government is *already* powerless to suppress the revolution, while the revolution is not *yet* strong enough to sweep away the Black-Hundred government. The decay of the tsar's government is complete. But even as it rots alive, it is contaminating Russia with the poison of its putrefaction. It is absolutely necessary, in contrast to the decay of the tsarist, counter-revolutionary forces, to *organise* the revolutionary forces at once, immediately, without the slightest delay. This organisation has been making splendid progress, particularly of late. This is evident from the formation of contingents of a revolutionary army (defence squads, etc.), the rapid development of Social-Democratic mass organisations of the proletariat, the establishment of peasants' committees by the revolutionary peasantry, and the first free meetings of our proletarian brothers in sailor's or soldier's uniform, who are paving for themselves a strenuous and difficult but true and bright way to freedom and to socialism.

What is lacking now is the unification of all the genuinely revolutionary forces, of all the forces that are already operating in revolutionary fashion. What is lacking is an all-Russian political centre, a fresh, living centre that is strong because it has struck deep roots in the people, a centre that enjoys the absolute confidence of the masses, that possesses tireless revolutionary energy and is closely linked with the organised revolutionary and socialist parties. Such a centre can be established only by the revolutionary proletariat, which has brilliantly carried through a political strike, which is now organising an armed uprising of the whole people, and which has won half freedom for Russia and will yet win full freedom for her.

The question may be asked: Why cannot the Soviet of Workers' Deputies become the embryo of such a centre? Is it because there are not only Social-Democrats in the Soviet? But this is an advantage, not a disadvantage. We have been speaking all the time of the need of a militant alliance of Social-Democrats and revolutionary bourgeois democrats. We have been speaking of it, and the workers have actually done it. It is splendid that they have done it. When I read in *Novaya Zhizn* a letter from *worker comrades* who belong to the Socialist-Revolutionary Party, and who protest against the Soviet being included in one of the parties, I could not help thinking that those worker comrades were right in many practical respects. It goes without saying that our views differ from theirs, and that a merger of Social-Democrats and Socialist-Revolutionaries is out of the question, but then there is no suggestion of it. We are deeply convinced that those workers who share Socialist-Revolutionary views and yet are fighting within the ranks of the proletariat are inconsistent, for they retain non-proletarian views while championing a truly proletarian cause. Their inconsistency we must combat, from the ideological point of view with the greatest determination, but in so doing we must see to it that the revolutionary cause, a vital, burning, living cause that is recognised by all and has brought all honest people together, does not suffer. We still consider the views of the Socialist-Revolutionaries to be revolutionary-democratic and not socialist. But for the sake of our militant aims, we must march together while fully retaining Party independence, and the Soviet is, and must be, a militant organisation. To expel devoted and honest revolutionary democrats at a time when we are carrying out a democratic revolution would be absurd, it would be folly. We shall have no difficulty in overcoming their inconsistency, for our views are supported by history itself, are supported at every step by reality. If our pamphlet has not taught them Social-Democracy, our revolution will. To be sure, those workers who remain Christians, who believe in God, and those intellectuals who defend mysticism (fie upon them!), are inconsistent too; but we shall not expel them from the Soviet or even from the Party, for it is our firm conviction that the actual struggle, and work within the ranks, will convince all elements possessing vitality that Marxism is the truth, and will cast aside all those who lack vitality. And we do not for one moment doubt our strength, the overwhelming strength of Marxists, in the Russian Social-Democratic Labour Party.

To my mind, the Soviet of Workers' Deputies, as a revolutionary centre providing political leadership, is not too broad an organisation but, on the contrary, a much too narrow one. The Soviet must proclaim itself the provisional revolutionary government, or form such a government, and must by all means enlist to this end the participation of new deputies not only from the workers, but, first of all, from the sailors and soldiers, who are everywhere seeking freedom; secondly, from the revolutionary peasantry, and thirdly, from the revolutionary bourgeois intelligentsia. The Soviet must select a strong nucleus for the provisional revolutionary government and reinforce it with representatives of all revolutionary parties and all revolutionary (but, of course, only revolutionary and not liberal) democrats. We are not afraid of so broad and mixed a composition – indeed, we want it, for unless the proletariat and the peasantry unite and unless the Social-Democrats and revolutionary democrats form a fighting alliance, the great Russian revolution cannot be fully successful. It will be a temporary alliance that is to fulfil clearly defined immediate practical tasks, while the more important interests of the socialist proletariat, its fundamental interests and ultimate goals, will be steadfastly upheld by the independent and consistently principled Russian Social-Democratic Labour Party.

1905: Socialism and Religion*

Present-day society is wholly based on the exploitation of the vast masses of the working class by a tiny minority of the population, the class of the landowners and that of the capitalists. It is a slave society, since the 'free' workers, who all their life work for the capitalists, are 'entitled' only to such means of subsistence as are essential for the maintenance of slaves who produce profit, for the safeguarding and perpetuation of capitalist slavery.

The economic oppression of the workers inevitably calls forth and engenders every kind of political oppression and social humiliation, the coarsening and darkening of the spiritual and moral life of the masses. The workers may secure a greater or lesser degree of political liberty to fight for their economic emancipation, but no amount of liberty will rid them of poverty, unemployment, and oppression until the power of capital is overthrown. Religion is one of the forms of spiritual oppression which everywhere weighs down heavily upon the masses of the people, overburdened by their perpetual work for others, by want and isolation. Impotence of the exploited classes in their struggle against the exploiters just as inevitably gives rise to the belief in a better life after death as impotence of the savage in his battle with nature gives rise to belief in gods, devils, miracles, and the like. Those who toil and live in want all their lives are taught by religion to be submissive and patient while here on earth, and to take comfort in the hope of a heavenly reward. But those who live by the labour of others are taught by religion to practise charity while on earth, thus offering them a very cheap way of justifying their entire existence as exploiters and selling them at a moderate price tickets to well-being in heaven. Religion is opium for the people. Religion is a sort of spiritual booze, in which the slaves of capital drown their human image, their demand for a life more or less worthy of man.

But a slave who has become conscious of his slavery and has risen to struggle for his emancipation has already half ceased to be a slave. The modern class-conscious worker, reared by large-scale factory industry and enlightened by urban life, contemptuously casts aside religious prejudices, leaves heaven to the priests and bourgeois bigots, and tries to win a better life for himself here on earth. The proletariat of today takes the side of socialism, which enlists science in the battle against the fog of religion, and frees the workers from their belief in life after death by welding them together to fight in the present for a better life on earth.

Religion must be declared a private affair. In these words socialists usually express their attitude towards religion. But the meaning of these words should be accurately defined to prevent any misunderstanding. We demand that religion be held a private affair so far as the state is concerned. But by no means can we consider religion a private affair so far as our Party is concerned. Religion must be of no concern to the state, and religious societies must have no connection with governmental authority. Everyone must be absolutely free to profess any religion he pleases, or no religion whatever, i.e., to be an atheist, which every socialist is, as a rule. Discrimination among citizens on account of their religious convictions is wholly intolerable. Even the bare mention of a citizen's religion in official documents should unquestionably be eliminated. No subsidies should be granted to the established church nor state allowances made to ecclesiastical and religious societies. These should become absolutely free associations of like-minded citizens, associations independent of the state. Only the complete fulfilment of these demands can put an end to the shameful and accursed past when the church lived in feudal dependence on the state, and Russian citizens lived in feudal dependence on the established church, when medieval, inquisitorial laws (to this day remaining in our criminal codes and on our statute-books) were in existence and were applied, persecuting men for their belief or disbelief, violating men's consciences, and linking cosy government jobs and government-derived incomes with the dispensation of this or that dope by the established church. Complete separation of Church and State is what the socialist proletariat demands of the modern state and the modern church.

The Russian revolution must put this demand into effect as a necessary component of political freedom. In this respect, the Russian revolution is in a particularly favourable position, since the revolting officialism of the police-ridden feudal autocracy has called forth discontent, unrest and indignation even among the clergy. However abject, however ignorant Russian Orthodox clergymen may have been, even they have now been awakened by the thunder of the downfall of the old, medieval order in Russia. Even they are joining in the demand for freedom, are protesting against bureaucratic practices and officialism, against the spying for the police imposed on the 'servants of God'. We socialists must lend this movement our support, carrying the demands of honest and sincere members of the clergy to their conclusion, making them stick to their words about freedom, demanding that they should resolutely break all ties between religion and the police. Either you are sincere, in which case you must stand for the complete separation of Church and State and of School and Church, for religion to be declared wholly and absolutely a private affair. Or you do not accept these consistent demands for freedom, in which case you evidently are still held captive by the traditions of the inquisition, in which case you evidently still cling to your cosy government jobs and government-derived incomes, in which case you evidently do not believe in the spiritual power of your weapon and continue to take bribes from the state. And in that case the class-conscious workers of all Russia declare merciless war on you.

So far as the party of the socialist proletariat is concerned, religion is not a private affair. Our Party is an association of class-conscious, advanced fighters for the emancipation of the working class. Such an association cannot and must not be indifferent to lack of class-consciousness, ignorance or obscurantism in the shape of religious beliefs. We demand complete disestablishment of the Church so as to be able to combat the religious fog with purely ideological and solely ideological weapons, by means of our press and by word of mouth. But we founded our association, the Russian Social-Democratic Labour Party, precisely for such a struggle against every religious bamboozling of the workers. And to us the ideological struggle is not a private affair, but the affair of the whole Party, of the whole proletariat.

If that is so, why do we not declare in our Programme that we are atheists? Why do we not forbid Christians and other believers in God to join our Party?

The answer to this question will serve to explain the very important difference in the way the question of religion is presented by the bourgeois democrats and the Social-Democrats.

Our Programme is based entirely on the scientific, and moreover the materialist, world-outlook. An explanation of our Programme, therefore, necessarily includes an explanation of the true historical and economic roots of the religious fog. Our propaganda necessarily includes the propaganda of atheism; the publication of the appropriate scientific literature, which the autocratic feudal government has hitherto strictly forbidden and persecuted, must now form one of the fields of our Party work. We shall now probably have to follow the advice Engels once gave to the German Socialists: to translate and widely disseminate the literature of the eighteenth-century French Enlighteners and atheists.

But under no circumstances ought we to fall into the error of posing the religious question in an abstract, idealistic fashion, as an 'intellectual' question unconnected with the class struggle, as is not infrequently done by the radical-democrats from among the bourgeoisie. It would be stupid to think that, in a society based on the endless oppression and coarsening of the worker masses, religious prejudices could be dispelled by purely propaganda methods. It would be bourgeois narrow-mindedness to forget that the yoke of religion that weighs upon mankind is merely a product and reflection of the economic yoke within society. No number of pamphlets and no amount of preaching can enlighten the proletariat, if it is not enlightened by its own struggle against the dark forces of capitalism.

Unity in this really revolutionary struggle of the oppressed class for the creation of a paradise on earth is more important to us than unity of proletarian opinion on paradise in heaven.

That is the reason why we do not and should not set forth our atheism in our Programme; that is why we do not and should not prohibit proletarians who still retain vestiges of their old prejudices from associating themselves with our Party. We shall always preach the scientific world-outlook, and it is essential for us to combat the inconsistency of various 'Christians'. But that does not mean in the least that the religious question ought to be advanced to first place, where it does not belong at all; nor does it mean that we should allow the forces of the really revolutionary economic and political struggle to be split up on account of third-rate opinions or senseless ideas, rapidly losing all political importance, rapidly being swept out as rubbish by the very course of economic development.

Everywhere the reactionary bourgeoisie has concerned itself, and is now beginning to concern itself in Russia, with the fomenting of religious strife – in order thereby to divert the attention of the masses from the really important and fundamental economic and political problems, now being solved in practice by the all-Russian proletariat uniting in revolutionary struggle. This reactionary policy of splitting up the proletarian forces, which today manifests itself mainly in Black-Hundred pogroms, may tomorrow conceive some more subtle forms. We, at any rate, shall oppose it by calmly, consistently and patiently preaching proletarian solidarity and the scientific world-outlook – a preaching alien to any stirring up of secondary differences.

The revolutionary proletariat will succeed in making religion a really private affair, so far as the state is concerned. And in this political system, cleansed of medieval mildew, the proletariat will wage a broad and open struggle for the elimination of economic slavery, the true source of the religious humbugging of mankind.

5
CREATION OF THE BOLSHEVIK PARTY

In the swirl of revolutionary turmoil and action, political positions of Mensheviks and Bolsheviks converged dramatically. In the course of 1905, the Mensheviks were temporarily swayed by a maverick member of their faction, Leon Trotsky, chairman of the Petersburg Soviet, whose views on the nature of the revolution, expressed in his theory of permanent revolution, overlapped to a significant degree with Lenin's. (Trotsky's theory, in some ways, went even further by seeing the possibility of the democratic revolution overflowing into a socialist revolution, assuming the revolution's spread to more industrialised capitalist countries.)[1] By 1906 the organisational differences that had separated Lenin from Martov also seemed to be evaporating, as the Mensheviks put forward a conception of 'democratic centralism' which the Bolsheviks also embraced. Lenin discussed the concept more than once, including in the brief article presented here, 'Freedom to Criticise and Unity of Action'.

In the wake of the defeat of the revolutionary upsurge, and a powerful re-consolidation of tsarist despotism that included maintaining increasingly threadbare and phony elements of the earlier democratic concessions (including different versions of the new parliament, or Duma), differences re-emerged within the RSDLP that were sharper than ever.

A decisive majority of the Mensheviks repudiated the revolutionary perspectives associated with Trotsky, returning with a vengeance to the notion of a worker–capitalist alliance. By 1907, the Mensheviks themselves had divided further, with some arguing that the RSDLP's underground organisation should be liquidated and that the party should restrict itself to legal activities – trade union work, building cultural and educational and social service efforts on behalf of the workers, and running for elections in the Duma. The Bolsheviks (and also some Mensheviks) indignantly argued that this amounted, for all practical purposes, to abandoning the revolutionary commitment to overthrow tsarism and was inconsistent with the RSDLP's Marxist programme. Lenin's unyielding position was that the 'liquidators' should be expelled from the RSDLP – a position naturally opposed by the 'liquidators' but also by most other Mensheviks (who feared that such expulsion would give the Bolsheviks control of the RSDLP).

In the same period, the Bolsheviks suffered a split. A substantial grouping led by Alexander A. Bogdanov and others rejected the idea of squandering energy in reform struggles, trade union work, and running for Duma elections, with some inclined to aggressively boycott the Duma and recall the RSDLP delegates already elected. The RSDLP's focus, they felt, should be on preparing and advancing revolutionary consciousness and armed struggle. Lenin and others around him, initially drawn to this view when they believed there would be a quick resurgence of the revolutionary wave, soon concluded that this 'ultra-left' path would make it impossible to build or maintain a mass base within the working class. An incredibly acrimonious internal struggle culminated in 1909, when Lenin and others organised a special conference that read the 'ultra-lefts' out of the ranks of the Bolshevik *faction* (or 'section', as Lenin labelled it in 1909). This was explained in a report 'The Extended Editorial Board Conference of *Proletary*', an excerpt of which appears here under the title 'Break with Ultra-Left Bolsheviks'.

The RSDLP was hopelessly divided by factions of liquidator and non-liquidator Mensheviks, Leninist and anti-Leninist Bolsheviks, and others – including a faction against factionalism led by Trotsky! Lenin and those around him concluded that effective revolutionary work could not be accomplished by such an entity, and in 1912 they reorganised themselves as the Russian Social-Democratic Labour Party distinctive from all other entities bearing that name – and which came to be known as the RSDLP (Bolsheviks). Lenin reported on this situation in 'Report to the International Socialist Bureau on the all-Russia Conference of the RSDLP' (reprinted here as 'Final Break with the Mensheviks'), explaining Bolshevik perspectives and intentions to the Socialist International (or Second International) to which all the world's Marxist-oriented socialist parties belonged.

All of the other factions of the RSDLP were indignant with Lenin's course of action and sought to recompose themselves as the real RSDLP. Their failure to maintain themselves as a coherent and functional entity, as opposed to disparate factions pulling in different directions, and the ability of the RSDLP (Bolsheviks) to become a cohesive and dynamic force in the working class from 1912 to 1914, is discussed in the excerpts from Lenin's 'Report to the Brussels Conference' (referring to another gathering of the Second International leadership), presented here under the title 'Report to Brussels'. Lenin's assertions here correspond to the recollections, many years later, of prominent Mensheviks ('they didn't even try to create a common organization', acknowledged Lydia Dan). Consider the comments of Boris Sapir:

The immense majority of Mensheviks in Russia were enthusiastically engrossed in founding and serving workers' organizations. They preferred to shelve underground activities even if they felt that this 'corrective' to the legal movement might in the long run prove necessary. Theoretically they probably agreed with Martov that the party in Russia should be 'an illegal organization of Social-Democratic elements fighting for an *open* labor movement,' that is, among other things, for its own open existence. In practice, however, little was done in this direction, and when the workers recovered from their post-1905 apathy, it was the Bolshevik underground apparatus that caught up most of the new [radicalized working-class] cadres in the legal organizations that the Mensheviks had created.[2]

The newly crystallised party, the RSDLP (Bolsheviks), popularised three demands dramatising their conception of a worker–peasant alliance that would lead a democratic revolution: (1) for an eight-hour workday; (2) for the redistribution of land to the peasants; and (3) for a constituent assembly to establish a democratic republic. Referring to a folktale about the world being balanced on the backs of three whales, these demands were nicknamed 'the three whales of Bolshevism'. As various historians have noted, Lenin's party rode the crest of a rising wave of working-class radicalisation, broken only by the calamity of the First World War.

Notes

1. This comes through clearly in a number of Menshevik accounts: Theodore Dan, *The Origins of Bolshevism* (New York: Schocken Books, 1970), 342–5; interviews with George Denike in Leopold H. Haimson (ed.), *The Making of Three Russian Revolutionaries, Voices from the Menshevik Past* (Cambridge: Cambridge University Press, 1987), 319–24; Solomon M. Schawarz, *The Russian Revolution in 1905: The Workers Movement and the Formation of Bolshevism and Menshevism* (Chicago: University of Chicago Press, 1967), 14–16, 246–54.

2. Boris Sapir, 'Notes and Reflections in the History of Menshevism', in Leopold H. Haimson (ed.), *The Mensheviks, From the Revolution of 1917 to the Second World War* (Chicago: University of Chicago Press, 1974), 356–7. Also see interviews with Lydia Dan and Boris Nicolaevsky, in Haimson (ed.), *The Making of Three Russian Revolutionaries*, 209, 286.

1906: Freedom to Criticise and Unity of Action*

The editors have received the following communication, signed by the Central Committee of the RSDLP.

'In view of the fact that several Party organisations have raised the question *of the limits within which the decisions of Party congresses may be criticised*, the Central Committee, bearing in mind that the interests of the Russian proletariat have always demanded the greatest possible unity in the tactics of the RSDLP, and that *this unity in the political activities* of the various sections of our Party is now more necessary than ever, is of the opinion:

(1) that in the Party press and at Party meetings, everybody must be allowed *full freedom* to express his personal opinions and to advocate his individual views;

(2) that at public political meetings members of the Party should refrain from conducting *agitation* that runs counter to congress decisions;

(3) that no Party member should at *such* meetings *call for action that runs counter to congress decisions*, or propose resolutions that are out of harmony with congress decisions.' (All italics ours.)

In examining the substance of this resolution, we see a number of queer points. The resolution says that 'at Party meetings' 'full freedom' is to be allowed for the expression of personal opinions and for criticism (§ 1), but at 'public meetings' (§ 2) 'no Party member should call for action that runs counter to congress decisions'. But see what comes of this: at Party meetings, members of the Party *have the right* to call for action that runs counter to congress decisions; but at public meetings they are *not* 'allowed' full freedom to 'express personal opinions'!!

Those who drafted the resolution have a totally wrong conception of the relationship between *freedom to criticise* within the Party and the Party's *unity of action*. Criticism within the limits of the *principles* of the Party Programme must be quite free (we remind the reader of what Plekhanov said on this subject at the Second Congress of the RSDLP), not only at Party meetings,

* *Collected Works*, Vol. 10: 442–3.

but also at public meetings. Such criticism, or such 'agitation' (for criticism is inseparable from agitation) cannot be prohibited. The Party's political action must be united. No 'calls' that violate the unity of definite actions can be tolerated either at public meetings, or at Party meetings, or in the Party press.

Obviously, the Central Committee has defined freedom to criticise inaccurately and too narrowly, and unity of action inaccurately and too broadly.

Let us take an example. The Congress decided that the Party should take part in the Duma elections. Taking part in elections is a very definite action. During the elections (as in Baku today, for example), no member of the Party *anywhere* has any right whatever to call upon the people to *abstain from voting*; nor can 'criticism' of the decision to take part in the elections be tolerated during this period, for it would in fact jeopardise success in the election campaign. *Before* elections have been announced, however, Party members *everywhere* have a perfect right to *criticise* the decision to take part in elections. Of course, the application of this principle in practice will sometimes give rise to disputes and misunderstandings; but *only* on the basis of *this* principle can *all* disputes and all misunderstandings be settled honourably for the Party. The resolution of the Central Committee, however, creates an impossible situation.

The Central Committee's resolution is essentially wrong and *runs counter to the Party Rules*. The principle of democratic centralism and autonomy for local Party organisations implies universal and full *freedom to criticise*, so long as this does not disturb the unity of *a definite action*; it rules out *all* criticism which disrupts or makes difficult the *unity* of an action decided on by the Party.

We think that the Central Committee has made a big mistake by publishing a resolution on this important question without first having it discussed in the Party press and by Party organisations; such a discussion would have helped it to avoid the mistakes we have indicated.

We call upon all Party organisations to discuss this resolution of the Central Committee now, and to express a definite opinion on it.

1909: Break with Ultra-Left Bolsheviks*

… The conference stated in its resolutions that tendencies were beginning to appear within the Bolshevik section which run counter to Bolshevism with its specific tactical principles. In our Party Bolshevism is represented by the Bolshevik *section*. But a section is not a party. A party can contain a whole gamut of opinions and shades of opinion, the extremes of which may be sharply contradictory. In the German party, side by side with the pronouncedly revolutionary wing of Kautsky, we see the ultra-revisionist wing of Bernstein. That is not the case within a section. A section in a party is a group of *like-minded persons* formed for the purpose primarily of influencing the party in a definite direction, for the purpose of securing acceptance for their principles in the party in the purest possible form. For this, real *unanimity of opinion* is necessary. The different standards we set for *party* unity and *sectional* unity must be grasped by everyone who wants to know how the question of the internal discord in the Bolshevik section really stands. …

Our immediate task is to preserve and consolidate the Russian Social-Democratic Labour Party. The very fulfilment of this great task involves one extremely important element: the combating of both varieties of *liquidationism* – liquidationism on the right and liquidationism on the left. The liquidators on the right say that no illegal RSDLP is needed, that Social-Democratic activities should be centred exclusively or almost exclusively on legal opportunities. The liquidators on the left go to the other extreme: legal avenues of Party work do not exist for them, illegality at any price is their 'be all and end all'. Both, in approximately equal degree, are liquidators of the RSDLP, for without methodical judicious *combination* of legal and illegal work in the present situation that history has imposed upon us, the 'preservation and consolidation of the RSDLP' is inconceivable. Liquidationism on the right, as we know, is rampant particularly in the Menshevik section, and partly in the Bund. But among the Mensheviks there have lately been

*   *Collected Works*, Vol. 15: 430, 432–4.

significant signs of a return to partyism, which must be welcomed: 'the minority of the [Menshevik] section', to quote the conference resolution, 'after running the full gauntlet of liquidationism, are now voicing their protest against it, and seeking anew solid party ground for their activities'.

What then are the tasks of the Bolsheviks in relation to this as yet small section of the Mensheviks who are fighting against liquidationism on the right? The Bolsheviks must undoubtedly seek *rapprochement* with this section of the membership, those who are Marxists and partyists. There is no question whatever of sinking our tactical differences with the Mensheviks. We are fighting and shall continue to fight most strenuously against Menshevik deviations from the policy of revolutionary Social-Democracy. Nor, needless to say, is there any question of the Bolshevik section dissolving its identity in the Party. The Bolsheviks have done a good deal to entrench their positions in the Party, but much remains to be done in the same direction. The Bolshevik section as a definite ideological trend in the Party must exist as before. But one thing must be borne firmly in mind: the responsibility of 'preserving and consolidating' the RSDLP, of which the resolution of the conference speaks, now rests primarily, if not entirely, on the Bolshevik section. All, or practically all, the *Party* work in progress, particularly in the localities, is now being shouldered by the Bolsheviks. And to them, as firm and consistent guardians of Party principle, now falls a highly important task. They must enlist in the cause of *building up the Party* all elements who are fitted to serve it. And in this hour of adversity it would be truly a crime on our part not to extend our hand to pro-Party people in other groups, who are coming out in defence of Marxism and partyism against liquidationism.

1912: Final Break with the Mensheviks[*]

The last few years have been years of indecision and disorganisation for the RSDLP. For three years the Party could not convene

---

[*]   *Collected Works*, Vol. 17: 503–5.

either a conference or a congress, and during the last two years the Central Committee has been unable to develop any activity. True enough, the Party has continued to exist, but only in the form of isolated groups in all the larger cities and, in view of the absence of a Central Committee, each of these groups has led a life of its own, somewhat isolated from the others.

Not so long ago, under the influence of the new awakening of the Russian proletariat, the Party again began to gain in strength, and quite recently we were able, at last, to convene a conference (something that had been impossible ever since 1908), at which the organisations of St Petersburg and Moscow, of the North-West and the South, the Caucasus and the central industrial region were represented. In all, 20 organisations established close ties with the Organising Commission convening this conference; that is to say, practically all the organisations, both Menshevik and Bolshevik, active in Russia at the present time.

During its 23 sessions the Conference, which assumed the rights and duties of the supreme authority of the Party, discussed all the questions on the agenda, among which were a number that were extremely important. The Conference made a comprehensive evaluation of the present political situation and of Party policy, this evaluation fully corresponding to the resolutions of the Conference held in 1908 and to the decisions of the Plenary Meeting of the Central Committee in 1910. The Conference devoted special attention to the Duma elections which are to be held in a few months' time, and adopted a resolution in three sections which gives a very explicit and detailed explanation of the intricate and involved election law, analyses the question of election agreements with other parties, and thoroughly elucidates the position and tactics of the Party in the forthcoming election campaign. The Conference also discussed and adopted resolutions on the questions of combating the famine, of workers' insurance, of trade unions, of strikes, etc.

Further, the Conference considered the question of the 'liquidators'. This trend denies the existence of the illegal Party, declares that the Party is already liquidated and that the attempts to revive the illegal Party are a reactionary utopia, and maintains that the Party can be revived only as a legally existing organisation. Nevertheless, this trend, which has broken with the illegal Party, has so far been unable to found a legally existing party. The Conference placed on record that for four years the Party had been waging a fight against this trend, that the Conference held in 1908 and the Plenary Meeting of the Central Committee in 1910 had both declared against the liquidators, and that in spite of all the attempts made by the Party, this trend continued to maintain its factional independence and to carry on a struggle against the Party in the columns of publications appearing legally. The Conference, therefore, declared that the liquidators, grouped around the magazines *Nasha Zarya* and *Dyelo Zhizni* (to which *Zhivoye Dyelo* should now be added), had placed themselves outside the ranks of the RSDLP.

Finally, the Conference elected a Central Committee and an editorial board for *Sotsial-Demokrat*, the Party's Central Organ. In addition, the Conference specially noted the fact that many groups abroad more or less adhering to socialism are, in any case, entirely divorced from the Russian proletariat and its socialist activity; consequently, these groups are absolutely irresponsible, and under no circumstances can they represent the RSDLP or speak in its name; that the Party does not hold itself in any way responsible or answerable for these groups, and that all relations with the RSDLP must be carried on solely through the Central Committee, whose address abroad is: Vladimir Ulyanov, 4, Rue Marie Rose, Paris XIV (for the Central Committee).

1914: Report to Brussels[*]

There are two bodies of opinion on what is at present taking place in the Russian Social-Democratic movement.

One opinion, expounded by Rosa Luxemburg in the proposal she made to the International Socialist Bureau last year (December 1913) and shared by the liquidators and the groups which support them, is as follows: in Russia the 'chaos' of factional strife reigns

[*] *Collected Works*, Vol. 20: 497–502, 503, 504, 505, 506–9, 513–15, 526–7.

among a multitude of factions, the worst of which, namely, the Leninist faction, is most active in fomenting a split. Actually, the differences do not preclude the possibility of joint activities. The road to unity lies through agreement or compromise among all trends and groups.

The other opinion, which we hold, is that there is nothing resembling 'chaos of factional strife' in Russia. The *only* thing we have there is a struggle against the liquidators, and it is *only* in the course of this struggle that a *genuinely* workers' Social-Democratic Party is being built up, which has already united the *overwhelming majority* – four-fifths – of the class-conscious workers of Russia. The illegal Party, in which the majority of the workers of Russia are organised, has been represented by the following conferences: the January Conference of 1912, the February Conference of 1913, and the Summer Conference of 1913. The legal organ of the Party is the newspaper *Pravda* (*Vérité*), hence the name Pravdist. Incidentally, this opinion was expressed by the St Petersburg worker who, at a banquet in St Petersburg which Comrade Vandervelde attended, stated that the workers in the factories of St Petersburg are united, and that outside of this unity of the workers there are only 'general staffs without armies'.

In the second part of my report I shall deal with the objective data which prove that ours is the correct opinion. And now I shall deal with the substance of liquidationism.

The liquidationist groups were formally expelled from the Party at the RSDLP Conference in January 1912, but the question of liquidationism was raised by our Party much earlier. A definite official resolution, binding upon the whole Party and unreservedly condemning liquidationism, was adopted by the All-Russia Conference of the RSDLP held as far back as December *1908*. In this resolution liquidationism is defined as follows:

(Liquidationism is) 'an attempt on the part of some of the Party intelligentsia to liquidate the existing organisation of the RSDLP and to substitute for it an amorphous federation acting at all cost within the limits of legality, even at the cost of openly abandoning the programme, tactics and traditions of the Party'.

From this it is evident that as far back as *1908* liquidationism was officially declared and recognised as an *intellectualist* trend, and that in substance it stood for the *renunciation* of the illegal Party and the *substitution*, or advocacy of the substitution, of a legal party for it.

The Central Committee's plenary meeting held in January *1910* once again *unanimously* condemned liquidationism as '*a manifestation of the influence of the bourgeoisie on the proletariat*'.

From this we see how mistaken is the opinion that our differences with the liquidators are no deeper and are less important than those between the so-called radicals and moderates in Western Europe. There is not a single – literally not a single – West-European party that has ever had occasion to adopt a general party decision against people who desired to *dissolve* the party and to *substitute* a new one for it!

Nowhere in Western Europe has there ever been, nor can there ever be, a question of whether it is permissible to bear the title of party member *and at the same time* advocate the dissolution of that party, to argue that the party is useless and unnecessary, and that another party be substituted for it. Nowhere in Western Europe does the question concern the very *existence* of the party as it does with us, i.e., whether that party is *to be or not to be*.

This is not disagreement over a question of organisation, of *how* the party should be built, but disagreement concerning the very *existence* of the party. Here, conciliation, agreement and compromise are totally out of the question.

We could not have built up our Party (to the extent of four-fifths) and cannot continue to build it otherwise than by relentlessly fighting those publicists who in the legal press fight against the 'underground' (i.e., the illegal Party), declare it to be an '*evil*', justify and eulogise desertion from it, and advocate the formation of an 'open party'.

In present-day Russia, where even the party of the extremely moderate liberals is not legal, our Party can exist only as an illegal party. The exceptional and unique feature of our position, which somewhat resembles that of the German Social-Democrats under the Anti-Socialist Law (although, even then, the Germans enjoyed a hundred times more legality than we do in Russia), is that our illegal Social-Democratic Labour Party consists of *illegal* workers' organisations (often called 'cells') which are surrounded by a more or less dense network of *legal* workers' associations (such as sick insurance societies, trade unions, educational associations, athletic clubs, temperance societies, and so forth). Most of these legal associations exist in the metropolis; in many parts of the provinces there are none at all.

Some of the illegal organisations are fairly large, others are quite small and in some cases they consist only of 'trusted agents'.

The legal associations serve to some extent as a *screen* for the illegal organisations and for the extensive, legal advocacy of the idea of working-class solidarity among the masses. Nation-wide contacts between the leading working-class organisations, the maintenance of a centre (the Central Committee) and the passing of precise Party resolutions on all questions – all these are of course carried out quite illegally and call for the utmost secrecy and trust-worthiness on the part of advanced and tested workers.

To come out in the legal press *against* the 'underground' or in favour of an 'open party' is simply to *disrupt* our Party, and we must regard the people who do this as *bitter enemies* of our Party.

Naturally, repudiation of the 'underground' goes hand in hand with repudiation of revolutionary tactics and advocacy of reformism. Russia is passing through a period of bourgeois revolutions. In Russia even the most moderate bourgeois – the Cadets and Octobrists – are decidedly dissatisfied with the government. But they are all enemies of revolution and detest us for 'demagogy', for striving again to lead the masses to the barricades as we did in 1905. They are all bourgeois who advocate only 'reforms' and spread among the masses the highly pernicious idea that reform is *compatible* with the present tsarist monarchy.

Our tactics are different. We make use of every reform (insurance, for example) and of every legal society. But we use them to develop the revolutionary consciousness and the revolutionary struggle of the masses. In Russia, where political freedom to this day does not exist, these words have far more direct implications for us than they have in Europe. Our Party conducts *revolutionary strikes*, which in Russia are growing as in no other country in the world. Take, for example, the month of May alone. In May 1912, 64,000 and in May 1914, 99,000 workers were involved in economic strikes.

The number involved in political strikes was: 364,000 in 1912 and 647,000 in 1914. The combination of political and economic struggle produces the revolutionary strike, which, by rousing the peasant millions, trains them for revolution. Our Party conducts campaigns of *revolutionary meetings* and *revolutionary street demonstrations*. For this purpose our Party distributes *revolutionary leaflets* and an *illegal newspaper*, the Party's Central Organ. The ideological unification of all these propaganda and agitation activities among the masses is achieved by the slogans adopted by the supreme bodies of our Party, namely: (1) an eight-hour day; (2) confiscation of the landed estates, and (3) a democratic republic. In the present situation in Russia, where absolute tyranny and despotism prevail and where all laws are suppressed by the tsarist monarchy, *only* these slogans can effectually unite and direct the entire propaganda and agitation of the Party aimed at effectually sustaining the revolutionary working-class movement.

It amuses us to hear the liquidators say, for example, that we are opposed to 'freedom of association', for we not only emphasised the importance of this point of our programme in a special resolution adopted by the January Conference of 1912, but we made ten times more effective use of the curtailed right of association (the insurance societies, for example) than the liquidators did. But when people tell us in the legal press that the slogans of confiscation of the land and of a republic cannot serve as subjects for agitation among the masses, we say that there can be no question of our Party's unity with *such* people, and such a group of publicists.

Since the purpose of this first part of my report is to explain the *gist* of our differences, I shall say no more on this point, except to remind you that the fourth part of my report will contain practical proposals, with an exact list of all the cases where the liquidators have departed from our Party's programme and decisions.

I shall not here go into the details of the history of the liquidators' *breakaway* from our illegal Party, the RSDLP, but will merely indicate the *three* main periods of this history.

First period: from the autumn of 1908 to January 1910. The Party combated liquidationism with the aid of precise, official, Party decisions condemning it.

Second period: from January 1910 to January 1912. The liquidators *hindered* the work of restoring the Central Committee of the Party; they disrupted the Central Committee of the Party and *dismissed* the last remnants of it, namely, the Technical Commission of the *Bureau* Abroad of the Central Committee. The Party committees *in Russia* then (autumn 1911) set up the Russian Organising Commission for the purpose of restoring the Party. That Commission convened the January Conference of 1912. The Conference restored the Party, elected a Central Committee and expelled the liquidationist group from the Party.

Third period: from January 1912 to the present time. The specific feature of this period is that a majority of four-fifths of the class-conscious workers of Russia have rallied around the decisions and bodies created by the January Conference of 1912. ...

In January 1912 the Conference of the RSDLP, which restored the illegal Party, was held. The liquidators and the groups abroad (including Plekhanov) greeted it with abuse. But what about the workers in Russia?

The answer to this question was provided by the Fourth Duma elections.

These elections were held in the autumn of 1912. Whereas in the Third Duma *50 per cent* (four out of eight) of the deputies elected by the worker curia belonged to our trend, in the Fourth Duma six out of nine, i.e., *67 per cent*, of the deputies elected by the worker curia were supporters of the Party. This proves that the masses of the workers sided with the Party and rejected liquidationism. ...

Daily newspapers are extremely important media of working-class *organisation*. They contain a vast amount of material proving this, i.e., the figures showing *the number of contributions received from workers' groups*. Both newspapers, the Pravdist (i.e., the Party) and the liquidationist, publish reports of financial contributions received from workers' groups. These reports are, for Russia, the best conceivable index – public and legal – of the actual state of *organisation* of the masses of the workers. ...

Here are the figures for the *whole* of 1913. The Pravdists received 2,181 money contributions from workers' groups, while the liquidators received 661. In 1914 (up to 13 May), the Pravdists had the support of 2,873 workers' groups, and the liquidators, of 671. Thus, the Pravdists organised 77 per cent of the workers' groups in 1913, and 81 per cent in 1914. ...

It is easy to give empty assurances, but it is very difficult to organise a genuine working-class newspaper that is really maintained by the workers. All the foreign comrades know this, and they are more experienced than we are. A real working-class newspaper, i.e., a newspaper that is really financed by the workers and which pursues the Party line, is a powerful instrument of organisation. ...

From 1 January to 13 May, 1914, both newspapers, as usual, published reports of collections, and our newspaper published a summary of these reports. Here are the results. *Pravda* collected R21,584.11, of which R18,934.10 came from workers' groups. Thus, 87 per cent of the contributions came from organised workers and only 13 per cent from the bourgeoisie. ...

The liquidators collected R12,055.89, of which R5,296.12 came from workers' groups, i.e., only 44 per cent – less *than half*. The liquidators get *more than half* their funds from bourgeois sources. ...

According to the figures Comrade Vandervelde obtained in St Petersburg and made public in the press, *Pravda* has a circulation of 40,000, while the liquidationist newspaper has one of 16,000. *Pravda* is maintained by the workers and pays its way, but the liquidationist newspaper is maintained by those whom our newspaper calls their *rich friends from among the bourgeoisie*. ...

To proceed. Here are the objective figures concerning the election of workers' representatives to the insurance bodies. We reject as mere liberalism all talk about political, constitutional reforms in present-day tsarist Russia and will have nothing to do with it; but we take advantage of *real* reforms, such as insurance, *in deed* and not in word. The *entire* workers' group on the All-Russia Insurance Board consists of *Pravda supporters*, i.e., of workers who have condemned and rejected liquidationism. During the election to this All-Russia Insurance Board, 47 out of the 57 delegates, i.e., 82 per cent, were Pravdists. During the election of the Metropolitan, St Petersburg, Insurance Board, 37 of the delegates were Pravdists and 7 were liquidators, the Pravdists constituting 84 per cent.

The same can be said about the trade unions. When they hear the talk of the Russian Social-Democrats abroad about the 'chaos of factional strife' in Russia (indulged in by Rosa Luxemburg, Plekhanov, Trotsky, and others), our foreign comrades perhaps imagine that the trade union movement in our country is split up.

Nothing of the kind.

In Russia there are no duplicate unions. Both in St Petersburg and in Moscow, the trade unions are *united*. The point is that in these unions the *Pravdists* completely *predominate*.

Not one of the 13 trade unions in Moscow is liquidationist.

Of the 20 trade unions in St Petersburg listed in our Workers' Calendar together with their membership, only the Draftsmen's, Druggist Employees' and Clerks' Unions, and half the members of the Printers' Union, are liquidationist; in all the other unions – Metalworkers', Textile Workers', Tailors', Woodworkers', Shop Assistants', and so forth – the Pravdists *completely* predominate. ...

Here are figures on the illegal press published abroad. *After* the liquidators' August Conference in 1912, our Party, up to June 1914, put out *five* issues of an illegal leading political newspaper; the *liquidators – nil*; the Socialist-Revolutionaries – *nine*. These figures do not include leaflets issued in Russia for revolutionary agitation during strikes, meetings and demonstrations.

In these five issues you will find mention of 44 illegal organisations of our Party; the liquidators – *nil*; the Socialist-Revolutionaries – *21* (mainly students and peasants).

Lastly, in October 1913, an independent Russian Social-Democratic Labour group was formed in the Duma, the aim of that group, unlike that of the liquidators, being to *carry out*, not flout, the will of the majority of the class-conscious workers of Russia. At that time *both* newspapers published *resolutions* from workers all over Russia supporting either the line of the Party group or that of the liquidationist group. The *signatures* to the resolutions in favour of the Pravdist, i.e., the Party group in the Duma, numbered 6,722, whereas those supporting the liquidationist group numbered 2,985 (including 1,086 signatures of Bundist workers and 719 of Caucasian workers). Thus, together with all their allies, the liquidators succeeded in collecting *less than one-third* of the signatures. ...

But let us assume for a moment that our numerous opponents (numerous in the opinion of the intellectualist groups and the Party groups living abroad) are right. Let us assume that we are 'usurpers', 'splitters', and so forth. In that case, would it not be natural to expect our opponents to prove, *not merely with words*, *but by the experience* of their activities and their unity, that we are wrong.

If we are wrong in asserting that the Party can only be built up by fighting the liquidationist groups, then should we not expect the groups and organisations which disagree with us to *prove from the experience of their* activities that unity with the liquidators is possible?

But the experience of our opponents shows this. In January 1912, our illegal Party was restored by our Conference, which was representative of the majority of organisations in Russia.

In March 1912, the following united in the columns of *Vorwärts* to abuse us:

the liquidators
the Bund
the Letts

the Poles
the Trotskyists
and the Vperyodists.

What a lot of 'trends' and 'groups', one might think! How easy it should have been for them to set the workers of Russia a good example by their unity!

But when steps were taken to convene the 'August' Conference of the liquidators, it was found that our opponents *could not* march in step.

Both the Poles and Plekhanov refused to attend the 'August' Conference of the liquidators.

Why?

Because they *could not* agree even on the meaning of the term: membership in the Party!

And so, when Plekhanov's group or Rosa Luxemburg or anybody else, assure themselves and others that *it is possible* to unite with the liquidators, we answer: dear comrades, you just try yourselves to 'unite' with the liquidators on a definition of Party membership, *not in word, but in deed.*

Further. The Vperyodists attended the August Conference, but afterwards *walked out* in protest and denounced it as a fiction.

Then, in February 1914, 18 months after the 'August Conference' of the liquidators, the Congress of the Lettish Party was held. The Letts had always been in favour of 'unity'. The Lettish workers *had wanted* to work with the liquidators and had proved this, not merely in word, but in deed, *by experience.*

And after 18 months' experience, the Letts, *while remaining strictly neutral*, declared at their congress that they were withdrawing from the August bloc because:

– as the resolution of the Lettish Congress reads:

'The attempt by the conciliators to unite at all costs with the liquidators (the August Conference of 1912) proved fruitless, and the uniters themselves became ideologically and politically dependent upon the liquidators.'

If anybody else wants to make the 'experiment of uniting with the liquidators', let them do so. We, however, declare that until the liquidators definitely abandon their liquidationist line, unity with them is absolutely impossible.

Lastly, Trotsky's group, the Caucasians under their leader An, and a number of other liquidators ('Em-El', for example) have practically *dropped out* of the August bloc and founded *their own* journal, *Borba*. This journal has no connection with the workers whatsoever, but by its very existence, by its criticism of the liquidators' opportunism, by its breakaway from the liquidators, this journal, which belongs to the group of former liquidators, *has proved* in deed and by experience that unity with the liquidators is impossible. ...

Formally, the situation is as follows. Our Party, which was restored at the January 1912 Conference in the teeth of the resistance from the liquidators' group, expelled that group. *After* this, after two-and-a-half years of the movement, the overwhelming majority of the class-conscious workers of Russia have approved of our Party line. We therefore have every reason to be convinced more firmly than ever that our line is correct, *and we shall not depart from it*. ...

Russia is passing through a period of bourgeois revolutions, during which small and unstable groups of intellectuals are sometimes inclined to regard themselves as Social-Democrats, or to support the opportunist trend in the Social-Democratic movement, which our Party has been fighting against for the past 20 years (Economism in 1895–1902, Menshevism in 1903–08, and liquidationism in 1908–14). The experience of the August (1912) bloc of liquidators and its break-down have shown that the liquidators and their defenders are absolutely incapable of forming any kind of party or organisation. The genuine workers' Social-Democratic Party of Russia which, in spite of enormous difficulties, has already united eight-tenths of the class-conscious workers (counting only Social-Democrats) or seven-tenths (counting Social-Democrats and Socialist-Revolutionaries) can be built up, and is being built up, only in the struggle against these groups.

6

IMPERIALIST WAR, NATIONAL LIBERATION, REVOLUTIONARY DEMOCRACY

The first reading in this section, 'The Historical Destiny of the Doctrine of Karl Marx', is a succinct and remarkable overview of Marxism's evolution as a distinctively revolutionary working-class orientation, through a contradictory phase of relative success and de-radicalisation, to a dynamic renewal in part through interaction with revolutionary upsurges among imperialist-dominated peoples outside of Europe. Written in 1913, it pushes against the Euro-centrism that characterised so many other Marxists, and it is suggestive of momentous developments about to impact on world history.

The First World War broke out in August 1914 – flaming through Europe as if it were a terrible back-draft from the long-violated colonies of the major European powers, with Germany and Austria-Hungary (allied also with the Turkish-based Ottoman Empire) engaged in lethal combat with an alliance that included Britain, France, Russia, and ultimately the United States. Among the 65 million men mobilised to fight, there were about 9 million – one soldier out of seven – combat deaths, with an additional 5 million reported missing, and 7 million suffering permanent disabilities (out of approximately 21 million wounded). This was a Total War, with the estimated civilian deaths resulting from the war exceeding the military casualties, with a total real economic cost estimated at $400 billion, and with the horrendous wreckage of cities, farmlands and countries, not to mention the brutalisation of life, leaving a lasting imprint on all that followed in the twentieth century.[1]

The socialist parties affiliated with the Second International had foreseen the possibility of such a war, and they had pledged to oppose it. It had been a touchstone of Marxists in all countries that the outbreak of such a war would prove that the time had come to replace capitalism with socialism through decisive revolutionary action. Instead the majorities of most of the Second International's member-parties declared allegiance to the 'patriotic' war efforts of their respective pro-capitalist governments. Some of the most prestigious representatives of 'Marxist orthodoxy' – such as Karl Kautsky and George Plekhanov – set aside their long-enunciated revolutionary commitments, in Kautsky's case to bow quietly before the patriotic slaughter, in Plekhanov's case to openly support the war effort of the Russian government and its allies.

Lenin helped to lead his Bolshevik organisation into intransigent opposition to the war, joining with minorities of anti-war socialists in other countries – although more determined than many of them to decisively and definitively break with those who had betrayed the revolutionary cause. He especially sought to understand and help others to understand why the war was happening and how it was that sectors of the labour and socialist movements (he angrily called them 'social-chauvinists' and 'social-patriots') had been drawn into supporting the war. What Lenin perceived as the dilution and distortion of Marxism manifested in the analyses of Kautsky and Plekhanov – men he had once respected greatly – was a focal-point of especially critical and scathing commentary. And, as always, he concentrated attention on the path forward for revolutionary socialists.

All of this found its way into *Socialism and War*, a 1915 pamphlet co-authored with a rising young co-thinker, Gregory Zinoviev, excerpts of which are presented here. One of the key issues Lenin felt compelled to clarify was the national question, since all combatants emphasised their claim to be defending the integrity and interests of 'the nation' and made ample use of nationalist ideology. Lenin saw the defence of the rights of oppressed nationalities as a vitally important component of the democratic programme (including a democratic republic, freedom of expression, women's rights). An intensified insistence on the centrality of democracy in the struggle for socialism can be found at the heart of his important essay 'The Revolutionary Proletariat and the Right of Nations to Self-Determination' (1915). Here he was taking issue with some revolutionary socialists – for example, the future Bolshevik Karl Radek (who used the pseudonym 'Parabellum') – whose views mirrored those of Rosa Luxemburg, holding that all forms of nationalism must be opposed. Lenin disagreed, insisting that a distinction must be made between the nationalism of oppressed nationalities (to be supported) and of oppressor nations (to be opposed).

Imperialism was the force that underlay and drove forward the nationalism of oppressor nations, Lenin held, and was the cause of the bloody calamity of global war. In his 1916 classic *Imperialism, The Highest Stage of Capitalism, A Popular Outline*, he drew on previous work by J.A. Hobson, a British left-liberal economist, Rudolf Hilferding, a prominent Austrian Marxist, and others to analyse the meaning, dynamics, and place in history of this phenomenon, which he saw as inseparable from the structure and functioning of modern-day capitalism. The excerpts from that work reproduced here begin with part of an introduction that was published later, when he could make essential points that war-time censorship had precluded. Matching Lenin's scholarship on imperialism is the final reading in this section, 'Statistics and Sociology', an unfinished work on nationalities offering additional insights especially on oppressed nationalities living in multi-national countries (among whom he includes African-Americans).

While the predominance of the Bolsheviks in the Russian workers' movement was shattered by war-time repression (their hegemony being replaced by pro-war factions among the Socialist-Revolutionaries and Mensheviks), the 'hard' revolutionary perspectives developed by Lenin's party would stand it in good stead as realities shifted when a disillusioned population turned against the war and against the tsarist order that had led the nation into this horrendous conflict.

Note

1. Louis L. Snyder, *The World in the Twentieth Century*, revised edn (Princeton, NJ: D. Van Nostrand Co., 1964), 35.

1913: The Historical Destiny of the Doctrine of Karl Marx*

The chief thing in the doctrine of Marx is that it brings out the historic role of the proletariat as the builder of socialist society. Has the course of events all over the world confirmed this doctrine since it was expounded by Marx?

Marx first advanced it in 1844. The Communist Manifesto of Marx and Engels, published in 1848, gave an integral and systematic exposition of this doctrine, an exposition which has remained the best to this day. Since then world history has clearly been divided into three main periods: (1) from the revolution of 1848 to the Paris Commune (1871); (2) from the Paris Commune to the Russian revolution (1905); (3) since the Russian revolution.

Let us see what has been the destiny of Marx's doctrine in each of these periods.

I

At the beginning of the first period Marx's doctrine by no means dominated. It was only one of the very numerous groups or trends of socialism. The forms of socialism that did dominate were in the main akin to our Narodism: in comprehension of the materialist basis of historical movement, inability to single out the role and significance of each class in capitalist society, concealment of the bourgeois nature of democratic reforms under diverse, quasi-socialist phrases about the 'people', 'justice', 'right', and so on.

The revolution of 1848 struck a deadly blow at all these vociferous, motley and ostentatious forms of pre-Marxian socialism. In all countries, the revolution revealed the various classes of society *in action*. The shooting of the workers by the republican bourgeoisie in Paris in the June days of 1848 finally revealed that the proletariat *alone* was socialist by nature. The liberal bourgeoisie dreaded the independence of this class a hundred times more than it did any kind of reaction. The craven liberals grovelled before reaction. The peasantry were content

*   *Collected Works*, Vol. 18: 582–5.

with the abolition of the survivals of feudalism and joined the supporters of order, wavering but occasionally between *workers' democracy and bourgeois liberalism*. All doctrines of *non*-class socialism and *non*-class politics proved to be sheer nonsense.

The Paris Commune (1871) completed this development of bourgeois changes; the republic, i.e., the form of political organisation in which class relations appear in their most unconcealed form, owed its consolidation solely to the heroism of the proletariat.

In all the other European countries, a more tangled and less complete development led to the same result – a bourgeois society that had taken definite shape. Towards the end of the first period (1848–71), a period of storms and revolutions, pre-Marxian socialism was *dead*. Independent *proletarian* parties came into being: the First International (1864–72) and the German Social-Democratic Party.

II

The second period (1872–1904) was distinguished from the first by its 'peaceful' character, by the absence of revolutions. The West had finished with bourgeois revolutions. The East had not yet risen to them.

The West entered a phase of 'peaceful' preparations for the changes to come. Socialist parties, basically proletarian, were formed everywhere, and learned to use bourgeois parliamentarism and to found their own daily press, their educational institutions, their trade unions and their co-operative societies. Marx's doctrine gained a complete victory and *began to spread*. The selection and mustering of the forces of the proletariat and its preparation for the coming battles made slow but steady progress.

The dialectics of history were such that the theoretical victory of Marxism compelled its enemies to *disguise themselves* as Marxists. Liberalism, rotten within, tried to revive itself in the form of socialist *opportunism*. They interpreted the period of preparing the forces for great battles as renunciation of these battles. Improvement of the conditions of the slaves to fight against wage slavery they took to mean the sale by the slaves of their right to liberty for a few pence. They cravenly preached 'social peace' (i.e., peace with the slaveowners), renunciation of the class struggle, etc. They had very many adherents among socialist members of parliament, various officials of the working-class movement, and the 'sympathising' intelligentsia.

III

However, the opportunists had scarcely congratulated themselves on 'social peace' and on the non-necessity of storms under 'democracy' when a new source of great world storms opened up in Asia. The Russian revolution was followed by revolutions in Turkey, Persia and China. It is in this era of storms and their 'repercussions' in Europe that we are now living. No matter what the fate of the great Chinese republic, against which various 'civilised' hyenas are now whetting their teeth, no power on earth can restore the old serfdom in Asia or wipe out the heroic democracy of the masses in the Asiatic and semi-Asiatic countries.

Certain people who were inattentive to the conditions for preparing and developing the mass struggle were driven to despair and to anarchism by the lengthy delays in the decisive struggle against capitalism in Europe. We can now see how short-sighted and faint-hearted this anarchist despair is.

The fact that Asia, with its population of 800 million, has been drawn into the struggle for these same European ideals should inspire us with optimism and not despair.

The Asiatic revolutions have again shown us the spinelessness and baseness of liberalism, the exceptional importance of the independence of the democratic masses, and the pronounced demarcation between the proletariat and the bourgeoisie of all kinds. After the experience both of Europe and Asia, anyone who speaks of non-class politics and non-class socialism, ought simply to be put in a cage and exhibited alongside the Australian kangaroo or something like that.

After Asia, Europe has also begun to stir, although not in the Asiatic way. The 'peaceful' period of 1872–1904 has passed, never to return. The high cost of living and the tyranny of the trusts are leading to an unprecedented sharpening of the economic struggle, which has set into movement even the British workers who have been most corrupted by liberalism. We see a political crisis brewing even in the most 'diehard', bourgeois-Junker country, Germany. The frenzied arming and the policy of imperialism are turning modern Europe into a 'social peace' which is more like a gunpowder barrel. Meanwhile the decay of *all* the bourgeois parties and the maturing of the proletariat are making steady progress.

Since the appearance of Marxism, each of the three great periods of world history has brought Marxism new confirmation and new triumphs. But a still greater triumph awaits Marxism, as the doctrine of the proletariat, in the coming period of history.

Pravda No. 50, 1 March 1913
Signed: *V. I.*

Published according
to the *Pravda* text

1915: Socialism and War*

Chapter I: The Principles of Socialism and the War of 1914–15

The Attitude of Socialists Towards Wars

Socialists have always condemned wars between nations as barbarous and brutal. Our attitude towards war, however, is fundamentally different from that of the bourgeois pacifists (supporters and advocates of peace) and of the anarchists. We differ from the former in that we understand the inevitable connection between wars and the class struggle within a country; we understand that wars cannot be abolished unless classes are abolished and socialism is created; we also differ in that we regard civil wars, i.e., wars waged by an oppressed class against the oppressor class, by slaves against slaveholders, by serfs against landowners, and by wage-workers against the bourgeoisie, as

---

* *Collected Works*, Vol. 21: 299–302, 304–5, 306–11, 315–17.

fully legitimate, progressive and necessary. We Marxists differ from both pacifists and anarchists in that we deem it necessary to study each war historically (from the standpoint of Marx's dialectical materialism) and separately. There have been in the past numerous wars which, despite all the horrors, atrocities, distress and suffering that inevitably accompany all wars, were progressive, i.e., benefited the development of mankind by helping to destroy most harmful and reactionary institutions (e.g., an autocracy or serfdom) and the most barbarous despotisms in Europe (the Turkish and the Russian). That is why the features historically specific to the present war must come up for examination.

The Historical Types of Wars in Modern Times

The Great French Revolution ushered in a new epoch in the history of mankind. From that time down to the Paris Commune, i.e., between 1789 and 1871, one type of war was of a bourgeois-progressive character, waged for national liberation. In other words, the overthrow of absolutism and feudalism, the undermining of these institutions, and the overthrow of alien oppression, formed the chief content and historical significance of such wars. These were therefore progressive wars; during such wars, all honest and revolutionary democrats, as well as all socialists, always wished success to that country (i.e., that bourgeoisie) which had helped to overthrow or undermine the most baneful foundations of feudalism, absolutism and the oppression of other nations. For example, the revolutionary wars waged by France contained an element of plunder and the conquest of foreign territory by the French, but this does not in the least alter the fundamental historical significance of those wars, which destroyed and shattered feudalism and absolutism in the whole of the old, serf-owning Europe. In the Franco-Prussian war, Germany plundered France but this does not alter the fundamental historical significance of that war, which liberated tens of millions of German people from feudal disunity and from the oppression of two despots, the Russian Tsar and Napoleon III.

The Difference Between Wars of Aggression and of Defence

The period of 1789–1871 left behind it deep marks and revolutionary memories. There could be no development of the proletarian struggle for socialism prior to the overthrow of feudalism, absolutism and alien oppression. When, in speaking of the wars of *such* periods, socialists stressed the legitimacy of 'defensive' wars, they always had these aims in mind, namely revolution against medievalism and serfdom. By a 'defensive' war socialists have always understood a '*just*' war in this particular sense (Wilhelm Liebknecht once expressed himself precisely in this way). It is only in this sense that socialists have always regarded wars 'for the defence of the fatherland', or 'defensive' wars, as legitimate, progressive and just. For example, if tomorrow, Morocco were to declare war on France, or India on Britain, or Persia or China on Russia, and so on, these would be 'just', and 'defensive' wars, *irrespective* of who would be the first to attack; any socialist would wish the oppressed, dependent and unequal states victory over the oppressor, slaveholding and predatory 'Great' Powers.

But imagine a slaveholder who owns 100 slaves warring against another who owns 200 slaves, for a more 'just' redistribution of slaves. The use of the term of a 'defensive' war, or a war 'for the defence of the fatherland', would clearly be historically false in such a case and would in practice be sheer deception of the common people, philistines, and the ignorant, by the astute slaveholders. It is in this way that the peoples are being deceived with 'national' ideology and the term of 'defence of the fatherland', by the present-day imperialist bourgeoisie, in the war now being waged between slaveholders with the purpose of consolidating slavery.

The War of Today is an Imperialist War

It is almost universally admitted that this war is an imperialist war. In most cases, however, this term is distorted, or applied to one side, or else a loophole is left for the assertion that this war may, after all, be bourgeois-progressive, and of significance to the national-liberation movement. Imperialism is the highest stage in the development of capitalism, reached only in the twentieth century. Capitalism now finds that the old national states, without whose formation it could not have overthrown feudalism, are too cramped for it. Capitalism has developed concentration to such a degree that entire branches of industry are controlled by syndicates, trusts and associations of capitalist multi-millionaires and almost the entire globe has been divided up among the 'lords of capital' either in the form of colonies, or by entangling other countries in thousands of threads of financial exploitation. Free trade and competition have been superseded by a striving towards monopolies, the seizure of territory for the investment of capital and as sources of raw materials, and so on. From the liberator of nations, which it was in the struggle against feudalism, capitalism in its imperialist stage has turned into the greatest oppressor of nations. Formerly progressive, capitalism has become reactionary. It has developed the forces of production to such a degree that mankind is faced with the alternative of adopting socialism or of experiencing years and even decades of armed struggle between the 'Great' Powers for the artificial preservation of capitalism by means of colonies, monopolies, privileges and national oppression of every kind. ...

'War is the Continuation of Politics by Other' (i.e., Violent) 'Means'

This famous dictum was uttered by Clausewitz, one of the profoundest writers on the problems of war. Marxists have always rightly regarded this thesis as the theoretical basis of views on the significance of any war. It was from this viewpoint that Marx and Engels always regarded the various wars.

Apply this view to the present war. You will see that for decades, for almost half a century, the governments and the ruling classes of Britain and France, Germany and Italy, Austria and Russia have pursued a policy of plundering colonies, oppressing other nations, and suppressing the working-class movement. It is this, and only this, policy that is being continued in the present war. In particular, the policy of both Austria and Russia, in peacetime as well as in war-time, is a policy of enslaving nations, not of liberating them. In China, Persia, India and other dependent countries, on the contrary, we have seen during the past decades a policy of rousing tens and hundreds of millions of people to a national life, of their liberation from the reactionary 'Great' Powers' oppression. A war waged on such a historical basis can even today be a bourgeois-progressive war of national liberation.

If the present war is regarded as a continuation of the politics of the 'Great' Powers and of the principal classes within them, a glance will immediately reveal the glaring anti-historicity, falseness and hypocrisy of the view that the 'defence-of-the-fatherland' idea can be justified in the present war. ...

What Social-Chauvinism Is

Social-chauvinism is advocacy of the idea of 'defence of the fatherland' in the present war. This idea logically leads to the abandonment of the class struggle during the war, to voting for war credits, etc. In fact, the social-chauvinists are pursuing an anti-proletarian, bourgeois policy; for they are actually championing, not 'defence of the fatherland' in the sense of combating foreign oppression, but the 'right' of one or other of the 'Great' Powers to plunder colonies and to oppress other nations. The social-chauvinists reiterate the bourgeois deception of the people that the war is being waged to protect the freedom and existence of nations, thereby taking sides with the bourgeoisie against the proletariat. Among the social-chauvinists are those who justify and varnish the governments and bourgeoisie of *one* of the belligerent groups of powers, as well as those who, like Kautsky, argue that the socialists of *all* the belligerent powers are equally entitled to 'defend the fatherland'. Social-chauvinism, which is, in effect, defence of the privileges, the advantages, the right to pillage and plunder, of one's 'own' (or any) imperialist bourgeoisie, is the utter betrayal of all socialist convictions and of the decision of the Basle International Socialist Congress.

The Basle Manifesto

The Manifesto on war unanimously adopted in Basle in 1912 has in view the very kind of war between Britain and Germany and their present allies, which broke out in 1914. The Manifesto openly declares that no plea of the interests of the people can serve to justify such a war waged 'for the sake of the profits of the capitalists and the ambitions of dynasties', on the basis of the imperialist, predatory policy of the Great Powers. The Manifesto openly declares that war is dangerous to 'governments' (all of them without exception), notes their fear of 'a proletarian revolution', and very definitely points to the example set by the Commune of 1871, and of October–December 1905, i.e., *to the examples of revolution and civil war.* Thus, the Basle Manifesto lays down, precisely for the present war, the tactics of the workers' revolutionary struggle on an international scale against their governments, the tactics of proletarian revolution. The Basle Manifesto repeats the statement in the Stuttgart resolution that, in the event of war, socialists must take advantage of the 'economic and political crisis' it will cause so as to 'hasten the downfall of capitalism', i.e., take advantage of the governments' war-time difficulties and the indignation of the masses, to advance the socialist revolution.

The social-chauvinists' policy, their justification of the war from the bourgeois-liberation standpoint, their sanctioning of 'defence of the fatherland', their voting for credits, entering cabinets, membership in governments, and so on and so forth, are downright treachery to socialism, which can be explained only, as we will soon show, by the victory of opportunism and of the national-liberal labour policy in the majority of European parties.

False References to Marx and Engels

The Russian social-chauvinists (headed by Plekhanov) make references to Marx's tactics in the war of 1870; the German (of the type of Lensch, David and Co.) – to Engels's statement in 1891 that, in the event of war against Russia and France combined, it would be the duty of the German socialists to defend their fatherland; finally, the social-chauvinists of the Kautsky type, who want to reconcile and legitimatise international chauvinism, refer to the fact that Marx and Engels, while condemning war, nevertheless, from 1854–55 to 1870–71 and 1876–77, always took the side of one belligerent state or another, once war had broken out.

All these references are outrageous distortions of the views of Marx and Engels, in the interest of the bourgeoisie and the opportunists, in just the same way as the writings of the anarchists Guillaume and Co. distort the views of Marx and Engels so as to justify anarchism. The war of 1870–71 was historically progressive on the part of Germany, until Napoleon III was defeated: the latter, together with the tsar, had oppressed Germany for years, keeping her in a state of feudal disunity. But as soon as the war developed into the plundering of France (the annexation of Alsace and Lorraine), Marx and Engels emphatically condemned the Germans. Even at the beginning of the war, Marx and Engels approved of the refusal of Bebel and Liebknecht to vote for war credits, and advised Social-Democrats not to merge with the bourgeoisie, but to uphold the independent class interests of the proletariat. To apply to the present imperialist war the appraisal of this bourgeois-progressive war of national-liberation is a mockery of the truth. The same applies with still greater force to the war of 1854–55, and to all the wars of the nineteenth century, when there existed *no* modern imperialism, *no* mature objective conditions for socialism, and *no* mass socialist parties *in any* of the belligerent countries, i.e., none of the conditions from which the Basle Manifesto deduced the tactics of 'proletarian revolution' *in connection* with a war between Great Powers.

Anyone who today refers to Marx's attitude towards the wars of the epoch of the *progressive* bourgeoisie and forgets Marx's statement that 'the workingmen have no country' – a statement that applies *precisely* to the epoch of the reactionary and outmoded bourgeoisie, to the epoch of the socialist revolution, is shamelessly distorting Marx, and is substituting the bourgeois point of view for the socialist.

The Collapse of the Second International

Socialists of all the world solemnly declared in Basle, in 1912, that they regarded the impending war in Europe as the 'criminal' and most reactionary deed of *all* the governments, which must hasten the downfall of capitalism by inevitably engendering a revolution against it. The war came, the crisis was there. Instead of revolutionary tactics, most of the Social-Democratic parties launched reactionary tactics, went over to the side of their respective governments and bourgeoisie. This betrayal of socialism signifies the collapse of the Second (1889–1914) International, and we must realise what caused this collapse, what brought social-chauvinism into being and gave it strength.

Social-Chauvinism is the Acme of Opportunism

Throughout the existence of the Second International, a struggle was raging within all the Social-Democratic parties, between their revolutionary and the opportunist wings. In a number of countries a split took place along this line (Britain, Italy, Holland, Bulgaria). Not one Marxist has ever doubted that opportunism expresses bourgeois policies within the working-class movement, expresses the interests of the petty bourgeoisie and the alliance of a tiny section of bourgeoisified workers with their '*own*' bourgeoisie, against the interests of the proletarian masses, the oppressed masses.

The objective conditions at the close of the nineteenth century greatly intensified opportunism, converted the utilisation of bourgeois legality into subservience to the latter, created a thin crust of a working-class officialdom and aristocracy and attracted numerous petty-bourgeois 'fellow travellers' to the Social-Democratic parties.

The war has speeded up this development and transformed opportunism into social-chauvinism, transformed the secret alliance between the opportunists and the bourgeoisie into an open one. Simultaneously, the military authorities have everywhere introduced martial law and have muzzled the mass of the workers, whose old leaders have nearly all gone over to the bourgeoisie.

Opportunism and social-chauvinism stand on a common economic basis – the interests of a thin crust of privileged workers and of the petty bourgeoisie, who are defending their privileged position, their 'right' to some modicum of the profits that their 'own' national bourgeoisie obtain from robbing other nations, from the advantages of their Great-Power status, etc.

Opportunism and social-chauvinism have the same politico-ideological content – class collaboration instead of class struggle, renunciation of revolutionary methods of struggle, helping one's 'own' government in its embarrassed situation, instead of taking advantage of these embarrassments so as to advance the revolution. If we take Europe as a whole and if we pay attention, not to individuals (even the most authoritative), we will find that it is the opportunist *trend* that has become the bulwark of social-chauvinism, whereas from the camp of the revolutionaries, more or less consistent protests against it are heard from almost all sides. And if we take, for example, the grouping of trends at the Stuttgart International Socialist Congress in 1907, we shall find that international Marxism was opposed to imperialism, while international opportunism was already in favour of it at that time.

Unity with the Opportunists Means an Alliance Between the Workers and Their 'Own' National Bourgeoisie and Splitting the International Revolutionary Working Class

In the past, before the war, opportunism was often looked upon as a legitimate, though 'deviationist' and 'extremist', component of the Social-Democratic Party. The war has shown the impossibility of this in the future. Opportunism has 'matured', and is now playing to the full its role as emissary of the bourgeois in the working-class movement. Unity with the opportunists has become sheer hypocrisy, exemplified by the German Social-Democratic Party. On every important occasion (e.g., the 4 August vote), the opportunists present an ultimatum, to which they give effect through their numerous links with the bourgeoisie, their majority on the executives of the trade unions, etc. Today *unity* with the opportunists *actually* means subordinating the working class to their 'own' national bourgeoisie, and an alliance with the latter for the purpose of oppressing other nations and of fighting for dominant-nation privileges; it means *splitting* the revolutionary proletariat of all countries.

No matter how hard, in individual circumstances, the struggle may be against the opportunists, who predominate in many organisations, whatever the specific nature of the purging of the workers' parties of opportunists in individual countries, this process is inevitable and fruitful. Reformist socialism is dying; regenerated socialism 'will be revolutionary, uncompromising and insurrectionary', to use the apt expression of the French Socialist Paul Golay. ...

Pacifism and the Peace Slogan

The temper of the masses in favour of peace often expresses the beginning of protest, anger and a realisation of the reactionary nature of the war. It is the duty of all Social-Democrats to utilise that temper. They will take a most ardent part in any movement and in any demonstration motivated by that sentiment, but they will not deceive the people with admitting the idea that a peace without annexations, without oppression of nations, without plunder, without the embryo of new wars among the present governments and ruling classes, is possible in the absence of a revolutionary movement. Such deception of the people would merely mean playing into the hands of the secret diplomacy of the belligerent governments and facilitating their counter-revolutionary plans. Whoever wants a lasting and democratic peace must stand for civil war against the governments and the bourgeoisie.

The Right of Nations to Self-Determination

The most widespread deception of the people by the bourgeoisie in the present war consists in their using the ideology of 'national liberation' to cloak the predatory aims. The British have promised the liberation of Belgium, the Germans – of Poland, etc. Actually, as we have seen, this is a war waged by the oppressors of most of the world's nations for the purpose of increasing and expanding that oppression.

Socialists cannot achieve their great aim without fighting against all oppression of nations. They must, therefore, unequivocally demand that the Social-Democratic parties of *oppressor* countries (especially of the so-called 'Great' Powers) should recognise and champion the *oppressed* nation's right to self-determination, in the specifically political sense of the term, i.e., the right to political secession. The socialist of a ruling or a colonial nation who does not stand for that right is a chauvinist.

The championing of this right, far from encouraging the formation of petty states, leads, on the contrary, to the freer, fearless and therefore wider and more universal formation of very large states and federations of states, which are more to the advantage of the masses and are more in keeping with economic development.

In their turn, the socialists of the *oppressed* nations must unfailingly fight for the complete unity of the *workers* of the oppressed and oppressor nationalities (this including organisational unity). The idea of the juridical separation of one nation from another (the so-called 'cultural-national autonomy' advocated by Bauer and Renner) is reactionary.

Imperialism is the epoch of the constantly increasing oppression of the nations of the world by a handful of 'Great' Powers; it is therefore impossible to fight for the socialist international revolution against imperialism unless the right of nations to self-determination is recognised. 'No nation can be free if it oppresses other nations' (Marx and Engels). A proletariat that tolerates the slightest violence by its 'own' nation cannot be a socialist proletariat.

1915: The Revolutionary Proletariat and the Rights of Nations to Self-Determination[*]

... The arguments advanced by Parabellum in support of his position boil down to an assertion that today all national problems,

[*]   *Collected Works*, Vol. 21: 407–9, 410–11, 413–14.

like those of Alsace-Lorraine, Armenia, etc., are problems of imperialism; that capital has outgrown the framework of national states; that it is impossible to turn the clock of history back to the obsolete ideal of national states, etc.

Let us see whether Parabellum's reasoning is correct.

First of all, it is Parabellum who is looking backward, not forward, when, in opposing working-class acceptance 'of the ideal of the national state', he looks towards Britain, France, Italy, Germany, i.e., countries where the movement for national liberation is a thing of the past, and not towards the East, towards Asia, Africa, and the colonies, where this movement is a thing of the present and the future. Mention of India, China, Persia, and Egypt will be sufficient.

Furthermore, imperialism means that capital has outgrown the framework of national states; it means that national oppression has been extended and heightened on a new historical foundation. Hence, it follows that, despite Parabellum, we must *link* the revolutionary struggle for socialism with a revolutionary programme on the national question.

From what Parabellum says, it appears that, *in the name of* the socialist revolution, he scornfully rejects a consistently revolutionary programme in the sphere of democracy. He is wrong to do so. The proletariat cannot be victorious except through democracy, i.e., by giving full effect to democracy and by linking with each step of its struggle democratic demands formulated in the most resolute terms. It is absurd to *contrapose* the socialist revolution and the revolutionary struggle against capitalism to a *single* problem of democracy, in this case, the national question. We must *combine* the revolutionary struggle against capitalism with a revolutionary programme and tactics on all democratic demands: a republic, a militia, the popular election of officials, equal rights for women, the self-determination of nations, etc. While capitalism exists, these demands – all of them – can only be accomplished as an exception, and even then in an incomplete and distorted form. Basing ourselves on the democracy already achieved, and exposing its incompleteness under capitalism, we demand the overthrow of capitalism, the expropriation of the bourgeoisie, as a necessary basis both for the abolition of the poverty of the masses and for the *complete* and *all-round* institution of *all* democratic reforms. Some of these reforms will be started before the overthrow of the bourgeoisie, others *in the course* of that overthrow, and still others after it. The social revolution is not a single battle, but a period covering a series of battles over all sorts of problems of economic and democratic reform, which are consummated only by the expropriation of the bourgeoisie. It is for the sake of this final aim that we must formulate *every one* of our democratic demands in a consistently revolutionary way. It is quite conceivable that the workers of some particular country will overthrow the bourgeoisie *before* even a single fundamental democratic reform has been fully achieved. It is, however, quite inconceivable that the proletariat, as a historical class, will be able to defeat the bourgeoisie, unless it is prepared for that by being educated in the spirit of the most consistent and resolutely revolutionary democracy.

Imperialism means the progressively mounting oppression of the nations of the world by a handful of Great Powers; it means a period of wars between the latter to extend and consolidate the oppression of nations; it means a period in which the masses of the people are deceived by hypocritical social-patriots, i.e., individuals who, under the pretext of the 'freedom of nations', 'the right of nations to self-determination', and 'defence of the fatherland', justify and defend the oppression of the majority of the world's nations by the Great Powers.

That is why the focal point in the Social-Democratic programme must be that division of nations into oppressor and oppressed which forms the *essence* of imperialism, and is *deceitfully* evaded by the social-chauvinists and Kautsky. This division is not significant from the angle of bourgeois pacifism or the philistine Utopia of peaceful competition among independent nations under capitalism, but it is most significant from the angle of the revolutionary struggle against imperialism. It is from this division that *our* definition of the 'right of nations to self-determination' must follow, a definition that is consistently democratic, revolutionary, and in *accord* with the general task of the immediate struggle for socialism. It is for that right, and in a struggle to achieve sincere recognition for it, that the Social-Democrats of the oppressor nations must demand that the oppressed nations should have the right of secession, for otherwise recognition of equal rights for nations and of international working-class solidarity would in fact be merely empty phrase-mongering, sheer hypocrisy. On the other hand, the Social-Democrats of the oppressed nations must attach prime significance to the unity and the merging of the workers of the oppressed nations with those of the oppressor nations; otherwise these Social-Democrats will involuntarily become the allies of their own national *bourgeoisie*, which always betrays the interests of the people and of democracy, and is *always* ready, in its turn, to annex territory and oppress other nations. ...

The imperialism of our days has led to a situation in which the Great-Power oppression of nations has become general. The view that a struggle must be conducted against the social-chauvinism of the dominant nations, who are now engaged in an imperialist war to enhance the oppression of nations, and are oppressing most of the world's nations and most of the earth's population – this view must be decisive, cardinal and basic in the national programme of Social-Democracy. ...

Russia is a prison of peoples, not only because of the military-feudal character of tsarism and not only because the Great-Russian bourgeoisie support tsarism, but also because the Polish, etc., bourgeoisie have sacrificed the freedom of nations and democracy in general for the interests of capitalist expansion. The Russian proletariat cannot march at the head of the people towards a victorious democratic revolution (which is its immediate task), or fight alongside its brothers, the proletarians of Europe, for a socialist revolution, without immediately demanding, fully and 'unreservedly' for all nations oppressed by tsarism, the freedom to secede from Russia. This we demand, not independently of our revolutionary struggle for socialism, but because this struggle will remain a hollow phrase if it is not linked up with a revolutionary approach to all questions of democracy, including the national question. We demand freedom of self-determination, *i.e.*, independence, *i.e.*, freedom of secession for the oppressed nations, not because we have dreamt of splitting up the country economically, or of the ideal of small states, but, on the contrary, because we want large states and the closer unity and even fusion of nations, only on a truly democratic, truly internationalist basis, which is inconceivable without the freedom to secede. Just as Marx, in 1869, demanded the separation of Ireland, not for a split between Ireland and Britain, but for a subsequent free union between them, not so as to secure 'justice for Ireland', but in the interests of the revolutionary struggle of the British proletariat, we in the same way consider the refusal of Russian socialists to demand freedom of self-determination for nations, in the sense we have indicated above, to be a direct betrayal of democracy, internationalism and socialism.

1916: Imperialism, the Highest Stage of Capitalism[*]

Preface to the French and German Editions (1920)

... It is proved in the pamphlet that the war of 1914–18 was imperialist (that is, an annexationist, predatory, war of plunder) on the part of both sides; it was a war for the division of the world, for the partition and repartition of colonies and spheres of influence of finance capital, etc.

Proof of what was the true social, or rather, the true class character of the war is naturally to be found, not in the diplomatic history of the war, but in an analysis of the *objective* position of the ruling *classes* in *all* the belligerent countries. In order to depict this objective position one must not take examples or isolated data (in view of the extreme complexity of the phenomena of social life it is always possible to select any number of examples or separate data to prove any proposition), but *all* the data on the *basis* of economic life in *all* the belligerent countries and the whole world.

It is precisely irrefutable summarised data of this kind that I quoted in describing the *partition of the world* in 1876 and 1914 (in Chapter VI) and the division of the world's *railways* in

[*]   *Collected Works*, Vol. 22: 189–91, 265–7, 271–4, 294–5, 298–303.

1890 and 1913 (in Chapter VII). Railways are a summation of the basic capitalist industries, coal, iron and steel; a summation and the most striking index of the development of world trade and bourgeois-democratic civilisation. How the railways are linked up with large-scale industry, with monopolies, syndicates, cartels, trusts, banks and the financial oligarchy is shown in the preceding chapters of the book. The uneven distribution of the railways, their uneven development – sums up, as it were, modern monopolist capitalism on a world-wide scale. And this summary proves that imperialist wars are absolutely inevitable under *such* an economic system, *as long as* private property in the means of production exists.

The building of railways seems to be a simple, natural, democratic, cultural and civilising enterprise; that is what it is in the opinion of the bourgeois professors who are paid to depict capitalist slavery in bright colours, and in the opinion of petty-bourgeois philistines. But as a matter of fact the capitalist threads, which in thousands of different intercrossings bind these enterprises with private property in the means of production in general, have converted this railway construction into an instrument for oppressing *a thousand million* people (in the colonies and semi-colonies), that is, more than half the population of the globe that inhabits the dependent countries, as well as the wage-slaves of capital in the 'civilised' countries.

Private property based on the labour of the small proprietor, free competition, democracy, all the catchwords with which the capitalists and their press deceive the workers and the peasants are things of the distant past. Capitalism has grown into a world system of colonial oppression and of the financial strangulation of the overwhelming majority of the population of the world by a handful of 'advanced' countries. And this 'booty' is shared between two or three powerful world plunderers armed to the teeth (America, Great Britain, Japan), who are drawing the whole world into *their* war over the division of *their* booty. ...

VII. Imperialism as a Special Stage of Capitalism

We must now try to sum up, to draw together the threads of what has been said above on the subject of imperialism. Imperialism emerged as the development and direct continuation of the fundamental characteristics of capitalism in general. But capitalism only became capitalist imperialism at a definite and very high stage of its development, when certain of its fundamental characteristics began to change into their opposites, when the features of the epoch of transition from capitalism to a higher social and economic system had taken shape and revealed themselves in all spheres. Economically, the main thing in this process is the displacement of capitalist free competition by capitalist monopoly. Free competition is the basic feature of capitalism, and of commodity production generally; monopoly is the exact opposite of free competition, but we have seen the latter being transformed into monopoly before our eyes, creating large-scale industry and forcing out small industry, replacing large-scale by still larger-scale industry, and carrying concentration of production and capital to the point where out of it has grown and is growing monopoly: cartels, syndicates and trusts, and merging with them, the capital of a dozen or so banks, which manipulate thousands of millions. At the same time the monopolies, which have grown out of free competition, do not eliminate the latter, but exist above it and alongside it, and thereby give rise to a number of very acute, intense antagonisms, frictions and conflicts. Monopoly is the transition from capitalism to a higher system.

If it were necessary to give the briefest possible definition of imperialism we should have to say that imperialism is the monopoly stage of capitalism. Such a definition would include what is most important, for, on the one hand, finance capital is the bank capital of a few very big monopolist banks, merged with the capital of the monopolist associations of industrialists; and, on the other hand, the division of the world is the transition from a colonial policy which has extended without hindrance to territories unseized by any capitalist power, to a colonial policy of monopolist possession of the territory of the world, which has been completely divided up.

But very brief definitions, although convenient, for they sum up the main points, are nevertheless inadequate, since we have to deduce from them some especially important features of the phenomenon that has to be defined. And so, without forgetting the conditional and relative value of all definitions in general, which can never embrace all the concatenations of a phenomenon in its full development, we must give a definition of imperialism that will include the following five of its basic features:

(1) the concentration of production and capital has developed to such a high stage that it has created monopolies which play a decisive role in economic life; (2) the merging of bank capital with industrial capital, and the creation, on the basis of this 'finance capital', of a financial oligarchy; (3) the export of capital as distinguished from the export of commodities acquires exceptional importance; (4) the formation of international monopolist capitalist associations which share the world among themselves, and (5) the territorial division of the whole world among the biggest capitalist powers is completed. Imperialism is capitalism at that stage of development at which the dominance of monopolies and finance capital is established; in which the export of capital has acquired pronounced importance; in which the division of the world among the international trusts has begun, in which the division of all territories of the globe among the biggest capitalist powers has been completed.

We shall see later that imperialism can and must be defined differently if we bear in mind not only the basic, purely economic concepts – to which the above definition is limited – but also the historical place of this stage of capitalism in relation to capitalism in general, or the relation between imperialism and the two main trends in the working-class movement. The thing to be noted at this point is that imperialism, as interpreted above, undoubtedly represents a special stage in the development of capitalism. To enable the reader to obtain the most well-grounded idea of imperialism, I deliberately tried to quote as extensively as possible *bourgeois* economists who have to admit the particularly incontrovertible facts concerning the latest stage of capitalist economy. With the same object in view, I have quoted detailed statistics which enable one to see to what degree bank capital, etc., has grown, in what precisely the transformation of quantity into quality, of developed capitalism into imperialism, was expressed. Needless to say, of course, all boundaries in nature and in society are conventional and changeable, and it would be absurd to argue, for example, about the particular year or decade in which imperialism 'definitely' became established. ...

'From the purely economic point of view,' writes Kautsky, 'it is not impossible that capitalism will yet go through a new phase, that of the extension of the policy of the cartels to foreign policy, the phase of ultra-imperialism', i.e., of a superimperialism, of a union of the imperialisms of the whole world and not struggles among them, a phase when wars shall cease under capitalism, a phase of 'the joint exploitation of the world by internationally united finance capital'.

We shall have to deal with this 'theory of ultra-imperialism' later on in order to show in detail how decisively and completely it breaks with Marxism. At present, in keeping with the general plan of the present work, we must examine the exact economic data on this question. 'From the purely economic point of view', is 'ultra-imperialism' possible, or is it ultra-nonsense?

If the purely economic point of view is meant to be a 'pure' abstraction, then all that can be said reduces itself to the following proposition: development is proceeding towards monopolies, hence, towards a single world monopoly, towards a single world trust. This is indisputable, but it is also as completely meaningless as is the statement that 'development is proceeding' towards the manufacture of foodstuffs in laboratories. In this sense the 'theory' of ultra-imperialism is no less absurd than a 'theory of ultra-agriculture' would be.

If, however, we are discussing the 'purely economic' conditions of the epoch of finance capital as a historically concrete epoch which began at the turn of the twentieth century, then the best reply that one can make to the lifeless abstractions of 'ultra-imperialism' (which serve exclusively a most reactionary aim: that of diverting attention from the depth of *existing* antagonisms) is to contrast them with the concrete economic realities of the present-day world economy. Kautsky's utterly meaningless talk about ultra-imperialism encourages, among other things, that profoundly mistaken idea which only brings grist to the mill of the apologists of imperialism, i.e., that the rule of finance capital *lessens* the unevenness and contradictions inherent in the world economy, whereas in reality it *increases* them.

R. Calwer, in his little book, *An Introduction to the World Economy*, made an attempt to summarise the main, purely economic, data that enable one to obtain a concrete picture of the internal relations of the world economy at the turn of the twentieth century. He divides the world into five 'main economic areas', as follows: (1) Central Europe (the whole of Europe with the exception of Russia and Great Britain); (2) Great Britain; (3) Russia; (4) Eastern Asia; (5) America; he includes the colonies in the 'areas' of the states to which they belong and 'leaves aside' a few countries not distributed according to areas, such as Persia, Afghanistan, and Arabia in Asia, Morocco and Abyssinia in Africa, etc.

Here is a brief summary of the economic data he quotes on these regions. [See table overleaf.]

We see three areas of highly developed capitalism (high development of means of transport, of trade and of industry): the Central European, the British and the American areas. Among these are three states which dominate the world: Germany, Great Britain, and the United States. Imperialist rivalry and the struggle between these countries have become extremely keen because Germany has only an insignificant area and few colonies; the creation of 'Central Europe' is still a matter for the future, it is being born in the midst of a desperate struggle. For the moment the distinctive feature of the whole of Europe is political disunity. In the British and American areas, on the other hand, political concentration is very highly developed, but there is a vast disparity between the immense colonies of the one and the insignificant colonies of the other. In the colonies, however, capitalism is only

Principal economic areas	Area (000,000 sq. km)	Population (000,000)	Transport		Trade	Industry		
			Railways (000 km)	Mercantile fleet (000,000 tons)	Imports and exports (000,000,000 marks)	Output (000,000 tons) Coal	Iron	Number of cotton spindles (000,000)
(1) Central Europe	27.6 (23.6)	388 (146)	204	8	41	251	15	26
(2) Britain	28.9 (28.6)	398 (355)	140	11	25	249	9	51
(3) Russia	22	131	63	1	3	16	3	7
(4) Eastern Asia	12	389	8	1	2	8	0.02	2
(5) America	30	148	379	6	14	245	14	19

beginning to develop. The struggle for South America is becoming more and more acute.

There are two areas where capitalism is little developed: Russia and Eastern Asia. In the former, the population is extremely sparse, in the latter it is extremely dense; in the former political concentration is high, in the latter it does not exist. The partitioning of China is only just beginning, and the struggle for it between Japan, the US, etc., is continually gaining in intensity.

Compare this reality – the vast diversity of economic and political conditions, the extreme disparity in the rate of development of the various countries, etc., and the violent struggles among the imperialist states – with Kautsky's silly little fable about 'peaceful' ultra-imperialism. Is this not the reactionary attempt of a frightened philistine to hide from stern reality? Are not the international cartels which Kautsky imagines are the embryos of 'ultra-imperialism' (in the same way as one 'can' describe the manufacture of tablets in a laboratory as ultra-agriculture in embryo) an example of the division *and the redivision* of the world, the transition from peaceful division to non-peaceful division and vice versa? Is not American and other finance capital, which divided the whole world peacefully with Germany's participation in, for example, the international rail syndicate, or in the international mercantile shipping trust, now engaged in *redividing* the world on the basis of a new relation of forces that is being changed by methods *anything but* peaceful? ...

Let us consider India, Indo-China and China. It is known that these three colonial and semi-colonial countries, with a population of 600–700 million, are subjected to the exploitation of the finance capital of several imperialist powers: Great Britain, France, Japan, the USA, etc. Let us assume that these imperialist countries form alliances against one another in order to protect or enlarge their possessions, their interests and their spheres of influence in these Asiatic states; these alliances will be 'inter-imperialist', or 'ultra-imperialist' alliances. Let us assume that *all* the imperialist countries conclude an alliance for the 'peaceful' division of these parts of Asia; this alliance would be an alliance of 'internationally united finance capital'. There are actual examples of alliances of this kind in the history of the twentieth century – the attitude of the powers to China, for instance. We ask, is it 'conceivable', assuming that the capitalist system remains intact – and this is precisely the assumption that Kautsky does make – that such alliances would be more than temporary, that they would eliminate friction, conflicts and struggle in every possible form?

The question has only to be presented clearly for any other than a negative answer to be impossible. This is because the only conceivable basis under capitalism for the division of spheres of influence, interests, colonies, etc., is a calculation of the *strength* of those participating, their general economic, financial, military strength, etc. And the strength of these participants in the division does not change to an equal degree, for the *even* development of different undertakings, trusts, branches of industry, or countries is impossible under capitalism. Half a century ago Germany was a miserable, insignificant country, if her capitalist strength is compared with that of the Britain of that time; Japan compared with Russia in the same way. Is it 'conceivable' that in ten or twenty years' time the relative strength of the imperialist powers will have remained unchanged? It is out of the question.

Therefore, in the realities of the capitalist system, and not in the banal philistine fantasies of English parsons, or of the German 'Marxist', Kautsky, 'inter-imperialist' or 'ultra-imperialist' alliances, no matter what form they may assume, whether of one imperialist coalition against another, or of a general alliance embracing *all* the imperialist powers, are *inevitably nothing* more than a 'truce' in periods between wars. Peaceful alliances prepare the ground for wars, and in their turn grow out of wars; the one conditions the other, producing alternating forms of peaceful and non-peaceful struggle on *one and the same* basis of imperialist connections and relations within world economics and world politics. …

X. The Place of Imperialism in History

We have seen that in its economic essence imperialism is monopoly capitalism. This in itself determines its place in history, for monopoly that grows out of the soil of free competition, and precisely out of free competition, is the transition from the capitalist system to a higher socio-economic order. We must take special note of the four principal types of monopoly, or principal manifestations of monopoly capitalism, which are characteristic of the epoch we are examining.

Firstly, monopoly arose out of the concentration of production at a very high stage. This refers to the monopolist capitalist associations, cartels, syndicates and trusts. We have seen the important part these play in present-day economic life. At the beginning of the twentieth century, monopolies had acquired complete supremacy in the advanced countries, and although the first steps towards the formation of the cartels were taken by countries enjoying the protection of high tariffs (Germany, America), Great Britain, with her system of free trade, revealed the same basic phenomenon, only a little later, namely, the birth of monopoly out of the concentration of production.

Secondly, monopolies have stimulated the seizure of the most important sources of raw materials, especially for the basic and most highly cartelised industries in capitalist society: the coal and iron industries. The monopoly of the most important sources of raw materials has enormously increased the power of big capital, and has sharpened the antagonism between cartelised and non-cartelised industry.

Thirdly, monopoly has sprung from the banks. The banks have developed from modest middleman enterprises into the monopolists of finance capital. Some three to five of the biggest banks in each of the foremost capitalist countries have achieved the 'personal link-up' between industrial and bank capital, and have concentrated in their hands the control of thousands upon thousands of millions which form the greater part of the capital and income of entire countries. A financial oligarchy, which throws a close network of dependence relationships over all the economic and political institutions of present-day bourgeois society without exception – such is the most striking manifestation of this monopoly.

Fourthly, monopoly has grown out of colonial policy. To the numerous 'old' motives of colonial policy, finance capital has added the struggle for the sources of raw materials, for the export of capital, for spheres of influence, i.e., for spheres for profitable deals, concessions, monopoly profits and so on, economic territory in general. When the colonies of the European powers, for instance, comprised only one-tenth of the territory of Africa (as was the case in 1876), colonial policy was able to develop – by methods other than those of monopoly – by the 'free grabbing' of territories, so to speak. But when nine-tenths of Africa had been seized (by 1900), when the whole world had been divided up, there was inevitably ushered in the era of monopoly possession of colonies and, consequently, of particularly intense struggle for the division and the redivision of the world.

The extent to which monopolist capital has intensified all the contradictions of capitalism is generally known. It is sufficient to mention the high cost of living and the tyranny of the cartels. This intensification of contradictions constitutes the most powerful driving force of the transitional period of history, which began from the time of the final victory of world finance capital.

Monopolies, oligarchy, the striving for domination and not for freedom, the exploitation of an increasing number of small or weak nations by a handful of the richest or most powerful nations – all these have given birth to those distinctive characteristics of imperialism which compel us to define it as parasitic or decaying capitalism. More and more prominently there emerges, as one of the tendencies of imperialism, the creation of the 'rentier state', the usurer state, in which the bourgeoisie to an ever-increasing degree lives on the proceeds of capital exports and by 'clipping coupons'. It would be a mistake to believe that this tendency to decay precludes the rapid growth of capitalism. It does not. In the epoch of imperialism, certain branches of industry, certain strata of the bourgeoisie and certain countries betray, to a greater or lesser degree, now one and now another of these tendencies. On the whole, capitalism is growing far more rapidly than before; but this growth is not only becoming more and more uneven in general, its unevenness also manifests itself, in particular, in the decay of the countries which are richest in capital (Britain).

In regard to the rapidity of Germany's economic development, Riesser, the author of the book on the big German banks, states: 'The progress of the preceding period (1848–70), which had not been exactly slow, compares with the rapidity with which the whole of Germany's national economy, and with it German banking, progressed during this period (1870–1905) in about the same way as the speed of the mail coach in the good old days compares with the speed of the present-day automobile … which is whizzing past so fast that it endangers not only innocent pedestrians in its path, but also the occupants of the car.' In its turn, this finance capital which has grown with such extraordinary rapidity is not unwilling, precisely because it has grown so quickly, to pass on to a more 'tranquil' possession of colonies which have to be seized – and not only by peaceful methods – from richer nations. In the United States, economic development in the last decades has been even more rapid than in Germany, *and for this very reason*, the parasitic features of modern American capitalism have stood out with particular prominence. On the other hand, a comparison of, say, the republican American bourgeoisie with the monarchist Japanese or German bourgeoisie shows that the most pronounced political distinction diminishes to an extreme degree in the epoch of imperialism – not because it is unimportant in general, but because in all these cases we are talking about a bourgeoisie which has definite features of parasitism.

The receipt of high monopoly profits by the capitalists in one of the numerous branches of industry, in one of the numerous countries, etc., makes it economically possible for them to bribe certain sections of the workers, and for a time a fairly considerable minority of them, and win them to the side of the bourgeoisie of a given industry or given nation against all the others. The intensification of antagonisms between imperialist nations for the division of the world increases this urge. And so there is created that bond between imperialism and opportunism, which revealed itself first and most clearly in Great Britain, owing to the fact that certain features of imperialist development were observable there much earlier than in other countries. Some writers, L. Martov, for example, are prone to wave aside the connection between imperialism and opportunism in the working-class movement – a particularly glaring fact at the present time – by resorting to 'official optimism' (*à la* Kautsky and Huysmans) like the following: the cause of the opponents of capitalism would be hopeless if it were progressive capitalism that led to the increase of opportunism, or, if it were the best-paid workers who were inclined towards opportunism, etc. We must have no illusions about 'optimism' of this kind. It is optimism in respect of opportunism; it is optimism which serves to conceal opportunism. As a matter of fact the extraordinary rapidity and the particularly revolting character of the development of opportunism is by no means a guarantee that its victory will be durable: the rapid growth of a painful abscess on a healthy body can only cause it to burst more quickly and thus relieve the body of it. The most dangerous of all in this respect are those who do not wish to understand that the fight against imperialism is a sham and humbug unless it is inseparably bound up with the fight against opportunism.

From all that has been said in this book on the economic essence of imperialism, it follows that we must define it as capitalism in transition, or, more precisely, as moribund capitalism. It is very instructive in this respect to note that bourgeois economists, in describing modern capitalism, frequently employ catchwords and phrases like 'interlocking', 'absence of isolation', etc.; 'in conformity with their functions and course of development', banks are 'not purely private business enterprises: they are more and more outgrowing the sphere of purely private business regulation'. And this very Riesser, whose words I have just quoted, declares with all seriousness that the 'prophecy' of the Marxists concerning 'socialisation' has 'not come true'!

What then does this catchword 'interlocking' express? It merely expresses the most striking feature of the process going on before our eyes. It shows that the observer counts the separate trees, but cannot see the wood. It slavishly copies the superficial, the fortuitous, the chaotic. It reveals the observer as one who is overwhelmed by the mass of raw material and is utterly incapable of appreciating its meaning and importance. Ownership of shares, the relations between owners of private property 'interlock in a haphazard way'. But underlying this interlocking, its very base, are the changing social relations of production. When a big enterprise assumes gigantic proportions, and, on the basis of an exact computation of mass data, organises according to plan the supply of primary raw materials to the extent of two-thirds, or three-fourths, of all that is necessary for tens of millions of people; when the raw materials are transported in a systematic and organised manner to the most suitable places of production, sometimes situated hundreds or thousands of miles from each other; when a single centre directs all the consecutive stages of processing the material right up to the manufacture of numerous varieties of finished articles; when these products are distributed according to a single plan among tens and hundreds of millions of consumers (the marketing of oil in America and Germany by the American oil trust) – then it becomes evident that we have socialisation of production, and not mere 'interlocking', that private economic and private property relations constitute a shell which no longer fits its contents, a shell which must inevitably decay if its removal is artificially delayed, a shell which may remain in a state of decay for a fairly long period (if, at the worst, the cure of the opportunist abscess is protracted), but which will inevitably be removed.

1917: Statistics and Sociology*

Foreword

Of the essays here presented for the reader's attention, some are published for the first time, others appeared in various periodicals before the war. They deal with a question which now, naturally, arouses especial interest – the significance and role of national movements, the relationship between the national and the international. The biggest drawback, one most frequently encountered in all the arguments on this question, is lack of concreteness and historical perspective. It has become customary to smuggle in every manner of contraband under cover of general phrases. We believe, therefore, that a few statistics will prove

* *Collected Works*, Vol. 23: 271–7.

anything but superfluous. A comparison with the lessons of the war of what we said before the war is not, in our view, unuseful. Unity of theory and perspective gives the essays continuity.

January 1917
The Author

Historical Background to National Movements

Facts are stubborn things, runs the English saying. It comes to mind, in particular, when a certain author waxes enthusiastic about the greatness of the 'nationality principle' in its different implications and relationships. What is more, in most cases the 'principle' is applied just as aptly, and is just as much in place, as the exclamation 'many happy returns of the day' by a certain folk-tale character at the sight of a funeral.

Precise facts, indisputable facts – they are especially abhorrent to this type of author, but are especially necessary if we want to form a proper understanding of this complicated, difficult and often deliberately confused question. But how to gather the facts? How to establish their connection and interdependence?

The most widely used, and most fallacious, method in the realm of social phenomena is to tear out *individual* minor facts and juggle with examples. Selecting chance examples presents no difficulty at all, but is of no value, or of purely negative value, for in each individual case everything hinges on the historically concrete situation. Facts, if we take them in their *entirety*, in their *interconnection*, are not only stubborn things, but undoubtedly proof-bearing things. Minor facts, if taken out of their entirety, out of their interconnection, if they are arbitrarily selected and torn out of context, are merely things for juggling, or even worse. For instance, when an author who was once a serious author and wishes to be regarded as such now too takes the fact of the Mongolian yoke and presents it as an example that explains certain events in twentieth-century Europe, can this be considered merely juggling, or would it not be more correct to consider it political chicanery? The Mongolian yoke is a fact of history, and one doubtlessly connected with the national question, just as in twentieth-century Europe we observe a number of facts likewise doubtlessly connected with this question. But you will find few people – of the type the French describe as 'national clowns' – who would venture, while claiming to be serious, to use this fact of the Mongolian yoke as an illustration of events in twentieth-century Europe.

The inference is clear: we must seek to build a reliable foundation of precise and indisputable facts that can be confronted to any of the 'general' or 'example-based' arguments now so grossly misused in certain countries. And if it is to be a real foundation, we must take not individual facts, but the *sum total* of facts, without *a single* exception, relating to the question under discussion. Otherwise there will be the inevitable, and fully justified, suspicion that the facts were selected or compiled arbitrarily, that instead of historical phenomena being presented in objective interconnection and interdependence and treated as a whole, we are presenting a 'subjective' concoction to justify what might prove to be a dirty business. This does happen … and more often than one might think.

Proceeding from these considerations, we have decided to begin with statistics, fully aware of course that statistics are deeply antipathetic to certain readers, who prefer 'flattering deception' to 'base truths', and to certain authors, who are prone to smuggle in political contraband under cover of 'general' disquisitions about internationalism, cosmopolitanism, nationalism, patriotism, etc.

Chapter 1: A Few Statistics

I

For a proper survey of the *whole* complex of data on national movements, we must take the *whole* population of the earth. And in so doing, two criteria must be established with the utmost accuracy and examined with the utmost fullness: first, national homogeneity or heterogeneity of the population of various states; second, division of states (or of state-like formations in cases where there is doubt that we are really dealing with a state) into politically independent and politically dependent.

Let us take the very latest data, published in 1916, and rely on two sources: one German, the *Geographical Statistical Tables* compiled by Otto Hübner, and one English, *The Statesman's Year-Book*. The first source will have to serve as a basis, for it contains much more comprehensive data on the question that interests us; the second we shall use to check and in some, mostly minor, cases to correct the first.

We shall begin our survey with the politically independent and nationally most homogeneous states. First and foremost among these is a group of *West-European* states, i.e., situated to the west of Russia and Austria.

Here we have 17 states of which five, however, though very homogeneous in national composition, are Lilliputian in size and population. These are Luxembourg, Monaco, San Marino, Liechtenstein and Andorra, with a combined population of only 310,000. Doubtlessly, it would be much more correct not to include them among the states under examination. Of the remaining twelve states, seven are absolutely homogeneous in national composition: in Italy, Holland, Portugal, Sweden and Norway, 99 per cent of the population are of one and the same nationality; in Spain and Denmark the proportion is 96 per cent. Then come three states with a nearly homogeneous national composition: France, England and Germany. In France, the Italians make up only 1.3 per cent, in areas annexed by Napoleon III by violating and falsifying the will of their people. England's annexed territory, Ireland, has a population of 4.4 million, which is less than one-tenth of the total (46.8 million). In Germany, out of a population of 64.9 million, the non-German element, which in practically all cases is just as nationally oppressed as the Irish in England, is represented by the Poles (5.47 per cent), Danes (0.25 per cent) and the population of Alsace-Lorrain (1.87 million). However, part of the latter (the exact proportion is not known) undoubtedly incline towards Germany, due not only to language, but also to economic interests and sympathies. All in all, about

5 million of Germany's population belong to alien, unequal and even oppressed nations.

Only two small states in Western Europe are of mixed national composition: Switzerland, whose population of somewhat less than 4 million consists of Germans (69 per cent), French (21 per cent) and Italians (8 per cent) – and Belgium (population less than 8 million; probably about 53 per cent Flemings and about 47 per cent French). It should be observed, however, that in spite of the high national heterogeneity in these countries, there can be no question of national oppression. In both countries all nationalities are equal under the constitution; in Switzerland this equality is fully implemented in practice; in Belgium there is inequality in relation to the Flemish population, though they make up the majority, but this inequality is insignificant compared, for instance, with what the Poles have to put up with in Germany, or the Irish in England, not to mention what has become customary in countries outside this group. That is why, incidentally, the term 'state of nationalities', to which the Austrian authors Karl Renner and Otto Bauer, opportunists on the national question, have given such wide currency, is correct only in a very restricted sense. Namely, if, on the one hand, we remember the special historical place of the majority of the countries of this type (which we shall discuss later) and, on the other, if we do not allow this term to obscure the fundamental difference between genuine national equality and national oppression.

Taking all the countries we have discussed, we get a group of twelve West-European states with a total population of 242 million. Of these 242 million only about 9.5 million, i.e., only 4 per cent, represent oppressed nations (in England and Germany). If we add together those sections of the population in all these countries that do not belong to the principal nationalities, we get about 15 million, i.e., 6 per cent.

On the whole, consequently, this group of states is characterised by the following: they are the most advanced capitalist countries, the most developed both economically and politically. Their cultural level, too, is the highest. In national composition most of these countries are homogeneous or nearly homogeneous.

National inequality, as a specific political phenomenon, plays a very insignificant part. What we have is the type of 'national state' people so often refer to, oblivious, in most cases, to the historically conditional and transitory character of this type in the general capitalist development of mankind. But that will be dealt with in its proper place.

It might be asked: Is this type of state confined to Western Europe? Obviously not. All its basic characteristics – economic (high and particularly rapid capitalist development), political (representative government), cultural and national – are to be observed also in the advanced states of America and Asia: the United States and Japan. The latter's national composition took shape long ago and is absolutely homogeneous: Japanese make up more than 99 per cent of the population. In the United States, the Negroes (and also the Mulattos and Indians) account for only 11.1 per cent. They should be classed as an oppressed nation, for the equality won in the Civil War of 1861–65 and guaranteed by the Constitution of the republic was in many respects increasingly curtailed in the chief Negro areas (the South) in connection with the transition from the progressive, pre-monopoly capitalism of 1860–70 to the reactionary, monopoly capitalism (imperialism) of the new era, which in America was especially sharply etched out by the Spanish-American imperialist war of 1898 (i.e., a war between two robbers over the division of the booty).

The white population of the United States makes up 88.7 per cent of the total, and of this figure 74.3 per cent are Americans and only 14.4 per cent foreign-born, i.e., immigrants. We know that the especially favourable conditions in America for the development of capitalism and the rapidity of this development have produced a situation in which vast national differences are speedily and fundamentally, as nowhere else in the world, smoothed out to form a single 'American' nation.

Adding the United States and Japan to the West-European countries enumerated above, we get 14 states with an aggregate population of 394 million, of which 26 million, i.e., 7 per cent, belong to unequal nationalities. Though this will be dealt with later, I might observe that at the turn of the century, i.e., in the period when capitalism was being transformed into imperialism, the majority of precisely these 14 advanced states made especially great strides in colonial policy, with the result that they now 'dispose' of a population of over 500 million in dependent and colonial countries.

II

The group of East-European states – Russia, Austria, Turkey (which geographically should now be considered among the Asian states, and economically a 'semi-colony'), and the six small Balkan states – Rumania, Bulgaria, Greece, Serbia, Montenegro and Albania – clearly reveal a fundamentally different picture. Not a *single* nationally fully homogeneous state! Only the small Balkan countries can be described as national states, though we should not forget that here, too, other nationalities comprise from 5 to 10 per cent, that very great numbers (compared with the total number of people belonging to the given nation) of Rumanians and Serbs live outside their 'own' states, and that, in general, the bourgeois-national development of Balkan statehood was not completed even by 'yesterday's' wars of 1911–12. There is not a *single* national state like Spain, Sweden, etc., among the small Balkan countries. And in the big East-European states, in all three, the proportion of their 'own', principal nationality is only 43 per cent. More than half the population of each of these three big states, 57 per cent, is made up of other nationalities (or, to use the official Russian term, of 'aliens'). Statistically, the difference between the West-European and East-European groups of states can be expressed as follows:

In the first group we have ten homogeneous or near homogeneous national states with an aggregate population of 231 million. There are only two heterogeneous states, but without national oppression and with constitutional and factual equality; their population is 11.5 million.

In the second group six states, with a population of 23 million, are nearly homogeneous; *three* states, with a population of 249 million, are heterogeneous or 'mixed' and without national equality.

On the whole, the proportion of the foreign-nationality population (i.e., not belonging to the principal nation[1] of the given state) is 6 per cent in Western Europe, and 7 per cent if we add the United States and Japan. In Eastern Europe, on the other hand, the proportion is 53 per cent![2]

---

1. The Great Hessians in Russia, the Germans and Hungarians in Austria, the Turks in Turkey. – *Lenin*
2. The manuscript breaks off here. – *Ed.*

7
1917 REVOLUTION

In February/March 1917, beginning with an uprising initiated by radicalising women workers on International Women's Day, a mass working-class insurgency demanding peace, freedom, and social justice overwhelmed the authorities of St Petersburg, was joined by troops (largely peasants in uniform) brought in to quell the crowds, and culminated in the forced abdication of Tsar Nicholas II and the collapse of the Russian monarchy, amid popular jubilation throughout the country. In the course of these events, soviets (democratic councils) once again arose in the working-class districts, at the same time many traditional politicians rallied – in part to stave off further radicalisation – to form a Provisional Government which promised to take matters in hand, organise elections for a Constituent Assembly (that would write a constitution for a democratic republic), and bring the revolution to a harmonious conclusion.

The Provisional Government contained elements from the upper classes, moderate conservatives and liberals, plus moderate socialists tied to the Socialist-Revolutionary Party (SRs) and Mensheviks. Despite anti-war sentiment, the Provisional Government was inclined to maintain Russia's involvement in the First World War. Despite the land hunger of the peasants, the Provisional Government was not inclined to confiscate and redistribute the land that was concentrated in the hands of the nobility. Despite terrible shortages of bread and other foodstuffs in the cities, the policies of the Provisional Government were unable to eliminate the causes of this problem (particularly the devastation of the war). When Lenin returned to Russia in April 1917, he presented at meetings of Bolsheviks and of all left-wing parties his 'April Theses' calling for a working-class revolution, supported by the peasantry, that would give all political power to the soviets and move forward to socialism.

While most of the non-Bolsheviks denounced this position as being crazy, most of the leading members of the Bolshevik party also sharply and openly disagreed. One of the most articulate of these was Lev Kamenev, who reminded Lenin and others that the traditional Bolshevik position was that the upcoming revolution would be a bourgeois-democratic revolution, pushed through by a 'revolutionary-democratic dictatorship of the proletariat and the peasantry', with a socialist revolution being a goal for the more distant future. In a campaign that soon won over a majority of his party, Lenin tirelessly argued for his new orientation – for example, in 'Letters on Tactics', which is excerpted here.

Along with winning a majority of Bolsheviks and others to a commitment to a revolution around such slogans as 'Overthrow the Provisional Government – All Power to the Soviets', which attracted growing numbers (including, most famously Leon Trotsky) to the ranks of the Bolshevik party, Lenin worked to advance his own understanding, and that of others, around a more radical comprehension of Marx's conceptions of state and revolution. This culminated in one of his most famous and important theoretical works, *The State and Revolution*, the bulk of whose opening chapter is reproduced here.

By October/November, after considerable turmoil and intense experiences, majorities in the soviets of Russia had been won to the Bolshevik proposals, which had been championed as well by a very substantial break-away from the SRs – the Left Socialist-Revolutionaries – as well as anarchists and even some left-wing Mensheviks. This resulted in the Bolshevik-led revolution that overthrew the Provisional Government and handed power over to the All-Russian Congress of the Soviets. Lenin issued a proclamation, reprinted here, 'To the Population' to take power into their own hands.

The new Soviet government (in which the Congress of Soviets established an executive body, headed by Lenin and consisting of a coalition of Bolsheviks and Left SRs) went ahead with elections for a long-awaited Constituent Assembly. But the results were odd. While the Bolsheviks won an overwhelming majority in working-class and urban areas (about 25 per cent of the total vote), the Socialist-Revolutionary Party won a decisive majority in the population-dense rural areas. While the peasants were basically voting for the SR programme of 'land to the peasants', this had been abandoned by much of the winning SR candidates list (drawn up before the split in the SR party). The programme the peasants were voting for was now represented by the Left SRs (who only had a fraction of the SR seats) and their Bolshevik allies. When the Constituent Assembly gathered in early January 1918, a majority of its representatives (Right SRs getting 40 per cent, with handfuls of Kadets, Mensheviks and others) were openly hostile to the notion that all power would be vested in the soviets. The Soviet government then dissolved the Constituent Assembly, with the backing not only of Bolsheviks, but also of Left SRs, anarchists, and many others, and with almost no popular outcry. Included here is Lenin's 'Speech on the Dissolution of the Constituent Assembly', explaining the situation to the central executive committee of the Soviets.

1917: Letters on Tactics*

First Letter: Assessment of the Present Situation

Marxism requires of us a strictly exact and objectively verifiable analysis of the relations of classes and of the concrete features peculiar to each historical situation. We Bolsheviks have always tried to meet this requirement, which is absolutely essential for giving a scientific foundation to policy.

'Our theory is not a dogma, but a guide to action', Marx and Engels always said, rightly ridiculing the mere memorising and repetition of 'formulas', that at best are capable only of marking out *general* tasks, which are necessarily modifiable by the *concrete* economic and political conditions of each particular *period* of the historical process.

What, then, are the clearly established objective *facts* which the party of the revolutionary proletariat must now be guided by in defining the tasks and forms of its activity?

Both in my first *Letter from Afar* ('The First Stage of the First Revolution') published in *Pravda* Nos 14 and 15, 21 and 22 March 1917, and in my theses, I define 'the specific feature of the present situation in Russia' as a period of *transition* from the first stage of the revolution to the second. I therefore considered the basic slogan, the 'task of the day' at *this* moment to be: 'Workers, you have performed miracles of proletarian heroism, the heroism of the people, in the civil war against tsarism. You must perform miracles of organisation, organisation of the proletariat and of the whole people, to prepare the way for your victory in the second stage of the revolution' (*Pravda* No. 15).

What, then, is the first stage?

It is the passing of state power to the bourgeoisie.

Before the February–March revolution of 1917, state power in Russia was in the hands of one old class, namely, the feudal landed nobility, headed by Nicholas Romanov.

After the revolution, the power is in the hands of a *different* class, a new class, namely, the *bourgeoisie*.

---

* *Collected Works*, Vol. 24: 43–5, 52, 53–4.

The passing of state power from one *class* to another is the first, the principal, the basic sign of a *revolution*, both in the strictly scientific and in the practical political meaning of that term.

To this extent, the bourgeois, or the bourgeois-democratic, revolution in Russia is *completed*.

But at this point we hear a clamour of protest from people who readily call themselves 'old Bolsheviks'. Didn't we always maintain, they say, that the bourgeois-democratic revolution is completed only by the 'revolutionary-democratic dictatorship of the proletariat and the peasantry'? Is the agrarian revolution, which is also a bourgeois-democratic revolution, completed? Is it not a fact, on the contrary, that it has *not even* started?

My answer is: The Bolshevik slogans and ideas *on the whole* have been confirmed by history; but *concretely* things have worked out *differently*; they are more original, more peculiar, more variegated than anyone could have expected.

To ignore or overlook this fact would mean taking after those 'old Bolsheviks' who more than once already have played so regrettable a role in the history of our Party by reiterating formulas senselessly *learned by rote* instead of *studying* the specific features of the new and living reality.

'The revolutionary-democratic dictatorship of the proletariat and the peasantry' has *already* become a reality[1] in the Russian revolution, for this 'formula' envisages only a *relation of classes*, and not a *concrete political institution implementing* this relation, this co-operation. 'The Soviet of Workers' and Soldiers' Deputies' – there you have the 'revolutionary-democratic dictatorship of the proletariat and the peasantry' already accomplished in reality.

This formula is already antiquated. Events have moved it from the realm of formulas into the realm of reality, clothed it with flesh and bone, concretised it and *thereby* modified it.

A new and different task now faces us: to effect a split *within* this dictatorship between the proletarian elements (the anti-defencist, internationalist, 'Communist' elements, who stand for a transition to the commune) and the *small-proprietor* or *petty-bourgeois*

1. In a certain form and to a certain extent.

elements (Chkheidze, Tsereteli, Steklov, the Socialist-Revolution-aries and the other revolutionary defencists, who are opposed to moving towards the commune and are in favour of 'supporting' the bourgeoisie and the bourgeois government).

The person who *now* speaks only of a 'revolutionary-democratic dictatorship of the proletariat and the peasantry' is behind the times, consequently, he has in effect *gone over* to the petty bourgeoisie against the proletarian class struggle; that person should be consigned to the archive of 'Bolshevik' pre-revolutionary antiques (it may be called the archive of 'old Bolsheviks').

The revolutionary-democratic dictatorship of the proletariat and the peasantry has already been realised, but in a highly original manner, and with a number of extremely important modifications. I shall deal with them separately in one of my next letters. For the present, it is essential to grasp the incontestable truth that a Marxist must take cognisance of real life, of the true facts of *reality*, and not cling to a theory of yesterday, which, like all theories, at best only outlines the main and the general, only *comes near* to embracing life in all its complexity.

'Theory, my friend, is grey, but green is the eternal tree of life.'

To deal with the question of 'completion' of the bourgeois revolution *in the old way* is to sacrifice living Marxism to the dead letter.

According to the old way of thinking, the rule of the bourgeoisie could and should be *followed* by the rule of the proletariat and the peasantry, by their dictatorship. ...

Comrade Kamenev's mistake is that even in 1917 he sees only *the past* of the revolutionary-democratic dictatorship of the proletariat and the peasantry. As a matter of fact its *future* has already begun, for the interests and policies of the wage-worker and the petty proprietor have *actually* diverged already, even in such an important question as that of 'defencism', that of the attitude towards the imperialist war. ...

I am deeply convinced that the Soviets will make the independent activity of the *masses* a reality more quickly and effectively than will a parliamentary republic (I shall compare the two types of states in greater detail in another letter). They will more effectively, more practically and more correctly decide what *steps* can be taken towards socialism and how these steps should be taken. Control over a bank, the merging of all banks into one, is *not yet* socialism, but it is *a step towards* socialism. Today such steps are being taken in Germany by the Junkers and the bourgeoisie against the people. Tomorrow the Soviet will be able to take these steps more effectively for the benefit of the people if the whole state power is in its hands.

What *compels* such steps?

Famine. Economic disorganisation. Imminent collapse. The horrors of war. The horrors of the wounds inflicted on mankind by the war.

1917: The State and Revolution[*]

Chapter 1: Class Society and the State

1. The State: A Product of the Irreconcilability of Class Antagonisms

What is now happening to Marx's theory has, in the course of history, happened repeatedly to the theories of revolutionary thinkers and leaders of oppressed classes fighting for emancipation. During the lifetime of great revolutionaries, the oppressing classes constantly hounded them, received their theories with the most savage malice, the most furious hatred and the most unscrupulous campaigns of lies and slander. After their death, attempts are made to convert them into harmless icons, to canonise them, so to say, and to hallow their *names* to a certain extent for the 'consolation' of the oppressed classes and with the object of duping the latter, while at the same time robbing the revolutionary theory of its *substance*, blunting its revolutionary edge and vulgarising it. Today, the bourgeoisie and the opportunists within the labour movement concur in this doctoring of Marxism. They omit, obscure or distort the revolutionary side of this theory, its revolutionary soul. They

* *Collected Works*, Vol. 25: 390–406.

push to the foreground and extol what is or seems acceptable to the bourgeoisie. All the social-chauvinists are now 'Marxists' (don't laugh!). And more and more frequently German bourgeois scholars, only yesterday specialists in the annihilation of Marxism, are speaking of the 'national-German' Marx, who, they claim, educated the labour unions which are so splendidly organised for the purpose of waging a predatory war!

In these circumstances, in view of the unprecedently widespread distortion of Marxism, our prime task is to *re-establish* what Marx really taught on the subject of the state. This will necessitate a number of long quotations from the works of Marx and Engels themselves. Of course, long quotations will render the text cumbersome and not help at all to make it popular reading, but we cannot possibly dispense with them. All, or at any rate all the most essential passages in the works of Marx and Engels on the subject of the state must by all means be quoted as fully as possible so that the reader may form an independent opinion of the totality of the views of the founders of scientific socialism, and of the evolution of those views, and so that their distortion by the 'Kautskyism' now prevailing may be documentarily proved and clearly demonstrated.

Let us begin with the most popular of Engels's works, *The Origin of the Family, Private Property and the State*, the sixth edition of which was published in Stuttgart as far back as 1894. We have to translate the quotations from the German originals, as the Russian translations, while very numerous, are for the most part either incomplete or very unsatisfactory.

Summing up his historical analysis, Engels says:

> The state is, therefore, by no means a power forced on society from without; just as little is it 'the reality of the ethical idea', 'the image and reality of reason', as Hegel maintains. Rather, it is a product of society at a certain stage of development; it is the admission that this society has become entangled in an insoluble contradiction with itself, that it has split into irreconcilable antagonisms which it is powerless to dispel. But in order that these antagonisms, these classes with conflicting economic interests, might not consume themselves and

society in fruitless struggle, it became necessary to have a power, seemingly standing above society, that would alleviate the conflict and keep it within the bounds of 'order'; and this power, arisen out of society but placing itself above it, and alienating itself more and more from it, is the state.

This expresses with perfect clarity the basic idea of Marxism with regard to the historical role and the meaning of the state. The state is a product and a manifestation of the *irreconcilability* of class antagonisms. The state arises where, when and insofar as class antagonism objectively *cannot* be reconciled. And, conversely, the existence of the state proves that the class antagonisms are irreconcilable.

It is on this most important and fundamental point that the distortion of Marxism, proceeding along two main lines, begins.

On the one hand, the bourgeois, and particularly the petty-bourgeois, ideologists, compelled under the weight of indisputable historical facts to admit that the state only exists where there are class antagonisms and a class struggle, 'correct' Marx in such a way as to make it appear that the state is an organ for the *reconciliation* of classes. According to Marx, the state could neither have arisen nor maintained itself had it been possible to reconcile classes. From what the petty-bourgeois and philistine professors and publicists say, with quite frequent and benevolent references to Marx, it appears that the state does reconcile classes. According to Marx, the state is an organ of class *rule*, an organ for the *oppression* of one class by another; it is the creation of 'order', which legalises and perpetuates this oppression by moderating the conflict between classes. In the opinion of the petty-bourgeois politicians, however, order means the reconciliation of classes, and not the oppression of one class by another; to alleviate the conflict means reconciling classes and not depriving the oppressed classes of definite means and methods of struggle to overthrow the oppressors.

For instance, when, in the revolution of 1917, the question of the significance and role of the state arose in all its magnitude as a practical question demanding immediate action, and, moreover, action on a mass scale, all the Social-Revolutionaries and Mensheviks descended at once to the petty-bourgeois theory that the 'state' 'reconciles' classes. Innumerable resolutions and articles by politicians of both these parties are thoroughly saturated with this petty-bourgeois and philistine 'reconciliation' theory. That the state is an organ of the rule of a definite class which *cannot* be reconciled with its antipode (the class opposite to it) is something the petty-bourgeois democrats will never be able to understand. Their attitude to the state is one of the most striking manifestations of the fact that our Socialist-Revolutionaries and Mensheviks are not socialists at all (a point that we Bolsheviks have always maintained), but petty-bourgeois democrats using near-socialist phraseology.

On the other hand, the 'Kautskyite' distortion of Marxism is far more subtle. 'Theoretically', it is not denied that the state is an organ of class rule, or that class antagonisms are irreconcilable. But what is overlooked or glossed over is this: if the state is the product of the irreconcilability of class antagonisms, if it is a power standing *above* society and '*alienating* itself *more and more* from it', it is clear that the liberation of the oppressed class is impossible not only without a violent revolution, *but also without the destruction* of the apparatus of state power which was created by the ruling class and which is the embodiment of this 'alienation'. As we shall see later, Marx very explicitly drew this theoretically self-evident conclusion on the strength of a concrete historical analysis of the tasks of the revolution. And – as we shall show in detail further on – it is this conclusion which Kautsky has 'forgotten' and distorted.

2. Special Bodies of Armed Men, Prisons, etc.

Engels continues:

> As distinct from the old gentile [tribal or clan] order, the state, first, divides its subjects *according to territory*. ...

This division seems 'natural' to us, but it costs a prolonged struggle against the old organisation according to generations or tribes.

> The second distinguishing feature is the establishment of a *public power* which no longer directly coincides with the population organising itself as an armed force. This special, public power is necessary because a self-acting armed organisation of the population has become impossible since the split into classes. ... This public power exists in every state; it consists not merely of armed men but also of material adjuncts, prisons, and institutions of coercion of all kinds, of which gentile [clan] society knew nothing. ...

Engels elucidates the concept of the 'power' which is called the state, a power which arose from society but places itself above it and alienates itself more and more from it. What does this power mainly consist of? It consists of special bodies of armed men having prisons, etc., at their command.

We are justified in speaking of special bodies of armed men, because the public power which is an attribute of every state 'does not directly coincide' with the armed population, with its 'self-acting armed organisation'.

Like all great revolutionary thinkers, Engels tries to draw the attention of the class-conscious workers to what prevailing philistinism regards as least worthy of attention, as the most habitual thing, hallowed by prejudices that are not only deep-rooted but, one might say, petrified. A standing army and police are the chief instruments of state power. But how can it be otherwise?

From the viewpoint of the vast majority of Europeans of the end of the nineteenth century, whom Engels was addressing, and who had not gone through or closely observed a single great revolution, it could not have been otherwise. They could not understand at all what a 'self-acting armed organisation of the population' was. When asked why it became necessary to have special bodies of armed men placed above society and alienating themselves from it (police and a standing army), the West-European and Russian philistines are inclined to utter a few phrases borrowed from

Spencer or Mikhailovsky, to refer to the growing complexity of social life, the differentiation of functions, and so on.

Such a reference seems 'scientific', and effectively lulls the ordinary person to sleep by obscuring the important and basic fact, namely, the split of society into irreconcilable antagonistic classes.

Were it not for this split, the 'self-acting armed organisation of the population' would differ from the primitive organisation of a stick-wielding herd of monkeys, or of primitive men, or of men united in clans, by its complexity, its high technical level, and so on. But such an organisation would still be possible.

It is impossible because civilised society is split into antagonistic, and, moreover, irreconcilably antagonistic classes, whose 'self-acting' arming would lead to an armed struggle between them. A state arises, a special power is created, special bodies of armed men, and every revolution, by destroying the state apparatus, shows us the naked class struggle, clearly shows us how the ruling class strives to restore the special bodies of armed men which serve it, and how the oppressed class strives to create a new organisation of this kind, capable of serving the exploited instead of the exploiters.

In the above argument, Engels raises theoretically the very same question which every great revolution raises before us in practice, palpably and, what is more, on a scale of mass action, namely, the question of the relationship between 'special' bodies of armed men and the 'self-acting armed organisation of the population'. We shall see how this question is specifically illustrated by the experience of the European and Russian revolutions.

But to return to Engels's exposition.

He points out that sometimes – in certain parts of North America, for example – this public power is weak (he has in mind a rare exception in capitalist society, and those parts of North America in its pre-imperialist days where the free colonist predominated), but that, generally speaking, it grows stronger:

> It [the public power] grows stronger, however, in proportion as class antagonisms within the state become more acute, and as adjacent

> states become larger and more populous. We have only to look at our present-day Europe, where class struggle and rivalry in conquest have tuned up the public power to such a pitch that it threatens to swallow the whole of society and even the state.

This was written not later than the early nineties of the last century, Engels's last preface being dated 16 June 1891. The turn towards imperialism – meaning the complete domination of the trusts, the omnipotence of the big banks, a grand-scale colonial policy, and so forth – was only just beginning in France, and was even weaker in North America and in Germany. Since then 'rivalry in conquest' has taken a gigantic stride, all the more because by the beginning of the second decade of the twentieth century the world had been completely divided up among these 'rivals in conquest', i.e., among the predatory Great Powers. Since then, military and naval armaments have grown fantastically and the predatory war of 1914–17 for the domination of the world by Britain or Germany, for the division of the spoils, has brought the 'swallowing' of all the forces of society by the rapacious state power close to complete catastrophe.

Engels could, as early as 1891, point to 'rivalry in conquest' as one of the most important distinguishing features of the foreign policy of the Great Powers, while the social-chauvinist scoundrels have ever since 1914, when this rivalry, many times intensified, gave rise to an imperialist war, been covering up the defence of the predatory interests of 'their own' bourgeoisie with phrases about 'defence of the fatherland', 'defence of the republic and the revolution', etc.!

3. The State: An Instrument for the Exploitation of the Oppressed Class

The maintenance of the special public power standing above society requires taxes and state loans. 'Having public power and the right to levy taxes,' Engels writes, the officials now stand, as organs of society, *above* society. The free, voluntary respect that was accorded to the organs of the gentile [clan] constitution does not satisfy them, even if they could gain it. ...

Special laws are enacted proclaiming the sanctity and immunity of the officials. 'The shabbiest police servant' has more 'authority' than the representative of the clan, but even the head of the military power of a civilised state may well envy the elder of a clan the 'unrestrained respect' of society.

The question of the privileged position of the officials as organs of state power is raised here. The main point indicated is: what is it that places them above society? We shall see how this theoretical question was answered in practice by the Paris Commune in 1871 and how it was obscured from a reactionary standpoint by Kautsky in 1912.

> Because the state arose from the need to hold class antagonisms in check, but because it arose, at the same time, in the midst of the conflict of these classes, it is, as a rule, the state of the most powerful, economically dominant class, which, through the medium of the state, becomes also the politically dominant class, and thus acquires new means of holding down and exploiting the oppressed class. ...

The ancient and feudal states were organs for the exploitation of the slaves and serfs; likewise, 'the modern representative state is an instrument of exploitation of wage-labor by capital. By way of exception, however, periods occur in which the warring classes balance each other so nearly that the state power as ostensible mediator acquires, for the moment, a certain degree of independence of both. ...' Such were the absolute monarchies of the seventeenth and eighteenth centuries, the Bonapartism of the First and Second Empires in France, and the Bismarck regime in Germany.

Such, we may add, is the Kerensky government in republican Russia since it began to persecute the revolutionary proletariat, at a moment when, owing to the leadership of the petty-bourgeois democrats, the Soviets have already become impotent, while the bourgeoisie are not yet strong enough simply to disperse them.

In a democratic republic, Engels continues, 'wealth exercises its power indirectly, but all the more surely', first, by means of the 'direct corruption of officials' (America); secondly, by means of an 'alliance of the government and the Stock Exchange' (France and America).

At present, imperialism and the domination of the banks have 'developed' into an exceptional art both these methods of upholding and giving effect to the omnipotence of wealth in democratic republics of all descriptions. Since, for instance, in the very first months of the Russian democratic republic, one might say during the honeymoon of the 'socialist' SRs and Mensheviks joined in wedlock to the bourgeoisie, in the coalition government, Mr Palchinsky obstructed every measure intended for curbing the capitalists and their marauding practices, their plundering of the state by means of war contracts; and since later on Mr Palchinsky, upon resigning from the Cabinet (and being, of course, replaced by another quite similar Palchinsky), was 'rewarded' by the capitalists with a lucrative job with a salary of 120,000 rubles per annum – what would you call that? Direct or indirect bribery? An alliance of the government and the syndicates, or 'merely' friendly relations? What role do the Chernovs, Tseretelis, Avksentyevs and Skobelevs play? Are they the 'direct' or only the indirect allies of the millionaire treasury-looters?

Another reason why the omnipotence of 'wealth' is more *certain* in a democratic republic is that it does not depend on defects in the political machinery or on the faulty political shell of capitalism. A democratic republic is the best possible political shell for capitalism, and, therefore, once capital has gained possession of this very best shell (through the Palchinskys, Chernovs, Tseretelis and Co.), it establishes its power so securely, so firmly, that *no* change of persons, institutions or parties in the bourgeois-democratic republic can shake it.

We must also note that Engels is most explicit in calling universal suffrage an instrument of bourgeois rule. Universal suffrage, he says, obviously taking account of the long experience of German Social-Democracy, is

> the gauge of the maturity of the working class. It cannot and never will be anything more in the present-day state.

The petty-bourgeois democrats, such as our Socialist-Revolutionaries and Mensheviks, and also their twin brothers, all the social-chauvinists and opportunists of Western Europe, expect just this 'more' from universal suffrage. They themselves share, and instil into the minds of the people, the false notion that universal suffrage 'in the *present-day* state' is really capable of revealing the will of the majority of the working people and of securing its realisation.

Here, we can only indicate this false notion, only point out that Engels's perfectly clear statement is distorted at every step in the propaganda and agitation of the 'official' (i.e., opportunist) socialist parties. A detailed exposure of the utter falsity of this notion which Engels brushes aside here is given in our further account of the views of Marx and Engels on the '*present-day*' state.

Engels gives a general summary of his views in the most popular of his works in the following words:

> The state, then, has not existed from all eternity. There have been societies that did without it, that had no idea of the state and state power. At a certain stage of economic development, which was necessarily bound up with the split of society into classes, the state became a necessity owing to this split. We are now rapidly approaching a stage in the development of production at which the existence of these classes not only will have ceased to be a necessity, but will become a positive hindrance to production. They will fall as they arose at an earlier stage. Along with them the state will inevitably fall. Society, which will reorganise production on the basis of a free and equal association of the producers, will put the whole machinery of state where it will then belong: into a museum of antiquities, by the side of the spinning-wheel and the bronze axe.

We do not often come across this passage in the propaganda and agitation literature of the present-day Social-Democrats. Even when we do come across it, it is mostly quoted in the same manner as one bows before an icon, i.e., it is done to show official respect for Engels, and no attempt is made to gauge the breadth and depth of the revolution that this relegating of 'the whole machinery of state to a museum of antiquities' implies. In most cases we do not even find an understanding of what Engels calls the state machine.

4. The 'Withering Away' of the State, and Violent Revolution

Engels's words regarding the 'withering away' of the state are so widely known, they are often quoted, and so clearly reveal the essence of the customary adaptation of Marxism to opportunism that we must deal with them in detail. We shall quote the whole argument from which they are taken.

> *The proletariat seizes from state power and turns the means of production into state property to begin with.* But thereby it abolishes itself as the proletariat, abolishes all class distinctions and class antagonisms, and abolishes also the state as state. Society thus far, operating amid class antagonisms, needed the state, that is, an organisation of the particular exploiting class, for the maintenance of its external conditions of production, and, therefore, especially, for the purpose of forcibly keeping the exploited class in the conditions of oppression determined by the given mode of production (slavery, serfdom or bondage, wage-labour). The state was the official represent-ative of society as a whole, its concentration in a visible corporation. But it was this only insofar as it was the state of that class which itself represented, for its own time, society as a whole: in ancient times, the state of slave-owning citizens; in the Middle Ages, of the feudal nobility; in our own time, of the bourgeoisie. When at last it becomes the real representative of the whole of society, it renders itself unnecessary. As soon as there is no longer any social class to be held in subjection, as soon as class rule, and the individual struggle for existence based upon the present anarchy in production, with the collisions and excesses arising from this struggle, are removed, nothing

more remains to be held in subjection – nothing necessitating a special coercive force, a state. The first act by which the state really comes forward as the representative of the whole of society – the taking possession of the means of production in the name of society – is also its last independent act as a state. State interference in social relations becomes, in one domain after another, superfluous, and then dies down of itself. The government of persons is replaced by the administration of things, and by the conduct of processes of production. The state is not 'abolished'. It withers away. This gives the measure of the value of the phrase 'a free people's state', both as to its justifiable use for a long time from an agitational point of view, and as to its ultimate scientific insufficiency; and also of the so-called anarchists' demand that the state be abolished overnight.

It is safe to say that of this argument of Engels's, which is so remarkably rich in ideas, only one point has become an integral part of socialist thought among modern socialist parties, namely, that according to Marx that state 'withers away' – as distinct from the anarchist doctrine of the 'abolition' of the state. To prune Marxism to such an extent means reducing it to opportunism, for this 'interpretation' only leaves a vague notion of a slow, even, gradual change, of absence of leaps and storms, of absence of revolution. The current, widespread, popular, if one may say so, conception of the 'withering away' of the state undoubtedly means obscuring, if not repudiating, revolution.

Such an 'interpretation', however, is the crudest distortion of Marxism, advantageous only to the bourgeoisie. In point of theory, it is based on disregard for the most important circumstances and considerations indicated in, say, Engels's 'summary' argument we have just quoted in full.

In the first place, at the very outset of his argument, Engels says that, in seizing state power, the proletariat thereby 'abolishes the state as state'. It is not done to ponder over the meaning of this. Generally, it is either ignored altogether, or is considered to be something in the nature of 'Hegelian weakness' on Engels's part. As a matter of fact, however, these words briefly express the experience of one of the greatest proletarian revolutions, the Paris Commune of 1871, of which we shall speak in greater detail in its proper place. As a matter of fact, Engels speaks here of the proletariat revolution 'abolishing' the *bourgeois* state, while the words about the state withering away refer to the remnants of the *proletarian* state *after* the socialist revolution. According to Engels, the bourgeois state does not 'wither away', but is 'abolished' by the proletariat in the course of the revolution. What withers away after this revolution is the proletarian state or semi-state.

Secondly, the state is a 'special coercive force'. Engels gives this splendid and extremely profound definition here with the utmost lucidity. And from it follows that the 'special coercive force' for the suppression of the proletariat by the bourgeoisie, of millions of working people by handfuls of the rich, must be replaced by a 'special coercive force' for the suppression of the bourgeoisie by the proletariat (the dictatorship of the proletariat). This is precisely what is meant by 'abolition of the state as state'. This is precisely the 'act' of taking possession of the means of production in the name of society. And it is self-evident that *such* a replacement of one (bourgeois) 'special force' by another (proletarian) 'special force' cannot possibly take place in the form of 'withering away'.

Thirdly, in speaking of the state 'withering away', and the even more graphic and colourful 'dying down of itself', Engels refers quite clearly and definitely to the period *after* 'the state has taken possession of the means of production in the name of the whole of society', that is, *after* the socialist revolution. We all know that the political form of the 'state' at that time is the most complete democracy. But it never enters the head of any of the opportunists, who shamelessly distort Marxism, that Engels is consequently speaking here of *democracy* 'dying down of itself', or 'withering away'. This seems very strange at first sight. But it is 'incomprehensible' only to those who have not thought about democracy *also* being a state and, consequently, also disappearing when the state disappears. Revolution alone can 'abolish' the bourgeois state. The state in general, i.e., the most complete democracy, can only 'wither away'.

Fourthly, after formulating his famous proposition that 'the state withers away', Engels at once explains specifically that this proposition is directed against both the opportunists and the anarchists. In doing this, Engels puts in the forefront that conclusion, drawn from the proposition that 'the state withers away', which is directed against the opportunists.

One can wager that out of every 10,000 persons who have read or heard about the 'withering away' of the state, 9,990 are completely unaware, or do not remember, that Engels directed his conclusions from that proposition *not* against anarchists *alone*. And of the remaining ten, probably nine do not know the meaning of a 'free people's state' or why an attack on this slogan means an attack on opportunists. This is how history is written! This is how a great revolutionary teaching is imperceptibly falsified and adapted to prevailing philistinism. The conclusion directed against the anarchists has been repeated thousands of times; it has been vulgarised, and rammed into people's heads in the shallowest form, and has acquired the strength of a prejudice, whereas the conclusion directed against the opportunists has been obscured and 'forgotten'!

The 'free people's state' was a programme demand and a catchword current among the German Social-Democrats in the seventies. This catchword is devoid of all political content except that it describes the concept of democracy in a pompous philistine fashion. Insofar as it hinted in a legally permissible manner at a democratic republic, Engels was prepared to 'justify' its use 'for a time' from an agitational point of view. But it was an opportunist catchword, for it amounted to something more than prettifying bourgeois democracy, and was also failure to understand the socialist criticism of the state in general. We are in favour of a democratic republic as the best form of state for the proletariat under capitalism. But we have no right to forget that wage slavery is the lot of the people even in the most democratic bourgeois republic. Furthermore, every state is a 'special force' for the suppression of the oppressed class. Consequently, *every* state is *not* 'free' and *not* a 'people's state'. Marx and Engels explained this repeatedly to their party comrades in the seventies.

Fifthly, the same work of Engels's, whose arguments about the withering away of the state everyone remembers, also contains an argument of the significance of violent revolution. Engels's historical analysis of its role becomes a veritable panegyric on violent revolution. This, 'no one remembers'. It is not done in modern socialist parties to talk or even think about the significance of this idea, and it plays no part whatever in their daily propaganda and agitation among the people. And yet it is inseparably bound up with the 'withering away' of the state into one harmonious whole.

Here is Engels's argument:

> ... That force, however, plays yet another role [other than that of a diabolical power] in history, a revolutionary role; that, in the words of Marx, it is the midwife of every old society which is pregnant with a new one, that it is the instrument with which social movement forces its way through and shatters the dead, fossilised political forms – of this there is not a word in Herr Dühring. It is only with sighs and groans that he admits the possibility that force will perhaps be necessary for the overthrow of an economy based on exploitation – unfortunately, because all use of force demoralises, he says, the person who uses it. And this in Germany, where a violent collision – which may, after all, be forced on the people – would at least have the advantage of wiping out the servility which has penetrated the nation's mentality following the humiliation of the Thirty Years' War. And this person's mode of thought – dull, insipid, and impotent – presumes to impose itself on the most revolutionary party that history has ever known!

How can this panegyric on violent revolution, which Engels insistently brought to the attention of the German Social-Democrats between 1878 and 1894, i.e., right up to the time of his death, be combined with the theory of the 'withering away' of the state to form a single theory?

Usually the two are combined by means of eclecticism, by an unprincipled or sophistic selection made arbitrarily (or to please the powers that be) of first one, then another argument, and in 99 cases out of 100, if not more, it is the idea of the 'withering away' that is placed in the forefront. Dialectics are replaced by eclecticism – this is the most usual, the most widespread practice to be met with in present-day official Social-Democratic literature in relation to Marxism. This sort of substitution is, of course, nothing new; it was observed even in the history of classical Greek philosophy. In falsifying Marxism in opportunist fashion, the substitution of eclecticism for dialectics is the easiest way of deceiving the people. It gives an illusory satisfaction; it seems to take into account all sides of the process, all trends of development, all the conflicting influences, and so forth, whereas in reality it provides no integral and revolutionary conception of the process of social development at all.

We have already said above, and shall show more fully later, that the theory of Marx and Engels of the inevitability of a violent revolution refers to the bourgeois state. The latter *cannot* be superseded by the proletarian state (the dictatorship of the proletariat) through the process of 'withering away', but, as a general rule, only through a violent revolution. The panegyric Engels sang in its honour, and which fully corresponds to Marx's repeated statements (see the concluding passages of *The Poverty of Philosophy* and the *Communist Manifesto*, with their proud and open proclamation of the inevitability of a violent revolution; see what Marx wrote nearly 30 years later, in criticising the Gotha Programme of 1875, when he mercilessly castigated the opportunist character of that programme) – this panegyric is by no means a mere 'impulse', a mere declamation or a polemical sally. The necessity of systematically imbuing the masses with *this* and precisely this view of violent revolution lies at the root of the *entire* theory of Marx and Engels. The betrayal of their theory by the now prevailing social-chauvinist and Kautskyite trends expresses itself strikingly in both these trends ignoring *such* propaganda and agitation.

The suppression of the bourgeois state by the proletarian state is impossible without a violent revolution. The abolition of the proletarian state, i.e., of the state in general, is impossible except through the process of 'withering away'.

A detailed and concrete elaboration of these views was given by Marx and Engels when they studied each particular revolutionary situation, when they analysed the lessons of the experience of each particular revolution. We shall now pass to this, undoubtedly the most important, part of their theory.

1917: To the Population – Take Power in Your Own Hands[*]

Comrades – workers, soldiers, peasants and all working people!

The workers' and peasants' revolution has definitely triumphed in Petrograd, having dispersed or arrested the last remnants of the small number of Cossacks deceived by Kerensky. The revolution has triumphed in Moscow too. Even before the arrival of a number of troop trains dispatched from Petrograd, the officer cadets and other Kornilovites in Moscow signed peace terms – the disarming of the cadets and the dissolution of the Committee of Salvation.

Daily and hourly reports are coming in from the front and from the villages announcing the support of the overwhelming majority of the soldiers in the trenches and the peasants in the uyezds for the new government and its decrees on peace and the immediate transfer of the land to the peasants. The victory of the workers' and peasants' revolution is assured because the majority of the people have already sided with it.

It is perfectly understandable that the landowners and capitalists, and the *top groups* of office employees and civil servants closely linked with the bourgeoisie, in a word, all the wealthy and those supporting them, react to the new revolution with hostility, resist its victory, threaten to close the banks, disrupt or bring to a standstill the work of the different establishments, and hamper the revolution in every way, openly or covertly. Every politically-conscious worker was well aware that we would inevitably encounter resistance of this kind. The entire Party press of the Bolsheviks has written about this on numerous occasions. Not for a single minute will the working classes be intimidated by this resistance; they will not falter in any way before the threats and strikes of the supporters of the bourgeoisie.

The majority of the people are with us. The majority of the working and oppressed people all over the world are with us. Ours is the cause of justice. Our victory is assured.

[*] *Collected Works*, Vol. 26: 296–8.

The resistance of the capitalists and the high-ranking employees will be smashed. Not a single person will be deprived of his property except under the special state law proclaiming nationalisation of the banks and syndicates. This law is being drafted. Not one of the working people will suffer the loss of a kopek; on the contrary, he will be helped. Apart from the strictest accounting and control, apart from levying the set taxes in full the government has no intention of introducing any other measure.

In support of these just demands the vast majority of the people have rallied round the Provisional Workers' and Peasants' Government.

Comrades, working people! Remember that now you yourselves are at the helm of state. No one will help you if you yourselves do not unite and take into *your* hands *all affairs* of the state. *Your* Soviets are from now on the organs of state authority, legislative bodies with full powers.

Rally around your Soviets. Strengthen them. Get on with the job yourselves; begin right at the bottom, do not wait for anyone. Establish the strictest revolutionary law and order, mercilessly suppress any attempts to create anarchy by drunkards, hooligans, counter-revolutionary officer cadets, Kornilovites and their like.

Ensure the strictest control over production and accounting of products. Arrest and hand over to the revolutionary courts all who dare to injure the people's cause, irrespective of whether the injury is manifested in sabotaging production (damage, delay and subversion), or in hoarding grain and products or holding up shipments of grain, disorganising the railways and the postal, telegraph and telephone services, or any resistance whatever to the great cause of peace, the cause of transferring the land to the peasants, of ensuring workers' control over the production and distribution of products.

Comrades, workers, soldiers, peasants and all working people! Take *all* power into the hands of *your* Soviets. Be watchful and guard like the apple of your eye your land, grain, factories, equipment, products, transport – all that from now onwards will be *entirely* your property, public property. Gradually, with the consent and approval of the majority of the peasants, in keeping

with their *practical* experience and that of the workers, we shall
go forward firmly and unswervingly to the victory of socialism – a
victory that will be sealed by the advanced workers of the most
civilised countries, bring the peoples lasting peace and liberate
them from all oppression and exploitation.

V. Ulyanov (Lenin)
Chairman of the Council of People's Commissars
5 November 1917, Petrograd

1918: Dissolution of the Constituent Assembly[*]

Comrades, the clash between Soviet power and the Constituent
Assembly results from the entire course of the Russian revolution,
which was confronted by the unprecedented task of reconstructing
society on socialist lines. After the events of 1905 there could be
no doubt that tsarism's day was over and that it had scrambled
out of the pit only because of the backwardness and ignorance
of the rural population. The Revolution of 1917 was marked on
the one hand by the transformation of the bourgeois imperialist
party into a republican party under the pressure of events, and
on the other hand, by the emergence of democratic organisations,
the Soviets, that had been formed in 1905; even then the socialists
had realised that the organisation of these Soviets was creating
something great, something new and unprecedented in the history
of world revolution. The Soviets, created solely by the initiative
of the people, are a form of democracy without parallel in any
other country of the world.

The revolution produced two forces – the union of the masses
for the purpose of overthrowing tsarism, and the organisations
of the working people. When I hear the enemies of the October
Revolution exclaim that the ideas of socialism are unfeasible
and utopian, I usually put to them a plain and simple question.
What in their opinion, I ask, are the Soviets? What gave rise to
these organisations of the people, which have no precedent in
the history of the development of world revolution? Not one

* *Collected Works*, Vol. 26: 437–41.

of them has been able to give a precise answer to this question. Defending the bourgeois system by inertia, they oppose these powerful organisations, the formation of which has never before been witnessed in any revolution in the world. All who are fighting the landowners are joining forces with the Soviets of Peasants' Deputies. The Soviets embrace all who do not wish to stand idle and are devoting themselves to creative work. They have spread their network over the whole country, and the denser this network of Soviets of the people, the less will it be possible to exploit the working people. For the existence of the Soviets is incompatible with a prosperous bourgeois system. That is the source of all the contradictions among the bourgeoisie, who are fighting our Soviets solely in their own interests.

The transition from capitalism to a socialist system entails a long and bitter struggle. Having overthrown tsarism, the Russian revolution was bound to go farther; it could not stop at the victory of the bourgeois revolution; for the war, and the untold sufferings it caused the exhausted peoples, created a soil favourable for the outbreak of the social revolution. Nothing, therefore, is more ludicrous than the assertion that the subsequent development of the revolution, and the revolt of the masses that followed, were caused by a party, by an individual, or, as they vociferate, by the will of a 'dictator'. The fire of revolution broke out solely because of the incredible sufferings of Russia, and because of the conditions created by the war, which sternly and inexorably faced the working people with the alternative of taking a bold, desperate and fearless step, or of perishing, of dying from starvation.

And revolutionary fire was manifest in the creation of the Soviets – the mainstay of the workers' revolution. The Russian people have made a gigantic advance, a leap from tsarism to the Soviets. That is a fact, irrefutable and unparalleled. While the bourgeois parliaments of all countries and states, confined within the bounds of capitalism and private property, have never anywhere supported a revolutionary movement, the Soviets, having lit the fire of revolution, imperatively command the people to fight, take everything into their own hands, and organise themselves. In the course of a revolution called forth by the strength of the

Soviets there are certain to be all kinds of errors and blunders. But everybody knows that revolutionary movements are always and inevitably accompanied by temporary chaos, destruction and disorder. Bourgeois society is the same war, the same shambles; and it was this circumstance that gave rise to and accentuated the conflict between the Constituent Assembly and the Soviets. Those who point out that we are now 'dissolving' the Constituent Assembly although at one time we defended it are not displaying a grain of sense, but are merely uttering pompous and meaningless phrases. At one time, we considered the Constituent Assembly to be better than tsarism and the republic of Kerensky with their famous organs of power; but as the Soviets emerged, they, being revolutionary organisations of the whole people, naturally became incomparably superior to any parliament in the world, a fact that I emphasised as far back as last April. By completely smashing bourgeois and landed property and by facilitating the final upheaval which is sweeping away all traces of the bourgeois system, the Soviets impelled us on to the path that has led the people to organise their own lives. We have taken up this great work of organisation, and it is well that we have done so. Of course, the socialist revolution cannot be immediately presented to the people in a clean, neat and impeccable form; it will inevitably be accompanied by civil war, sabotage and resistance. Those who assert the contrary are either liars or cowards. The events of 20 April, when the people, without any directions from 'dictators' or parties, came out independently and solidly against the government of compromisers, showed even then that the bourgeoisie were weak and had no solid support. The masses sensed their power, and to placate them the famous game of ministerial leapfrog began, the object of which was to fool the people. But the people very soon saw through the game, particularly after Kerensky, both his pockets stuffed with predatory secret treaties with the imperialists, began to move the armies for an offensive. Gradually the activities of the compromisers became obvious to the deceived people, whose patience began to be exhausted. The result was the October Revolution. The people learned by experience, having suffered torture, executions and wholesale shootings and it is nonsense for the butchers to assert that the Bolsheviks, or certain 'dictators', are responsible for the revolt of the working people. They are given the lie by the split that is occurring among the people themselves at congresses, meetings, conferences, and so forth. The people have not yet fully understood the October Revolution. This revolution has shown in practice how the people must take into their own hands, the hands of the workers' and peasants' state, the land, the natural resources, and the means of transport and production. Our cry was, All power to the Soviets; it is for this we are fighting. The people wanted the Constituent Assembly summoned, and we summoned it. But they sensed immediately what this famous Constituent Assembly really was. And now we have carried out the will of the people, which is – All power to the Soviets. As for the saboteurs, we shall crush them. When I came from Smolny, that fount of life and vigour, to the Taurida Palace, I felt as though I were in the company of corpses and lifeless mummies. They drew on all their available resources in order to fight socialism, they resorted to violence and sabotage, they even turned knowledge – the great pride of humanity – into a means of exploiting the working people. But although they managed to hinder somewhat the advance towards the socialist revolution, they could not stop it and will never be able to. Indeed the Soviets that have begun to smash the old, outworn foundations of the bourgeois system, not in gentlemanly, but in a blunt proletarian and peasant fashion, are much too strong.

To hand over power to the Constituent Assembly would again be compromising with the malignant bourgeoisie. The Russian Soviets place the interests of the working people far above the interests of a treacherous policy of compromise disguised in a new garb. The speeches of those outdated politicians, Chernov and Tsereteli, who continue whining tediously for the cessation of civil war, give off the stale and musty odour of antiquity. But as long as Kaledin exists, and as long as the slogan 'All power to the Constituent Assembly' conceals the slogan 'Down with Soviet power', civil war is inevitable. For nothing in the world will make us give up Soviet power! And when the Constituent Assembly again revealed its readiness to postpone all the painfully urgent problems and tasks that were placed before it by the Soviets, we told the Constituent Assembly that they must not be postponed for one single moment. And by the will of Soviet power the Constituent Assembly, which has refused to recognise the power of the people, is being dissolved. The Ryabushinskys have lost their stakes; their attempts at resistance will only accentuate and provoke a new outbreak of civil war.

The Constituent Assembly is dissolved. The Soviet revolutionary republic will triumph, no matter what the cost.

8

WORLD REVOLUTION

The Russian Revolution was followed by a combination of civil war and foreign military intervention, both designed to bring an end to Soviet power. Some who initiated the civil war claimed an allegiance to the recently-dissolved Constituent Assembly – this was particularly the case for certain elements among the Right SRs and the right-wing of the Mensheviks – but others were functioning out of loyalty to components of the old social order: in some cases to tsarism and the landed nobility, in some cases to capitalism, in some cases to the authority of the Russian Orthodox Church, in some cases to a more elemental authoritarianism, ultra-nationalism, and anti-Semitism typical among the old Black Hundreds, and to a large extent mixtures of these. The various World Powers, far more sympathetic to the more sinister of these counter-revolutionary elements than to the revolutionary democracy represented by the Bolshevik Revolution, intervened powerfully and generously on their behalf.

In the desperate situation, Lenin's Bolsheviks (renaming themselves the Russian Communist Party) established emergency dictatorial measures, particularly when the Left SRs sharply broke with the Soviet government over policy differences having to do with the Russian withdrawal from the First World War, and when Left SRs and many Mensheviks engaged in campaigns to discredit the Bolshevik remnant in the Soviet government.

Yet Lenin and his co-thinkers were convinced it was only the spread of the revolution to other countries that could guarantee the success of Russia's revolution. They expended considerable energy to explain their situation to workers around the world, to encourage them to learn the lessons of their own oppression and class-struggle experiences, to learn from the horrors of the imperialist World War, and to prepare their own socialist revolutions. An interesting example of this is the first reading in this chapter, Lenin's 'Letter to American Workers' (1918).

The devastation of the First World War helped to create pre-conditions for working-class radicalisation and the heightened possibility of socialist revolutions. The betrayals of the old Socialist International, and the political disorientation generated by the old socialist parties, now made necessary the 1919 creation of a Communist International. This would help establish Communist Parties throughout the world for the purpose of training and preparing growing sectors of the working class and the oppressed peoples for revolutionary insurgencies on the Russian model. Just as the Second International had necessarily replaced the First International (the International Workingmen's Association led by Marx), so was it time for the Third International to take its place in history. These are among the ideas offered in the excerpts from 'The Third International and Its Place in History'.

The last two readings in this chapter deal with debates that arose inside of the Communist International. Some would-be Communists conflated the profoundly democratic October/November revolution with the dictatorial measures of the civil war, ignoring the years of struggle that enabled the Bolsheviks to become a force capable of winning a majority of the population to the revolutionary establishment of soviet power. Not comprehending the profoundly democratic commitments over decades that had been essential to the Bolshevik success, many of the new adherents to the Communist cause in various countries saw the Bolshevik Revolution as the model for a revolutionary short-cut. In a manner reminiscent of the 'ultra-left' Bolsheviks arising after Russia's 1905 upsurge (and with whom Lenin broke in 1909), these new 'left-wing' Communists were inclined to reject trade union struggles, united fronts, reform struggles, patient educational efforts among the masses of working people and their allies, electoral campaigns within bourgeois democratic republics, etc. Instead, they assumed that through determined and decisive action, a Communist-led revolutionary minority could simply take power and impose a new order.

In the excerpts of *'Left-Wing' Communism, An Infantile Disorder* (1920) and 'Speech on Tactics of the Communist International' (1921), we see Lenin sharply polemicising against what he sees as seriously mistaken comrades. What comes through is his conviction, which can be traced back to the 1890s, that the struggle for reforms is an essential component of revolutionary strategy, and that genuinely democratic perspectives, capable of giving power to the workers and the oppressed, are inseparable from the struggle for socialism.

1918: Letter to American Workers[*]

Comrades! A Russian Bolshevik who took part in the 1905 Revolution, and who lived in your country for many years afterwards, has offered to convey my letter to you. I have accepted his proposal all the more gladly because just at the present time the American revolutionary workers have to play an exceptionally important role as uncompromising enemies of American imperialism – the freshest, strongest and latest in joining in the world-wide slaughter of nations for the division of capitalist profits. At this very moment, the American multimillionaires, these modern slaveowners have turned an exceptionally tragic page in the bloody history of bloody imperialism by giving their approval – whether direct or indirect, open or hypocritically concealed, makes no difference – to the armed expedition launched by the brutal Anglo-Japanese imperialists for the purpose of throttling the first socialist republic.

The history of modern, civilised America opened with one of those great, really liberating, really revolutionary wars of which there have been so few compared to the vast number of wars of conquest which, like the present imperialist war, were caused by squabbles among kings, landowners or capitalists over the division of usurped lands or ill-gotten gains. That was the war the American people waged against the British robbers who oppressed America and held her in colonial slavery, in the same way as these 'civilised' bloodsuckers are still oppressing and holding in colonial slavery hundreds of millions of people in India, Egypt, and all parts of the world.

About 150 years have passed since then. Bourgeois civilisation has borne all its luxurious fruits. America has taken first place among the free and educated nations in level of development of the productive forces of collective human endeavour, in the utilisation of machinery and of all the wonders of modern engineering. At the same time, America has become one of the foremost countries in regard to the depth of the abyss which lies between the handful

* *Collected Works*, Vol. 28: 62–75.

of arrogant multimillionaires who wallow in filth and luxury, and the millions of working people who constantly live on the verge of pauperism. The American people, who set the world an example in waging a revolutionary war against feudal slavery, now find themselves in the latest, capitalist stage of wage-slavery to a handful of multimillionaires, and find themselves playing the role of hired thugs who, for the benefit of wealthy scoundrels, throttled the Philippines in 1898 on the pretext of 'liberating' them, and are throttling the Russian Socialist Republic in 1918 on the pretext of 'protecting' it from the Germans.

The four years of the imperialist slaughter of nations, however, have not passed in vain. The deception of the people by the scoundrels of both robber groups, the British and the German, has been utterly exposed by indisputable and obvious facts. The results of the four years of war have revealed the general law of capitalism as applied to war between robbers for the division of spoils: the richest and strongest profited and grabbed most, while the weakest were utterly robbed, tormented, crushed and strangled.

The British imperialist robbers were the strongest in number of 'colonial slaves'. The British capitalists have not lost an inch of 'their' territory (i.e., territory they have grabbed over the centuries), but they have grabbed all the German colonies in Africa, they have grabbed Mesopotamia and Palestine, they have throttled Greece, and have begun to plunder Russia.

The German imperialist robbers were the strongest in organisation and discipline of 'their' armies, but weaker in regard to colonies. They have lost all their colonies, but plundered half of Europe and throttled the largest number of small countries and weak nations. What a great war of 'liberation' on both sides! How well the robbers of both groups, the Anglo-French and the German capitalists, together with their lackeys, the social-chauvinists, i.e., the socialists who went over to the side of '*their own*' bourgeoisie, have 'defended their country'!

The American multimillionaires were, perhaps, richest of all, and geographically the most secure. They have profited more than all the rest. They have converted all, even the richest, countries into their tributaries. They have grabbed hundreds of billions of dollars. And every dollar is sullied with filth: the filth of the secret treaties between Britain and her 'allies', between Germany and her vassals, treaties for the division of the spoils, treaties of mutual 'aid' for oppressing the workers and persecuting the internationalist socialists. Every dollar is sullied with the filth of 'profitable' war contracts, which in every country made the rich richer and the poor poorer. And every dollar is stained with blood – from that ocean of blood that has been shed by the 10 million killed and 20 million maimed in the great, noble, liberating and holy war to decide whether the British or the German robbers are to get most of the spoils, whether the British or the German thugs are to be *foremost* in throttling the weak nations all over the world.

While the German robbers broke all records in war atrocities, the British have broken all records not only in the number of colonies they have grabbed, but also in the subtlety of their disgusting hypocrisy. This very day, the Anglo-French and American bourgeois newspapers are spreading, in millions and millions of copies, lies and slander about Russia, and are hypo-critically justifying their predatory expedition against her on the plea that they want to 'protect' Russia from the Germans!

It does not require many words to refute this despicable and hideous lie; it is sufficient to point to one well-known fact. In October 1917, after the Russian workers had overthrown their imperialist government, the Soviet government, the government of the revolutionary workers and peasants, openly proposed a just peace, a peace without annexations or indemnities, a peace that fully guaranteed equal rights to all nations – and it proposed such a peace to *all* the belligerent countries.

It was the Anglo-French and the American bourgeoisie who refused to accept our proposal; it was they who even refused to talk to us about a general peace! It was *they* who betrayed the interests of all nations; it was they who prolonged the imperialist slaughter!

It was they who, banking on the possibility of dragging Russia back into the imperialist war, refused to take part in the peace negotiations and thereby gave a free hand to the no less predatory German capitalists who imposed the annexationist and harsh Brest Peace upon Russia!

It is difficult to imagine anything more disgusting than the hypocrisy with which the Anglo-French and American bourgeoisie are now 'blaming' us *for* the Brest Peace Treaty. The very capitalists of those countries which could have turned the Brest negotiations into general negotiations for a general peace are now our 'accusers'! The Anglo-French imperialist vultures, who have profited from the plunder of colonies and the slaughter of nations, have prolonged the war for nearly a whole year after Brest, and yet they 'accuse' *us*, the Bolsheviks, who proposed a just peace to all countries, they accuse *us*, who tore up, published and exposed to public disgrace the secret, criminal treaties concluded between the ex-tsar and the Anglo-French capitalists.

The workers of the whole world, no matter in what country they live, greet us, sympathise with us, applaud us for breaking the iron ring of imperialist ties, of sordid imperialist treaties, of imperialist chains – for breaking through to freedom, and making the heaviest sacrifices in doing so – for, as a socialist republic, although torn and plundered by the imperialists, keeping *out* of the imperialist war and raising the banner of peace, the banner of socialism for the whole world to see.

Small wonder that the international imperialist gang hates us for this, that it 'accuses' us, that all the lackeys of the imperialists, including our Right Socialist-Revolutionaries and Mensheviks, also 'accuse' us. The hatred these watchdogs of imperialism express for the Bolsheviks, and the sympathy of the class-conscious workers of the world, convince us more than ever of the justice of our cause.

A real socialist would not fail to understand that for the sake of achieving victory over the bourgeoisie, for the sake of power passing to the workers, for the sake of *starting* the world proletarian revolution, we *cannot* and must *not* hesitate to make the heaviest sacrifices, including the sacrifice of part of our territory, the sacrifice of heavy defeats at the hands of imperialism. A real socialist would have proved by *deeds* his willingness for 'his' country to make the greatest sacrifice to give a real push forward to the cause of the socialist revolution.

For the sake of 'their' cause, that is, for the sake of winning world hegemony, the imperialists of Britain and Germany have not hesitated to utterly ruin and throttle a whole number of countries, from Belgium and Serbia to Palestine and Mesopotamia. But must socialists wait with 'their' cause, the cause of liberating the working people of the whole world from the yoke of capital, of winning universal and lasting peace, until a path without sacrifice is found? Must they fear to open the battle until an easy victory is 'guaranteed'? Must they place the integrity and security of 'their' bourgeois-created 'fatherland' above the interests of the world socialist revolution? The scoundrels in the international socialist movement who think this way, those lackeys who grovel to bourgeois morality, thrice stand condemned.

The Anglo-French and American imperialist vultures 'accuse' us of concluding an 'agreement' with German imperialism. What hypocrites, what scoundrels they are to slander the workers' government while trembling because of the sympathy displayed towards us by the workers of 'their own' countries! But their hypocrisy will be exposed. They pretend not to see the difference between an agreement entered into by 'socialists' with the bourgeoisie (their own or foreign) *against the workers*, against the working people, and an agreement entered into *for the protection* of the workers who have defeated their bourgeoisie, with the bourgeoisie of one national colour *against the bourgeoisie* of another colour in order that the proletariat may take advantage of the antagonisms between the different groups of bourgeoisie.

In actual fact, every European sees this difference very well, and, as I shall show in a moment, the American people have had a particularly striking 'illustration' of it in their own history. There are agreements and agreements, there are *fagots et fagots*, as the French say.

When in February 1918 the German imperialist vultures hurled their forces against unarmed, demobilised Russia, who had relied on the international solidarity of the proletariat before the world revolution had fully matured, I did not hesitate for a moment to enter into an 'agreement' with the French monarchists. Captain Sadoul, a French army officer who, in words, sympathised with the Bolsheviks, but was in deeds a loyal and faithful servant of French imperialism, brought the French officer de Lubersac to see me. 'I am a monarchist. My only aim is to secure the defeat of Germany', de Lubersac declared to me. 'That goes without saying (*cela va sans dire*)', I replied. But this did not in the least prevent me from entering into an 'agreement' with de Lubersac concerning certain services that French army officers, experts in explosives, were ready to render us by blowing up railway lines in order to hinder the German invasion. This is an example of an 'agreement' of which every class-conscious worker will approve, an agreement in the interests of socialism. The French monarchist and I shook hands, although we knew that each of us would willingly hang his 'partner'. But for a time our interests coincided. Against the advancing rapacious Germans, *we*, in the interests of the Russian and the world socialist revolution, utilised the equally rapacious counter-interests of *other* imperialists. In this way we served the interests of the working class of Russia and of other countries, we strengthened the proletariat and weakened the bourgeoisie of the whole world, we resorted to the methods, most legitimate and essential in *every* war, of manoeuvre, stratagem, retreat, in anticipation of the moment when the rapidly maturing proletarian revolution in a number of advanced countries *completely matured*.

However much the Anglo-French and American imperialist sharks fume with rage, however much they slander us, no matter how many millions they spend on bribing the Right Socialist-Revolutionary, Menshevik and other social-patriotic newspapers, *I shall not hesitate one second* to enter into a *similar* 'agreement' with the German imperialist vultures if an attack upon Russia by Anglo-French troops calls for it. And I know perfectly well that my tactics will be approved by the class-conscious proletariat of Russia, Germany, France, Britain, America – in short, of the whole civilised world. Such tactics will ease the task of the socialist revolution, will hasten it, will weaken the international bourgeoisie, will strengthen the position of the working class which is defeating the bourgeoisie.

The American people resorted to these tactics long ago to the advantage of their revolution. When they waged their great war of liberation against the British oppressors, they had also against them the French and the Spanish oppressors who owned a part of what is now the United States of North America. In their arduous war for freedom, the American people also entered into 'agreements' with some oppressors against others for the purpose of weakening the oppressors and strengthening those who were fighting in a revolutionary manner against oppression, for the purpose of serving the interests of the oppressed *people*. The American people took advantage of the strife between the French, the Spanish and the British; sometimes they even fought side by side with the forces of the French and Spanish oppressors against the British oppressors; first they defeated the British and then freed themselves (partly by ransom) from the French and the Spanish.

Historical action is not the pavement of Nevsky Prospekt, said the great Russian revolutionary Chernyshevsky. A revolutionary would not 'agree' to a proletarian revolution only 'on the condition' that it proceeds easily and smoothly, that there is, from the outset, combined action on the part of the proletarians of different countries, that there are guarantees against defeats, that the road of the revolution is broad, free and straight, that it will not be necessary during the march to victory to sustain the heaviest casualties, to 'bide one's time in a besieged fortress', or to make one's way along extremely narrow, impassable, winding and dangerous mountain tracks. Such a person is no revolutionary, he has not freed himself from the pedantry of the bourgeois intellectuals; such a person will be found constantly slipping into the camp of the counter-revolutionary bourgeoisie, like our Right Socialist-Revolutionaries, Mensheviks and even (although more rarely) Left Socialist-Revolutionaries.

Echoing the bourgeoisie, these gentlemen like to blame us for the 'chaos' of the revolution, for the 'destruction' of industry, for the unemployment and the food shortage. How hypocritical these accusations are, coming from those who welcomed and supported the imperialist war, or who entered into an 'agreement' with Kerensky who continued this war! It is this imperialist war that is the cause of all these misfortunes. The revolution engendered by the war cannot avoid the terrible difficulties and suffering bequeathed it by the prolonged, ruinous, reactionary slaughter of the nations. To blame us for the 'destruction' of industry, or for the 'terror', is either hypocrisy or dull-witted pedantry; it reveals an inability to understand the basic conditions of the fierce class struggle, raised to the highest degree of intensity that is called revolution.

Even when 'accusers' of this type do 'recognise' the class struggle, they limit themselves to verbal recognition; actually, they constantly slip into the philistine utopia of class 'agreement' and 'collaboration'; for in revolutionary epochs the class struggle has always, inevitably, and in every country, assumed the form of *civil war*, and civil war is inconceivable without the severest destruction, terror and the restriction of formal democracy in the interests of this war. Only unctuous parsons – whether Christian or 'secular' in the persons of parlour, parliamentary socialists – cannot see, understand and feel this necessity. Only a lifeless 'man in the muffler' can shun the revolution for this reason instead of plunging into battle with the utmost ardour and determination at a time when history demands that the greatest problems of humanity be solved by struggle and war.

The American people have a revolutionary tradition which has been adopted by the best representatives of the American proletariat, who have repeatedly expressed their complete solidarity with us Bolsheviks. That tradition is the war of liberation against the British in the eighteenth century and the Civil War in the nineteenth century. In some respects, if we only take into consideration the 'destruction' of some branches of industry and of the national economy, America in 1870 was *behind* 1860. But what a pedant, what an idiot would anyone be to deny on *these* grounds the immense, world-historic, progressive and revolutionary significance of the American Civil War of 1863–65!

The representatives of the bourgeoisie understand that for the sake of overthrowing Negro slavery, of overthrowing the rule of the slaveowners, it was worth letting the country go through long years of civil war, through the abysmal ruin, destruction and terror that accompany every war. But now, when we are confronted with the vastly greater task of overthrowing capitalist *wage*-slavery, of overthrowing the rule of the bourgeoisie – now, the representatives and defenders of the bourgeoisie, and also the reformist socialists who have been frightened by the bourgeoisie and are shunning the revolution, cannot and do not want to understand that civil war is necessary and legitimate.

The American workers will not follow the bourgeoisie. They will be with us, for civil war against the bourgeoisie. The whole history of the world and of the American labour movement strengthens my conviction that this is so. I also recall the words of one of the most beloved leaders of the American proletariat, Eugene Debs, who wrote in the *Appeal to Reason*, I believe towards the end of 1915, in the article 'What Shall I Fight For' (I quoted this article at the beginning of 1916 at a public meeting of workers in Berne, Switzerland) – that he, Debs, would rather be shot than vote credits for the present criminal and reactionary war; that he, Debs, knows of only one holy and, from the proletarian standpoint, legitimate war, namely: the war against the capitalists, the war to liberate mankind from wage-slavery.

I am not surprised that Wilson, the head of the American multi-millionaires and servant of the capitalist sharks, has thrown Debs into prison. Let the bourgeoisie be brutal to the true international-ists, to the true representatives of the revolutionary proletariat! The more fierce and brutal they are, the nearer the day of the victorious proletarian revolution.

We are blamed for the destruction caused by our revolution. ... Who are the accusers? The hangers-on of the bourgeoisie, of that very bourgeoisie who, during the four years of the imperialist war, have destroyed almost the whole of European culture and have reduced Europe to barbarism, brutality and starvation. These bourgeoisie now demand we should not make a revolution on these ruins, amidst this wreckage of culture, amidst the wreckage and ruins created by the war, nor with the people who have been brutalised by the war. How humane and righteous the bourgeoisie are!

Their servants accuse us of resorting to terror. ... The British bourgeoisie have forgotten their 1649, the French bourgeoisie have forgotten their 1793. Terror was just and legitimate when the bourgeoisie resorted to it for their own benefit against feudalism. Terror became monstrous and criminal when the workers and poor peasants dared to use it against the bourgeoisie! Terror was just and legitimate when used for the purpose of substituting one exploiting minority for another exploiting minority. Terror became monstrous and criminal when it began to be used for the purpose of overthrowing *every* exploiting minority, to be used in the interests of the vast actual majority, in the interests of the proletariat and semi-proletariat, the working class and the poor peasants!

The international imperialist bourgeoisie have slaughtered 10 million men and maimed 20 million in 'their' war, the war to decide whether the British or the German vultures are to rule the world.

If *our* war, the war of the oppressed and exploited against the oppressors and the exploiters, results in half a million or a million casualties in all countries, the bourgeoisie will say that the former casualties are justified, while the latter are criminal.

The proletariat will have something entirely different to say.

Now, amidst the horrors of the imperialist war, the proletariat is receiving a most vivid and striking illustration of the great truth taught by all revolutions and bequeathed to the workers by their best teachers, the founders of modern socialism. This truth is that no revolution can be successful unless *the resistance of the exploiters is crushed*. When we, the workers and toiling peasants, captured state power, it became our duty to crush the resistance of the exploiters. We are proud we have been doing this. We regret we are not doing it with sufficient firmness and determination.

We know that fierce resistance to the socialist revolution on the part of the bourgeoisie is inevitable in all countries, and that this resistance will *grow* with the growth of this revolution. The proletariat will crush this resistance; during the struggle against the resisting bourgeoisie it will finally mature for victory and for power.

Let the corrupt bourgeois press shout to the whole world about every mistake our revolution makes. We are not daunted by our mistakes. People have not become saints because the revolution has begun. The toiling classes who for centuries have been oppressed, downtrodden and forcibly held in the vice of poverty, brutality and ignorance cannot avoid mistakes when making a revolution. And, as I pointed out once before, the corpse of bourgeois society cannot be nailed in a coffin and buried. The corpse of capitalism is decaying and disintegrating in our midst, polluting the air and poisoning our lives, enmeshing that which is new, fresh, young and virile in thousands of threads and bonds of that which is old, moribund and decaying.

For every 100 mistakes we commit, and which the bourgeoisie and their lackeys (including our own Mensheviks and Right Socialist-Revolutionaries) shout about to the whole world, 10,000 great and heroic deeds are performed, greater and more heroic because they are simple and inconspicuous amidst the everyday life of a factory district or a remote village, performed by people who are not accustomed (and have no opportunity) to shout to the whole world about their successes.

But even if the contrary were true – although I know such an assumption is wrong – even if we committed 10,000 mistakes for every 100 correct actions we performed, even in that case our revolution would be great and invincible, and *so it will be in the eyes of world history*, because, *for the first time*, not the minority, not the rich alone, not the educated alone, but the real people, the vast majority of the working people, are *themselves* building a new life, are *by their own experience* solving the most difficult problems of socialist organisation.

Every mistake committed in the course of such work, in the course of this most conscientious and earnest work of tens of millions of simple workers and peasants in reorganising their whole life, every such mistake is worth thousands and millions of 'lawless' successes achieved by the exploiting minority – successes in swindling and duping the working people. For only *through* such mistakes will the workers and peasants *learn* to build the new life, learn to do *without* capitalists; only in this way will they hack a path for themselves – through thousands of obstacles – to victorious socialism.

Mistakes are being committed in the course of their revolutionary work by our peasants, who at one stroke, in one night, 25–26 (old style) October 1917, entirely abolished the private ownership of land, and are now, month after month, overcoming tremendous difficulties and correcting their mistakes themselves, solving in a practical way the most difficult tasks of organising new conditions of economic life, of fighting the kulaks, providing land for the *working people* (and not for the rich), and of changing to *communist* large-scale agriculture.

Mistakes are being committed in the course of their revolutionary work by our workers, who have already, after a few months, nationalised almost all the biggest factories and plants, and are learning by hard, everyday work the new task of managing whole branches of industry, are setting the nationalised enterprises going, overcoming the powerful resistance of inertia, petty-bourgeois mentality and selfishness, and, brick by brick, are laying the foundation of *new* social ties, of a *new* labour discipline, of a *new* influence of the workers' trade unions over their members.

Mistakes are committed in the course of their revolutionary work by our Soviets, which were created as far back as 1905 by a mighty upsurge of the people. The Soviets of Workers and Peasants are a new *type* of state, a new and higher *type* of democracy, a form of the proletarian dictatorship, a means of administering the state *without* the bourgeoisie and *against* the bourgeoisie. For the first time democracy is here serving the people, the working people, and has ceased to be democracy for the rich as it still is in all bourgeois republics, even the most democratic. For the first time, the people are grappling, on a scale involving 100 million, with the problem of implementing the dictatorship of the proletariat and semi-proletariat – a problem which, if not solved, makes socialism *out of the question*.

Let the pedants, or the people whose minds are incurably stuffed with bourgeois-democratic or parliamentary prejudices, shake their heads in perplexity about our Soviets, about the absence of direct elections, for example. These people have forgotten nothing and have learned nothing during the period of the great upheavals of 1914–18. The combination of the proletarian dictatorship with the new democracy for the working people – of civil war with the widest participation of the people in politics – such a combination cannot be brought about at one stroke, nor does it fit in with the outworn modes of routine parliamentary democracy. The contours of a new world, the world of socialism, are rising before us in the shape of the Soviet Republic. It is not surprising that this world does not come into being ready-made, does not spring forth like Minerva from the head of Jupiter.

The old bourgeois-democratic constitutions waxed eloquent about formal equality and right of assembly; but our proletarian and peasant Soviet Constitution casts aside the hypocrisy of formal equality. When the bourgeois republicans overturned thrones they did not worry about formal equality between monarchists and republicans. When it is a matter of overthrowing the bourgeoisie, only traitors or idiots can demand formal equality of rights for the bourgeoisie. 'Freedom of assembly' for workers and peasants is not worth a farthing when the best buildings belong to the bourgeoisie. Our Soviets have *confiscated* all the good buildings in town and country from the rich and have *transferred* all of them to the workers and peasants for *their* unions and meetings. This is our *freedom* of assembly – for the working people! This is the meaning and content of our Soviet, our socialist Constitution!

That is why we are all so firmly convinced that no matter what misfortunes may still be in store for it, our Republic of Soviets is *invincible*.

It is invincible because every blow struck by frenzied imperialism, every defeat the international bourgeoisie inflict on us, rouses more and more sections of the workers and peasants to the struggle, teaches them at the cost of enormous sacrifice, steels them and engenders new heroism on a mass scale.

We know that help from you will probably not come soon, comrade American workers, for the revolution is developing in different countries in different forms and at different tempos (and it cannot be otherwise). We know that although the European proletarian revolution has been maturing very rapidly lately, it may, after all, not flare up within the next few weeks. We are banking on the inevitability of the world revolution, but this does not mean that we are such fools as to bank on the revolution inevitably coming on a *definite* and early date. We have seen two great revolutions in our country, 1905 and 1917, and we know revolutions are not made to order, or by agreement. We know that circumstances brought *our* Russian detachment of the socialist proletariat to the fore not because of our merits, but because of the exceptional backwardness of Russia, and that *before* the world revolution breaks out a number of separate revolutions may be defeated.

In spite of this, we are firmly convinced that we are invincible, because the spirit of mankind will not be broken by the imperialist slaughter. Mankind will vanquish it. And the first country to *break* the convict chains of the imperialist war was *our* country. We sustained enormously heavy casualties in the struggle to break these chains, but we *broke* them. We are *free from* imperialist dependence, we have raised the banner of struggle for the complete overthrow of imperialism for the whole world to see.

We are now, as it were, in a besieged fortress, waiting for the other detachments of the world socialist revolution to come to our relief. These detachments *exist*, they are *more numerous* than ours, they are maturing, growing, gaining more strength the longer the brutalities of imperialism continue. The workers are breaking away from their social traitors – the Gomperses, Hendersons, Renaudels, Scheidemanns and Renners. Slowly but surely the workers are adopting communist, Bolshevik tactics and are marching towards the proletarian revolution, which alone is capable of saving dying culture and dying mankind.

In short, we are invincible, because the world proletarian revolution is invincible.

N. Lenin
20 August 1918

1919: The Third International and Its Place in History[*]

… The First International (1864–72) laid the foundation of an international organisation of the workers for the preparation of their revolutionary attack on capital. The Second International (1889–1914) was an international organisation of the proletarian movement whose growth proceeded in *breadth*, at the cost of a temporary drop in the revolutionary level, a temporary strengthening of opportunism, which in the end led to the disgraceful collapse of this International.

The Third International actually emerged in 1918, when the long years of struggle against opportunism and social-chauvinism, especially during the war, led to the formation of Communist Parties in a number of countries. Officially, the Third International was founded at its First Congress, in March 1919, in Moscow. And the most characteristic feature of this International, its mission of fulfilling, of implementing the precepts of Marxism, and of achieving the age-old ideals of socialism and the working-class movement – this most characteristic feature of the Third International has manifested itself immediately in the fact that the new, third, 'International Working Men's Association' *has already begun to develop*, to a certain extent, into a *union of Soviet Socialist Republics*.

The First International laid the foundation of the proletarian, international struggle for socialism.

The Second International marked a period in which the soil was prepared for the broad, mass spread of the movement in a number of countries.

The Third International has gathered the fruits of the work of the Second International, discarded its opportunist, social-chauvinist, bourgeois and petty-bourgeois dross, and *has begun to implement* the dictatorship of the proletariat.

The international alliance of the parties which are leading the most revolutionary movement in the world, the movement of the proletariat for the overthrow of the yoke of capital, now

[*]   *Collected Works*, Vol. 29: 306–8, 310–12.

rests on an unprecedentedly firm base, in the shape of several *Soviet republics*, which are implementing the dictatorship of the proletariat and are the embodiment of victory over capitalism on an international scale.

The epoch-making significance of the Third, Communist International lies in its having begun to give effect to Marx's cardinal slogan, the slogan which sums up the centuries-old development of socialism and the working-class movement, the slogan which is expressed in the concept of the dictatorship of the proletariat.

This prevision and this theory – the prevision and theory of a genius – are becoming a reality. ...

A new era in world history has begun.

Mankind is throwing off the last form of slavery: capitalist, or wage, slavery.

By emancipating himself from slavery, man is for the first time advancing to real freedom.

How is it that one of the most backward countries of Europe was the first country to establish the dictatorship of the proletariat, and to organise a Soviet republic? We shall hardly be wrong if we say that it is this contradiction between the backwardness of Russia and the 'leap' she has made over bourgeois democracy to the highest form of democracy, to Soviet, or proletarian, democracy – it is this contradiction that has been one of the reasons (apart from the dead weight of opportunist habits and philistine prejudices that burdened the majority of the socialist leaders) why people in the West have had particular difficulty or have been slow in understanding the role of the Soviets.

The working people all over the world have instinctively grasped the significance of the Soviets as an instrument in the proletarian struggle and as a form of the proletarian state. But the 'leaders', corrupted by opportunism, still continue to worship bourgeois democracy, which they call 'democracy' in general.

Is it surprising that the establishment of the dictatorship of the proletariat has brought out primarily the 'contradiction' between the backwardness of Russia and her 'leap' *over* bourgeois democracy? It would have been surprising had history granted us the establishment of a new form of democracy *without* a number of contradictions. …

Leadership in the revolutionary proletarian International has passed for a time – for a short time, it goes without saying – to the Russians, just as at various periods of the nineteenth century it was in the hands of the British, then of the French, then of the Germans.

I have had occasion more than once to say that it was easier for the Russians than for the advanced countries *to begin* the great proletarian revolution, but that it will be more difficult for them *to continue* it and carry it to final victory, in the sense of the complete organisation of a socialist society.

It was easier for us to begin, firstly, because the unusual – for twentieth-century Europe – political backwardness of the tsarist monarchy gave unusual strength to the revolutionary onslaught of the masses. Secondly, Russia's backwardness merged in a peculiar way the proletarian revolution against the bourgeoisie with the peasant revolution against the landowners. That is what we started from in October 1917, and we would not have achieved victory so easily then if we had not. As long ago as 1856, Marx spoke, in reference to Prussia, of the possibility of a peculiar combination of proletarian revolution and peasant war. From the beginning of 1905 the Bolsheviks advocated the idea of a revolutionary-democratic dictatorship of the proletariat and the peasantry. Thirdly, the 1905 revolution contributed enormously to the political education of the worker and peasant masses, because it familiarised their vanguard with 'the last word' of socialism in the West and also because of the revolutionary action of the masses. Without such a 'dress rehearsal' as we had in 1905, the revolutions of 1917 – both the bourgeois, February revolution, and the proletarian, October revolution – would have been impossible. Fourthly, Russia's geographical conditions permitted her to hold out longer than other countries could have done against the superior military strength of the capitalist, advanced countries. Fifthly, the specific attitude of the proletariat towards the peasantry facilitated the transition from the bourgeois revolution to the socialist revolution, made it easier for the urban proletarians to influence the semi-proletarian, poorer sections of the rural working people. Sixthly, long schooling in strike action and the experience of the European mass working-class movement facilitated the emergence – in a profound and rapidly intensifying revolutionary situation – of such a unique form of proletarian revolutionary organisation as the *Soviets*.

This list, of course, is incomplete; but it will suffice for the time being.

Soviet, or proletarian, democracy was born in Russia. Following the Paris Commune a second epoch-making step was taken. The proletarian and peasant Soviet Republic has proved to be the first stable socialist republic in the world. As a *new type of state* it cannot die. It no longer stands alone.

For the continuance and completion of the work of building socialism, much, very much is still required. Soviet republics in more developed countries, where the proletariat has greater weight and influence, have every chance of surpassing Russia once they take the path of the dictatorship of the proletariat.

The bankrupt Second International is now dying and rotting alive. Actually, it is playing the role of lackey to the world bourgeoisie. It is a truly yellow International. Its foremost ideological leaders, such as Kautsky, laud *bourgeois* democracy and call it 'democracy' in general, or – what is still more stupid and still more crude – 'pure democracy'.

Bourgeois democracy has outlived its day, just as the Second International has, though the International performed historically necessary and useful work when the task of the moment was to train the working-class masses within the framework of this bourgeois democracy.

No bourgeois republic, however democratic, ever was or could have been anything but a machine for the suppression of the working people by capital, an instrument of the dictatorship of the bourgeoisie, the political rule of capital. The democratic bourgeois republic promised and proclaimed majority rule, but it could never put this into effect as long as private ownership of the land and other means of production existed.

'Freedom' in the bourgeois-democratic republic was actually freedom *for the rich*. The proletarians and working peasants could and should have utilised it for the purpose of preparing their forces to overthrow capital, to overcome bourgeois democracy, but *in fact* the working masses were, as a general rule, unable to enjoy democracy under capitalism.

Soviet, or proletarian, *democracy* has for the first time in the world created democracy for the masses, for the working people, for the factory workers and small peasants.

Never yet has the world seen political power wielded by the *majority* of the population, power *actually* wielded by this majority, as it is in the case of Soviet rule.

1920: 'Left-Wing' Communism, An Infantile Disorder[*]

II. An Essential Condition of the Bolsheviks' Success

It is, I think, almost universally realised at present that the Bolsheviks could not have retained power for two and a half months, let alone two and a half years, without the most rigorous and truly iron discipline in our Party, or without the fullest and unreserved support from the entire mass of the working class, that is, from all thinking, honest, devoted and influential elements in it, capable of leading the backward strata or carrying the latter along with them. ...

Would it not be better if the salutations addressed to the Soviets and the Bolsheviks were *more frequently* accompanied by a *profound analysis* of the reasons *why* the Bolsheviks have been able to build up the discipline needed by the revolutionary proletariat?

As a current of political thought and as a political party, Bolshevism has existed since 1903. Only the history of Bolshevism during the *entire* period of its existence can satisfactorily explain why it has been able to build up and maintain, under most difficult conditions, the iron discipline needed for the victory of the proletariat.

[*]   *Collected Works*, Vol. 31: 23, 24–31, 91–3, 95–7.

The first questions to arise are: how is the discipline of the proletariat's revolutionary party maintained? How is it tested? How is it reinforced? First, by the class-consciousness of the proletarian vanguard and by its devotion to the revolution, by its tenacity, self-sacrifice and heroism. Second, by its ability to link up, maintain the closest contact, and – if you wish – merge, in certain measure, with the broadest masses of the working people – primarily with the proletariat, *but also with the non-proletarian* masses of working people. Third, by the correctness of the political leadership exercised by this vanguard, by the correctness of its political strategy and tactics, provided the broad masses have seen, *from their own experience*, that they are correct. Without these conditions, discipline in a revolutionary party really capable of being the party of the advanced class, whose mission it is to overthrow the bourgeoisie and transform the whole of society, cannot be achieved. Without these conditions, all attempts to establish discipline inevitably fall flat and end up in phrase-mongering and clowning. On the other hand, these conditions cannot emerge at once. They are created only by prolonged effort and hard-won experience. Their creation is facilitated by a correct revolutionary theory, which, in its turn, is not a dogma, but assumes final shape only in close connection with the practical activity of a truly mass and truly revolutionary movement.

The fact that, in 1917–20, Bolshevism was able, under unprecedentedly difficult conditions, to build up and successfully maintain the strictest centralisation and iron discipline was due simply to a number of historical peculiarities of Russia.

On the one hand, Bolshevism arose in 1903 on a very firm foundation of Marxist theory. The correctness of this revolutionary theory, and of it alone, has been proved, not only by world experience throughout the nineteenth century, but especially by the experience of the seekings and vacillations, the errors and disappointments of revolutionary thought in Russia. For about half a century – approximately from the forties to the nineties of the last century – progressive thought in Russia, oppressed by a most brutal and reactionary tsarism, sought eagerly for a correct revolutionary theory, and followed with the utmost diligence and thoroughness each and every 'last word' in this sphere in Europe and America. Russia achieved Marxism – the only correct revolutionary theory – through the *agony* she experienced in the course of half a century of unparalleled torment and sacrifice, of unparalleled revolutionary heroism, incredible energy, devoted searching, study, practical trial, disappointment, verification, and comparison with European experience. Thanks to the political emigration caused by tsarism, revolutionary Russia, in the second half of the nineteenth century, acquired a wealth of international links and excellent information on the forms and theories of the world revolutionary movement, such as no other country possessed.

On the other hand, Bolshevism, which had arisen on this granite foundation of theory, went through 15 years of practical history (1903–17) unequalled anywhere in the world in its wealth of experience. During those 15 years, no other country knew anything even approximating to that revolutionary experience, that rapid and varied succession of different forms of the movement – legal and illegal, peaceful and stormy, underground and open, local circles and mass movements, and parliamentary and terrorist forms. In no other country has there been concentrated, in so brief a period, such a wealth of forms, shades, and methods of struggle of *all* classes of modern society, a struggle which, owing to the backwardness of the country and the severity of the tsarist yoke, matured with exceptional rapidity, and assimilated most eagerly and successfully the appropriate 'last word' of American and European political experience.

III. The Principal Stages in the History of Bolshevism

The years of preparation for revolution (1903–05). The approach of a great storm was sensed everywhere. All classes were in a state of ferment and preparation. Abroad, the press of the political exiles discussed the theoretical aspects of *all* the fundamental problems of the revolution. Representatives of the three main classes, of the three principal political trends – the liberal-bourgeois, the petty-bourgeois-democratic (concealed behind 'social-democratic' and 'social-revolutionary' labels), and the proletarian-revolutionary – anticipated and prepared the impending open class struggle by waging a most bitter struggle on issues of programme and tactics. *All* the issues on which the masses waged an armed struggle in 1905–07 and 1917–20 can (and should) be studied, in their embryonic form, in the press of the period. Among these three main trends there were, of course, a host of intermediate, transitional or half-hearted forms. It would be more correct to say that those political and ideological trends which were genuinely of a class nature crystallised in the struggle of press organs, parties, factions and groups; the classes were forging the requisite political and ideological weapons for the impending battles.

The years of revolution (1905–07). All classes came out into the open. All programmatical and tactical views were tested by the action of the masses. In its extent and acuteness, the strike struggle had no parallel anywhere in the world. The economic strike developed into a political strike, and the latter into insurrection. The relations between the proletariat, as the leader, and the vacillating and unstable peasantry, as the led, were tested in practice. The Soviet form of organisation came into being in the spontaneous development of the struggle. The controversies of that period over the significance of the Soviets anticipated the great struggle of 1917–20. The alternation of parliamentary and non-parliamentary forms of struggle, of the tactics of boycotting parliament and that of participating in parliament, of legal and illegal forms of struggle, and likewise their interrelations and connections – all this was marked by an extraordinary wealth of content. As for teaching the fundamentals of political science to masses and leaders, to classes and parties alike, each month of this period was equivalent to an entire year of 'peaceful' and 'constitutional' development. Without the 'dress rehearsal' of 1905, the victory of the October Revolution in 1917 would have been impossible.

The years of reaction (1907–10). Tsarism was victorious. All the revolutionary and opposition parties were smashed. Depression, demoralisation, splits, discord, defection, and pornography took the place of politics. There was an ever greater drift towards philosophical idealism; mysticism became the garb of counter-revolutionary sentiments. At the same time, however, it was this great defeat that taught the revolutionary parties and the revolutionary class a real and very useful lesson, a lesson in historical dialectics, a lesson in an understanding of the political struggle, and in the art and science of waging that struggle. It is at moments of need that one learns who one's friends are. Defeated armies learn their lesson.

Victorious tsarism was compelled to speed up the destruction of the remnants of the pre-bourgeois, patriarchal mode of life in Russia. The country's development along bourgeois lines proceeded apace. Illusions that stood outside and above class distinctions, illusions concerning the possibility of avoiding capitalism, were scattered to the winds. The class struggle manifested itself in a quite new and more distinct way.

The revolutionary parties had to complete their education. They were learning how to attack. Now they had to realise that such knowledge must be supplemented with the knowledge of how to retreat in good order. They had to realise – and it is from bitter experience that the revolutionary class learns to realise this – that victory is impossible unless one has learned how to attack and retreat properly. Of all the defeated opposition and revolutionary parties, the Bolsheviks effected the most orderly retreat, with the least loss to their 'army', with its core best preserved, with the least significant splits (in point of depth and incurability), with the least demoralisation, and in the best condition to resume work on the broadest scale and in the most correct and energetic manner. The Bolsheviks achieved this only because they ruthlessly exposed and expelled the revolutionary phrase-mongers, those who did not wish to understand that one had to retreat, that one had to know how to retreat, and that one had absolutely to learn how to work legally in the most reactionary of parliaments, in the most reactionary of trade unions, co-operative and insurance societies and similar organisations.

The years of revival (1910–14). At first progress was incredibly slow, then, following the Lena events of 1912, it became somewhat more rapid. Overcoming unprecedented difficulties, the Bolsheviks thrust back the Mensheviks, whose role as bourgeois agents in the working-class movement was clearly realised by the entire bourgeoisie after 1905, and whom the bourgeoisie therefore supported in a thousand ways against the Bolsheviks. But the Bolsheviks would never have succeeded in doing this had they not followed the correct tactics of combining illegal work with the utilisation of 'legal opportunities', which they made a point of doing. In the elections to the arch-reactionary Duma, the Bolsheviks won the full support of the worker curia.

The First Imperialist World War (1914–17). Legal parliamentarianism, with an extremely reactionary 'parliament', rendered most useful service to the Bolsheviks, the party of the revolutionary proletariat. The Bolshevik deputies were exiled to Siberia. All shades of social-imperialism, social-chauvinism, social-patriotism, inconsistent and consistent internationalism, pacifism, and the revolutionary repudiation of pacifist illusions found full expression in the Russian émigré press. The learned fools and the old women of the Second International, who had arrogantly and contemptuously turned up their noses at the abundance of 'factions' in the Russian socialist movement and at the bitter struggle they were waging among themselves, were unable – when the war deprived them of their vaunted 'legality' in *all* the advanced countries – to organise anything even approximating such a free (illegal) interchange of views and such a free (illegal) evolution of correct views as the Russian revolutionaries did in Switzerland and in a number of other countries. That was why both the avowed social-patriots and the 'Kautskyites' of all countries proved to be the worst traitors to the proletariat. One of the principal reasons why Bolshevism was able to achieve victory in 1917–20 was that, since the end of 1914, it has been ruthlessly exposing the baseness and vileness of social-chauvinism and 'Kautskyism' (to which Longuetism in France, the views of the Fabians and the leaders of the Independent Labour Party in Britain, of Turati in Italy, etc., correspond), the masses later becoming more and more convinced, from their own experience, of the correctness of the Bolshevik views.

The second revolution in Russia (February to October 1917). Tsarism's senility and obsoleteness had (with the aid of the blows and hardships of a most agonising war) created an incredibly destructive force directed against it. Within a few days Russia was transformed into a democratic bourgeois republic, freer – in war conditions – than any other country in the world. The leaders of the opposition and revolutionary parties began to set up a government, just as is done in the most 'strictly parliamentary' republics; the fact that a man had been a leader of an opposition party in parliament – even in a most reactionary parliament – *facilitated* his subsequent role in the revolution. ...

As history would have it, the Soviets came into being in Russia in 1905; from February to October 1917 they were turned to a false use by the Mensheviks, who went bankrupt because of their inability to understand the role and significance of the Soviets, today the idea of Soviet power has emerged *throughout the world* and is spreading among the proletariat of all countries with extraordinary speed. Like our Mensheviks, the old heroes of the Second International are *everywhere* going bankrupt, because they are incapable of understanding the role and significance of the Soviets. Experience has proved that, on certain very important questions of the proletarian revolution, *all* countries will inevitably have to do what Russia has done.

Despite views that are today often to be met with in Europe and America, the Bolsheviks began their victorious struggle against the parliamentary and (in fact) bourgeois republic and against the Mensheviks in a very cautious manner, and the preparations they made for it were by no means simple. At the beginning of the period mentioned, we did *not* call for the overthrow of the government but explained that it was impossible to overthrow it *without* first changing the composition and the temper of the Soviets. We did not proclaim a boycott of the bourgeois parliament, the Constituent Assembly, but said – and following the April (1917) Conference of our Party began to state officially in the name of the Party – that a bourgeois republic with a Constituent Assembly would be better than a bourgeois republic without a Constituent Assembly, but that a 'workers' and peasants" republic, a Soviet republic, would be better than any bourgeois-democratic, parliamentary republic. Without such thorough, circumspect and long preparations, we could not have achieved victory in October 1917, or have consolidated that victory. ...

X. Several Conclusions

... It is now essential that Communists of every country should quite consciously take into account both the fundamental objectives of the struggle against opportunism and 'Left' doctrinairism, and the *concrete features* which this struggle assumes and must inevitably assume in each country, in conformity with the specific character of its economics, politics, culture, and national composition (Ireland, etc.), its colonies, religious divisions, and so on and so forth. Dissatisfaction with the Second International is felt everywhere and is spreading and growing, both because of its opportunism and because of its inability or incapacity to create a really centralised and really leading centre capable of directing the international tactics of the revolutionary proletariat in its struggle for a world Soviet republic. It should be clearly realised that such a leading centre can never be built up on stereotyped, mechanically equated, and identical tactical rules of struggle. As long as national and state distinctions exist among peoples and countries – and these will continue to exist for a very long time to come, even after the dictatorship of the proletariat has been established on a world-wide scale – the unity of the international tactics of the communist working-class movement in all countries demands, not the elimination of variety or the suppression of national distinctions (which is a pipe dream at present), but an application of the *fundamental* principles of communism (Soviet power and the dictatorship of the proletariat), which will *correctly modify* these principles in certain *particulars*, correctly adapt and apply them to national and national-state distinctions. ...

The proletarian vanguard has been won over ideologically. That is the main thing. Without this, not even the first step towards victory can be made. But that is still quite a long way from victory. Victory cannot be won with a vanguard alone. To throw only the vanguard into the decisive battle, before the entire class, the broad masses, have taken up a position either of direct support for the vanguard, or at least of sympathetic neutrality towards it and of precluded support for the enemy, would be, not merely foolish but criminal. Propaganda and agitation alone are not enough for an entire class, the broad masses of the working people, those oppressed by capital, to take up such a stand. For that, the masses must have their own political experience. Such is the fundamental law of all great revolutions, which has been confirmed with compelling force and vividness, not only in Russia but in Germany as well. To turn resolutely towards communism, it was necessary, not only for the ignorant and often illiterate masses of Russia, but also for the literate and well-educated masses of Germany, to realise from their own bitter experience the absolute impotence and spinelessness, the absolute helplessness and servility to the bourgeoisie, and the utter vileness of the government of the paladins of the Second International; they had to realise that a dictatorship of the extreme reactionaries (Kornilov in Russia; Kapp and Co. in Germany) is inevitably the only alternative to a dictatorship of the proletariat. …

History as a whole, and the history of revolutions in particular, is always richer in content, more varied, more multiform, more lively and ingenious than is imagined by even the best parties, the most class-conscious vanguards of the most advanced classes. This can readily be understood, because even the finest of vanguards express the class-consciousness, will, passion and imagination of tens of thousands, whereas at moments of great upsurge and the exertion of all human capacities, revolutions are made by the class-consciousness, will, passion and imagination of tens of millions, spurred on by a most acute struggle of classes. Two very important practical conclusions follow from this: first, that in order to accomplish its task the revolutionary class must be able to master *all* forms or aspects of social activity without exception (completing after the capture of political power – sometimes at great risk and with very great danger – what it did not complete before the capture of power); second, that the revolutionary class must be prepared for the most rapid and brusque replacement of one form by another.

One will readily agree that any army which does not train to use all the weapons, all the means and methods of warfare that the enemy possesses, or may possess, is behaving in an unwise or even criminal manner. This applies to politics even more than it does to the art of war. In politics it is even harder to know in advance which methods of struggle will be applicable and to our advantage in certain future conditions. Unless we learn to apply all the methods of struggle, we may suffer grave and sometimes even decisive defeat, if changes beyond our control in the position of the other classes bring to the forefront a form of activity in which we are especially weak. If, however, we learn to use all the methods of struggle, victory will be certain, because we represent the interests of the really foremost and really revolutionary class, even if circumstances do not permit us to make use of weapons that are most dangerous to the enemy, weapons that deal the swiftest mortal blows. Inexperienced revolutionaries often think that legal methods of struggle are opportunist because, in this field, the bourgeoisie has most frequently deceived and duped the workers (particularly in 'peaceful' and non-revolutionary times), while illegal methods of struggle are revolutionary. That, however, is wrong. The truth is that those parties and leaders are opportunists and traitors to the working class that are unable or unwilling (do not say, 'I can't'; say, 'I shan't') to use illegal methods of struggle in conditions such as those which prevailed, for example, during the imperialist war of 1914–18, when the bourgeoisie of the freest democratic countries most brazenly and brutally deceived the workers, and smothered the truth about the predatory character of the war. But revolutionaries who are incapable of combining illegal forms of struggle with *every* form of legal struggle are poor revolutionaries indeed. It is not difficult to be a revolutionary when revolution has already broken out and is in spate, when all people are joining the revolution just because they are carried away, because it is the vogue, and sometimes even from careerist motives. After its victory, the proletariat has to make most strenuous efforts, even the most painful, so as to 'liberate' itself from such pseudo-revolutionaries. It is far more difficult – and far more precious – to be a revolutionary when the conditions for direct, open, really mass and really revolutionary struggle *do not yet exist*, to be able to champion the interests of the revolution (by propaganda, agitation and organisation) in non-revolutionary bodies, and quite often in downright reactionary bodies, in a non-revolutionary situation, among the masses who are incapable of immediately appreciating the need for revolutionary methods of action. To be able to seek, find and correctly determine the specific path or the particular turn of events that will *lead* the masses to the real, decisive and final revolutionary struggle – such is the main objective of communism in Western Europe and in America today.

1921: Speech on Tactics of the Communist International[*]

… We Russians are already sick and tired of these Leftist phrases. We are men of organisation. In drawing up our plans, we must proceed in an organised way and try to find the correct line. It is, of course, no secret that our theses are a compromise. And why not? Among Communists, who have already convened their Third Congress and have worked out definite fundamental principles, compromises under certain conditions are necessary. …

Terracini says that we were victorious in Russia although the Party was very small. He is dissatisfied with what is said in the theses about Czechoslovakia. Here there are 27 amendments, and if I had a mind to criticise them I should, like some orators, have to speak for not less than three hours. … We have heard here that in Czechoslovakia the Communist Party has 300,000–400,000 members, and that it is essential to win over the majority, to create an invincible force and continue enlisting fresh masses of workers. Terracini is already prepared to attack. He says: if there are already 400,000 workers in the party, why should we want more? Delete! He is afraid of the word 'masses' and wants to eradicate it. Comrade Terracini has understood very little of

* *Collected Works*, Vol. 32: 468, 470–1, 473, 474–7.

the Russian revolution. In Russia, we were a small party, but we had with us in addition the majority of the Soviets of Workers' and Peasants' Deputies throughout the country. Do you have anything of the sort? We had with us almost half the army, which then numbered at least 10 million men. Do you really have the majority of the army behind you? Show me such a country! If these views of Comrade Terracini are shared by three other delegations, then something is wrong in the International! Then we must say: 'Stop! There must be a decisive fight! Otherwise the Communist International is lost.' ...

We were victorious in Russia, and with such ease, because we prepared for our revolution during the imperialist war. That was the first condition. Ten million workers and peasants in Russia were armed, and our slogan was: an immediate peace at all costs. We were victorious because the vast mass of the peasants were revolutionarily disposed against the big landowners. ...

If it is said that we were victorious in Russia in spite of not having a big party, that only proves that those who say it have not understood the Russian revolution and that they have absolutely no understanding of how to prepare for a revolution.

Our first step was to create a real Communist Party so as to know whom we were talking to and whom we could fully trust. ...

Our first task is to create a genuinely revolutionary party and to break with the Mensheviks. But that is only a preparatory school. ...

The second stage, after organising into a party, consists in learning to prepare for revolution. In many countries we have not even learned how to assume the leadership. We were victorious in Russia not only because the undisputed majority of the working class was on our side (during the elections in 1917 the overwhelming majority of the workers were with us against the Mensheviks), but also because half the army, immediately after our seizure of power, and nine-tenths of the peasants, in the course of some weeks, came over to our side; we were victorious because we adopted the agrarian programme of the Socialist-Revolutionaries instead of our own, and put it into effect. Our victory lay in the fact that we carried out the Socialist-Revolutionary programme; that is why this victory was so easy. ...

In spite of the fact that the majority so rapidly came to be on our side, the difficulties confronting us after our victory were very great. Nevertheless we won through because we kept in mind not only our aims but also our principles, and did not tolerate in our Party those who kept silent about principles but talked of aims, 'dynamic tendencies' and the 'transition from passivity to activity'. ...

I have been speaking too long as it is; hence I wish to say only a few words about the concept of 'masses'. It is one that changes in accordance with the changes in the nature of the struggle. At the beginning of the struggle it took only a few thousand genuinely revolutionary workers to warrant talk of the masses. If the party succeeds in drawing into the struggle not only its own members, if it also succeeds in arousing non-party people, it is well on the way to winning the masses. During our revolutions there were instances when several thousand workers represented the masses. In the history of our movement, and of our struggle against the Mensheviks, you will find many examples where several thousand workers in a town were enough to give a clearly mass character to the movement. You have a mass when several thousand non-party workers, who usually live a philistine life and drag out a miserable existence, and who have never heard anything about politics, begin to act in a revolutionary way. If the movement spreads and intensifies, it gradually develops into a real revolution. We saw this in 1905 and 1917 during three revolutions, and you too will have to go through all this. When the revolution has been sufficiently prepared, the concept 'masses' becomes different: several thousand workers no longer constitute the masses. This word begins to denote something else. The concept of 'masses' undergoes a change so that it implies the majority, and not simply a majority of the workers alone, but the majority of all the exploited. Any other kind of interpretation is impermissible for a revolutionary, and any other sense of the word becomes incomprehensible. It is possible that even a small party, the British or American party, for example, after it has thoroughly studied the course of political development and become acquainted with the life and customs of the non-party masses, will at a favourable moment evoke a revolutionary movement (Comrade Radek has pointed to the miners' strike as a good example). You will have a mass movement if such a party comes forward with its slogans at such a moment and succeeds in getting millions of workers to follow it. I would not altogether deny that a revolution can be started by a very small party and brought to a victorious conclusion. But one must have a knowledge of the methods by which the masses can be won over. For this thoroughgoing preparation of revolution is essential. But here you have comrades coming forward with the assertion that we should immediately give up the demand for 'big' masses. They must be challenged. Without thoroughgoing preparation you will not achieve victory in any country. Quite a small party is sufficient to lead the masses. At certain times there is no necessity for big organisations.

But to win, we must have the sympathy of the masses. An absolute majority is not always essential; but what is essential to win and retain power is not only the majority of the working class – I use the term 'working class' in its West-European sense, i.e., in the sense of the industrial proletariat – but also the majority of the working and exploited rural population. Have you thought about this? Do we find in Terracini's speech even a hint at this thought? He speaks only of 'dynamic tendency' and the 'transition from passivity to activity'. Does he devote even a single word to the food question? And yet the workers demand their victuals, although they can put up with a great deal and go hungry, as we have seen to a certain extent in Russia. We must, therefore, win over to our side not only the majority of the working class, but also the majority of the working and exploited rural population. Have you prepared for this? Almost nowhere. ...

The comrades ought to learn to wage a real revolutionary struggle. The German workers have already begun this. Hundreds of thousands of proletarians in that country have been fighting heroically. Anyone who opposes this struggle should be immediately expelled. But after that we must not engage in empty word-spinning but must immediately begin to learn, on the basis of the mistakes made, how to organise the struggle better. We must not conceal our mistakes from the enemy. Anyone who is afraid of this is no revolutionary. On the contrary, if we openly declare to the workers: 'Yes, we have made mistakes', it will mean that they will not be repeated and we shall be able better to choose the moment. And if during the struggle itself the majority of the working people prove to be on our side – not only the majority of the workers, but the majority of all the exploited and oppressed – then we shall really be victorious.

9

REACHING FOR SOCIALISM, RESISTING BUREAUCRACY

The isolation of revolutionary Russia – thanks to the intense hostility of the capitalist powers and their success in repressing (often murderously) revolutionary upsurges following the First World War – helped to block the realisation of the revolutionary-democratic vision that had animated Lenin and his comrades. The devastation of the First World War, the incredibly violent Russian civil war, and the combined aggression of military intervention and economic blockade by anti-Bolshevik governments resulted in economic collapse and extreme social crisis, in turn brutalising political realities in the early Soviet Republic. Excessive self-confidence and blind spots in the ideological perspectives of the Bolsheviks made it more difficult for them, under such circumstances, to resist authoritarian temptations. Their giving way to such temptations was justified in the name of revolutionary necessity and expediency. The resulting tragedy has been suggested in sections of the editor's essay in Part One of this volume.

While Lenin's thought in the final six years of his active political life very much bears the marks of this tragic authoritarianism, there is also powerful evidence of his continuing revolutionary-democratic commitments, consistent with all he had struggled for over the previous 20 years and more. These qualities are evident in the readings one finds in this final chapter. As with his other writings and speeches, we find here an intense effort to express ideas clearly and directly, to connect the ideas with practical action, but also to compel his practical-minded readers and listeners to think more broadly, to consider more deeply, to take the long view of history.

What is strikingly absent from these selections is any claim that a socialist economy had been established by the Soviet government. As with other Marxists, Lenin believed that socialism would only be possible on the basis of a high level of economic development and in a global context in which other sectors of the world economy were moving, in tandem with revolutionary Russia, in a transition from capitalism to socialism. A careful examination of his writings reveals that initially he envisioned a form of 'mixed economy' in which a significant capitalist sector of the economy (under watchful 'workers' control', to be sure) would exist for some time, and that the sudden shift to the extreme statist measures of 'War Communism' adopted with the flare-up of civil war and foreign intervention was not seen by him as constituting socialism. Instead he conceived of the Soviet economic reality as a variant of 'state capitalism', which he concluded would be a necessary pre-condition for the transition to socialism. At the same time, he believed that the Communist Party and Soviet regime could and must be constantly reaching in the direction of socialism – by elevating the material condition, the education, the consciousness, and the democratic participation in government of increasingly broad layers of workers and peasants.

In the excerpts of his 1919 address 'Tasks of the Working Women's Movement in the Soviet Republic', Lenin elaborates on various dimensions of women's liberation, placing this in the broader context of achieving the radical-democratic goals of the Russian Revolution and building up the country's economy. In the excerpts of addresses delivered in the same year to the All-Russian Conference on Adult Education, we first see him commenting on practical efforts to increase literacy among the largely illiterate population, and then placing such matters in a broad historical context. This includes: considering the brutal circumstances of the Russian civil war; acknowledging the real possibility that the Russian Revolution might be defeated, but insisting that this would not negate its value; comparing the Russian with the French revolutionary experience; comparing proletarian with capitalist discipline; and focusing on the dictatorship of the proletariat as a means for establishing working-class control over society while forging an essential alliance with the peasantry.

The brief excerpts from 'On the Trade Unions' at the end of 1920 and 'The Party Crisis' at the beginning of 1921 reflect the fact that in this period a number of intense debates had cropped up in Bolshevik ranks. On the one hand, Trotsky (whose central contribution had been organising and leading to victory the Red Army) had veered in a more centralising direction than Lenin, arguing for 'the militarisation of labour' and the subordination of trade unions to the state, under the logic that workers should not require protection from their own 'workers' state'. On the other hand, a fiercely anti-bureaucratic faction, the Workers Opposition led by Alexander Shlyapnikov and Alexandra Kollontai, argued that the state was actually controlled by bureaucracy not workers. They called for subordination of the state to the trade unions (a notion which Lenin tagged as 'syndicalism' and viewed as dangerously impractical). Yet this position resonated among many workers and found echoes in other

Party currents, including 'Left Communists' associated with Nikolai Bukharin and 'Democratic Centralists' associated with Timothy V. Sapronov.

We see Lenin arguing against Trotsky by pointing out that since 1917 the Soviet state had evolved into something that was no longer simply a 'workers' state', but instead was 'a workers' state with bureaucratic distortions', which indeed required that a certain amount of autonomy be allowed the trade unions for the purpose of protecting the workers. And while we also see him warning against 'ideological discord' that could give aid to the Soviet government's enemies, and against the 'syndicalist deviation' that might 'kill the Party', he also emphasises the necessity of conducting 'a long and arduous' struggle against bureaucracy.

These comments preceded a major reorientation which Lenin helped to bring about in Soviet government policy as the civil war came to an end – from the repressive and militarised economics of 'War Communism' to the New Economic Policy (NEP). The much greater openness to individual and market initiatives allowed by NEP, especially beneficial to small businessmen in urban areas and to the peasantry, contributed to the emergence of inequalities, but it also dramatically revitalised the economy and improved living standards. Accompanying this, despite an end to the brutal 'Red Terror' and a flourishing of greater cultural diversity, there was the final elimination of organised political opposition to the government. There had been fluctuating and severe curtailments during the civil war, but elements of the Mensheviks, Left SRs, and anarchists – all substantial forces up to early 1918 – had been able to maintain some open presence in Soviet political life. But especially with a mini-civil war within the working class, in the form of the 1921 uprising – in the former Bolshevik stronghold of Kronstadt (outside of Petersburg) – and suppression of the uprising, all of these non-Bolshevik political currents were systematically closed down. The Tenth Congress of the Russian Communist Party (1921) also voted to ban organised factions within its own ranks. This combination – a dramatically improving economic situation and the closing off of opportunities for organised political criticism and dissent – contributed to the corrupting bureaucratic tendencies against which Lenin was polemicising.

In his last article, 'Better Fewer, But Better' (published in March 1923), and presented here in its entirety, Lenin goes further than ever in his critical estimate of the Soviet state's bureaucratic distortions. His remarks focus on the bureaucratisation of the Workers' and Peasants' Inspection, which Lenin had helped establish in 1919. It had been designed to expose abuses of power, inefficiency, and corruption in the state apparatus. But under the leadership of Joseph Stalin it had itself degenerated into a bureaucratic, meddlesome, corrupt entity quite unable to function as the instrument of worker–peasant control over the bureaucracy that Lenin had intended. In this article he typically placed the problem in its historical, cultural, and global-political context, and offered practical proposals. But his comments were also seen as an incredibly negative reflection on Stalin, who had a few months earlier been elevated to the newly-created and potentially quite powerful position of the Russian Communist Party's General Secretary.

In fact, this article was part of a last, desperate campaign by a now gravely incapacitated Lenin, who had suffered three strokes and realised that his life would soon end. With the assistance of Krupskaya and in alliance with Trotsky (other leading Bolsheviks seemingly oblivious to the looming danger), Lenin moved against what he perceived as the regime's bureaucratic-authoritarian disorientation in general, and against Stalin in particular. In addition to the sally against bureaucracy, Lenin targeted a Stalin-supported proposal that would ease the government monopoly on foreign trade, and also protested repressive policies toward the oppressed Georgian nationality by Stalin and others close to him. Lenin's opinion of Stalin had dramatically deteriorated since being able to observe him in his new position of power. 'Stalin is too rude and this defect, although quite tolerable in our midst and in dealings among us Communists, becomes intolerable in a Secretary-General.' He suggested that Stalin be removed and replaced by someone 'more tolerant, more loyal, more polite and more considerate to comrades, less capricious, etc'.[1]

Another stroke brought an end to Lenin's efforts, and after several agonised months a final stroke killed him – at which point Stalin led the way in establishing a Lenin cult. Among those who resisted this was Krupskaya, Lenin's widow, who wrote:

> Comrades, workers and peasants! I have a great request to make to you: do not allow your grief for Ilyich to express itself in the external veneration of his person. Do not build memorials to him, [have] palaces named after him, [do not hold] magnificent celebrations in his memory, etc. All of this meant so little to him in his lifetime: he found it all so trying. Remember how much poverty and disorder we still have in our country. If you want to honor the name of Vladimir Ilyich – build day care centers, kindergartens, homes, schools … etc., and most importantly – try in all things to fulfill his legacy …[2]

Instead, the Lenin cult ballooned into a form of secular religion utilised to enhance the authority of the bureaucratic dictatorship that was to become the hallmark of the Union of Soviet Socialist Republics.

To find the fulfilment of Lenin's legacy, one must look elsewhere – in the struggles for freedom, democracy, and social justice which have continued, since his death, in his native land and throughout the world.

Notes

1. Lenin, 'Letter to the Congress', *Collected Works*, Vol. 36 (Moscow: Progress Publishers, 1971), 596.
2. Ronald W. Clark, *Lenin, A Political Biography* (New York: Harper and Row, 1988), 487.

1919: Tasks of the Working Women's Movement[*]

… I should like to say a few words about the general tasks facing the working women's movement in the Soviet Republic, those that are, in general, connected with the transition to socialism, and those that are of particular urgency at the present time. Comrades, the question of the position of women was raised by Soviet power from the very beginning. It seems to me that any workers' state in the course of transition to socialism is laced with a double task. The first part of that task is relatively simple and easy. It concerns those old laws that kept women in a position of inequality as compared to men.

Participants in all emancipation movements in Western Europe have long since, not for decades but for centuries, put forward the demand that obsolete laws be annulled and women and men be made equal by law, but none of the democratic European states, none of the most advanced republics have succeeded in putting it into effect, because wherever there is capitalism, wherever there is private property in land and factories, wherever the power of capital is preserved, the men retain their privileges. It was possible to put it into effect in Russia only because the power of the workers has been established here since 25 October 1917. From its very inception Soviet power set out to be the power of the working people, hostile to all forms of exploitation. It set itself the task of doing away with the possibility of the exploitation of the working people by the landowners and capitalists, of doing away with the rule of capital. Soviet power has been trying to make it possible for the working people to organise their lives without private property in land, without privately-owned factories, without that private property that everywhere, throughout the world, even where there is complete political liberty, even in the most democratic republics, keeps the working people in a state of what is actually poverty and wage-slavery, and women in a state of double slavery.

Soviet power, the power of the working people, in the first months of its existence effected a very definite revolution in

* *Collected Works*, Vol. 30: 40–4.

legislation that concerns women. Nothing whatever is left in the Soviet Republic of those laws that put women in a subordinate position. I am speaking specifically of those laws that took advantage of the weaker position of women and put them in a position of inequality and often, even, in a humiliating position, i.e., the laws on divorce and on children born out of wedlock and on the right of a woman to summon the father of a child for maintenance.

It is particularly in this sphere that bourgeois legislation, even, it must be said, in the most advanced countries, takes advantage of the weaker position of women to humiliate them and give them a status of inequality. It is particularly in this sphere that Soviet power has left nothing whatever of the old, unjust laws that were intolerable for working people. We may now say proudly and without any exaggeration that apart from Soviet Russia there is not a country in the world where women enjoy full equality and where women are not placed in the humiliating position felt particularly in day-to-day family life. This was one of our first and most important tasks. ...

We see that equality is proclaimed in all democratic republics but in the civil laws and in laws on the rights of women – those that concern their position in the family and divorce – we see inequality and the humiliation of women at every step, and we say that this is a violation of democracy specifically in respect of the oppressed. Soviet power has implemented democracy to a greater degree than any of the other, most advanced countries because it has not left in its laws any trace of the inequality of women. ...

Laws alone, of course, are not enough, and we are by no means content with mere decrees. In the sphere of legislation, however, we have done everything required of us to put women in a position of equality and we have every right to be proud of it. The position of women in Soviet Russia is now ideal as compared with their position in the most advanced states. We tell ourselves, however, that this is, of course, only the beginning.

Owing to her work in the house, the woman is still in a difficult position. To effect her complete emancipation and make her the equal of the man it is necessary for the national economy to be socialised and for women to participate in common productive labour. Then women will occupy the same position as men.

Here we are not, of course, speaking of making women the equal of men as far as productivity of labour, the quantity of labour, the length of the working day, labour conditions, etc., are concerned; we mean that the woman should not, unlike the man, be oppressed because of her position in the family. You all know that even when women have full rights, they still remain factually downtrodden because all housework is left to them. In most cases housework is the most unproductive, the most barbarous and the most arduous work a woman can do. It is exceptionally petty and does not include anything that would in any way promote the development of the woman.

In pursuance of the socialist ideal we want to struggle for the full implementation of socialism, and here an extensive field of labour opens up before women. We are now making serious preparations to clear the ground for the building of socialism, but the building of socialism will begin only when we have achieved the complete equality of women and when we undertake the new work together with women who have been emancipated from that petty, stultifying, unproductive work. This is a job that will take us many, many years.

This work cannot show any rapid results and will not produce a scintillating effect.

We are setting up model institutions, dining-rooms and nurseries, that will emancipate women from housework. And the work of organising all these institutions will fall mainly to women. It has to be admitted that in Russia today there are very few institutions that would help woman out of her state of household slavery. There is an insignificant number of them, and the conditions now obtaining in the Soviet Republic – the war and food situation about which comrades have already given you the details – hinder us in this work. Still, it must be said that these institutions that liberate women from their position as household slaves are springing up wherever it is in any way possible.

We say that the emancipation of the workers must be effected by the workers themselves, and in exactly the same way the emancipation of working women is a matter for the working women themselves. The working women must themselves see to it that such institutions are developed, and this activity will bring about a complete change in their position as compared with what it was under the old, capitalist society.

In order to be active in politics under the old, capitalist regime special training was required, so that women played an insignificant part in politics, even in the most advanced and free capitalist countries. Our task is to make politics available to every working woman. Ever since private property in land and factories has been abolished and the power of the landowners and capitalists overthrown, the tasks of politics have become simple, clear and comprehensible to the working people as a whole, including working women. In capitalist society the woman's position is marked by such inequality that the extent of her participation in politics is only an insignificant fraction of that of the man. The power of the working people is necessary for a change to be wrought in this situation, for then the main tasks of politics will consist of matters directly affecting the fate of the working people themselves.

Here, too, the participation of working women is essential – not only of party members and politically-conscious women, but also of the non-party women and those who are least politically conscious. Here Soviet power opens up a wide field of activity to working women.

1919: Comments to Congress on Adult Education*

... I am sure that there is not another sphere of Soviet activity in which such enormous progress has been made during the past 18 months as in the sphere of adult education. Undoubtedly, it has been easier for us and for you to work in this sphere than in others. Here we had to cast aside the old obstacles and the old

* *Collected Works*, Vol. 29: 335–8, 371–4.

hindrances. Here it was much easier to do something to meet the tremendous demand for knowledge, for free education and free development, which was felt most among the masses of the workers and peasants; for while the mighty pressure of the masses made it easy for us to remove the external obstacles that stood in their path, to break up the historical bourgeois institutions which bound us to imperialist war and doomed Russia to bear the enormous burden that resulted from this war, we nevertheless felt acutely how heavy the task of re-educating the masses was, the task of organisation and instruction, spreading knowledge, combating that heritage of ignorance, primitiveness, barbarism and savagery that we took over. In this field the struggle had to be waged by entirely different methods; we could count only on the prolonged success and the persistent and systematic influence of the leading sections of the population, an influence which the masses willingly submit to, but often we are guilty of doing less than we could do. I think that in taking these first steps to spread adult education, education, free from the old limits and conventionalities, we had at first to contend with two obstacles. The first was the plethora of bourgeois intellectuals ... testing their individual theories ... and ... very often the most absurd ideas were hailed as something new, and the supernatural and incongruous were offered as purely proletarian art and proletarian culture. ...

The second was also inherited from capitalism. The broad masses of the petty-bourgeois working people who were thirsting for knowledge, broke down the old system, but could not propose anything of an organising or organised nature. ...

When we raised the question of mobilising literate persons, the most striking thing was the brilliant victory achieved by our revolution without immediately emerging from the limits of the bourgeois revolution. It gave freedom for development to the available forces, but these available forces were petty bourgeois and their watch-word was the old one – each for himself and God for all – the very same accursed capitalist slogan which can never lead to anything but Kolchak and bourgeois restoration. If we review what we are doing to educate the illiterate, I think we shall have to draw the conclusion that we have done very little, and that our duty in this field is to realise that the organisation of proletarian elements is essential. It is not the ridiculous phrases which remain on paper that matter, but the introduction of measures which the people need urgently and which would compel every literate person to regard it his duty to instruct several illiterate persons. This is what our decree says; but in this field hardly anything has been done. ...

At present we must combat the survivals of disorganisation, chaos, and ridiculous departmental wrangling. This must be our main task. We must take up the simple and urgent matter of mobilising the literate to combat illiteracy. We must utilise the books that are available and set to work to organise a network of libraries which will help the people to gain access to every available book; there must be no parallel organisations, but a single, uniform planned organisation. This small matter reflects one of the fundamental tasks of our revolution. If it fails to carry out this task, if it fails to set about creating a really systematic and uniform organisation in place of our Russian chaos and inefficiency, then this revolution will remain a bourgeois revolution because the major specific feature of the proletarian revolution which is marching towards communism is this organisation – for all the bourgeoisie wanted was to break up the old system and allow freedom for the development of peasant farming, which revived the same capitalism as in all earlier revolutions.

Since we call ourselves the Communist Party, we must understand that only now that we have removed the external obstacles and have broken down the old institutions have we come face to face with the primary task of a genuine proletarian revolution in all its magnitude, namely, that of organising tens and hundreds of millions of people. After the 18 months' experience that we all have acquired in this field, we must at last take the right road that will lead to victory over the lack of culture, and over the ignorance and barbarism from which we have suffered all this time. ...

I will now deal with the last question on my list, that of the defeat and victory of the revolution. Kautsky, whom I mentioned to you as the chief representative of the old, decayed socialism, does not understand the tasks of the dictatorship of the proletariat. He reproached us, saying that a decision taken by a majority might have ensured a peaceful issue. A decision by a dictatorship is a decision taken by military means. Hence, if you do not win by force of arms you will be vanquished and annihilated, because in civil war no prisoners are taken, it is a war of extermination. This is how terrified Kautsky tried to 'terrify' us.

Quite right. What you say is true. We confirm the correctness of your observation and there is nothing more to be said. Civil war is more stern and cruel than any other war. This has been the case throughout history since the time of the civil wars in ancient Rome; wars between nations always ended in a deal between the propertied classes, and only during civil war does the oppressed class exert efforts to exterminate the oppressing class, to eliminate the economic conditions of this class's existence.

I ask you, what is the 'revolutionary' worth who tries to scare those who have started the revolution with the prospect that it might suffer defeat? There has never been, there is none, there will not be, nor can there be a revolution which did not stand some risk of defeat. A revolution is a desperate struggle of classes that has reached the peak of ferocity. The class struggle is inevitable. One must either reject revolution altogether or accept the fact that the struggle against the propertied classes will be sterner than all other revolutions. Among socialists who are at all intelligent there was never any difference of opinion on this point. A year ago, when I analysed the apostasy that lay behind Kautsky's statements I wrote the following. Even if – this was in September last year – even if the imperialists were to overthrow the Bolshevik government tomorrow we would not for a moment repent that we had taken power. And not a single class-conscious worker who represents the interests of the masses of the working people would repent, or have any doubt that, in spite of it all, our revolution had triumphed; the revolution triumphs if it brings to the forefront the advanced class which strikes effectively at exploitation. Under such circumstances, the revolution triumphs even if it suffered defeat. This may sound like juggling with words; but to prove the truth of it, let us take a concrete example from history.

Take the great French Revolution. It is with good reason that it is called a great revolution. It did so much for the class that it served, for the bourgeoisie, that it left its imprint on the entire nineteenth century, the century which gave civilisation and culture to the whole of mankind. The great French revolutionaries served the interests of the bourgeoisie although they did not realise it for their vision was obscured by the words 'liberty, equality and fraternity'; in the nineteenth century, however, what they had begun was continued, carried out piecemeal and finished in all parts of the world.

In a matter of 18 months our revolution has done ever so much more for our class, the class we serve, the proletariat, than the great French revolutionaries did.

They held out in their own country for two years, and then perished under the blows of united European reaction, under the blows of the united hordes of the whole world, who crushed the French revolutionaries, reinstated the legitimate monarch in France, the Romanov of the period, reinstated the landowners, and for many decades later crushed every revolutionary movement in France. Nevertheless, the great French Revolution triumphed.

Everybody who studies history seriously will admit that although it was crushed, the French Revolution was nevertheless triumphant, because it laid down for the whole world such firm foundations of bourgeois democracy, of bourgeois freedom, that they could never be uprooted.

In a matter of 18 months our revolution has done ever so much more for the proletariat, for the class which we serve, for the goal towards which we are striving – the overthrow of the rule of capital – than the French Revolution did for its class. And that is why we say that even if we take the hypothetically possible worst contingency, even if tomorrow some lucky Kolchak were to exterminate the Bolsheviks to the last man, the revolution would still be invincible. And what we say is proved by the fact that the new type of state organisation produced by this revolution has achieved a moral victory among the working class all over the world and is already receiving its support. When the prominent French bourgeois revolutionaries perished in the struggle they were isolated, they were not supported in other countries. All the European states turned against them, chief among them England, although it was an advanced country. After only 18 months of Bolshevik rule, our revolution succeeded in making the new state organisation which it created, the Soviet organisation, comprehensible, familiar and popular to the workers all over the world, in making them regard it as their own.

I have shown you that the dictatorship of the proletariat is an inevitable, essential and absolutely indispensable means of emerging from the capitalist system. Dictatorship does not mean only force, although it is impossible without force, but also a form of the organisation of labour superior to the preceding form. That is why in my brief speech of greeting at the opening of the Congress I emphasised this fundamental, elementary and extremely simple task *of organisation*; and that is why I am so strongly opposed to all these intellectual fads and 'proletarian cultures'. As opposed to these fads I advocate the ABC of organisation. Distribute grain and coal in such a way as to take care of every pood – this is the object of proletarian discipline. Proletarian discipline is not discipline maintained by the lash, as it was under the rule of the serf-owners, or discipline maintained by starvation, as it is under the rule of the capitalists, but comradely discipline, the discipline of the labour unions. If you solve this elementary and extremely simple problem of organisation, we shall win, for then the peasants – who vacillate between the workers and the capitalists, who cannot make up their minds whether to side with the people of whom they are still suspicious, but cannot deny that these people are creating a more just organisation of production under which there will be no exploitation, and under which 'freedom' of trade in grain will be a crime against the state, who cannot make up their minds whether to side with these people or with those who, as in the good old days, promise freedom to trade which is alleged to mean also freedom to work in any way one pleased – the peasants, I say, will whole-heartedly side with us. When the peasants see that the proletariat is organising its state power in such a way as to maintain order – and the peasants want this and demand it, and they are right in doing so, although this desire for order is connected with much that is confused and reactionary, and with many prejudices – they, in the long run, after considerable vacillation, will follow the lead of the workers. The peasants cannot simply and easily pass from the old society to the new overnight. They are aware that the old society ensured 'order' by ruining the working people and making slaves of them. But they are not sure that the proletariat can guarantee order. More cannot be expected of these downtrodden, ignorant and disunited peasants. They will not believe words and programmes. And they are quite right not to believe words, for otherwise there would be no end to frauds of every kind. They will believe only deeds, practical experience. Prove to them that you, the united proletariat, the proletarian state, the proletarian dictatorship, are able to distribute grain and coal in such a way as to husband every pood, that you are able to arrange matters so that every pood of surplus grain and coal is distributed not by the profiteers ... but shall be fairly distributed, supplied to starving workers, even to sustain them during periods of unemployment when the factories and workshops are idle. Prove that you can do this. This is the fundamental task of proletarian culture, of proletarian organisation. Force can be used even if those who resort to it have no economic roots, but in that case, history will doom it to failure. But force can be applied with the backing of the advanced class, relying on the loftier principles of the socialist system, order and organisation. *In that case, it may suffer temporary failure, but in the long run it is invincible.*

If the proletarian organisation proves to the peasants that it can maintain proper order, that labour and bread are fairly distributed and that care is being taken to husband every pood of grain and coal, that we workers are able to do this with the aid of our comradely, trade union discipline, that we resort to force in our struggle only to protect the interests of labour, that we take grain from profiteers and not from working people, that we want to reach an understanding with the middle peasants, the working peasants, and that we are ready to provide them with all we can at present – when the peasants see all this, their alliance with the working class, their alliance with the proletariat, will be indestructible. And this is what we aim at.

1920: On the Trade Unions[*]

… While betraying this lack of thoughtfulness, Comrade Trotsky falls into error himself. He seems to say that in a workers' state it is not the business of the trade unions to stand up for the material and spiritual interests of the working class. That is a mistake. Comrade Trotsky speaks of a 'workers' state'. May I say that this is an abstraction. It was natural for us to write about a workers' state in 1917; but it is now a patent error to say: 'Since this is a workers' state without any bourgeoisie, against whom then is the working class to be protected, and for what purpose?' The whole point is that it is not quite a workers' state. That is where Comrade Trotsky makes one of his main mistakes. We have got down from general principles to practical discussion and decrees, and here we are being dragged back and prevented from tackling the business at hand. This will not do. For one thing, ours is not actually a workers' state but a workers' and peasants' state. And a lot depends on that. …

Our Party Programme … shows that ours is a workers' state *with a bureaucratic twist to it*. We have had to mark it with this dismal, shall I say, tag. There you have the reality of the transition. Well, is it right to say that in a state that has taken this shape in practice the trade unions have nothing to protect, or that we can do without them in protecting the material and spiritual interests of the massively organised proletariat? No, this reasoning is theoretically quite wrong. It takes us into the sphere of abstraction or an ideal we shall achieve in 15 or 20 years' time, and I am not so sure that we shall have achieved it even by then. What we actually have before us is a reality of which we have a good deal of knowledge, provided, that is, we keep our heads, and do not let ourselves be carried away by intellectualist talk or abstract reasoning, or by what may appear to be 'theory' but is in fact error and misap-

[*]   *Collected Works*, Vol. 32: 24–5.

prehension of the peculiarities of transition. We now have a state under which it is the business of the massively organised proletariat to protect itself, while we, for our part, must use these workers' organisations to protect the workers from their state, and to get them to protect our state. Both forms of protection are achieved through the peculiar interweaving of our state measures and our agreeing or 'coalescing' with our trade unions.

1921: The Party Crisis*

... While dealing with the 30 December discussion, I must correct another mistake of mine. I said: 'Ours is not actually a workers' state but a workers' and peasants' state.' Comrade Bukharin immediately exclaimed: 'What kind of a state?' In reply I referred him to the Eighth Congress of Soviets, which had just closed. I went back to the report of that discussion and found that I was wrong and Comrade Bukharin was right. What I should have said is: 'A workers' state is an abstraction. What we actually have is a workers' state, with this peculiarity, firstly, that it is not the working class but the peasant population that predominates in the country, and, secondly, that it is a workers' state with bureaucratic distortions.' ...

Communism says: The Communist Party, the vanguard of the proletariat, leads the non-Party workers' masses, educating, preparing, teaching and training the masses ('school' of communism) – first the workers and then the peasants – to enable them eventually to concentrate in their hands the administration of the whole national economy. ...

Our platform up to now has been: Do not defend but rectify the bureaucratic excesses. The fight against bureaucracy is a long and arduous one. Excesses can and must be rectified at once. It is not those who point out harmful excesses and strive to rectify them but those who resist rectification that undermine the prestige of the military workers and appointees. ... On this basis, let us vigorously work together for practical results.

* *Collected Works*, Vol. 32: 48, 50, 52, 53.

We have now added to our platform the following: We must combat the ideological discord and the unsound elements of the opposition who talk themselves into repudiating all 'militarisation of industry', and not only the 'appointments method', which has been the prevailing one up to now, but all 'appointments', that is, in the last analysis, repudiating the *Party*'s leading role in relation to the non-Party masses. We must combat the syndicalist deviation, which will kill the Party unless it is entirely cured of it.

The Entente[1] capitalists will surely try to take advantage of our Party's malaise to mount another invasion, and the Socialist-Revolutionaries, to hatch plots and rebellions. We need have no fear of this because we shall all unite as one man, without being afraid to admit the malaise, but recognising that it demands from all of us a greater discipline, tenacity and firmness at every post. By the time the Tenth Congress of the RCP meets in March, and after the Congress, the Party will not be weaker, but stronger.

1923: Better Fewer, But Better[*]

In the matter of improving our state apparatus, the Workers' and Peasants' Inspection should not, in my opinion, either strive after quantity or hurry. We have so far been able to devote so little thought and attention to the efficiency of our state apparatus that it would now be quite legitimate if we took special care to secure its thorough organisation, and concentrated in the Workers' and Peasants' Inspection a staff of workers really abreast of the times, i.e., not inferior to the best West-European standards. For a socialist republic this condition is, of course, too modest. But our experience of the first five years has fairly crammed our heads with mistrust and scepticism. These qualities assert themselves involuntarily when, for example, we hear people dilating at too great length and too flippantly on 'proletarian' culture. For a start, we should be satisfied with real bourgeois culture; for a start we

---

1. *Entente* or the 'Allies' – Britain, France, the USA, Japan and other countries that took part in the intervention against Soviet Russia. It should not be confused with *Entente cordiale*, the alliance of France and Great Britain and, later, tsarist Russia.

* *Collected Works*, Vol. 33: 487–502.

should be glad to dispense with the crude types of pre-bourgeois culture, i.e., bureaucratic culture or serf culture, etc. In matters of culture, haste and sweeping measures are most harmful. Many of our young writers and Communists should get this well into their heads.

Thus, in the matter of our state apparatus we should now draw the conclusion from our past experience that it would be better to proceed more slowly.

Our state apparatus is so deplorable, not to say wretched, that we must first think very carefully how to combat its defects, bearing in mind that these defects are rooted in the past, which, although it has been overthrown, has not yet been overcome, has not yet reached the stage of a culture, that has receded into the distant past. I say culture deliberately, because in these matters we can only regard as achieved what has become part and parcel of our culture, of our social life, our habits. We might say that the good in our social system has not been properly studied, understood, and taken to heart; it has been hastily grasped at; it has not been verified or tested, corroborated by experience, and not made durable, etc. Of course, it could not be otherwise in a revolutionary epoch, when development proceeded at such break-neck speed that in a matter of five years we passed from tsarism to the Soviet system.

It is time we did something about it. We must show sound scepticism for too rapid progress, for boastfulness, etc. We must give thought to testing the steps forward we proclaim every hour, take every minute and then prove every second that they are flimsy, superficial and misunderstood. The most harmful thing here would be haste. The most harmful thing would be to rely on the assumption that we know at least something, or that we have any considerable number of elements necessary for the building of a really new state apparatus, one really worthy to be called socialist, Soviet, etc.

No, we are ridiculously deficient of such an apparatus, and even of the elements of it, and we must remember that we should not stint time on building it, and that it will take many, many years.

What elements have we for building this apparatus? Only two. First, the workers who are absorbed in the struggle of socialism. These elements are not sufficiently educated. They would like to build a better apparatus for us, but they do not know how. They cannot build one. They have not yet developed the culture required for this; and it is culture that is required. Nothing will be achieved in this by doing things in a rush, by assault, by vim or vigour, or in general, by any of the best human qualities. Secondly, we have elements of knowledge, education and training, but they are ridiculously inadequate compared with all other countries.

Here we must not forget that we are too prone to compensate (or imagine that we can compensate) our lack of knowledge by zeal, haste, etc.

In order to renovate our state apparatus we must at all costs set out, first, to learn, secondly, to learn, and thirdly, to learn, and then see to it that learning shall not remain a dead letter, or a fashionable catch-phrase (and we should admit in all frankness that this happens very often with us), that learning shall really become part of our very being, that it shall actually and fully become a constituent element of our social life. In short, we must not make the demands that were made by bourgeois Western Europe, but demands that are fit and proper for a country which has set out to develop into a socialist country.

The conclusions to be drawn from the above are the following: we must make the Workers' and Peasants' Inspection a really exemplary institution, an instrument to improve our state apparatus.

In order that it may attain the desired high level, we must follow the rule: 'Measure your cloth seven times before you cut.'

For this purpose, we must utilise the very best of what there is in our social system, and utilise it with the greatest caution, thoughtfulness and knowledge, to build up the new People's Commissariat.

For this purpose, the best elements that we have in our social system – such as, first, the advanced workers, and, second, the really enlightened elements for whom we can vouch that they will not take the word for the deed, and will not utter a single word that goes against their conscience – should not shrink from admitting any difficulty and should not shrink from any struggle in order to achieve the object they have seriously set themselves.

We have been bustling for five years trying to improve our state apparatus, but it has been mere bustle, which has proved useless in these five years, of even futile, or even harmful. This bustle created the impression that we were doing something, but in effect it was only clogging up our institutions and our brains.

It is high time things were changed.

We must follow the rule: Better fewer, but better. We must follow the rule: Better get good human material in two or even three years than work in haste without hope of getting any at all.

I know that it will be hard to keep to this rule and apply it under our conditions. I know that the opposite rule will force its way through a thousand loopholes. I know that enormous resistance will have to be put up, that devilish persistence will be required, that in the first few years at least work in this field will be hellishly hard. Nevertheless, I am convinced that only by such effort shall we be able to achieve our aim; and that only by achieving this aim shall we create a republic that is really worthy of the name of Soviet, socialist, and so on, and so forth.

Many readers probably thought that the figures I quoted by way of illustration in my first article [How We Should Reorganise the Workers' and Peasants' Inspection] were too small. I am sure that many calculations may be made to prove that they are. But I think that we must put one thing above all such and other calculations, i.e., our desire to obtain really exemplary quality.

I think that the time has at last come when we must work in real earnest to improve our state apparatus and in this there can scarcely be anything more harmful than haste. That is why I would sound a strong warning against inflating the figures. In my opinion, we should, on the contrary, be especially sparing with figures in this matter. Let us say frankly that the People's Commissariat of the Workers' and Peasants' Inspection does not at present enjoy the slightest authority. Everybody knows that no other institutions are worse organised than those of our Workers' and Peasants' Inspection, and that under present conditions nothing can be expected from this People's Commissariat. We must have this firmly fixed in our minds if we really want to create within a few years an institution that will, first, be an exemplary institution, secondly, win everybody's absolute confidence, and, thirdly, prove to all and sundry that we have really justified the work of such a highly placed institution as the Central Control Commission. In my opinion, we must immediately and irrevocably reject all general figures for the size of office staffs. We must select employees for the Workers' and Peasants' Inspection with particular care and only on the basis of the strictest test. Indeed, what is the use of establishing a People's Commissariat which carries on anyhow, which does not enjoy the slightest confidence, and whose word carries scarcely any weight? I think that our main object in launching the work of reconstruction that we now have in mind is to avoid all this.

The workers whom we are enlisting as members of the Central Control Commission must be irreproachable Communists, and I think that a great deal has yet to be done to teach them the methods and objects of their work. Furthermore, there must be a definite number of secretaries to assist in this work, who must be put to a triple test before they are appointed to their posts. Lastly, the officials whom in exceptional cases we shall accept directly as employees of the Workers' and Peasants' Inspection must conform to the following requirements:

First, they must be recommended by several Communists.

Second, they must pass a test for knowledge of our state apparatus.

Third, they must pass a test in the fundamentals of the theory of our state apparatus, in the fundamentals of management, office routine, etc.

Fourth, they must work in such close harmony with the members of the Central Control Commission and with their own secretariat that we could vouch for the work of the whole apparatus.

I know that these requirements are extraordinarily strict, and I am very much afraid that the majority of the 'practical' workers in the Workers' and Peasants' Inspection will say that these requirements are impracticable, or will scoff at them. But

I ask any of the present chiefs of the Workers' and Peasants' Inspection, or anyone associated with that body, whether they can honestly tell me the practical purpose of a People's Commissariat like the Workers' and Peasants' Inspection? I think this question will help them recover their sense of proportion. Either it is not worthwhile having another of the numerous reorganisations that we have had of this hopeless affair, the Workers' and Peasants' Inspection, or we must really set to work, by slow, difficult and unusual methods, and by testing these methods over and over again, to create something really exemplary, something that will win the respect of all and sundry for its merits, and not only because of its rank and title.

If we do not arm ourselves with patience, if we do not devote several years to this task, we had better not tackle it at all.

In my opinion we ought to select a minimum number of the higher labour research institutes, etc., which we have baked so hastily, see whether they are organised properly, and allow them to continue working, but only in a way that conforms to the high standards of modern science and gives us all its benefits. If we do that it will not be utopian to hope that within a few years we shall have an institution that will be able to perform its functions, to work systematically and steadily on improving our state apparatus, an institution backed by the trust of the working class, of the Russian Communist Party, and the whole population of our Republic.

The spade-work for this could begin at once. If the People's Commissariat of the Workers' and Peasants' Inspection accepted the present plan of reorganisation, it could not take the preparatory steps and work methodically until the task is completed, without haste, and not hesitating to alter what has already been done.

Any half-hearted solution would be extremely harmful in this matter. A measure for the size of the staff of the Workers' and Peasants' Inspection based on any other consideration would, in fact, be based on the old bureaucratic considerations, on old prejudices, on what has already been condemned, universally ridiculed, etc.

In substance, the matter is as follows:

REACHING FOR SOCIALISM **343**

Either we prove now that we have really learned something about state organisation (we ought to have learned something in five years), or we prove that we are not sufficiently mature for it. If the latter is the case, we had better not tackle the task.

I think that with the available human material it will not be immodest to assume that we have learned enough to be able to systematically rebuild at least one People's Commissariat. True, this one People's Commissariat will have to be the model for our entire state apparatus.

We ought to at once announce a contest in the compilation of two or more textbooks on the organisation of labour in general, and on management in particular. We can take as a basis the book already published by Yermansky, although it should be said in parentheses that he obviously sympathises with Menshevism and is unfit to compile textbooks for the Soviet system.

We can also take as a basis the recent book by Kerzhentsev, and some of the other partial textbooks available may be useful too.

We ought to send several qualified and conscientious people to Germany, or to Britain, to collect literature and to study this question. I mention Britain in case it is found impossible to send people to the USA or Canada.

We ought to appoint a commission to draw up the preliminary programme of examinations for prospective employees of the Workers' and Peasants' Inspection; ditto for candidates to the Central Control Commission.

These and similar measures will not, of course, cause any difficulties for the People's Commissar or the collegium of the Workers' and Peasants' Inspection, or for the Presidium of the Central Control Commission.

Simultaneously, a preparatory commission should be appointed to select candidates for membership of the Central Control Commission. I hope that we shall now be able to find more than enough candidates for this post among the experienced workers in all departments, as well as among the students of our Soviet higher schools. It would hardly be right to exclude one or another category beforehand. Probably preference will have to be given to a mixed composition for this institution, which should combine many qualities, and dissimilar merits. Consequently, the tasks of drawing up the list of candidates will entail a considerable amount of work. For example, it would be least desirable for the staff of the new People's Commissariat to consist of people of one type, only of officials, say, or for it to exclude people of the propagandist type, or people whose principal quality is sociability or the ability to penetrate into circles that are not altogether customary for officials in this field, etc.

I think I shall be able to express my idea best if I compare my plan with that of academic institutions. Under the guidance of their Presidium, the members of the Central Control Commission should systematically examine all the paper and documents of the Political Bureau. Moreover, they should divide their time correctly between various jobs in investigating the routine in our institutions, from the very small and privately-owned offices to the highest state institutions. And lastly, their functions should include the study of theory, i.e., the theory of organisation of the work they intend to devote themselves to, and practical work under the guidance of other comrades or of teachers in the higher institutes for the organisation of labour.

I do not think, however, that they will be able to confine themselves to this sort of academic work. In addition, they will have to prepare themselves for working which I would not hesitate to call training to catch, I will not say rogues, but something like that, and working out special ruses to screen their movements, their approach, etc.

If such proposals were made in West-European government institutions they would rouse frightful resentment, a feeling of moral indignation, etc.; but I trust that we have not become so bureaucratic as to be capable of that. NEP has not yet succeeded in gaining such respect as to cause any of us to be shocked at the idea somebody may be caught. Our Soviet Republic is of such recent construction, and there are such heaps of the old lumber still lying around that it would hardly occur to anyone to be shocked at the idea that we should delve into them by means of ruses, by means of investigations sometimes directed to rather remote sources or in a roundabout way. And even if it did occur to anyone to be shocked by this, we may be sure that such a person would make himself a laughing-stock.

Let us hope that our new Workers' and Peasants' Inspection will abandon what the French call *pruderie*, which we may call ridiculous primness, or ridiculous swank, and which plays entirely into the hands of our Soviet and Party bureaucracy. Let it be said in parentheses that we have bureaucrats in our Party offices as well as in Soviet offices.

When I said above that we must study and study hard in institutes for the higher organisation of labour, etc., I did not by any means imply 'studying' in the schoolroom way, nor did I confine myself to the idea of studying only in the schoolroom way. I hope that not a single genuine revolutionary will suspect me of refusing, in this case, to understand 'studies' to include resorting to some semi-humourous trick, cunning device, piece of trickery or something of that sort. I know that in the staid and earnest states of Western Europe such an idea would horrify people and that not a single decent official would even entertain it. I hope, however, that we have not yet become as bureaucratic as all that and that in our midst the discussion of this idea will give rise to nothing more than amusement.

Indeed, why not combine pleasure with utility? Why not resort to some humourous or semi-humorous trick to expose something ridiculous, something harmful, something semi-ridiculous, semi-harmful, etc.?

It seems to me that our Workers' and Peasants' Inspection will gain a great deal if it undertakes to examine these ideas, and that the list of cases in which our Central Control Commission and its colleagues in the Workers' and Peasants' Inspection achieved a few of their most brilliant victories will be enriched by not a few exploits of our future Workers' and Peasants' Inspection and Central Control Commission members in places not quite mentionable in prim and staid textbooks.

How can a Party institution be amalgamated with a Soviet institution? Is there not something improper in this suggestion?

I do not ask these questions on my own behalf, but on behalf of those I hinted at above when I said that we have bureaucrats in our Party institutions as well as in the Soviet institutions.

But why, indeed, should we not amalgamate the two if this is in the interests of our work? Do we not all see that such an amalgamation has been very beneficial in the case of the People's Commissariat of Foreign Affairs, where it was brought about at the very beginning? Does not the Political Bureau discuss from the Party point of view many questions, both minor and important, concerning the 'moves' we should make in reply to the 'moves' of foreign powers in order to forestall their, say, cunning, if we are not to use a less respectable term? Is not this flexible amalgamation of a Soviet institution with a Party institution a source of great strength in our politics? I think that what has proved its usefulness, what has been definitely adopted in our foreign politics and has become so customary that it no longer calls forth any doubt in this field, will be at least as appropriate (in fact, I think it will be much more appropriate) for our state apparatus as a whole. The functions of the Workers' and Peasants' Inspection cover our state apparatus as a whole, and its activities should affect all and every state institution without exception: local, central, commercial, purely administrative, educational, archival, theatrical, etc. – in short, all without any exception.

Why then should not an institution, whose activities have such wide scope, and which moreover requires such extraordinary flexibility of forms, be permitted to adopt this peculiar amalgamation of a Party control institution with a Soviet control institution?

I see no obstacles to this. What is more, I think that such an amalgamation is the only guarantee of success in our work. I think that all doubts on this score arise in the dustiest corners of our government offices, and that they deserve to be treated with nothing but ridicule.

Another doubt: is it expedient to combine educational activities with official activities? I think that it is not only expedient, but necessary. Generally speaking, in spite of our revolutionary attitude towards the West-European form of state, we have allowed ourselves to become infected with a number of its most harmful and ridiculous prejudices; to some extent we have been deliberately infected with them by our dear bureaucrats, who counted on being able again and again to fish in the muddy waters of these prejudices. And they did fish in these muddy waters to so great an extent that only the blind among us failed to see how extensively this fishing was practised.

In all spheres of social, economic and political relationships we are 'frightfully' revolutionary. But as regards precedence, the observance of the forms and rites of office management, our 'revolutionariness' often gives way to the mustiest routine. On more than one occasion, we have witnessed the very interesting phenomenon of a great leap forward in social life being accompanied by amazing timidity whenever the slightest changes are proposed.

This is natural, for the boldest steps forward were taken in a field which was long reserved for theoretical study, which was promoted mainly, and even almost exclusively, in theory. The Russian, when away from work, found solace from bleak bureaucratic realities in unusually bold theoretical constructions, and that is why in our country these unusually bold theoretical constructions assumed an unusually lopsided character. Theoretical audacity in general constructions went hand in hand with amazing timidity as regards certain very minor reforms in office routine. Some great universal agrarian revolution was worked out with an audacity unexampled in any other country, and at the same time the imagination failed when it came to working out a tenth-rate reform in office routine; the imagination, or patience, was lacking to apply to this reform the general propositions that produced such brilliant results when applied to general problems.

That is why in our present life reckless audacity goes hand in hand, to an astonishing degree, with timidity of thought even when it comes to very minor changes.

I think that this has happened in all really great revolutions, for really great revolutions grow out of the contradictions between the old, between what is directed towards developing the old, and the very abstract striving for the new, which must be so new as not to contain the tiniest particle of the old.

And the more abrupt the revolution, the longer will many of these contradictions last.

The general feature of our present life is the following: we have destroyed capitalist industry and have done our best to raze to the ground the medieval institutions and landed proprietorship, and thus created a small and very small peasantry, which is following the lead of the proletariat because it believes in the results of its revolutionary work. It is not easy for us, however, to keep going until the socialist revolution is victorious in more developed countries merely with the aid of this confidence, because economic necessity, especially under NEP, keeps the productivity of labour of the small and very small peasants at an extremely low level. Moreover, the international situation, too, threw Russia back and, by and large, reduced the labour productivity of the people to a level considerably below pre-war. The West-European capitalist powers, partly deliberately and partly unconsciously, did everything they could to throw us back, to utilise the elements of the Civil War in Russia in order to spread as much ruin in the country as possible. It was precisely this way out of the imperialist war that seemed to have many advantages. They argued somewhat as follows: 'If we fail to overthrow the revolutionary system in Russia, we shall, at all events, hinder its progress towards socialism.' And from their point of view they could argue in no other way. In the end, their problem was half-solved. They failed to overthrow the new system created by the revolution, but they did prevent it from at once taking the step forward that would have justified the forecasts of the socialists, that would have enabled the latter to develop the productive forces with enormous speed, to develop all the potentialities which, taken together, would have produced socialism; socialists would thus have proved to all and sundry that socialism contains within itself gigantic forces and that mankind had now entered into a new stage of development of extraordinarily brilliant prospects.

The system of international relationships which has now taken shape is one in which a European state, Germany, is enslaved by the victor countries. Furthermore, owing to their victory, a number of states, the oldest states in the West, are in a position to make some insignificant concessions to their oppressed classes – concessions which, insignificant though they are, nevertheless heard the revolutionary movement in those countries and create some semblance of 'class truce'.

At the same time, as a result of the last imperialist war, a number of countries of the East, India, China, etc., have been completely jolted out of the rut. Their development has definitely shifted to general European capitalist lines. The general European ferment has begun to affect them, and it is now clear to the whole world that they have been drawn into a process of development that must lead to a crisis in the whole of world capitalism.

Thus, at the present time we are confronted with the question – shall we be able to hold on with our small and very small peasant production, and in our present state of ruin, until the West-European capitalist countries consummate their development towards socialism? But they are consummating it not as we formerly expected. They are not consummating it through the gradual 'maturing' of socialism, but through the exploitation of some countries by others, through the exploitation of the first of the countries vanquished in the imperialist war combined with the exploitation of the whole of the East. On the other hand, precisely as a result of the first imperialist war, the East has been definitely drawn into the revolutionary movement, has been definitely drawn into the general maelstrom of the world revolutionary movement.

What tactics does this situation prescribe for our country? Obviously the following. We must display extreme caution so as to preserve our workers' government and to retain our small and very small peasantry under its leadership and authority. We have the advantage that the whole world is now passing to a movement that must give rise to a world socialist revolution. But we are labouring under the disadvantage that the imperialists have succeeded in splitting the world into two camps; and this split is made more complicated by the fact that it is extremely difficult for Germany, which is really a land of advanced, cultured, capitalist development, to rise to her feet. All the capitalist powers of what is called the West are pecking at her and preventing her from rising. On the other hand, the entire East, with its hundreds of millions of exploited working people, reduced to the last degree of human suffering, has been forced into a position where its physical and material strength cannot possibly be compared with the physical, material and military strength of any of the much smaller West-European states.

Can we save ourselves from the impending conflict with these imperialist countries? May we hope that the internal antagonisms and conflicts between the thriving imperialist countries of the East will give us a second respite as they did the first time, when the campaign of the West-European counter-revolution in support of the Russian counter-revolution broke down owing to the antagonisms in the camp of the counter-revolutionaries of the West and the East, in the camp of the Eastern and Western exploiters, in the camp of Japan and the USA?

I think the reply to this question should be that the issue depends upon too many factors, and that the outcome of the struggle as a whole can be forecast only because in the long run capitalism itself is educating and training the vast majority of the population of the globe for the struggle.

In the last analysis, the outcome of the struggle will be determined by the fact that Russia, India, China, etc., account for the overwhelming majority of the population of the globe. And during the past few years it is this majority that has been drawn into the struggle for emancipation with extraordinary rapidity, so that in this respect there cannot be the slightest doubt what the final outcome of the world struggle will be. In this sense, the complete victory of socialism is fully and absolutely assured.

But what interests us is not the inevitability of this complete victory of socialism, but the tactics which we, the Russian Communist Party, we the Russian Soviet Government, should pursue to prevent the West-European counter-revolutionary states from crushing us. To ensure our existence until the next military conflict between the counter-revolutionary imperialist West and the revolutionary and nationalist East, between the most civilised countries of the world and the Orientally backward countries which, however, compromise the majority, this majority must become civilised. We, too, lack enough civilisation to enable us to pass straight on to socialism, although we do have the political requisites for it. We should adopt the following tactics, or pursue the following policy, to save ourselves.

We must strive to build up a state in which the workers retain leadership of the peasants, in which they retain the confidence of the peasants, and by exercising the greatest economy remove every trace of extravagance from our social relations.

We must reduce our state apparatus to the utmost degree of economy. We must banish from it all traces of extravagance, of which so much has been left over from tsarist Russia, from its bureaucratic capitalist state machine.

Will not this be a reign of peasant limitations?

No. If we see to it that the working class retains its leadership over the peasantry, we shall be able, by exercising the greatest possible thrift in the economic life of our state, to use every saving we make to develop our large-scale machine industry, to develop electrification, the hydraulic extraction of peat, to complete the Volkhov Power Project, etc.

In this, and in this alone, lies our hope. Only when we have done this shall we, speaking figuratively, be able to change horses, to change from the peasant, muzhik horse of poverty, from the horse of an economy designed for a ruined peasant country, to the horse which the proletariat is seeking and must seek – the horse of large-scale machine industry, of electrification, of the Volkhov Power Station, etc.

That is how I link up in my mind the general plan of our work, of our policy, of our tactics, of our strategy, with the functions of the reorganised Workers' and Peasants' Inspection. This is what, in my opinion, justifies the exceptional care, the exceptional attention that we must devote to the Workers' and Peasants' Inspection in raising it to an exceptionally high level, in giving it a leadership with Central Committee rights, etc., etc.

And this justification is that only by thoroughly purging our government machine, by reducing it to the utmost everything that is not absolutely essential in it, shall we be certain of being able to keep going. Moreover, we shall be able to keep going not on the level of a small-peasant country, not on the level of universal limitation, but on a level steadily advancing to large-scale machine industry.

These are the lofty tasks that I dream of for our Workers' and Peasants' Inspection. That is why I am planning for it the amalgamation of the most authoritative Party body with an 'ordinary' People's Commissariat.

INDEX

Printed and bound by CPI Group (UK) Ltd, Croydon, CR0 4YY

13/04/2025

14656488-0004